A GENEALOGICAL COLLECTION OF SOUTH CAROLINA WILLS and RECORDS
VOLUME I

Compiled by
MISS PAULINE YOUNG

Southern Historical Press, Inc.
Greenville, South Carolina

This volume was reproduced from
An 1955 edition located in the
Publisher's private Library

All rights reserved. No part of this publication may be reproduced,
stored in a retrieval system, transmitted in any form, posted
on to the web in any form or by any means without
the prior written permission of the publisher.

Please direct all correspondence and orders to:
www.southernhistoricalpress.com
or
SOUTHERN HISTORICAL PRESS, Inc.
PO Box 1267
375 West Broad Street
Greenville, SC   29601
southernhistoricalpress@gmail.com

Originally published: Liberty, SC 1955
Copyright 1955 by Pauline Young
          & The Silas Emmett Lucas, Jr.
ISBN #0-89308-037-3
All rights Reserved.
Printed in the United States of America

This book is lovingly

DEDICATED

to Randall in remembrance of the happiness that we shared together in life, the one person who always understood me . . . tho he has departed into the unknown, his memory I will always cherish.

WILL OF JONATHAN AMORY, VOL. 1 PAGE 5
PROBATE JUDGE'S OFFICE, CHARLESTON, S. C.

In ye Name of God Amen ye twenty third Day of November & year of our Lord God on Thousand Six hundred Ninety Seven I Jonathan Amory of ye Province of Carolina Merch.t being weak in Body yet of Sound and Perfect Memory, praised be God do make this my Last Will & Testem.t in manner & form following (Vizt) First I Bequeath my Soul & Spirit into ye hands of almighty God my Heavenly Father & my Body to ye Earth to be buried at ye Discretion of my Executrix & my worldly Estate to be disposed of as follows I Give & Bequeath unto my Son Joseph Croskeys all ye Piece of Land that lyeth next ye Rattrapp wch was bought of Andrew Lawson & lyeth on ye Left hand of ye Broad path as you goe into ye Country to him & his assignes for ever. I likewise request my Executrix to make a Title to him of ye piece of Land which lyes next to my dwelling house which I gave to him with my Daughter I also give him my best Silver headed Cane. I give to Sarah Rhett daughter to Capt. Willm. Rhett ten Pounds pd. into ye hands of Mother to buy her a gould Chain I Give to Doctr. Atkin Williamson ten Pounds, I give unto Doctr. Thomas Todd ten Pounds, I give to ye Poor of Charles Town fifteen Pounds I Give & Bequeath to Thomas Noble Twenty Pounds I Give unto my Loveing Wife Martha my Dwelling house in charles Towne & all ye Land paled in about ye Same dureing her Natural Life and after her Death I Give, Grant & Devise ye sd House & Land to my Sons Thomas and Robert Amory & ye Survivours of them their Heirs & assigns for Ever, I Give and Bequeath unto my Sd Loveing Wife all her Wearing Apparell & all ye Plate and household goods belonging to my Sd Dwelling House I Give & Bequeath unto my Daughter, Sarah Amory Ye Sum of three hundreds Pounds & to my Daughter Ann ye Like Sum of three hundred Pounds, All ye rest and residue of my Estate both reall & prsonall in this World, I give grant & Devise to my Loveing Wife Martha and my two Sons Thomas & Robert Amorys to be equally Divided between Them Share & Share alike, I also Nominate and appoint my my Said Wife Martha Sole Executrix during her Life & after her Decease I Nominate and appoint my two Sons Thomas & Robert my Executors I Do also Impower and authorize my sd Executrix to Sell & Dispose forever all or any part of my real Estate Provided that the Shares of ye Money raised thereby be Secured to my Sons Behoofe In Witness Whereof I have hereunto set my hand and Seal, day year & Place above Exprest.

Sealed Published and   Jonathan Amory (SEAL)
Declared In the Presence of
Geo. Logan
Fra. Fidling
Joane Hearne

Memorand. That this Day personally appeared before me George Logan & Fra. Fidling ye within Witnesses & Did on ye holy Evangelists Declare that they did See ye within named Joanathan Amory Sign Seal & publish ye Within to be his Last Will and Testam.t and that ye said Jonathan Amory was of Sound Memory at ye time of his So Doing.

Recorded Oct. 1699.

WILL OF MARTHA AMORY, VOL. 1 PAGE 7
PROBATE JUDGES OFFICE, CHARLESTON, S. C.

In the Name of God Amen I Martha Amory of Charles Town in South Carolina Widdo. being weak in Body but of Sound and Perfect Memory praise be given to Almighty God for ye Same Do make & Ordain this my Last Will and Testamt. in Manner and form following, first I bequeath my Soul & Spirit into ye hands of ye Ever Blessed God my merciful Creator yt made me & Inspired me with ye Breath of Life and of my Blessed Lord & Saviour Jesus Christ who redeemed me with his Precious Blood beseeching him to receive ye Same unto ye hands of his Mercy hopeing & assuredly believing ye Salvation of my Soul through ye alone Merits of Jesus Christ my Blessed Saviour And my Body I Comitt to ye Earth to be decently buried at ye Discretion of my hereafter mentioned Executrix being in full & Certain Hope of a Resurrection to a Glorious Immortality in ye Great Day of our Saviours Second Comeing to Judge ye World And for my Estate which it hath Pleased God to bestow upon me in this World I do give and Dispose of ye Same as followeth (Vizt) Impis I will yt my Just Debts & funerall Expences shall be first paid and Discharged. Items I Do Give and Bequeath unto my Dear friend Mrs. Sarah Rhett my gold Watch, & my Horse and Horse Netts & my White quilted petticoat. Item I do give and Bequeath unto yt Minister of ye Church of England who shall Succeed ye late Reverend Mr. Samuel Marshall deceased as Rector or Minister of ye Church of Charles Towne in South Carolina ye Sum of Tenn Pounds Carolina money. Item I Do Give & Bequeath unto ye Poor of Charles Town in Carolina ye Sum of Tenn Pounds Carolina Moneys. Item I Do Give & Bequeath unto William Rhett Junr. ye Son of Capt. Willm. Rhett ye Sum of five Pounds Carolina Moneys to buy a Ring Item I Do Give & Bequeath to Sarah Rhett Junr daughter ye sd. Capt. Willm. Rhett ye Sum of Twenty Pounds Carolina Money Item I Do Give and Bequeath unto my Son in Law Thomas Amory my Largest Silver Tankard. Item I Do give and Bequeath unto my daughter Sarah my gold girdle Buckle & a Gold Lockett and Six Silver Spoones. Item I do Give & Bequeath to my Daughter Ann my Gold Shoe Buckles & a gold Button of my Night raile & Six Silver Spoones. Item As To remaining part of my third part of my deceased Husbands Estate Left me by his Last Will and Testamt. & all other my Estate whatsoever my Will is yt ye Same be divided into three equal Parts, One third of which I do Give devise & Bequeath unto my Son in Law Thomas Amory & my son Robt Amory to be equally divided between them But if my Son in Law Thomas Amory dye without Isue of his Body lawfully Begotten Then my Will is that his part shall be equally divided between my Son Robert & my daughter Sarah & Ann or the Survivors of them and ye other two thirds I do Give to my daughters Sarah & Ann Amory to be equally divided between them and my Will is that if my sd Son Robert or either of my Said Daughters Sarah & Ann shall Depart this Life before ye Age of Twneyt one years or day of Marriage That then That part of him or her That is deceased shall be equally divided between ye two Survivors. Itm I Do Dominate & appoint my dearly beloved friend Sarah Rhett ye Wife of Capt. William Rhett of Charles Town in Carolina Executrix and my Beloved Son Robert Amory Executor of this my Last Will & Testamt & my Will is yt ye Education of my Children Robert Sarah and An shall be

at ye Sole Ordering and Disposall of my sd Executrix Sarah Rhett and yt dureing ye Minority of my Son Robert Amory ye Sole Execution of this my Last will and Testamt be solely in ye Said Sarah Rhett as fully and as amply as if She was Sole Executrix of ye Same In Witness where of I ye first above named Martha Amory have to this my last Will and Testamt. Sett my hand & Seal Dated ye Thirtieth day of October In ye Year of our Lord 1699.
Signed, Sealed & Declared   Martha Amory (SEAL)
by ye above named Martha
Amory as her last Will and
Testamt. in ye Presence
Joseph Croskeys
Robert Dacres
Jane Trott
The Mark of
Susanna Jackson
Nicholas Trott

    Memorandum: this Thirteenth Day of November Anno Dom; Personally Came & appeared before me Nicholas Trott Esq. Mr. Joseph Croskeys & Mr. Robt Dacres & on their oaths on ye holy Evangelists taken Say that they & every & either of them did See & were personally Prest. When Mrs Martha Amory ye Above Testatrix did Sign Seal Publish & Declare ye above written to be & Contain her last Will & Testament & yt at ye Doing thereof she was of Sound & prfect mind & memory.
Capt e t Jurat
Joseph Blake

WILL OF ALEXANDER SHAW, VOL. 10 PAGE 687
PROBATE JUDGES OFFICE, CHARLESTON, S. C.

South Carolina

    IN THE NAME OF GOD AMEN I Alexander Shaw of St. Bartholamews Parish Colleton County & province aforesaid Planter being weak in Body But of perfect sound mind and memory and Calling to mind the mortality of the Body and Well knowing it is appointed for all men once to Die do make and ordain this my Last Will and Testament in manner and form following (that is to say) FIRST & PRINCIPALLY I recommend my soul to Almighty God hoping thro' the merits of my Saviour pardon and forgivness of all my Sins, my Body I Recommend to the Earth to be Interr'd in a decent and Christian Like manner at the Discretion of my Executor or Executrix hereafter mentioned and as to what worldly Estate it hath pleased Amighty God to Betsow upon me I Give and Bequeath as follows It is my Will and desire that all my Lawfull Debts and funeral Charges Be first Discharged.

    ITEM I Will and Bequeath one full third part of my Personal Estate to my Well Beloved Wife Martha Shaw to her and her forever in Lieu of her Dower.

    ITEM I Will and Bequeath to my Well Beloved sister sister formerly Ann Gray now Ann Atkins and her Issue by William Gray deceas'd (that is) John, William Alexander & Martha Gray, another full third of my personal Estate to be equally Divided between the said John, William, Alexander, and Martha Grays or the survivors of them at the discease of Ann Atkins to them and their Heirs forever.

ITEM L Will and Bequeath the other one third part of my Personal Estate to my Beloved Sister Martha Newman During her natural Life & at her Demise to Her Issue John George Alexander & Susannah Newman & Ann Newman now Filput Martha Newman other wise Smith to be equally divided between them to them and their Heirs forever.

ITEM I Give and Bequeath unto Thos. Filput One Tract of Land Containing Five Hundred Acres on Savannah River in Granville County to him and his Heirs forever And if in Case it Shall appear here-after that any other Lands in this province shall prove my property I give and Bequeath all such Land or lands to my well beloved Wife Martha Shaw Her & her Heirs forever.

AND LASTLY I Constitute and appoint Well Beloved Wife Martha Shaw Executrix and Wm. McTier Thos. Filput John Newman John & Wm. Gray Exors to this my Last Will and Testament hereby Revoking all former wills by me made.

IN WITNESS whereof I have Hereunto Set my Hand and Seal this Sixteenth Day of April in the Year of our Lord One Thousand Seven Hundred and Sixty Five and in the fifty Year of the Reign of our Sovereign Lord George the third of Great Brittain france & Ireland King Defender of the faith & ca & ca.

Signed Sealed Delivered Published.
& Pronounced in presence of us   Alexr. Shaw (SEAL)
Thos. Holman   Wm. Day
Mary Hohnan   Jno. Hugh's

Proved by Virtue of a Didmus directed to George Johnston Esqr. this fourteenth day of June 1765.

WILL OF ANN ABBOTT, VOL. 47 PAGE 756
PROBATE JUDGE'S OFFICE, CHARLESTON, S. C.

I do hereby make this my last Will, and give Charles, My slave, and all the property of which May die Seized and possessed to my Son Thomas H. Abbott, after payment of my debts, Constituting him Executor with full power to Sell.

Witness my Hand and Seal at Charleston this Twelfth day of March 1853.
                                                  Ann Abbott (LS)

Signed, Sealed, delivered and published by the Testator as and for her last Will in presence of the Subscribers, who in her presence and in the presence of each other, have Subscribed their Names as Witnesses.
Dan. Horlbeck
Henry Horlbeck   PROVED MARCH 11, 1856.
Ann G. Horlbeck

WILL OF ELIZABETH B. KEITH PACK. 182
CLERK OF COURTS OFFICE, PICKENS, S. C.

In the name of God, Amen.

I Elizabeth B. Keith of Pickens Village in the State of South Carolina being Somewhat weak and feeble and knowing it is appointed for man as also for woman to die, and having a desire to dispose of my worldly Estate which was left me by my beloved Husband W. L. Keith late of Pickens Dist.

do make this my last Will and Testament in Maner following Viz:

1st. I desire that all my just debts and funeral expenses be paid out of my Estate by my Executors after me Death.

2nd. I give to my Grand daughter Elizabeth L. Allen one negro girl Emme, and I also direct my Executors to retain enough of my Estate to finish & complete her Education, if her Education Should not be completed before my death, and my Executors is hereby directed to se that she does have an Education—Sufficiently to be as they adjudge Equal to any of my daughters heretofore. I also give hur two fether beds & Sufficient furniture. It may be asked why I have given the foregoing property to my Said Loving Grand Daughter—I will here Say the will of my late Husband W. L. Keith Decst. will does not allow her an equal Share without my making the bequest, which I think is justly due hur & I therefore give it to hur with the following proviso, that is She dies before She comes to be of proper age or twenty one years of age—or if She dies after that time without having an heir the Said property & all it increas Shal Relap to my Estate to be divided among my lawful heirs.

3d. I direct and Desire that my Executors as Soon after my Death as is a reasonable time, to cause all my Efects & Estate both Real & personal to be appraised and Sold as they may think most advantageous and Equally divided agreeable to the wishes and directions of the last will and Testament of my Husband William L. Keith which I desire to be Equal to Each & Every of my heirs as so directed.

Lastly, I constitute and appoint Joseph J. Norton my Son William C. Keith & Joseph B. Reid of this my last will and Testament to carry the Same into Effect agreeable to the meaning & intent of the Same Will.

In testimony where unto I have here unto Set my hand and affixed my Seal. Hereby published and declared to be the last Will and Testament of Elizabeth B. Keith hereby Revoking all former Wills by me heretofore made in the presence of us.

Nathl. Reid
J. P. Reid
J. B. Reid
                                                        E. B. Keith (SEAL)

South Carolina

Pickens District) Personally appeared Joseph B. Reid before me, and being duly Sworn Saith on oath that he was present and did see E. B. Keith Sign and Seal the foregoing instrument as, and for, her last Will and Testament, that J. P. Reid and Nathl. Reid were present and Saw the Same, that they all three Signed their names to the Same as Witnesses in presence of each other and the Testatrix.

Sworn to before me   Joseph B. Reid
29th Decr 1863
W. E. Holcombe
  O.P.D.

WILLIAM L. KEITH PACK. 182 EQUITY
CLERK OF COURTS OFFICE, PICKENS, S. C.

Wm. L. Keith died in 1856. Left a widow Elizabeth Brown Keith & 7 children to wit, Elliott M., Thomas J., Marville L., Col. William C., John R. and Eliza Ann Earle, wife of Dr. James B. Earle, Mary Isabella Keith . . .

Thomas J. Keith died August 5, 1862 . . . Elliott M. Keith died in Sept. 1862 intestate leaving a widow Mary R. Keith and five children all of whom are minors to wit, Flora C. Keith, Virginia Elvira Keith, Calhoun Wm. Keith, Elizabeth M. Keith, Elliott M. Keith Jr. . . . On June 29, 1863, Marvel L. Keith & William C. Keith were mentioned as being absent from the state . . . John R. Keith, Thomas J. Keith, Elliott M. Keith the testators three sons died during the year 1862, each intestate, the two former unmarried and the latter married. Elizabeth B. Keith his widow died in December 1863, not having entered into a second marriage . . . List of lands belonging to the said Major W. L. Keith viz. "Cheohee" containing 2,470 acres sold to Gen. J. W. Harrison. Homestead town lots & 128 acres land adjoining sold to J. E. Hagood. One acre lot in front of dwelling house sold to M. F. Mitchell. . . .

JOHN B. CLAYTON TO THOMAS J. KEITH PACK. 182 DEED TO 811 ACRES CLERK OF COURTS OFFICE, PICKENS, S. C.

THE STATE OF SOUTH CAROLINA

Know all men by these Presents, that I, John B. Clayton, assignee of Thomas D. Garvin of Pickens District in the State aforesaid, in consideration of Fifty Dollars and fifty cents to me paid by Thomas J. Keith do grant, bargain, sell and release unto the said Thomas J. Keith all Thos. D. Garvins interest, to All that Piece, Parcel or Tract of land situate, lying and being in the State and District aforesaid on Devils Fork waters of Keowee River containing according to the plat annexed to the original grant Eight hundred and eleven acres, originally granted to Jeremiah Field and Fred'k N. Garvin on the third day of December One thousand eight hundred and thirty two. The form and boundaries of which will more fully appear by reference to the said original Grant and the Plat thereto annexed. Together with all and singular the Rights, Members, Hereditaments and Appurtenances to the said premises belonging, or in any wise incident or appertaining. To have and to hold all and singular the premises before mentioned, unto the said Thomas J. Keith, his Heirs and Assigns forever. And I do hereby bind myself, my Heirs, Executors, and Administrators, to warrant and forever defend all and singular the said premises unto the said Thomas J. Keith his Heirs and Assigns, against myself and my Heirs lawfully claiming or to claim the same, or any part thereof and against no other person whatsoever.

Witness my Hand and Seal this twenty seventh day of January in the year of our Lord one thousand eight hundred and fifty nine and in the Eighty third year of the Independence of the United States of America.
Signed, Sealed and Delivered
in the presence of   J. B. CLAYTON (SEAL)
W. M. Hadden   Assignee
J. J. Norton
The State of South Carolina

Pickens District) Personally appeared before me W. M. Hadden and made oath that he saw J. B. Clayton sign, seal and deliver the within Deed of Conveyance, for the use and purposes therein mentioned, and that J. J. Norton together with said Deponent, was a subscribing witness thereto.
Sworn to and subscribed before me,
this 27th day of January 1859.   W. M. Hadden

J. J. Norton
Not. Pub. for P. D.

WILL OF WILLIAM L. KEITH PACK. 182
CLERK OF COURTS OFFICE, PICKENS, S. C.
FEBRUARY 21, 1856

IN THE NAME OF GOD AMEN.

I William L. Keith of Pickens Village in the State of South Carolina being weak and feeble and knowing it is appointed for man to die and having a desire to dispose of my worldly estate which it hath pleased God to Bless me with do make this my last will and Testament in manner following viz.

1st. I desire that all my just debts and funeral expenses be paid out of my estate by my Executrix and Executors after my death.

2nd. I have heretofore given my son Elliott M. Keith an Education and property what I intend for him to have at present.

3rd. I have heretofore given my son Marville L. Keith an Education and property what I intend for him to have, Except three hundred dollars I direct my Executrix and Executors to pay him as soon as convenient in place of the office I built for him and the small piece of Land I intended for him.

4th. I have heretofore given my daughter Eliza A. Earle what property I emtend for her to have at present.

5th. Elizabeth J. Allen who is dead and left one heir Elizabeth L. Allen about four years of age is provided for out of the property that was heretofore given to her mother by Trust deed I desire that her Trustee take the said Trust property and sell the males and hire the females or sell them as the Trustee may think best and keep the money at interest for the said E. L. Allen until she comes of age.

6th. I have heretofore given to my son Thomas J. Keith what property I intend for him to have (Except he is to have Two hundred dollars to be paid to him out of my Estate when it is convenient, also two cows and calves and one Bed and furniture by my Executrix and Executors to make him equal to the Balance of his Brothers and Sisters.

7th. I give and bequeath to my beloved daughter Mary J. Keith my Negro girl chain Jenney and her child Joe and Patts two children Joe and Lucy one gold watch worth one Hundred dollars one good Horse two cows and calves and two Beds and furniture to her and her heirs and assigns forever.

8th. I give and bequeath to my son William C. Keith my Negro Boy Bob and Negro girl Nancy and Five hundred dollars in money and all his expenses to be paid by my Executrix and Executors until he graduates and one bed and furniture and two cows and calves and one good Horse.

9th. I give and bequeath to my beloved son John R. Keith my Negro Boy Bill and Betsey and at his mother's death I give him my Oolenoy plantation containing one hundred and fifty acres and a small tract adjoining known as the Huwary? tract containing eight acres more or less to him his heirs and assigns with the following Proviso he is not to have possession of the said Land until his mothers death also one Bed and furniture a good Horse and two cows and calves.

10th. I give and bequeath to my beloved Grandson Calhoun William Keith

Five hundred dollars in money to be paid to his Father E. M. Keith by my Executrix and Executors as soon as convenient and his father to keep it on interest until the said C. W. Keith arrives at full age and then to pay it to him with the Interest.

11th. I give and bequeath to my beloved Grandson Broadwell William Keith Five Hundred dollars in money to be paid to his Father Marville L. Keith by my Executrix and Executors as soon as convenient and his Father to keep it at Interest until the said B. W. Keith arrives at full age and then to be paid to him with the Interest.

12th. I give and bequeath to my beloved Grandson William Robison Earle Five Hundred dollars in money to be paid to his father James W. Earle by my Executrix and Executors as soon as convenient and his Father to keep it at interest until the said W. R. Earle arrives of full age and then pay it to him with the Interest.

13th. I give and bequeath to my beloved wife Elizabeth Brown Keith all the balance of my Real Estates all Lands or parts of Lands now owned or belonging to me in any way whatever together with all my Slaves or Negroes that is not disposed of in this instrument together with all my money cash Notes or accounts of every description, also all my household furniture plantation tools and every other thing that belongs to me of every kind or description that is not disposed of in this instrument during her life or Widowhood with the following instructions. That she be at full Liberty at any time during her single life to Swap sell devise as she may think fit and proper any of said property devised to her and if the said property become any way burthensome or ungovernable to make a sale and sell off such portion as she and the Executors may think best I further direct my said Wife and Executors that if any of the property devised to my son William or daughter Mary or son John should die before they arrive of full age and receive it I direct it to be made up to them out of my Estate by other property to the value of the property so dead or valueless. I further direct my said wife Elizabeth not to sell my Cheohee plantation during her life unless it can be sold for Ten thousand dollars or more and I desire my Executors if the said Cheohee plantation is not sold by my wife and them before her death if they think it advisable to let the said Tract of Land lie for Ten years if they think it best for the interest of the estate. Should my said wife marry I only give and bequeath to her my Oolenoy plantation Darby and Patt his wife old Chaney Lucy and her children Jinney and Jenney and Ben and as much stock as will support the place to have during her life and at her death to be sold and equally divided between my Seven children viz. Elliott Marville Eliza Thomas William Mary and John. I further direct my said wife Elizabeth to try to make my children as equal as she can should any of my children become deceased that is not of full years and become unable to make a support that she provide for them as she thinks best for there benefit. I direct my said wife to set old Chaney at full Liberty at her death and she is provided for and the other old Servants put them in as easy circumstances as she can should my said wife remain Single during her life she is to have the full control and management of all the property so devised to her and to dispose of the same at her will and pleasure though I desire that she doe equal Justice to all of our seven children as she can.

Lastly I constitute and appoint my beloved wife Elizabeth B. Keith my Executrix and my son Elliott M. Keith and my son Thomas J. Keith my Executors of this my last will and Testament to carry the same into effect agreeable to the meaning of the said will.

In testimony whereunto I have hereunto set my hand and affixed my seal, Hereby published and declared   W. L. Keith (SEAL)
to be the last will and testament of
William L. Keith hereby revoking all
former Wills by me heretofore made
in Presence of us.

Tho. R. Brackenridge   James George
M. F. Mitchell   Wesley Phillips
South Carolina
Pickens District) In the Court of Ordinary.

   I certify that the foregoing is a true copy of the last will and testament of W. L. Keith dessd. which has been duly Probated in the court of ordinary, the original will now remaining in my office.

Given under my hand and Seal of office this 11th day of June 1866.
                             W. E. Holcombe O. P. D.

L. W. ALLEN TO J. W. EARLE PACK. 182 DEED OF TRUST
CLERK OF COURTS OFFICE, PICKENS, S. C.

The State of South Carolina

   Know all men by these presents That I Lafayett W. Allen of Pickens District and State aforesaid for and in consideration of the natural love good will and affection which I the said Lafayett W. Allen has for and toward my little Daughter Elizabeth Luella Allen who is about five years of age and where of is hereby acknowledged Have bargained sold and in plain open market delivered and by these presents do hereby bargain sell and in plain open market deliver unto the said Dr. James W. Earle trustee the following negro slaves viz Sarah a yellow Girl about eighteen years of age, Ben a boy about fourteen years of age, Jim a boy about Twelve years of age and Letty a girl about four years of age, Together with their increase. To have and to hold the said Sarah, Ben, Jim and Letty and all the future increase of the Females if there should be any unto the said J. W. Earle in Trust for the sole benefit and enjoyment of my said Daughter Elizabeth L. Allen during her natural life, and after her death to such Heir or Heirs as she may leave to be equally divided amongst them share and share alike should the said Elizabeth Luella Allen leave no heir of her own body or die before she should arrive of full age, that then and in that case the said negro slaves and their increase is to revert to Wm. L. Keith his Heirs or assigns Executors or Administrators and become a part of his Estate agreeable to the meaning and intention of any former deed heretofore sealed and accepted my myself, if the said Dr. James W. Earle trustee die before the said Elizabeth Luella Allen arrives of full age, that then and in that case his Heirs Executors or Administrators shall and may have full power and authority to take the said slaves into their possession and the same retain and hold until a new Trustee may be appointed to act in his stead, it is further covananted and agreed that if the said negro slaves should be attempted to be removed from the said District of Pickens or State that then and in that case the said J. W. Earle Trustee shall have full power and authority to take the same into his own possession it is further agreed that the said J. W. Earle shall see that the said negro slaves be humanely and well treated, it is further agreed and I do hereby direct the said J. W. Earle to act and do with the said negro slaves as he thinks will be most to the advantage of the said E. L. Allen, and the Trustee is hereby directed to do all in his power for the safety or seeing to and securing the said property and the increase to the said Elizabeth L. Allen in every respect, fully in the said matter.

In witness whereof I the said Lafayett W. Allen have hereunto set his hand & seal this eleventh day of May in the year of our Lord one thousand eight hundred and fifty four and in the seventy eighth year of American Independence.

Signed Sealed & delivered   L. W. Allen (SEAL)
In the presence of
J. A. Jenkins
D. B. McAllister
State of South Carolina

Pickens District) I James W. Earle the Trustee named in the annexed deed of trust, do hereby signify my acceptance to the Trust therein specified and stated.

Witness my hand and seal this eleventh day of May in the year of our Lord one thousand eight hundred and fifty four.

In the presence of   J. W. Earle (SEAL)
J. A. Jenkins
D. B. McAllister

RECORDED IN BOOK G, PAGE 460. CERTIFIED MAY 25, 1854. COPIED FROM ORIGINAL RECORD.

PETITION OF THE FEMALES OF PICKENS COUNTY PACK 181 NO. 7
CLERK OF COURTS OFFICE, PICKENS, S. C.

To the County Commissioners of Pickens County South Carolina.

Your humble Petitioners a portion of the females of your County respectfully represent that when we take a retrospective view of the eventful ten years that have just passed, we are alarmd at the awful increase of crime in our midst, and feel constrained to raise our humble voice in behalf of suffering humanity. Scarcely a day passes but we hear of some horrid crime having been perpetrated by some one while under the baleful influence of intoxicating drinks. The sad tragedy that has recently occurred in our immediate vicinity should nerve every one of our feebleses to sound the tension of alarm, that it may be heard throughout hill and dale of our sunny clime.

While we stood near the lifeless form of that youthful officer of the law on last Sabbath listening to the heart rending shrieks of that motherless sister and affectionate wife, and heard the loud lamentations of that bereaved father, when we beheld the burning tears streaming down the manly cheek of so many whom we never knew before to weep, our fortitude well nigh forsook us, but when that prattling boy too young to realize his great loss, and to his widowed mother as they passed from the grave, "Ma! are you not going with Pa?" what heart could fail to have melted into tenderness, while thus reflecting on the scene before us. Our minds could but carry us to that mountain grave yard where he who fell simultaneously with our neighbor was lowered in the silent tomb surrounded by the weeping widow, mother, sisters and brother, and a large concourse of sympathizing friends.

We need not tell you the cause of all this wo; but permit us to humbly request you to refuse the granting of license to any one, to retail that "liquid fire" which is so rapidly consuming the very vitals of our County, our State and even our entire nation. Thousands of our Citizens annually sink to the drunkards grave. It is not the SELFISH that so often and so readily fall victims to intemperance, but remember, Oh? we pray you remember that many of our noblest, our highly gifted young men sink prematurely to the drunkards tomb. We appeal to you in this sad extremity in behalf of the lonely widow, the sorrowing parent, and weeping orphan, and implore you as conservators of the peace, as lovers of your race, and as immortal beings accountable to God for your actions, to arrest to the utmost extent of your power this one fruitful source of crime by granting no license to sell intoxicating drinks.

Think us not unreasonable. We and our children are the principle sufferers. Though many of us are blessed with sober husbands, fathers, sons and brothers, we can but deeply sympathize with those of our sex who see their dearest friends on the road to destruction. We are not in sane on this subject, as Paul said, "We are not mad but speak the words of truth and soberness." Shut down we pray you, this one dire flood gate, and obstruct as far as practicable that stream of woe now flowing through the length and breadth of our land hurling thousands of our fellow beings into the grave of the drunkard. Suffering wives, mothers and sisters will repay in tears of gratitude and prayers to God for his blessings on you and your families, and Heavens Dome will echo with angels shouts of rejoicing o'er the great good you shall have accomplished. For this as in duty bound we will ever pray. March 1871.

Elizabeth Jones
Mary Dickson
Ann Dickson
Sarah Lesley
Justina Lesley
M. A. Mims
E. R. Mims
H. Jones
Louisa Jones
Sarah Hughes
Mary Hughes
Mary S. Gillam

Jessie L. Gilliam
Carrie C. Gillam
Della Folger
Mary Smith
Elizbaeth Hendricks
Martha A. Clayton
Laura M. O'Dell
Martha O'Dell
Corrie Folger
M. C. Briggs
E. Smith
M. P. Folger

GEORGE B. THOMAS & GEORGE W. O'NEAL PACK. 181 NO. 21
TAVERN LICENSE
CLERK OF COURT'S OFFICE, PICKENS, S. C.

To Hon Board of County Commissioners Pickens County.

We the undersigned most respectfully petition your Honorable Board for a license to retail spiritious liquors for six months at William L. Rogers store commencing on the 10th of June 1869 and your petitioners will ever pray.

George B. Thomas
George W. Oneal

We the undersigned free holders recommend Messrs George Thomas, G. W. O'Neal as suitable persons to retail spiritious liquors and in our opinion will comply with the law in such case made & provided.

Wm. L. Rogers
W. S. Kirksey
W. G. Blassingame

WILLIAM BARTON PACK 181 NO. 30
TAVERN LICENSE
CLERK OF COURT'S OFFICE, PICKENS, S. C

Pickens County, S. C.
Jan. 1st, 1869

To the Honorable Booard of Commissioners for Pickens County.

The undersigned respectfully ask your honorable body the liberty to retail spiritious liquors near King Mills.

Wm. Barton

The undersigned recommend Wm. Barton as being a man in every respect suitable to retail spirits.

M. M. Arnold
Samuel Chapman
A. Ramsay

WILLIAM L. ROGERS PACK. 181 NO. 29
TAVERN LICENSE
CLERK OF COURTS OFFICE, PICKENS, S. C.

To the Board of County Commissioners for Pickens County.

The undersigned petition your Honorable Board for a license to retail spiritious at his house now occupied by him from the 1st day of November 1868 to 1st of May 1869 and your petitioner will ever pray.

Jany 19, 1869   Wm. L. Rogers

We the undersigned Free Holders of Pickens County recommend William L. Rogers as a proper & suitable person to retail spiritious liquors, and that he will comply with the law in such case made & provided.
Jany 19, 1869

H. Philpot
Riley Ferguson
R. A. Bowen
Robert Craig

His house was near the Court House.

ANDREW J. VANDERGRIFT PACK. 181 NO. 16
TAVERN LICENSE

To the Clerk of Court's Office, Pickens, S. C.

The undersigned Andrew J. Vandergrift most respectfully petition your Honorable Board for a license to retail spiritious liquors by the drink at the Wool Factory of William McDades in Pickens County for the term of Twelve Months commencing on the 23 day of this month, and your petitioner will ever pray &c.

March 22, 1870   A. J. Vandergrift

We the undersigned free holders recommend Mr. A. J. Vandergrift as a suitable person to retail spiritious liquors at McDades Factory and will comply with the law relating to the same.

March 23, 1870

George R. Burgess
J. J. Hunt
William McDade

J. F. WILSON PACK. 181 NO. 19
TAVERN LICENSE
CLERK OF COURTS OFFICE, PICKENS, S. C.

To the Honorable Board of County Commissioners for Pickens County.

The undersigned most respectfully petition your Honorable Board for a license to retail spiritious liquors by the drink in your county on the Pendleton Road near Dr. H. C. Miller's house and your petitioner will ever pray &c.

Dec. 31, 1868   J. F. Wilson

We the undersigned Free Holders recommend J. F. Wilson as a fit and proper person to retail spiritious liquors by the drink and believe that he will comply with the law in such case made and provided.

E. H. Lawrence
Jeremiah Looper

J. BROWN KIRKSEY PACK. 181 NO. 14
TAVERN LICENSE
CLERK OF COURTS OFFICE, PICKENS, S. C.

To the Honorable Board of County Commissioners for Pickens County.

The undersigned petitions your honorable body to grant Licenses to retail spiritious liquors at Table Mountain, Pickens Co. S. C. for the term of twelve (12) months commencing May the first 1870 to May first 1871.

J. Brown Kirksey

We the undersigned free holders of Pickens County do hereby recommend J. Brown Kirksey as being a suitable person to retail liquor at Table Mountain, S. C.

Isaac Williams
J. Hester
G. K. Hendricks

A. J. STEWART & J. E. NIMMONS PACK. 181 NO. 26
TAVERN LICENSE
CLERK OF COURTS OFFICE, PICKENS, S. C.

To the Honorable Board of County Commissioners for Pickens County.

The undersigned A. J. Stewart and James Nimmons trading under the name firm and style of Stewart & Nimmons most respectfully petition your Honorable Board for a license to retail spiritious liquors in the west corner of the village of Pickens on Main Street, for the term of twelve months from the date and your petitioners will ever pray &c.
Jany 14, 1869

                                      A. J. Stewart
                                      J. E. Nimmons

AUSTIN DAY PACK. 181 NO. 18
TAVERN LICENSE
CLERK OF COURTS OFFICE, PICKENS, S. C.

To the Honorable Board of County Commissioners for Pickens County.

The undersigned most respectfully petition your Honorable Board for a license to retail spiritious liquors at my home at Cedar Rock until the 1st day of May next and your petitioner will ever pray &c.
Feby 24, 1869   Austin Day

We the undersigned Free Holders recommend Mr. Austin Day as a fit and suitable person to retail spiritious liquors and that in our opinion he will comply with the laws in such case made & provided.

                                      A. S. Smith
                                      J. V. B. Duncan
                                      A. Hollingsworth

R. M. CASEY & C. W. YOUNG PACK. 181 NO. 12
TAVERN LICENSE
CLERK OF COURTS OFFICE, PICKENS, S. C.

To the Honorable Board of County Commissioners for Pickens County.

We the undersigned most respectfully petition your Honorable Board for a license to retail Spiritious Liquors at or near Dr. H. C. Millers in Pickens County for the Term of three months commencing on the 1st day of April next and your petitioner will ever pray &c.
March 28, 1870

                                      R. M. Casey
                                      C. W. Young

We the undersigned Free Holders of Pickens County take great pleasure in recommending R. M. Casey & C. W. Young as suitable and proper persons to retail spiritious liquors and we believe will keep a decent and respectable Bar Room.

                                      F. V. Clayton
                                      H. Philpot
                                      W. E. Holcombe

JOSEPH A. BATES PACK. 181 NO. 13
TAVERN LICENSE
CLERK OF COURTS OFFICE, PICKENS, S. C.

To the Honorable Board of County Commissioners for Pickens County.

The undersigned most respectfully petition your board for a license to retail spiritious liquors at his Hotel at Table Rock for the term of three months commencing on the 18th day of July 1870 and your petitioner will ever pray &c.

July 4, 1870   Joseph A. Bates

We the undersigned recommend Joseph A. Bates, as a fit and proper person to retail spiritious liquors at his Hotel at Table Rock.

July 4, 1870   (No names signed.)

JESSE CRENSHAW PACK. 181 NO. 28
TAVERN LICENSE
CLERK OF COURTS OFFICE, PICKENS, S. C.

To the Honorable Board of County Commissioners for Pickens County.

The undersigned most respectfully petition your Board for a license to retail spiritious liquor at his house in said county from the 12 day of Feby 1869 to 1st of May 1869, and your petitioner will ever pray &c.

March 23, 1869   Jesse Crenshaw

We the undersigned recommend Jesse Crenshaw as a fit and suitable person to retail spiritious liquors.

                     B. F. Morgan
                     John Julian
                     Wm. M. Jones
                     County Commissioners Office
                     Pickens May 3, 1869

Mr. Jesse Crenshaw

I am instructed by the Board of County Commissioners to notify you that unless you comply with the law in relation to Retailing Spiritious Liquors that the law will be enforced against you.

By order of the Board

                     J. E. Hagood, Clerk

Mr. J. E. Hagood

Dear Sir, I have neglected returning the paper back to you but I hope that it will be right. I have not sold the amount of ten gallons of whiskey since I taken oute lisones the black aids rumors has running mee and all so I am redy to pay what ever I ow at eny time when ever I now how to pay too and allso I hope that you will bee as strict on others as you ar on mee I have not solde no whiskey sence the firste of May and dont expect to till I get new papers.

                     yours truly
                     Jesse Crenshaw

this 10th May 1869

A. R. BRADEEN PACK. 181 NO. 8
TAVERN LICENSE
CLERK OF COURTS OFFICE, PICKENS, S. C.

To the Honorable Board of County Commissioners of Pickens County.

The humble petition of the undersigned a Citizen of Pickens County.

Respectfully petition your Honorable Board for a Tavern License to retail liquors at the house now occupied by him on the Air Line Rail Road, and near the public road, between Mrs. Maddens and Cato Hallums.

Your petitioner is prepared to keep a Tavern and has at least two spare beds and necessary bedding, more than are required for the family of the said applicant, and I am well provided with house room and stabling and provender for four horses.

May 20, 1872   A. R. Bradeen

We the undersigned residing in the neighborhood, where the said A. R. Bradeen proposes to open a Tavern license and we certify that the said A. R. Bradeen is a gentleman of good repute for honesty and sobriety, and is known to us to have at least two spare beds and necessary bedding, more than is required for the family of the said applicant, and is well provided with house room stabling and provender for four horses.

May 20, 1872

                                    Benj. J. Johnston
                                    S. W. Clayton
                                    F. V. Clayton

JOHN HOWARD PACK. 181 NO. 25
TAVERN LICENSE
CLERK OF COURTS OFFICE, PICKENS, S. C.

To the Honorable Board of County Commissioners for Pickens County.

The undersigned most respectfully petition your Honorable Board for a license to retail spiritious liquors at his house on Cedar Rock Road from old Pickens for the term of four months from the 1 day of Jany 1869 and your petitioner will ever pray.

Feby 8, 1869

                                         his
                                    John X Howard
                                         mark

We the undersigned free holders most respectfully recommend Mr. John Howard as a proper person to retail spiritious liquors at his home and that in our opinion he will comply with the law in such case made and provided.

Feby 8, 1869

Thos. R. Brackenridge   John Craig
Isaac Durham   J. W. Vickery
J. M. Hunnicut   John F. Byrd
Lewis M. Jones   Robert Craig

SAMUEL A. McCRACKIN PACK. 181 NO. 24
TAVERN LICENSE
CLERK OF COURTS OFFICE, PICKENS, S. C.

To the Honorable Board of County Commissioners for Pickens County.

The undersigned Samuel A. McCracken of Pickensville most respectfully petition your board for a license to retail spiritious liquors by the drink at Pickensville for the term of three months commencing on the 15 Inst and your

Petitioner will ever pray.
Oct. 15, 1869 S. A. McCracken
We the undersigned certify that Samuel A. McCracken is a suitable person to retail liquors by the drink and will obey the laws in such case made & provided.

his
William X Stegall
mark
W. E. Holcombe

Oct. 15, 1869
Test J. E. Hagood

MOSES S. EMERSON PACK. 181 NO. 23
TAVERN LICENSE
CLERK OF COURTS OFFICE, PICKENS, S. C.

To Honorable Board of County Commissioners of Pickens County.

The undersigned most respectfully petition your board for a license to retail spiritious liquors by the drink at Cedar Rock for three months from the 18 day of August 1869 and your petitioner will ever pray &c.

Aug. 23, 1869 M. S. Emerson

We the undersigned recommend Moses Emerson as a suitable person to retail spiritious liquors at Cedar Rock.

A. S. Smith
J. V. Durham

Aug. 23, 1869

JAMES PERRY LOOPER & BENSON GILSTRAP PACK. 181 NO. 34
CLERK OF COURTS OFFICE, PICKENS, S. C.
TAVERN LICENSE

The State of South Carolina
Pickens County.)
To the Honorable Board of County Commissioners of Pickens County.

The humble petition of the undersigned Citizens of the County and State aforesaid.

Respectfully petition your Honorable Board for a Tavern License to keep a Tavern and retail Spiritious Liquors at the house whereon we now live at at the forks of the Greenville and Pickensville Road just outside of the corporate limits of the Village of Pickens for twelve months from this date.

Your petitioners is prepared to keep a Tavern, and has at least two spare beds and necessary bedding more than are required for the families of the applicants and are well provided with house room and stabling and provender for four horses.

J. Perry Looper
B. B. Gilstrap

March 22, 1873
We the undersigned Citizens residing in the neighborhood, where the said J. Perry Looper and B. B. Gilstrap proposes to open and keep a Tavern License, and we certify that the said J. Perry Looper and B. B. Gilstrap are

gentlemen of good repute for honesty and sobriety, and is known to us to have at least two spare beds, and necessary bedding, more than are required for the families of the said applicants, and is well provided with house room stabling and provender for four horses.
March 22, 1873

Wm. McDade
E. H. Griffin
E. B. Hendrix
Isaac Langston

J. Riley Ferguson
Joab Mauldin
Jeremiah Looper

JOHN M. HENDRICKS PACK. 181 NO. 5
TAVERN LICENSE
CLERK OF COURTS OFFICE, PICKENS, S. C.

To the Honorable Board of County Commissioners of Pickens County.

The Humble Petition of the undersigned a Citizen of Pickens County.

Respectfully petition your Honorable for a Tavern License to keep a Tavern and Retail Spiritious Liquors at my house where I now live on the main road from Pickens to Slabtown for one year. Your petitioner is prepared to keep a Tavern and has at least two spare beds, and necessary bedding, more than are required for the family of the said applicant, and I am well provided with house room and stabling and provender for four horses.
June 1, 1872   John M. Hendricks

We the undersigned Citizens residing in the neighborhood, where the said John M. Hendricks proposes to open a Tavern and keep a Tavern License and we certify that the said John M. Hendricks is a gentleman of good repute for honesty and sobriety, and is known to us, to have at least two spare beds and necessary bedding, more than are required for the family of the said applicant, and is well provided with house room stabling and provender for four horses.
June 1, 1872

F. M. Couch
Abner Mullinix
Calvin O'Dell
Elias Kennemore
Lot Kennemore

T. M. WELBORN PACK. 181 NO. 6
TAVERN LICENSE
CLERK OF COURTS OFFICE, PICKENS, S. C.

To the Honorable Board of County Commissioners of Pickens County.

The Humble Petition of the undersigned, a Citizen of Pickens County in the State of South Carolina, most respectfully petition your Honorable Board for a Tavern License, to retail Spiritious Liquors at the house now occupied by him at Pickensville and known as the Pickensville Hotel, situated at Pickensville. Your petitioner is prepared to keep a Tavern, and is now keeping one, and has at least two spare beds, and the necessary bedding, more than are required for the family of the said applicant, are well provided with house room & stabling and provender for four or more horses.

April 30, 1872   T. M. Welborn

We the undersigned Citizens and Free Holders residing in the neighborhood where the said Thomas M. Welborne proposes to open & carry on a Tavern License and we certify that the said Thomas M. Welborne is a gentleman of good repute for honesty and sobriety, and is known to us to have in his Tavern at least two spare beds, and necessary bedding, more than are required for the family of the said applicant, and is well provided with house room, stabling and provender for at least four or more horses.

April 30, 1872

                        R. J. Gilliland
                        Stephen B. Watson
                        Jacob Pickle
                        J. M. Rankley

J. BROKN KIRKSEY PACK. 181 NO. 33
TAVERN LICENSE
CLERK OF COURTS OFFICE, PICKENS, S. C.

The State of South Carolina
Pickens County.)
To the Honorable Board of County Commissioners of Pickens County.

The humble petition of the undersigned a citizen of Pickens County respectfully petition your honorable Board for a Tavern License to keep a Tavern and Retail Spiritious Liquors at my house whereon I live on main road from Pumpkintown to Pickensville for one year.

Your petitioner is prepared to keep a Tavern and has at least two spare beds and necessary bedding, more than are required for the family of the said applicant and am well provided with house room and stabling and provender for four horses.

December 4, 1872   J. Brown Kirksey

We the undersigned Citizens residing in the neighborhood, where the said J. Brown Kirksey prepares to open a Tavern and keep a Tavern License, and we certify that the said J. Brown Kirksey is a gentleman of good repute for honesty and sobriety and is known to us to have at least two spare beds and necessary bedding more than are required for the family of the said applicant and is well provided with house room stabling and provender for four horses.

December 4, 1872

                       S. D. Keith
                       J. B. Hester
                       Wm. M. Jones
                       J. B. Sutherland
                       J. S. Jones
                       Simeon E. Burgess

R. J. PARRIS PACK. 181 NO. 3
TAVERN LICENSE
CLERK OF COURTS OFFICE, PICKENS, S. C.

To the Honorable Board of County Commissioners of Pickens County.

The Humble Petition of the undersigned, most respectfully petition your

Honorable Board, for a Tavern License to Retail Spirtious Liquors at the house near to Easleys Bridge in Pickens County the house known as the Love House on Easley Bridge Road. Your petitioner is prepared to keep a Tavern, and has at least two spare beds and the necessary bedding, more than are required for the family of said applicant and I am well provided with house room and stabling and provender for four or more horses.

May 1872   R. J. Parris

We the undersigned Citizens residing in the neighborhood where the said R. J. Parris proposes to open a Tavern & keep a License and we certify that the said R. J. Parris is a gentleman of good repute for honesty and sobriety, and is known to us to have at least two spare beds, and necessary bedding, more than are required for the family of the said applicant, and is well provided with provisions, with house room, stabling and provendor for four horses.

May 1872

W. D. Garrison
G. B. Puckett
T. C. Spencer
John Jones
O. W. Garrison
P. F. Suddeth

Pickens Ct.
Mr. J. E. Hagood Esq. May the 21st 1872

Sir I have complied with the law throughout & you will please send me the license forthwith to Mr. Jno. Gosset Georges Creek P. O. & oblige.

Yours truly
R. J. Parris

May 23d 1872
Jas. E. Hagood Esq.

Dear Sir,
You will please make out and send by the mail carrier (Mr. Bell) a license for Jasper Parris to Retail Spit. Liquors. He has paid me the money for the same.

Respectfully &c
John T. Gossett

ESTATE OF SILAS KIRKSEY PACK. 180
CLERK OF COURTS OFFICE, PICKENS, S. C.

William L. Keith admnr. of the estate of Silas Kirksey sheweth that he departed this life on Oct. 10, 1853, that previous to his death on March 16, 1852, filed his bill in the court against William Kirksey, Sr., David Garvin & his wife Nancy Garvin, who was formerly Nancy Kirksey, Jared Kirksey, Isaac Kirksey and Mary Kirksey being the heirs of Jarod Kirksey decd., Robert Kirksey, William Kirksey, Jr., Thomas J. Hallum and his wife Catherine Hallum, formerly Catharine Kirksey, Christopher Kirksey, B. F. Holland and his wife Penelope Holland, formerly Penelope Kirksey stating therein that Fair Kirksey the brother of said Silas Kirksey departed this life intestate on the 24th April 1845. That shortly thereafter Silas Kirksey applied to the Ord. of Anderson District where the said Fair Kirksey died, for Letters of Admnr. upon his estate.

HARDY GILSTRAP & JAMES P. LOOPER PACK. 181 NO. 1
PETITION FOR PERMISSION TO KEEP A TAVERN LICENSE
CLERK OF COURTS OFFICE, PICKENS, S. C.

To the Hon. Board of County Commissioners of Pickens County.

The humble petition of the undersigned Citizens of Pickens County most respectfully petition your Honorable Board for a Tavern License to retail spiritious Liquors at the house now occupied by us, situate in the forks of Greenville and Pickensville Road, and just outside of the incorporation of the Village of Pickens. Your petitioner is prepared to keep a Tavern and has at least two spare beds and necessary bedding, more than are required for the family of the said applicants, and we are well provided with house room, and stabling and provender for four horses.

March 22, 1872

       H. Gilstrap

       J. Perry Looper

We the undersigned Citizens residing in the neighborhood where the said Hardy Gilstrap and James P. Looper proposes to open a Tavern License, and we certify that the said Hardy Gilstrap and James P. Looper are gentlemen of good repute for honesty and sobriety and is known to us to have at least two spare beds and necessary bedding more than are required for the families of the said applicants, and is well provided with house room, stabling and provender for four horses.

March 22, 1872

J. E. Hagood

       E. R. Griffin

       L. Hughes

       Thos. Perkins

       Z. Smith

Bond.

The State of South Carolina

Pickens County)

Know all men by these presents, That we Hardy Gilstrap, James P. Looper, E. H. Griffin Sgr. and D. F. Bradley of Pickens County acknowledge ourselves to owe to John T. Gossett, Jacob Lewis and Robert Craig, Commissioners of Pickens County and their Successors in office, the sum of one thousand dollars, to which payment well and truly to be made, we bind ourselves and every of us each and every of our heirs Executors and administrators jointly and severeally by these presents. Witness our hands and seals this the 22 Day of March in the year of our Lord one thousand Eight Hundred & Seventy two (1872).

The condition of this recognizance is such that whereas Hardy Gilstrap and James P. Looper is licensed to keep a Tavern in the House occupied by them in the forks of the Greenville and Pickensville Road just outside of the incorporation of the Village of Pickens, for the space of one year from the date hereof. Now if the said Hardy Gilstrap and James P. Looper during the continuance of the said license, shall not keep a disorderly house, nor suffer or permit any unlawful gaming in or about the said house and premises, nor violate the law, concerning the traffic in Spiritious Liquors, but shall during the said time in all things use and maintain good order and rule, and feed and provide good wholesome and sufficient lodging diet and entertainment for mare & stabling and provender for horses, and observe the directions of the law relating to the keeping of taverns, then this Recognizance to be void otherwise to remain in full force and virtue.

Given under our hands & seals the day and year above written. In presence of J. E. Hagood

       H. Gilstrap (SEAL)
       J. Perry Looper (SEAL)
       D. F. Bradley (SEAL)
       E. H. Griffin (SEAL)

"SLAVE PAPERS," PACK. 179
CLERK OF COURTS OFFICE, PICKENS, S. C.

No. 1 Dennis Dodd made oath that on or about the 3rd of Nov. inst. that Lewis a slave of James M. Crawford did commit a larceny by stealing about a bushel of corn, which he believes was his own, but Lewis said he had taken it from his master, to buy tobacco and pay the corn for it . . . No. 2. On Aug. 29, 1851 Sarah Gant made oath that on the 22nd of inst. that Berry a slave belonging to Mrs. Sarah Mancill was on the side of the highway between Mrs. Mancills & Lewis Hills was with his pants a loose strip so as to show his nakedness. Hariet Haris sworn says, as she went to schoole one morning the boy was on the fence with his pants downs and ask some in fair qustions to her & then jumped off the fence and and said something to her and she says she did not under stand what he said & then she returned back home on account of the boys conduct. Nancy Clarintine Gant says, "He was between Mrs. Mancills and Lewis Hill on the fence with his pants down and said he wanted some . . . He was found guilty and sentenced to 15 lashes well laid on his back . . . No. 3. On March 14, 1855 Mrs. Sarah Ann McConnel wife of J. B. W. McConnel of Pickens Dist. made oath that Jerry a negro slave belonging to William N. Martin of Anderson Dist. came to our house and assaulted me and committed a rape on my person and left taking off with him some clothing and a hat . . . No. 4. On March 21, 1855 W. W. King made oath that Gill a slave and Nero a slave belonging to C. Lay has been carring corn off at nights and selling it for liquor and also Gill has been retaling liquor at church. (Uame not plain) sworn says, Gill came to my house and called me out of bed and wanted to sell me some corn for liquor had a bag with something in it. Said it was corn. Said one of Mrs. Walkers negroes was with him, had no order or pass from his master. I told him that I had no liquor, he asked me where he could get any liquor, I told him that he could get it from Messer Madden if he had an order. I saw Madden since and asked him if Gill had been there that night he said he had not. W. W. Knight sworn says, Mr. Manly told me he wanted me to come down to the ditch where he was ditching as he had something to tell me, he told me what he had seen and heard wit Mr. Lays negroes the night before. I went to the field where Mr. Lays negroes were at work, asked Gill if he was out from home last night, he said he was not, I asked him if he was not at our house, he said he believed he was there a little bit. I asked him if he had a bag of corn last night he said not. I remarked to him that a white man had seen him with a bag of corn last night, he said that no white man that God ever put a gut in had seen him with a bag of corn that night . . . No. 5. On Sept. 1, 1853 James Zachary made oath that on Aug. 25th, Jim and Green two slaves belonging to Thomas Murphey did on that day break open his house and did steal and carry away he thinks about 40 lbs. bacon but does not know the exact amount. Simpson L. Fountain says that Jim came down to the mill for meal he had there and did not leave until next morning, as he knows of, and in the morning got his meal and left. The negroes were found guilty and sentenced to 39 lashes on the bare back and ordered to leave the neighborhood of Walhalla . . . No. 6. On Dec. 13, 1853 Alvin Jenkins made oath that Sol the property of Mrs. Violet Bowman did in a very insolent manner resist his authority & threatened him with blows. He states that some days before the 16th Sept. 1853 Milly a negro woman the wife of Sol, was ordered by him to go to work, if she did not he would correct her. Sd. boy Solomn said to him that if there was any lick struck, he would strike the next. On Sept. 16, 1853 while I was correcting some small negroes Solomon said that I had whipped them enough, and put his hands in his pants as though it were for his knife, and believes it was his intention to use it in case I further corrected them. He further states that in a difficulty between Mr. John Bowman and said Solomon broke loose and said that he would go after his young master Mr. Smithson who had promised that in case any difficulty arose, he would come and thresh the ground with them, Solomon went off immediately and brought Mr. Smithson with him, who said if I whipped Solomon I would have to whip him also. The jury found Solomon guilty and sentenced him to 50 lashes well laid on now, and imprisoned at home during the Christmas holidays or within the enclosure of his master, in case he does not stay at home he is to have 75 lashes . . . No. 7. On July 1, 1852 Larkin Nix made oath that Alf & Abe slaves of John Ariail was concerned in stoning his housefl At the time it was done on Sunday night, June 20, 1852 Larkin Nix states that he heard some one of the company say less stone the house. Jasper Hawthorne said, "That a crowd passed his house about 10 o'clock the night the house was stoned, he did not know whether they were negroes or white men. Elihu Griffin said, "That a crowd passed his house about 11 o'clock that he did not know whether there was any negroes along or not. The jury found the negroes guilty and sentenced them to 30 lashes apiece on there bare backs well laid on . . . No. 8. On Sept. 12, 1854 Benjamin Durham made oath that Perry Burdin a free boy of color did on the 11th Sept. 1854 came to Mr. M. Mauldins griss mill which mill the said B. Durham had in his care and after some conversation said boy said that is not the truth and opened his knife in his pocket and called him the said B. Durham a damned son of a bich with other abusive language and also threw a rock which came very near striking him and swore that if Durham followed him any further he would cut his guts out and also held his knife open in his hand at the time. The jury found the boy guilty and sentenced him to five lashes with a hickory on his bare back well layed on . . . No. 9. Wm. R. Pitts a constable of Pickens Dist. was ordered to deliver into the custody of said jail the body of Spensor a slave who was found strolling about thru the country with a white woman of loose habits and having in his possession two horses one of which is a stallion . . . No. 10. On May 14, 1855 Caroline Boren made oath that on April 15th last, Berry the property of William Hunter did come to where her son Hamp was fishing and did raise a fuss with him and took a brush and beat him. The jury found the boy not guilty . . . No. 11. On Nov. 27, 1852 Israel Mayfield made oath that he believes that Henry a slave belonging to Leonard Capehart did on Aug. 8th take and carry away from his patch several watermellons one a very large one . . . No. 12. On Jan. 29, 1850 James White made oath that he believes that Parris a slave the property of Thomas Alexander did on the night of the 25th Inst. commit an assault on the person of Milly Oglesby a free woman of color. Milly Oglesby says that she was waked up between morning and day, heard Rachel hollowing murder and said Paris was choking her, went out to meet them. Rachel went into Mrs. Calhouns house, Paris tried to go in after her. I pushed him back several times and then Paris struck me. They then went on down to next house & Paris followed. They ordered him out of the house but he would not go. Pushed him several times, tried to get him out. Paris made many threats said he would have his money or kill some of them, also threatened to burn down her house, he struck her and bit her finger. Mrs. Calhoun sworn said Rachel & Paris came to her house quarreling, ordered them not to come in her house. Milly pushed Paris out and against the door. Paris struck Milly. Milly tried to keep peace. Paris said he wanted them to go home & give up his money. Milly had been staying with her since Christmas. Lucinda Kelly says, Saw Paris at her mothers house, saw him strike Milly . . . Tom a slave of W. L. Keith said he was at Millys the night the money was stolen. Saw no fighting between them. The jury found Paris guilty and sentenced him to 25 lashes on his bare back . . . No. 13. On Jany. 26, 1850 Susannah Carver made oath that she believes that Gabriel Shoemate a free person of color has within the last week grossly slandered her and her daughter Polly Carver with the following words, that he Gabriel Shoemate and the said Susannah Carver were trying to root out David James for her & her daughter to get his house to live in, so that the said Gabriel might have the use of her said daughter Polly . . . No. 14. On Sept. 26, 1850 G. W. Farr made oath that he believes that Frances a negro woman belonging to Clary Turner & Rebuen a negro boy belonging to G. W. Farr did steal some money from him between 25 & 40 dollars. G. W. Farr sworn says, "That Frances told him she had met with one of her old friends & he paid her 2 dollars & she bought those things with, afterwards she told me how she did come by these things that old Uncle Abraham had let her have the money. The jury found them guilty and sentenced them to be tied and strip their bare backs and that each have fifty lashes.

ESTATE OF JOSHUA CHAPMAN BOX 44 NO. 492
PROBATE JUDGE'S OFFICE, PICKENS CO. S. C.

Estate admnr. Aug. 10, 1857 by Samuel Chapman, Abraham Sargent, J. E. Hagood, E. E. Alexander who are bound unto W. J. Parsons Ord. Pickens Dist. in sum of $2,000.00 . . . Summons in petition Joseph Merck & wife vs. Joel Chapman. To Elizabeth Chapman, Jacob Chapman, Rachel Chapman, Isaac A. Chapman, Margaret Chapman, Samuel Chapman, David Garret & wife Elizabeth and the heirs of Giles Chapman decd. viz. John F. Chapman and Mary E. Chapman were required to appear before the Ord. to show cause why the real estate of Samuel Chapman should not be sold . . . Dated Aug. 4, 1858 . . . Owned 192 acres of land more or less lying on Shoal Creek bounded by lands of Carter Clayton, Samuel Chapman & others . . . On April 15, 1861 Obadiah J. Wigington and Ruth his wife of Cobb County, Georgia appointed Samuel Chapman of Pickens Disrtict their Attorney. The widow was Elizabeth Chapman . . . J. Merck & wife Susannah were heirs . . . Feb. 19, 1858 Heirs out of the state were viz. Thomas McKinney & wife Mary, Joel Chapman, Israil Chapman, O. J. Wigington & wife Ruth. On August 2, 1869 Susannah Merck, Elizabeth Garrett, Jacob Chapman, Toliver Roper & wife Mary E., David Tompkins & wife Mary, Clinton Hollingsworth and wife Elizabeth were required to appear before the Ordinary on the 6th Sept. 1869 to show cause why the real estate of Joshua Chapman situated on Shoal Creek waters of 12 Mile River should not be sold . . . On June 27, 1869 states that Toliver Roper & wife Mary E. were heirs of Giles Chapman decd. David Tompkins & wife Mary, Clinton Hollingsworth & wife Elizabeth R. were heirs of Isaac Chapman decd. . . . Joel Chapman resides in Tennessee . . . Mary McKinney resides in Georgia.

ESTATE OF DELLA CHAPMAN BOX 48 NO. 531
PROBATE JUDGES OFFICE, PICKENS CO. S. C.

Estate admnr. March 29, 1858 by F. N. Garvin, J. N. Lawrence who are bound unto W. J. Parsons Ord. Pickens Dist. in sum of $300.00.

ESTATE OF JOHN CHAPMAN BOX 9 NO. 118
PROBATE JUDGE'S OFFICE, PICKENS, S. C.

Estate admnr. April 6, 1840 by Samuel Chapman, Joshua Chapman, Moses Hendrix who are bound unto James H. Dendy Ord. Pickens Dist. in sum $1,000.00 . . . Samuel Chapman was a son of said John Chapman . . . Left a widow and children, but no names given. (Loose paper found probably goes in this package). April 8, 1843 Rhodey Chapman recd. $317.00 from estate of her father John Chapman decd.

ESTATE OF BENJAMIN CHAPMAN BOX 23 NO. 271
PROBATE JUDGES OFFICE, PICKENS CO. S. C.

Estate admnr. Oct. 18, 1850 by General F. N. Garvin, William Smith Esq., J. A. Doyle who are bound unto William D. Steele Ord. Pickens Dist. in sum of $2,800.00 . . . Expend: 1849 Paid W. A. Chapman for 2 years of work at $10.00 per month $240.00. . . . Amelia J. wife of William A. Mauldin was a dtr. of said decd. Sarah Chapman, Rebecca Swords, Thomas H. Chapman, J. W. Chapman, Martha E. Fennell, George Chapman, Benjamin P. Chapman, Green E. Chapman, Cynthia Hinton, Elvira Smith were legatees.

ESTATE OF GILES CHAPMAN BOX 25 NO. 294
PROBATE JUDGES OFFICE, PICKENS CO. S. C.

Estate admnr. March 24, 1845 by Lucy Eleanor Chapman, John O'Briant, W. L. Keith who are bound unto William D. Steele Drd. Pickens Dist. in sum of $400.00 . . . Lucy E. Chapman later married a Evins? Left a widow and 2 children . . . Expend: July 26, 1866 Paid Mary E. R. Chapman her share $81.85 . . . Due estate of John F. Chapman decd. $81.85 less amount of Confederate money paid for coll. for heirs at his special instance & request $75.00.

ESTATE OF JOHN CHAPMAN BOX 40 NO. 454
PROBATE JUDGE'S OFFICE, PICKENS CO. S. C.

Estate admnr. Nov. 23, 1855 by Samuel Chapman, F. N. Garvin, David Freeman who are bound unto W. J. Parsons Ord. Pickens Dist. in sum of $500.00. Left a widow, Caroline Chapman and 3 heirs, no names given.

ESTATE OF JOSEPH CHAPMAN SR. BOX 6 NO. 75
PROBATE JUDGES OFFICE, PICKENS, S. C.

Estate admnr. Feb. 1, 1863 by Col. Benjamin Hagood, John Burdine, William L. Keith who are bound unto James M. Dendy Ord. Pickens Dist. in sum of $25,000.00. (One way looked like thousand & then a hundred).
State of Georgia
Hall County) Know all men by these presents that I Joseph Chapman of the State of S. C. and Pendleton Dist. do most solemnly affirm before me John E. Rivers or Rieves? J. P. for Hall Co. that at the intermarriage of my dtr. Polly to Wm. Ladd I gave up to the said Wm. Ladd $800.00 in property and part negroes and the said Wm. Ladd undertook to keep a stud horse for me in the Co. of Harbersham, Ga. for 1 yr. and I have lent him money & sold him other property the bal. of what he made of the horse and of what money I lent him & property sold him long after his marriage amts. in all to $250.00 besides the $800.00 given him at his marriage aforesd. I further affirm that the cause of this affidavits being made in Ga. was the removal of the sd. Wm. Ladd out of the State of Ga. as I was fully determined to have a sett. with him and in order to deal justly with all my chn. is a further cause of doing so. And I further most solemnly affirm that I never in tend hereafter to give sd. Ladd one cent with as a s. l. or stranger. Sworn before me this 5 Mar. 1827.
J. E. Rivers?

                his
             Jos. X Chapman
               mark

The legattes of said Joseph Chapman were: George Chapman, William Chapman, John Chapman, Jeremiah Chapman, Solomon & Elizabeth Magee, William Lynch, William Ladd, Nancy Patterson, John Garner, . . . Archibald Chapman was Attorney for Joseph Chapman, Enoch Chapman, John Chapman, George Chapman, John Henson, Samuel Sullivan, John Garner.

BIBLE RECORDS IN POSSESSION OF
MR. CHARLES NEWTON DURHAM, AGE 80 YEARS
PICKENS, PICKENS COUNTY, S. C.

FATHER—LORENO YOUNG DURHAM was born August 25, 1847 and dept. this life Feb. 11, 1920.

MOTHER—SARAH ANN DURHAM was born November 14, 1849.
BROTHER—JULIUS NEWTON DURHAM was born March 26, 1872.
"ME"—CHARLES NEWTON DURHAM was born January 21, 1874.
GRANDFATHER—CHARLES DURAM was born May 11, 1810.
GRANDMOTHER—REBECCA YOUNG was born September 12, 1812.
MY OLDEST BOY—COURTNAY McILROY DURHAM was born Oct. 13, 1895.
MY OLDEST DAU.—HORTENCE DURHAM was borned Sept. the 19, 1897.

MARRIAGES

CHARLES DURHAM and JANIE McWHORTER were united by me in the Parsonage at Pickens Courthouse on the 4 day of November in the year of our Lord 1894.

In presence of
G. R. Shaffer
Signed
H. Ernest McWhorter

Lorenzo Y. Durham and Sarah A. Hawthorne were married January 24, 1867.

Charles N. Durham and Janie McWhorter was married by Rev. G. R. Shaffer in the Parsonage at Pickens C. H. S. C. November 4, 1894.

DEATHS

Julius N. Durham died March 27, 1872.
Jasper N. Hawthorne departed this life March 4, 1856.
Charles Durham departed this life Nov. 19, 1884.
Rebecca Durham departed this life July 14, 1896.
L. R. Durham dept. this life Feb. 11, 1920.
Sarah A. Durham departed this life December 29, 1932.
"MY OWN BOYS." William Homer Durham was borned Oct. 2, 1899.
Charles Harold Durham was borned March 2, 1902.

ESTATE OF JOHN W. MASON APT. 84 NO. 897
WALHALLA COURTHOUSE, OCONEE CO. S. C.

Estate administered Dec. 6. 1897 by Wallace W. Cornog?, W. C. Mason and J. R. Earle who are bound unto E. L. Herndon Ord. Oconee County in sum $518.00 . . . John W. Mason died April 9, 1897 in Franklin County, Georgia. His widow was Julia Mason. Children viz. John W. and Carry C. Mason minors under 14 years. Had half an interest . . . 128 acres . . . known as the Cleveland Place in Center Township, Oconee Co. adjoining lands of William Cleveland, B. J. Maret, Robert Isbell and E. C. Maret.

ESTATE OF JOEL MASON APT. 13 NO. 148
WALHALLA COURTHOUSE, OCONEE CO. S. C.

On Sept. 26, 1861 Frances Mason recd. $26.18 her share of her late husband Joel Mason decd. estate. Heirs were: Frances Mason widow, B. C. Whisenant & wife Milly, Samuel Lyles & wife Mary W., D. L. Lyles and wife Martha Ann, Charles W. Mason all residents of Pickens Dist. & of age except

Charles Mason. Dated Oct. 19, 1859.

ESTATE OF AMBROSE MASON BOX 12 NO. 420
PROBATE JUDGES OFFICE. ANDERSON, S. C.

Abstract of Will . . . Will dated April 4, 1837. Proven June 5, 1837. Witness, James Young Sr., Jesse Bradberry, Abraham Meridith . . . Ment. Estate to Jenny Payne . . . Expend. July 25, 1849 Paid Lucinda Mason $19.19½ . . . Oct. 24, 1849 Paid Ester Mason $14.40. July 25, 1849 Paid Mary Mason $19.19½. Paid Kitty Mason $19.19½ . . . On Feb. 1, 1845 Elijah Kees of Pickens Dist. saith that Elizabeth Cox was his half sister & had a female illegimate child & when about 3 years old she married James Mason & the child took the name of Nancy Mason and when the child came to maturity she had a illegimate female child Milinday and she married John Vills? Jr. and the said child Malinday is about to try to become one of the heirs of Ambrose Mason decd. . . . James Bradberry of Habersham County, Georgia married a sister of Ambrose Mason. Dated Jan. 17, 1842 . . . William King of Anderson applied for Letters of Admnr.

WILL OF WILLIAM SPENCER VOL. 6 PAGE 482
PROBATE JUDGE'S OFFICE, CHARLESTON, S. C.

In the Name of God Amen the nineteenth day of February in the year of our Lord one thousand Seven hundred & fifty one I William Spencer of James Island in Berkley County Planter Being Sick and Weak in body but of Perfect mind and memory thanks be given unto God therefore calling to mind the mortality of my Body and Knowing that it is appointed for all men once to die do make and ordain this my Last Will & Testament that is to say Principally and first of all I Give & Recommend my Soul into the hands of God that Gave it and my Body I Recommend to the Earth to be buried in a Decent Christian burial at the discretion of my Exors nothing doubting but at the General Resurrection I Shall Receive the same again by the Almighty Power of God and as Touching Such Worldly Estate wherewith it hath pleased God to bless me with in this life I Give & Dispose of the same in the following manner and form. ITEM. I Give and Bequeath unto my Beloved Wife Sarah Spencer one negro man named Robin and a girl named Flower & all the Cattle & Sheep of her mark her Riding horse her bed and furniture two Cedar Chests her Poultry. Item. I Leave her the use of a Room in the Dwelling house during her widow hood. Item. I Leave her a Wench named Hannah the use of her During her widowhood or the day of her Death which shall be in Lieu of a Child part. ITEM. I Give and Bequeath unto my son William Spencer the plantation whereon I now live & the two Islands fronting the Sea to him and his heirs of his body. Item. I Give and Bequeath unto my Son John Spencer Sixty acres of Land belonging to the tract that he now lives on to him and the heirs forever. ITEM. My Will is that the tract of Land Containing two hundred Acres Joyning to John Stanyarne's Land to be sold and pay my Debts if any. Item. My will is that the Tract of Land Containing two hundred Acres joyning to Mrs. Coles Land to be Sold to pay my Debts if any. Item. My will is that my Personal Estate shall be Justly appraised and

Equally Divided amongst my Children John Spencer, William Spencer, Ann Sandiford, Sarah Holmes. ITEM. My Will is that after my funeral charges is paid and my Estate is Divided that all my Children as before mentioned shall equally pay all my Debts also I give Eighty Pounds Current to be put out to Interest for the Support of Poor Children at a Christian School at the Discretion of my Exors and I Give twenty pounds Currency for the Repairing of the meeting house on James Island whenever wanted for that use and also my will is that if either of my Children should die without issue then that share before Bequeathed Shall be Divided among the Surviving Children and Lastly I do Constitute appoint my Beloved Wife Sarah Spencer, John Spencer, William Spencer, John Sandiford, John Holmes to be my Exors to this my Last Will & Testament In Witness whereof I have Set my hand and Seal the day & year above written.

William Spencer (L. S.)

Jno Mathewes
Mary Samvays
Mary Vanderwicke
   O (Her Mark)   PROVED APRIL 12, 1751.

WILL OF JOSEPH SPENCER VOL. 5 PAGE 585
PROBATE JUDGES OFFICE, CHARLESTON, S. C.

IN THE NAME OF GOD AMEN the twentieth day of June in the Year of our Lord one thousand Seven hundred and forty six I Joseph Spencer of James Island St. Andrews Parish and Province of South Carolina being very Sick and weak of Body but of perfect mind and Memory know that it is appointed by the all wise God for all men once to die do make and Ordain this My Last Will and Testament And first of all I give and Recommend my Soul to God who gave it; And my Body I recommend to the Earth to be buried in a Christian manner at the Discretion of my Executors, there to wait the glorious resurrection through the migh Power of God, And as to my Worldly Estate I give Demife and Difpofe of the Same in manner and form Following Imprimis, I will and Order that all my Just Debts and funeral Charges be paid so soon after my decease as pofsible by my Executors hereinafter named Item I give and bequeath unto my dearly beloved brother William Spencer and to his Heirs for Ever all that Tract of Land on which I now dwell, consisting of one hundred and forty Acres more or lefs, together with my dwelling Houfe Out Houfes, and all other the Appurtenances thereto belonging and being on the premifses, Except what is hereafter Excepted Item I give and bequeath unto my dear friend Mary Dill, Daughter of Elizabeth Dill, One Cedar Chest now being in the Dwelling house of the said Elizabeth Dill, together with all the things which are therein at the time of my decease. Item my Will is, and I hereby Order, that the Land which I bought of Captain Robert Rivers, lately in the Pofsefsion of Stephen Rufsell, and containing about fifty two Acres and half more or lefs, together with all my moveables and personal Estate be Immediately by my Executors Put to Sale, and what monies may arise from Such Sale to be applied to paying all my Just Debts and funeral Charges and the remainder to be given as follows, that is to say

I will and Order that my Executors do make three Equal parts or Division of such Money as may be left after my Just Debts are difcharged as aforesaid Item I Give bequeath unto my dearly beloved Sifter, One part or moiety of the said money, and the other two parts or moietys, I give and bequeath unto my dear and well beloved friend Mary Dill Daughter of Elizabeth Dill aforesaid Item I constitute nominate and appoint my Brother William Spencer Executor, together with my friend Mary Dill aforesaid Executrix to this my last will and Testament disannulling all former Wills and Testaments by me made and Ratifying this and no other to be my last Will and Testament in Witness whereof I have hereunto Set my hand and Seal the day and year first above written.

The within Will and Testament of Joseph Spencer contain two Sides of this Sheet of Paper was Signed Sealed Published and declared, by the said Joseph Spencer to be his last Will and Testament before us who in presence of the said Testator have witnefsed the Same.

Joseph Spencer (SEAL)

Samuel Stent
Jofeph Rivers
Will Gough

This will was proved before his Excellency the 11th July 1746 by the Oaths of Will Gough, Saml Stent and Joseph Rivers.

WILL OF OLIVER SPENCER VOL. 6 PAGE 356
PROBATE JUDGE'S OFFICE, CHARLESTON, S. C.

In the name of God Amen, I Oliver Spencer of the Parish of Christ in Berkley County in the Province of South Carolina, Cord-weiner being sick in Body but of perfect mind & memory thanks be to God for the Same And now calling to mind the uncertainty of this Life that it is appointed once for all men to Die have constituted this my last Will and Testament in manner and form following, But Principally & first of all I Recommend my Soul into the hands of God that gave it and my Body to the Earth to be buried in a Christian Like Manner at the discretion of my Executors nothing doubting but at the General Resurrection I shall receive the same again by the mighty Power of God and as touching such worldly Estate where with it hath pleased God to bless me with in this Life I give devise and dispose of the same in the following manner and form. IMPRIMIS. It is my full Intent and meaning that all my Debts and Funeral Charges be paid as soon may Possible be after my Decease & before any of my Estate be divided. 2dly. Item. It is my Will and request that my beloved Wife Rebecca Spencer do live where I now reside and have a Room of her own Choosing in the House with a Feather Bed and Furniture and one Negro Fellow named Prince during the time that she continues a Widow or keeps my name up and after that to be equally divided among my Children that is viz. Oliver, John, Elizabeth, Martha, Ann and Susannah. 3dly. Item. I do give unto my Dearly deloved Sons viz. Oliver & John One hundred & thirteen acres & half of Land equally to be divided betwixt them and do desire that the Land be not pillaged by any Persons until they come to age only Oliver to have that part where the house I now dwell in stands to them and their or either of their Heirs forever. and further I do desire that two Sons that is Oliver and John do when they or either of them shall come to age pay unto my three Daughters viz. Rebecca, Royer, Sarah Evans & Hannah Spencer Ten Pounds Current money of the Province afsd. 4thly. Item. It is my Will and pleasure further that my Loving Wife do with the advice and consent of my Executors here under mentioned sell and dispose as she shall think most convenient towards paying my Lawfull Debts Three Negroes viz. Toney Marrels & Bess with what sovr. of my Personal Estate not be fore mentioned & whatever if not sold to be equally divided among my children when they come of age as before mentioned viz. Oliver John Elizabeth Martha Ann and Susannah. 5thly. And Lastly I do constitute Ordain & appoint my Loving Wife my beloved Son Oliver Spencer & Capt. William Hendrick to be my true & Lawful Executors to this my last Will & Testament utterly disallowing and do make void all other Wills or Testamoneys Legacys & bequests whatsoever by me in any wise made AS WITNESS my hand this twenty third day of Nov. in the Year of our Lord one thousand seven hundred & forty Eight.

Oliver Spencer (L. S.)

Signed Sealed Published & Pronounced by the said Oliver Spencer to be his last Will & Testament in presence of us.
William Sheers
The mark of) S. Stephen Callebuff
Henry Varnor
PROVED MAY 25th, 1750.

ESTATE OF ROBERT SPENCER NO. 383
PROBATE JUDGE'S OFFICE, GEORGETOWN, S. C.

Estate administered Feb. 21, 1874 by B. J. Hazard, S. R. Carr, Thomas M. Merrimon who are bound unto R. O. Bush Ord. in sum of $200.00 . . . Died in 1874 . . . Heirs, children viz. Isaiah Spencer now about 20 years old, Sarah Spencer about 17 years old, Elizabeth Spencer now about 15 years old, Emeline Spencer about 12 years of age.

WILL OF JOHN SPENCER VOL. 19 PAGE 46
PROBATE JUDGE'S OFFICE, CHARLESTON, S. C.

South Carolina
IN THE NAME OF GOD AMEN I John Spencer of Christ Parish Planter being at this time of sound disposing Mind Memory and Under standing do make & declare this my last Will and Testament in manner and form following that is to say, First I Will that my Just Debts & funeral Expenses be duly paid and satisfied. Item I give and bequeath unto Peter Rya the son of Peter deceased the sum of Five Shillings sterling in full of all Claims and Demands he can or may against my Estate either real or Personally to his heirs Exors or Assigns forever. Item, I give and bequeath unto William Rya the sum of Five Shillings Sterling in full of all Claims and Demands he can or may have against my Estate either Real or Personally to his Heirs Exors and Assigns forever. Item, I give and Bequeath unto Richard Rya the sum of Five shillings Sterling in full of all demands he can or may have against my Estate

either Real or Personally to his heirs Exors and Assigns forever. Item I give and bequeath unto Elizabeth Quelch Niece of Capt. Andrew Quelch all that plantation or tract of Land Containing Seventy Acres more or less to her, her heirs Exors & Assigns forever. Item, I give and bequeath unto the said Elizabeth Quelch all the Remainder of my Estate not before mentioned goods Chattles Horse Cows and affects whatsoever to her Heirs Exors and Assigns for for ever. I do hereby Nominate and appoint Elizabeth Quelch Executrix of this my last Will and Testament & hereby Revoking all former and other Will or Wills by me heretofore made declaring this only to be my last Will and Testament. IN WITNESS whereof I have hereunto set my Hand and Seal the thirtieth day of September in the Year of our Lord one Thousand seven hundred and Eighty. Signed Sealed Published by the Testator for & as his last Will and Testament in the presence of us who at his request & in his presence have unto subscribed Our names.

Martha Bolton John Spencer (LS)
John Elliott
Jacob Remington PROVED NOV. 21, 1780

WILL OF SEBASTIAN SPENCER VOL. 33 PAGE 1281
PROBATE JUDGES OFFICE, CHARLESTON, S. C.

16-F. S

No. 16) South Carolina. In the Name of God Amen. I Sebastain Spencer, of the Village of Hampstead, in the Parish of Saint Phillip, in the State aforesaid, do make my last Will & testament in manner and form following. I do hereby authorize & impower my Executor herein after named, to sell and dispose of my whole Estate both real and Personal, on such terms as he shall think most for the benefit & advantage of my Legatees herein after named. Item I give to a free Woman of Colour, named Amy, formerly belonging to, & emancipated by me, the sum of Two hundred Dollars; And all the rest, residue and remainder of my Estate both real and Personal, whatsoever and wheresoever. I give, devise & bequeath to my Friends Mrs. Catherine Ehney, Mrs. Ann B. Chitty, Mrs. Ann Friend, Mrs. Catherine Stoll, Mrs. Mary Stone, & Miss Catherine Lindershine for ever, to be equally divided amongst them, share and share alike, And lastly I do, hereby nominate constitute and appoint my friend Mr. Thomas Raine sole Executor of this my last Will & Testament, hereby revoking all former Wills by me made, and declaring this only to be my last Will & Testament. In Witness whereof I have hereunto set my hand and Seal the Twelfe day of August, in the Year of our Lord One thousand eight hundred & Seventeen.

Sebastain x Spencer (SEAL)
Hist Mark

Signed, Sealed, Published, Pronounced & declared by the Testator to be his last Will & Testament in the Presence of us, who, in his Presence, & in the Presence of each other, have, athis request, Signed our Names as Witnesses hereto.

B. Hinrickson
Jams. Smith
Benjn. Elfe PROVED AUGUST 30, 1817.

WILL OF JOSEPH SPENCER VOL 12 PAGE 656
PROBATE JUDGES OFFICE, CHARLESTON, S. C.

In the Name of God Amen. I Joseph Spencer of the Parish of St. James Santee in perfect Mind & Memory thanks be given unto God calling unto Mind the Mortality of my Body & knowing that it is appointed for all Men once to die, I do make & Ordain this my last Will & Testament that is to say Principally & first of all, I give & Recommend to the Earth to be Buried in a decent Christian like Manner at the Discretion of my Exors, Not doubting but at the General Resurrection I shall Receive the same again by the Mighty Power of God, And as Touching such Worldly Estate wherewith it has pleased God to bless me with in this life, I give devise & Bequeath the same in Manner & form following. Item I give devise & Bequeath to my beloved Wife Ann Spencer (after all my lawful Debts are paid) all & Singular my whole Estate both Real & Personal, Consisting of Lands, Moneys, Negroes, Goods & Chattells, & I give devise & Bequeath the same accordingly. Item my Will is that what I have herein above given & Bequeathed to my beloved Wife Ann Spencer, Shall be no longer than during her Natural Life & Power & at her Death by her last Will & Testament she shall have full Power to give & dispose of the same to such of her Children by me as she shall think proper, And I do here by Nominate Ordain & Appoint my beloved Wife Ann Spencer, & my Sister Jane Mary Spencer Executrix of this my last Will & Testament & I do hereby Disannul Revoke & make Void all other former Wills by me at any time heretofore made and I do publish and declare this to be my only last Will and Testament.

In Witness whereof I have hereunto Set my Hand & Seal, this tenth day of May & in the Year of our Lord one thousand Seven Hundred & Sixty Nine.

Jos. Spencer (l. s.)

Signed, Sealed, Published & Declared
by the Testator Joseph Spencer to be his only last Will and
Testament. Signed & Sealed in the Presence of
Jas. Calladon
Lambt. Sheilds
Isaac Dutart

Proved by the Hon. Wm. Bull Esq. Lt. Gov. to Paul Douxsaint Esq. the 12th Dec. 1769.

ESTATE OF WILLIAM SATTERFIELD NO. 654
ANDERSON COURTHOUSE, S. C.

Estate admnr. Dec. 6, 1813 by Rachel Satterfield, Thomas W. Satterfield who are bound unto John Harris Ord. of Pendleton Dist. in the sum $500.00. Citation published at Wilsons Meeting House . . . William Law, Lot Warren, Elijah Satterfield, Thomas W. Satterfield Jr., Lewice? Jones were all legatess.

ESTATE OF WILLIAM WALLACE NO. 783
ANDERSON COURTHOUSE, S. C.

Estate admnr. Sept. 26, 1799 by Thomas Hamilton, Andrew Hamilton,

Archibald Hamilton & Robert Lemon who are bound unto the Judges of Pendleton Dist. in the sum $2,000.00 . . . Letitia Wallace bought at the sale. . . .

ESTATE OF ROBERT R. WALLACE NO. 1462
ANDERSON COURTHOUSE, S. C.

Estate admnr. Oct. 8, 1855 by John T. Wallace, A. E. Reed, James A. Drake who are bound unto the Ord. Anderson Dist. in sum $1200.00 . . . John T. Wallace a brother to decd. . . . 1856 To amount recd. of Ebenezer Wallace on note $39.02 . . . Feb. 15, 1858 one note held by Mary Jane Wallace worth $351.11. . . .

ESTATE OF JOHN T. WALLACE NO. 2053
ANDERSON COURTHOUSE, S. C.

Estate admnr. March 2, 1869 by James A. Drake, Jasper Brown, T. L. Clinkscales who are bound unto W. W. Humphreys Ord. in $2,000.00 . . . Dec. 22, 1868 states that Letitia C. Wallace admnrx. had married James J. Harkness. Left a widow Letitia and a child Lilly Ola who was 11 years old. . .

ESTATE OF W. A. WALLACE NO. 2327

On Feb. 16, 1867 S. A. Wallace wanted William Augustus Wallace to be the guardian of Ida Tecoa, Laura Cannon Major minors under 21 years and children of the said S. A. Wallace & children of Joab W. Major. decd. . . .

WILL OF WILLIAM THRUSTON APT. 7 FILE NO. 489
PROBATE JUDGES OFFICE, GREENVILLE COURTHOUSE, S. C.

IN THE NAME OF GOD AMEN,
I, William Thruston, of the District of Greenville and State of South Carolina being weak in body but of sound mind and memory do make and ordain this my last will and Testament in manner and form followin.

1st. I give and bequeath to my beloved wife Rebecca Thruston one Negro Girl named Phoeby and one called Dicy two feather beds with as much furniture as she may choose to take my large trunk, Desk and book case with as much household and kitchen furniture as she may choose to take for her own use, also my Riding Chear & harness a horse beast of her own choosing, during her natural life in Leiu and right of her dowry; and at the death of my wife I give and bequeath the Said Negro Girl Dicy & her increase to my grandaughter Rebecca Thruston to her and her Heirs forever, and all the balance above named to my wife to be sold & equally divided among all my children.

2nd. I Give and bequeath to my Grand Son William Thruston Son of John Thruston one Hundred Dollars.

3rd. I Give and bequeath to my Grand Son William Thruston Son of Street Thruston one Negro boy called George to him and his heirs forever the Said Negro to remain in posesion of my Son Street Thruston till William

4th. I Give and bequeath to my Grand Son William Thruston Son of Beverly Thruston one hundred dollars.

5th. I give and bequeath to my grand Son Lewis Thruston Son of Richard Thruston one hundred dollars.

It is my will and desire that the above named Legacies be kept at Interest by my Executors untill my said Grand Sons shall respectively arrive to lawful age. It is also my will and desire that my Negro man Peter and my Negro Woman Doll be allowed to choose which of my children they will live with.

6th. It is my will and desire that all the balance of my Estate both real and personal of every nature & kind be sold (vis) the personal property on a credit of twelve months and my Land whereon I now live on a credit of one and two years and the money arising from said sale and also the debts that is due me after all my just debts are paid be equally divided between all my children namely William John Street Richard & Beverly—but it is to be understood the above named Legacies are first to be paid before the division is made between my said children.

Lastly I do nominate and appoint my son William Thruston & my friend Spartan Goodlett Executors of this my last will and testament.

In testimony whereof I have hereunto set my hand and seal this tenth day of May Eighteen Hundred and twenty six.

It is also my desire that there be no Inventory or appraisement made of my Estate. . . .

Signed Sealed and declared to be his last will & testament by the Said Testator in presence of us who at his request and in his presence & in presence of eath other have witnessed the same.

David Johnson　　　　　　　　　　William Thruston (L. S.)
Martha N. Goodlett
Spartan Goodlett
PROBATED FEBRUARY 15, 1828.
S. Goodlett.　　　　　　　RECORDED IN WILL BOOK B. PAGES 101-102.

WILL OF JOSEPH BOYD CASE 9 FILE 361
YORK COUNTY COURTHOUSE, YORK, S. C.

The State of South Carolina York District I Joseph Boyd of the State District aforesaid being in my perfect sinces & memory & in a common State of health but Calling to mind that all men have Once to Die & of all such Estate as God has been pleased to bless me with I desire to be disposed of in the following manner Viz. I will & bequeath to my wife Sara Boyd the plantation on which I Now Live also three Negroes honest Jim Falls & Dinah to be her Property During her natural life the Negroes Not to be Removed out of sd State without Leave of the Executors.

2 I will and bequeth to Daughter Maryan Mannon ten Dollars.

3 I will & bequeth to my son James Lee Boyd two Negro boys Jep & Sandee allso one hundred & fifty Dollars in Cash.

4 I will & bequeth to my four youngest Daughters Sally Jinny Clark Eliza Livena & Peggy all the Remaining part of my Real & Personal Estate to be Equally Divided between them the Said property to Remain the hands of the Executors Until they mary and then one Negro to be given Each one as

they marry or become of lawful age in one year after the first one is married and especial divide to take place.

5 I will & bequth to my wife Sary boyd one third part of all my house & kitchen furniture also one third part of all my Stock & Farming Utensils and Do hereby constitute & ordain this my last Will and Testament I do also Nominate & appoint my Son James Lee Boyd & Robert Mannor my Executors to Cary this my last will into Effect In witness whereof I have hereunto set my hand & Seal this twenty third day of January 1822.
Witness Present
Jno. Ellis   Jos Boyd (SEAL)
Thomas Clark
PROBATED JUNE 4, 1822. WILL BOOK "G" PAGE 81.

WILL OF ZADOCK DARBY CASE 16 FILE 670
YORK COUNTY COURTHOUSE, YORK, S. C.

I Zadock Darby of York District and State of South Carolina being in perfect health, of sound & disposing mind, memory and understanding, but believing all men has to die do make and declare this, my last Will and testament in the manner and form following Viz.—

1st I give & bequeath unto my beloved Wife Mary Darby the one half of the plantation whereon I now live including the dewling house and spring during her life time and at her death to my grand Son Zadock D. Smith to have and to hold the Same for ever. Also to my wife Mary Darby my negroe man Simon his wife Fanny and her two Children Garland & Sarah and my negroe boy Jim. Also all my stock including Horses Cattle, hogs, Sheep, etc. house hold and Kitchen furniture Also all my implements of husbandry including Waggon geers, and Every thing appertaining or made use of as empliments of husbandry & the crop on my farm above mentioned and also my wearing apperal provided never the less and my will is that she pays all my Just debts, and reserves Two hundred Dollars to be hereafter disposed of in my will.

2dly I give and bequeath to my Daughter Delilah Darby alias Delilah Gingles the plantation whereon she now lives during her life time and at her death to be equally divided between her children—Note the two hundred Dollars which as reserved or exacted of my wife Mary Darby is to be placed in the hands of my Executors & by them put out to Intrust—the Interest of which is to be paid Annually to the Said Delilah Gingles at their discretion.—

3dly I give and bequeath unto my Daughter Jane Darby alias Jane Smith the other half of the plantation I now live on during her life time and at her death to My Grand Son Zadock D. Smith to have and to hold the Same for ever. Also to my Daughter Jane Smith all the ballance of my negroes namely Frederick, Charity, & her younges Child not yet named and John and Hamilton to have and to hold the Same for ever—I do hereby nominate constitute and appoint my beloved Wife Mary Darby Williams Campbell of York District S. C. and Isaac Price of Mecklinburg Co. North Carolina to be the Executors completion of his education I will & direct my Executors to pay him the sum of two hundred dollars—this sum & all the money necessary to give him his education & profession, to be taken out of the funds arising from the labor of my slaves & the occupation of my lands as above stated.

of this my last will and testament, hereby revoking and making void all and Every other will and wills at any time heretofore by me made and do declare this to be my last will and testament.

In testimony hereof I have hereunto Set my hand and afixed my seal this 27th day of July in the year of our Lord one thousand Eight hundred and twenty four—

witness present   Zadock Darby (SEAL)
David Johnston
John Glen
Franklin Glen

PROBATED NOV. 6, 1824. WILL BOOK "G" PAGE 150.

WILL OF JOHN MILLER CASE 7 FILE 278
YORK COUNTY COURTHOUSE, YORK, S. C.

South Carolina

York District) In the name of God Amen I John Miller being desirous of setling my worldly affairs & of sound & disposing mind & memory do make & ordain this my last will & testament in manner & form following viz

Item 1. I will and desire that my negroes & all my other personal property of what kind soever, except as hereinafter stated, be Kept together on my farm or farms after my death & continue to work the same until my youngest child arrives to the age of fourteen years. Should the said youngest child die before arriving at the age of fourteen, then the property above named, except as herein after stated, is to be kept together until the next youngest child arrives at the age of fourteen, or should he or she die until the next youngest arrives at that age.

Item 2 I give & devise to my sons, John, James G., Dickson, Thomas & Calvin, all my lands to them & their heirs forever—upon the condition howe'r & with the restriction, that my negroes as above stated continue to occupy and work the same until my youngest child arrives to the age of fourteen, or the next youngest, if the said youngest child should die.

Item 3 I will & desire that my family, except such members of the same as may marry, continue upon the lands & with the negroes, until the time hereinafter stated, for the division of my estate.

Item 4 Out of the income arising from the labour of my slaves & the occupation of my land, I will & desire my family who remain on the land as above stated, to be decently & comfortably maintained & cloathed—The remainder after defraying the expenses mention in Item 5 & Item 6 of this my will ,to be let out at interest by my Executors they taking note for the same with good security.

Item 5 I will & desire that my son Charles Gerome, receive a good classical education, and that he study some one of the learned professions—and on the completion of his education I will & direct my executors to pay him the sum of two hundred dollars—this sum & all the money necessary to give him his education & profession to be taken out of the funds arising from the labor of my slaves & the occupation of my lands as above stated.

Item 6 I would wish & so direct such of my sons as may be of age & single at my death to remain onm y plantation & take charge of the negroes & that each one for the said service, should receive out of the proceeds of the crop the sum of one hundred & fifty dollars per annum & I will direct my executors to pay them the said sum.

Item 7 Should any of my children who are now single marry before my youngest child arrives to the age of fourteen years, or the next youngest in case of the death of the youngest, I will & desire that my Executors give to such child or children so marrying, on their marriage a negro boy—a negro woman and a small boy or girl, having regard to the quality so as to make the portions of each child as nearly equal as may be and for this purpose my executors are hereby directed to select out of all my negroes, except Julia & Caroline, the negroes to be given as above, and have them appraised by three disinterested persons and at the price fixed by such persons, such children shall account as hereafter stated.

Item 8. When my youngest child arrives to the age of fourteen or the next youngest in case of the death of such youngest child, I will & direct, Three negroes to be given to each one of my children by my present wife, except such as may have received them from my executors as stated above in Item 7 to be selected & appraised as stated in said 7th Item of my will These of my said children who receive the most valuable negroes, must account for the difference to these who receive the less valuable.

Item 9 All the residue, rest & remainder of my property I will & desire to be divided & disposed of as follows viz I give & bequeath to my wife all my household furniture to be divided amongst her & her children as she sees fit I will & desire all the rest & remainder of my property money etc. to be divided equally amongst my wife & all my children, she taking a portion equal to a child & in full satisfaction of all claim of Dower in my land—The division to be made by my Executors and the division of the negroes, stock etc. to be made as above described in Item 7th—And also so as to include in my wife's share a negro woman called Julia, the same who is now her cook wench—and in that of my son Calvin a negro girl called Carolina. Item 10 Should either if my son John, James G. Dickson, Thomas or Calvin, marry before my youngest child arrives to the age of fourteen years, or my next youngest in case of the death of the youngest, such son so marrying, shall be at liberty & have the right to live on some one of my farms & work the same, including a proportionate part of good and inferior land, until the time fixed for a division of my land & estate. Item 11 It is my wish & desire that all monies which may be let out at interest at my death, be loaned out by my executors until a division of my estate they securing the payment of the same by taking note & good security. Item 12 I further will & direct that on the marrying of any of my children before the division of my estate as above stated, and on their taking the three negroes, above bequeathed to them, the selection shall be made so as not to include my Blacksmith called Jim Williams & my carpenter called Jack Williams, who are to remain on the plantation with my wife until the division of my estate.

Item 13 I further give & bequeath to each one of my children by my present wife two horses two cows & calves, to be given to them on marrying or at the division of my estate, on the same terms & in the same manner as the three slaves bequeathed to each of them.

Item 14 I will & desire the remainder of my property after taking out that bequeathed in the last item, to be divided & disposed of as directed in the 9th item of this my will.

Item 15 I hereby appoint my wife Mildred Executrix & my sons Joseph & John & my friend G. W. Williams Executors of this my last will & testament—witness my hand & seal 23d Jany. 1840.

Signed Sealed, published & declared as & for his last will & testament in presence of us, who in presence of each other & in the presence of Testator, signed our names as witnesses thereto at his request on this the 23d day of January 1840.

John Miller (LS)

Jas. Kuykendal
W. C. Beatty
F. H. Wood

Probated June 7, 1847. WILL BOOK "3" PAGE 158.

WILL OF THOMAS BOYD SR. CASE 4 FILE 50
YORK COUNTY COURTHOUSE, YORK, S. C.

In the name of God Amen. I Thomas Boyd Snr. of the District of York & State of South Carolina being in good health and sound mind and memory, do this tenth day of November in the year of our Lord one thousand eight hundred and thirty four, make and ordain this my last will and testament in the manner and form following:

Item 1 Will and bequeath to my beloved wife Elizabeth Boyd during her natural life The house I now live in and the tract of land whereon it is situate adjoining lands of James Boyd, Samuel Smith, William Boyd, Robert Boyd and Aquilla Dyson (with the exception of the priviledge to be hereafter mentioned to my daughter Nancy Smith on said land) Also I Will and bequeath to my wife Elizabeth for and during her natural life the following Negro slaves Viz. Virgil, Bacchus, Amanda, Mitchel & Melinda. Also I Will & bequeath to my wife Elizabeth Boyd all my house hold and kitchen furniture, Stock of horses, horned cattle, hogs, sheep, Geece, wagon and gear, Farming gear of every description, all my farming tools of every description, loom and tackle ect. This last request to my wife shall be subject to certain legacies to be hereafter mentioned to some of my children which I allow her to furnish out of the above property. Also I will & bequeath unto my Wife Elizabeth Boyd, All my corn, wheat, Cotton, and crop of every description which may be in my fields not gathered or growing at the time of my decease. Also all provisions, Wheat corn and Meat ect and all provender on hands at the time of my decease. In consideration of the above request to my wife I allow her to pay all my Just debts—Item I will & bequeath to my Son John Boyd, my wearing apparel, having given him heretofore all that I allow him of my estate except the above—

Item I Will & bequeath to my daughter Nancy Smith the priviledge of living in the house wherein she now resides on my land, to have the use of a spring. And fire wood ect, and as much land as she and her children can cultivate, convenient and adjacent to her house. This priviledge to continue so long as she may live separate from her husband, Wm. Smith, and no longer. Also during the time she lives separate from him I allow her mother the priviledge to furnish her yearly in Ten dollars worth of provisions yearly during her mothers life, which annuity I allow to be continued by my son Bennett Franklin Boyd so soon as he becomes possessed of my lands after the death of his mother during the life of the said Nancy or her separation from her husband—

Item I have given my son Thomas Jefferson Boyd all that I allow him.

Item I have given my son Robert Boyd all that I allow him, But it is my will and desire that he should at the time of my youngest child is twenty one years old—if my wife is then dead or at her death, That he should take my negro boy Virgil at what he may be valued at, at that time, which amount he shall pay over to my executor for the use of my daughters herein after to be mentioned.

Item, To my son James Boyd I have given him all that I allow him of my estate.

Item To my son Wm. Boyd I have given him all that I allow him of my estate, But it is my wish and desire that he should take my negro boy Bacchus, when my youngest child is twenty one years old if my wife should be then deceased, if not at her demise, at a valuation of what he is then worth which amount he shall pay into the hands of my executors for the use of my daughters to be hereinafter named.

Item I Will and bequeath to my son Bennet Franklin Boyd at the death of his mother the plantation I live on (subject to the incumbrances of my daughter Nancy the priviledge mentioned of living on the land heretofore named, & to my five daughters to be hereafter named that is the house where I live to be a home to them while they are single. Also I Will & bequeath to my said son Bennet Franklin Boyd, after the decease of his mother my Negro Boy Mitchel, I also allow his mother to give him my Cup board and Clock—

Item To my five daughters Viz Jane, Elizabeth, Mary, Rachel & Louisa I Will & bequeath that they shall each be furnished with a Bed & furniture Bureau, a horse worth at least fifty dollars, a saddle and bridle, Spinning wheel these articles I allow to be furnished by their mother at such time as they may want them or stand in need of them—The last mentioned Legacies to my daughters I allow my wife to furnish out of the property here to fore named to her—

I also Will & bequeath to my said five daughters viz Jane, Elizabeth, Mary, Rachel & Louisa—to be equally divided among them The valuation of Virgil & Bacchus Also the following negroes with their increase Amanda & Melinda to be equally divided among the five said daughters last named said Division to take place at the time my youngest child is twenty one years old—If my wife is then deceased, if not to take place at her decease.

My Will is that the said five daughters last named shall have the priviledge of living and remaining in the house where I now live so long as they live single if they see proper—They are not to be deprived of said house for a home until they marry—

Item My threshing Machine on the land I have given to my son William— my will and desire is that it remain there for the use of all my children who may wish to use it—Also I will constitute and appoint my Wife Elizabeth Boyd my Executrix and my son John Boyd Executor of this my last will and testament.

In Witness whereof I have hereunto set my hand and affixed my seal the date and year first above written.

Signed in the presence of   Thomas Boyd (L. S.)
Wm. Moore.
John McGill
John Glenn
Wm. Campbell
     PROBATED MAY 7, 1838. WILL BOOK "2" PAGE 19.

WILL OF JAMES PLAXICO CASE 14 FILE 591
YORK COUNTY COURTHOUSE, YORK, S. C.

In the Name of God Amen I James Plaxico of the state of South Carolina York District being weak in boddy but of sound and disposing mind & Memory thanks, be given unto God. Calling unto mind the Mortality of my body, and knowing that it is appointed for all men once to die do make & ordain this my last Will and testament That is to say principally and first of all I Give and recommend my Soul into the hand of Almighty God that gave it and my boddy I recommend to the earth to be buried in a deacent and Christian manner at the discretion of my executors nothing doubting but at the general resurrection I shall receive the same again my the might—power of God. And as touching such worldly estate werewith it has pleased God to bless me in this life I give devise and dispose of in the following manner and form:

First I give and bequeath unto my two sons John T. Plaxico & James G. Plaxico all my lands or real estate the crop now on hands of last year and likewise the crop now growing at present. Also all my debts due the Estate and bind them of this devize to settle or pay all just debts against my Estate.

2d. I give and bequeath unto my son John T. Plaxico my negro man named Billey, a small girl named adaline, One bed and furniture, and cow & calf.

3d. I give and bequeath unto my Sone James G. Plaxico my negro woman named Viney A Small girl named Margaret, one bed & furniture and a cow and calf.

4th. I give unto my executors four hundred dollars in trust for Pamela Garison and her children to be paid to her as they may think advisable for her & their benefit Should it not all be paid during her lifetime I allow the Ballanc to B divided among them equally.

5th. I give and bequeath unto my daughter Jane Plaxico my negro girl named Clarissa two beds and furniture, feathers for another bed which she hase now on hands one Bureau two cows and calves, and a horse and saddle and while she remains single her living off the land for a home & a support with the labour of her Girl Clarissa.

6th. I give and bequeath unto m y son Henry G. Plaxico a negro girel named liza and one hundred dollars to be paid him in money if he comes back to live in this countery if not I alow him four hundred fifty dollars out of my estate in money or property at valuation as may suit him.

7th. I give and bequeath unto my sons John and James all the ballance of my personal estate to be devided between them equally.

8th. I do ordain and constitute my sons John T. Plaxico & James G. Plaxico to be my legal and lawful executors of this my last will & testament and I do hereby utterly disallow & disanul all & every other form or testament Wills legacies and bequests & executors by me in any way before named willed and bequeathed ratufying and conferming this and no other to be my last will and testament in witness whereof I have hereunto set my hand and seal this twenty seventh day of December one thousand eight hundred and forty eight.

Signed sealed published pronounced and declared by the said James Plexico as his last will and testament in the presence of us who in his presence and in the presence of each other have hereunto subscribed our names.
Test   James Plaxico (SEAL)
    Jas. S. Hemphill
    John P. Hood
    John S. Plaxco
PROBATED JANUARY 16, 1850. WILL BOOK "3" PAGE 211.

WILL OF WILLIAM WHERRY CASE 14 FILE 611
YORK COUNTY COURTHOUSE, YORK, S. C.

In the name of God amen I William Wherry of York District State of South Carolina being of sound and disposing mind and Memory, but weak in body and calling to mind the uncertainty of life and being desirous to dispose of all such worldly estate as it hath pleased God to bless me with do make and ordain this my last will and testament in manner following that is to say I Desire my Executor herein after named to sell of My personal property, after my decease suficient to pay all my just Debts and funeral Expenses. After the payment of all my Just Debts and funeral Expenses I Give to my wife Elizabeth Wherry the whole of my estate as well real as personal for and during the term of her natural life and after her decease I Give Devise and bequeath unto my Daughter Elizabeth Wherry the plantation on which I now reside to her and her heirs forever. The ballance or rest of my Estate not herein before disposed of I Leave to be equally Divided amongst My Children And Lastly I do constitute and appoint my son Andrew Wherry Executor of this my Last will and testament by me heretofore made In testimony whereof I have hereunto set my hand and seal this the twenty third Day of February in the year of our Lord one thousand eight hundred and fifty.

Signed sealed published and declared as and for the last will and testament of the above named.
William Wherry in the presence of us   Wm. Wherry (SEAL)
HARVEY H. DRENNON
ARCHABALD STEELE
MATHEW H. WILLIAMS
    PROBATED MARCH 12, 1850. WILL BOOK "3" PAGE 212.

WILL OF JAMES DARNAL CASE 16 FILE 664
YORK COUNTY COURTHOUSE, YORK, S. C.

South Carolina

York District) In the Name of God Amen I James Darnal of the State and District aforesaid Being in a low and declining state of Health but of sound mind and disposing memory do make and ordain this my last Will and Testament in Manner and form following (viz) I give and bequeath to my Daughter Susan Sturgis One Negro Girl which shee now has in possession and this with what other property shee has heretofore recd. I allow for her full part of my Estate To my Son William Darnal I give and bequeath my mare named Kiney and this I Allow for his full part To my Daughter Hanah I give and bequeath one Negroe boy named Joe likewise one Bed three Coverleds one white counter pain and three sheets and this is to be her full part of my estate. To my Daughter Cinthy I Give and Bequath one Negroe Girl named Hariet To my Daughter Elizabeth I Give and Bequeath one Negroe boy Name Si My Land and My Negroe Woman Ann My Stock of every kind household furniture plantation tools and whatever else I die possessed of not heretofore named I allow to be sold as soon as convenient after my decease and out of the money arising from the sale I allow my Just debts to be paid To my Son Franklin I allow the one third of the price of what my land may sell for this I allow for his full part And to my Son John I allow the other two thirds of the price of the land the price of all the other property directed be sold I allow to be equally divided share & share alike alike amongst my three Youngest Children (Viz) Senthy, John and Elizabeth so much of it as is necessary to be applied for their support and schooling at the discreation of my Executor—And I do hereby Nominate and appoint William Sturges my Son in law Sole Executor of this my last Will and Testament Hereby Revoking and disanuling all other Wills by me heretofore made In testimony whereof and in conformation of every part of the I do hereunto set my hand and seal this 11th day of January In the Year of our Lord One Thousand Eigh hundred and thirty one 1831.

Signed Sealed & pronounced　　　　　　　　　　Jaes Darnal (LS)
In presence of us
John Cauthen
James Hutchison
Leroy Hutchison

My Mare not named in the above I will to my Son Franklin done before signing.

WILL OF RICHARD BARNETTE CASE 4 FILE 153
YORK COUNTY COURTHOUSE, YORK, S. C.

In the name of God Amen

I Richard Barnette being of sound & disposing mind & memory & calling to mind the uncertainty of life do make & ordain this my last will & Testament in manner & form following Viz.

1st. I desire that the whole of my Estate shall be in the possession & at the disposal of my wife Frances Parham Bonnette during her natural life or widowhood after the discharge of all my Just & lawful debts which debts shall be paid by the sale of such property as my Executor shall think it most convenient to spare.

2nd. As soon as either of the above named acurrences shall transpire I mean the death or Marriage of my wife my will is that my land shall be Equally divided between my two sons Jno. Allen Bonnette & Joseph Josiah Bonnette by valuation so that they shall not have actually more of my property than an equal dividend with the rest of my children & my wife if living.

3rd. It is my will & intention that my wife & each of my children shall have an equal & proportionable share of my whole Estate & that Each one shall take possession of his or her Legacy as soon as he or She Shall attain to the age of twenty one years or be married.

All the rest of my property both real & personal of whatsoever kind it may be not above particularly disposed of as well as that which may accrue as the result of rents, hire, or labour I give & bequeath to my heirs and their assigns forever to be disposed of as the above named Estate.

Lastly I do constitute & appoint my wife Frances P. Bonnette my Executrix & Joel S. Bonnette my Executor of this my last will & Testament by me heretofore made in testimony whereof I have set my hand & affixed my seal this 29th day of October 1834.

R. Barnett (L. S.)

Signed sealed & declared
in presence of us
A. G. Laurence (L. S.)
H. I. Cathcart (L. S.)
J. S. Barnett (L. S.)

PROBATED NOV. 15, 1834. WILL BOOK "G" PAGE 467.
WILL OF ELIZABETH LUSK CASE 59 FILE 670
YORK COUNTY COURTHOUSE, YORK, S. C.

IN THE NAME OF GOD AMEN The seventh day of October in the year of our Lord one thousand seven hundred and seventy I Elisabeth Lusk of the County of Tryon widow, being very sick and weak in body but of perfect mind and memory thanks Be given to God there fore calling unto mind the mortality of my body and knowing that it is appointed for all men once to die, do make and ordain this my last will and testament that is to say principally and first of all I give and recommend my soul into the hands of God that gave it and for my body I recomend it to the earth to be intered in a Christian like and decent manner at the descreation of my Executors and as toutching such worldly estate wherewith it hath pleased God to bless me in this life I give and bequeath and dispose of the same in the following manner and form—

Imprimis I gave and bequeath to my beloved son Robert Lusk one young gray horse.

Item I give and bequeath to my beloved son Samuel Lusk twinty bushels of corn now in the hand of Hugh McCleland.

Item I give and bequeath to my son in law Hugh McCleland twinty bushels of corn.

Item I give and bequeath to my beloved daughter Elizabeth McCleland a black gown and a mantle.

Item I give and bequeath unto my son in law Hugh Whiteside a Roan Colt.

Item I give and bequeath to my beloved daughter Margaret Whiteside one woman's saddle.

Item I give and bequeath unto my beloved son James Lusk all and singular the remainder of my Estate Real and personal.

My son Robert Lusk and son in law Hugh Whiteside before mentioned I constitute and appoint my Executors of this my last will and testament and do hereby utterly disalow revoke and disanul all and every other former testaments and wills and executors by me in any wise before this named.

In witness Whereof I have hereunto set my hand and seal the day and year first above written.

Sign-d Seal-d and Deliver-d   Elizabeth her X Lusk
                     mark

In presents of us
Samuel Neeley
  her
Dorcas X Wharey
  mark
  her
Martha X Workman
  mark

RECORDED FEB. 12, 1798. BOOK "A" PAGE 176.

WILL OF JAMES FEEMSTER CASE 18 FILE 742
YORK COUNTY COURTHOUSE, YORK, S. C.

In the name of God Amen. I James Feemster of the District of York and State of South Carolina being sick of body but of sound and disposing mind, memory and understanding praised be God for the same do make this my last Will in manner and form following:

First I give and devise unto my Three sons William, Joseph and James D. Feemster the plantation whereon I now live to be so divided among them as to make the share of each when added to the plantation or parcel of Land which I have previously deeded to each of them of equal value this division may be done by themselves or whom soever they call to assist them in making it,

Second As relates to my personal Estate I will to my two single daughters Mary and Nancy Feemster in kind as mush as will be equal to what my two married daughters Prudence Brown and Lettitia Gaston received at their marriage and thirdly I give to my daughter Jane Leech three Hundred dollars to be placed at interest for her until called for by her or her representative Fourthly I give to my four daughters Prudence Brown, Lettitia Gaston, Mary Feemster and Nancy Feemster each the sum of seven hundred dollars— And after the Legacies are paid over I will that the balance of my property be equally divided among my children Prudence Brown, Lettitia Gaston, William Feemster, Joseph Feemster, James B. Feemster and Mary and Nancy Feemster share and share alike. And now that I have specified my bequests I wish to make known my wishes respecting that part of my property which consists of Black persons and in the first place I order and ordain that old Mariah be comfortably maintained out of my estate and in the next place as it has been the under with me and my family that the little motherless child

Caroline which has been nursed by my daughter Mary Feemster should and ought of right to belong to her the said Mary Feemster and I do hereby acknowledge and confirm the aforesaid understanding and claim And thirdly as the Black person belonging to me have been long in the family and it would appear a harshness to force them contrary to their desires to leave the family— Therefore I will and ordain that where any or all of them wish and make choice to live with any of my children (when the arrangement can possibly be made) that the said negro or negroes so choosing shall be appraised with my other personal property and shall be given to the child or children whom the make choice of aforesaid at the appraisal, And in the close I will that my Just debts and funeral expenses with one year provision and necessaries for my two daughters Mary and Nancy Feemster with the sum sufficient to maintain Mariah during life be provided for before any other division or payment is made. And I do nominate constitute and appoint my three sons William Joseph and James B. Feemster sole executors of this my last Will & testament revoking all other wills and declaring this my last will and testament. Signed sealed declared and published by the above named James Feemster the Twenty third day of September in the year of our Lord one thousand eight hundred and thirty four as and for his last Will in presence of us who in in his presence and at his request have subscribed our names as witnesses.

William Jamison
Thos. K. McKnight
J. J. Foster

James Feemster (LS)

PROBATED OCT. 22, 1834. WILL BOOK "G" PAGE 463.

WILL OF ROBERT McNEELY CASE 71 FILE 3513
YORK COUNTY COURTHOUSE, YORK, S. C.

The Last Will and Testament of Robert McNeely In the name of God Amen. I Robert McNeely of York District & of the State of South Carolina being sick but of perfect mind and memory do make this my Last will and Testament Item 1st I will and be queath to my son James McNeely one Hundred acres of Land lying on the North East part of the plantation on which I now Live I also will and bequeath unto my Daughter Jemima one Hundred Acres of Land Lying on the North Side of Same plantation or Tract of Land I also will and Bequeath to my Daughter Eliza Ann one Hundred Acres Lying on the West side of Same Tract or parcel & I further Will & Bequeath unto my Wife Margaret the Balance of my Land which part Contains the Dwelling House and other improvements I also will and bequeath unto my wife Margaret all my Stock, or Horses Cows Hogs, Sheep and all other Property of which I may be possessed at my Death to be to her use untill her Death at which time I will and Bequeath it to my Daughters Mary & Jane I do also by this my Last will and Testament Constitute make & ordain N. P. Kennedy Executor of this my Last Will and Testament In Witness wher of I have hereunto set my hand and seal this Twelfth day of November in the year of our Lord one Thousand Eight Hundred & Forty Two.

In presence of
Samuel G. Brown

Robert McNeely (LS)

John Johnson
Th Miller
    PROBATED NOV. 21, 1842. WILL BOOK "3" PAGE 48.

WILL OF THOMAS BRIDGES CASE 9 PACK. 367
YORK COUNTY COURTHOUSE, S. C.

    In the name of God Amen I Thomas Bridges of the State of South Carolina and District of york being very sick and weak of body but of perfect Mind and memory thanks be given unto God Calling unto mind the Mortality of my body and knowing that it is appointed for all Men once to die do make and ordain this my last will and Testament—That is to say principally and first of all I give and Recommend my Soul into the hands of Almighty God that gave it and my body I Recommend to the Earth to be buried in decent Christian Burial at the discretion of my Executor and as touching Such worldly Estate wherewith it has pleased God to bless me in this life I give devise and dispose of the same in the following maner and form first I give and bequeath to my son Thomas Bridges one half of my Real Estate it being divided acording to quanty and Quality Including the Improvments the other half to my other two sons Edmond and Robert Bridges alowing my Said Son Thomas to take the moyaty last mentioned Should he think proper So to do by paying to the sd Edmond and Robert Bridges the valuation thereof farther I give and bequeath unto my said Son Thomas one half of the Stock of Hogs also half the Money and Money Debts Reducting two hundred Dollars, also five head of neet Cattle towit two Steers a Cow and Claf and a yearlin one Gray Gilding bed and furniture als half the corn on hand half the farming utentials and half the Beaken.

    I give and bequeath to my Daughter Dicy White one Bed and furniture— All the remaining part of my Estate I will to be sold on a Credit of twelve months and one third of the amount of sd Sale I give and beqath to my Daughter Dicy White aforesaid the other two thirds of the amount of Sale I give to my three Sons Edmond Robert and Thomas Bridges equally and I do hereby constitute make and ordain the above named Thomas Bridges Sole Executor of this my Last Will and testament Ratifying and confirming this and no other to be my last will and Testament in witness whereof I have hereunto Set my hand and Seal this the 19th day of April in the year of our Lord one thousand Eight hundred and thirty one Signed sealed published pronounced by the said Thomas Bridges as his last Will and testament in the presence of us and in the presence of each other have hereunto subscribed our names.

George Plaxco   Thos. Bridges (LS)
William Bridges
James Moreland
    PROBATED MAY 23, 1831. WILL BOOK "G" PAGE 341.

WILL OF JOHN RATCHFORD CASE 24 FILE 1006
YORK COUNTY COURTHOUSE, YORK, S. C.

    The last Will and Testament of John Ratchford
    I John Ratchford of York District State of South Carolina in view of the

Shortness of life, under ni influence Save a Sense of duty to make and publish this my last will and Testament, And first I direct that my body be decently interred in such place as circumstances may require or friends Select in a manner corresponding with my estate and Situation in life And as to Such worldly estate as it has pleased God to intrust me with I dispose of the same as follows:

First I direct that all my debts and funeral expenses be paid as Soon after my decease as possible out of the first moneys that Shall come into the hands of my executors from any portion of my estate real or personal, and I hereby vest in my executors full power and authority to dispose of such portions of my estate as they under the circumstances may deem most expedient as will Satisfy all Just and lawful demands against me. Secondly, After the payment of these my debts and funeral expenses, every item of my estate of which I may die Seised or possessed both real and personal I will and bequeath to my beloved wife Sarah Catharine Ratchford to be hers, to hold possess and dispose of in Such manner as to her may Seem proper. And I do hereby make and ordain my esteemed friend and Kinsman A. S. Wallace and my wife Sarah Catharine Ratchford, executors of this my last will and Testament in testimony whereof I John Ratchford the testator have to this my will Set my hand and Seal this seventeenth day of May A. D. one thousand eight hundred and fifty three.

John Ratchford (SEAL)

Signed Sealed and delivered in presence of us who have signed in the presence of each other.
J. H. Walker
James M. Pardue
G. H. Letson

PROBATED OCT. 29, 1853. WILL BOOK "3" PAGE 265.

WILL OF JANE BOYD CASE 13 FILE 567
YORK COUNTY COURTHOUSE, YORK, S. C.

In the name of God, Amen, the twenty sixth day of October 1847 I Jane Boyd, of the District of York and State of South Carolina, being very sick and weak in body but of perfect mind and memory Blessed be Almighty God for the same do make and publish this my last Will and Testament in manner and form as follows Viz.

First. I give and bequeath unto my daughter Mary one Negro girl named Violet to her and her heirs forever.

2nd. I give and bequeath unto my daughter Margaret one Negro boy named Sam to her and her heirs forever.

3rd. I further give and bequeath to my daughter Margaret my young sorrel horse—

4th. I direct my negro boy John together with all my other property of what nature and kind soever to be sold and all my just debts to be paid out of the money arising therefrom. The balance after paying sd debts to be equally divided between my daughters Jincy and Pemilia and my Grandson Andrew N. Smith.

5th. I do constitute and appoint my friends John Glenn and Rufus J. Boyd executors of this my last will and testament.

In witness whereof I have hereunto set my hand and affixed my seal the day and year above writin.

Signed, Sealed Published and declared by the said Jane Boyd as her last will and testament in the presence of us who were present at the time of signing and sealing there of.

Wm. H. Johnston
T. M. Boyd
John A. Laney

Jane X Boyd (L. S.)
her   mark

PROBATED NOV. 28, 1849. WILL BOOK "3" PAGE 210

WILL OF WILLIAM DAVIS CASE 16 FILE 669
YORK COUNTY COURTHOUSE, YORK, S. C.

In the Name of God amen I William Davis sener of the State of South Carolina York District Being low in Health of body but of Sound mind and memory thanks be given to God Calling to mind the mortality of my body and knowing that it is appointed for all Men once to die do Make and ordain this my last will and testament that is to say principally and first of all I give and recommend my Soul into the hand of Almighty God that gave it and my body to the Earth to be buried in a decent Christian Burial at the discretion of my Executors Nothing Doubting but at the general Resirrection I Shall Receive the Same again by the mighty power of God—and as touching such Worldly Estate Wherewith it hast pleased God to bless me with in this life I give demise and despose of the same in the following manner and form I Do give and bequeath unto my Dear ond loveing Wife Martha Davis her bed and furniture and one Milk Cow and her Mentainance of the plantation as along as She lives I also give to my son francis C. Davis two dollars also my Daughter Anne Scott and my son John Davis two dollars to each also my son William davis I give one Cow and the rest of my personal property to be Equally Devided amongst the rest of my Children younger then William ither by praisement or by Sale as the Can agree amongst them selves also I give my plantation to my son Thomas Davis and to Maintain his Mother of the same as long as She doth live I also give to my grand daughter Martha E. Davis that Cow the have of mine and I do also apoint and ordain my son francis and Joe McKenzie Jun Executors of this my Last will and Testament.

Sign in presence of this 23rd day November 1820.

Jos McKenzie Jun
Edwin McKenzie
John D. McCall

William X Davis
his   mark

PROBATED DEC. 9, 1820. WILL BOOK "G" PAGE 32.

WILL OF GEORGE DUGLASS CASE 17 FILE 693
YORK COURTHOUSE, S. C.

In the NAME of GOD Amen. . . .

I George Duglass of the State of South Carolina York District planter

Being weak and in an Imparfect State of Body but of perfect mind and memory thanks be given unto God Calling unto mind the Mortality of my Body and knoing that it is apointed for all men Once to die do make and ordain this my Last will and Testament that is to Say principally I give and Recommend my Soul into the hand of Almighty God that Gave it and my body I Recommend to the Earth to be buried in Decent Christian Manner at the Discretion of my Executors Nothing Doubting but at the General Resurrection I Shall Receive the Same again by the Mioty power of God and as Tuching Such worldly Estate Whare with it has pleased God to Bless me in this Life I Gave Demise and dispose of the Same in the Following Manner and form First I Leave my Beloved wife in full Possession of all that I am now in possession of for the purpose of Scooling and Supporting my Children and for portioning of to the best advantage Such of my Children as my See proper to take to themselves and thus to Remain During Life or widowhood and when Either of these takes place I Alow my property to be Sold and Each to have their Eaqual Share I Likewise Constitute and ordain Elizabeth my Beloved wife and Thos. H. Duglass my Sole Executors of this my Last will and Testament in witness whareof I have hereunto Set my hand and Seal this May 7th year of our Lord one Thousand Eight hundred & Fifteen Signed Sealed and Declared by the Said George Duglass to be his Last will and Testament in Preasanc of

Nathaniel Henderson George Duglass (SEAL)
James H. Barton
    Probated July 13, 1816.
    WILL BOOK "D" PAGE 121.

WILL OF JOHN DURHAM WILL BOOK "G" PAGE 315
YORK COUNTY COURTHOUSE, YORK, S. C.

The State of South Carolina, York District.

In the name of God! Amen. I John Durham of the State and District aforesaid being of sound and disposing mind and memory and desirous to dispose of all my estate, do make and publish the following as my last will & testament.

Imprimis. I will and devise to my son George G. Durham his heirs and assigns forever My dwelling house and the appurtenances together with Three hundred acres of land surrounding and adjacent thereto to be laid off by the said George G. Durham Wheresoever he may choose out of all My lands provided the farm shall be in a body and shall surround and include the dwelling and to be laid off as soon as convenient after my decease.

Item. I will and devise to my daughter Elizabeth Durham her heirs and assigns forever. The tract of land purchased by me from Alexander Eakin Containing about sixty five acres And I also will and devise to the said Elizabeth Durham her heirs and assigns One hundred acres of land in addition to the above to be by her chosen and laid off from all my lands not herein before devised provided the farm shall be in a body & and she will make her election within a convenient time after my death—

Item. I will and devise to Hugh Currence his heirs and assigns forever one hundred acres of land to be laid off to him from my lands adjoining the line of his land the said quantity of one hundred acres shall be so allotted and surveyed as to extend the whole distance along his line which adjoins to my land.

Item. I will and desire that the whole of the remainder of my lands not herein before disposed of shall be laid off and surveyed into lots which Shall be be most proper and convenient for Sale and for that purpose O appoint my Friends David Watson, Duncan McCollum and William Berry to make such division into lots and request that they will perform this my wish and in case of their refusal of the refusal or inability of a majority to do the same then my executors or a majority of them are hereby directed to act in like manner—My Executors or a majority of them are hereby directed to sell the said land in lotts at public sale on a credit of Twelve months and upon such sale they are authorized to execute titles to the purchaser. The proceeds of the said sales shall be divided into four shares, and I bequeath the same viz. One fourth part thereof to the Chlidren of my deceased daughter Jane Stevenson Share & share alike—One fourth part to Hugh Currence, One fourth part to George Durham and the remaining fourth part to Elizabeth Durham.

Item. It is my Will and I do hereby direct that all my negro slaves not herein after Specially bequeathed shall be divided by my aforesaid friends David Watson, Duncan McCollum & Wm. Berry or any two of them into three lots, of vlaue as nearly equal as may be having regard to their relationship And to be valued by them—My Son George G. Durham My daughter Elizabeth Durham & Hugh Currence Shall by lot determine to which of the said lots or parcel of Negroes they shall be respective-ly entitled and the said parcel of Negroes so drawn by lot I do hereby give and bequeath to the aforesaid George D. Durham Elizabeth Durham and Hugh Currence their heirs and assigns respectively & severally, And in case either of them should die after my decease and before the division can b emade then his or her legal representatives are authorized to act in their stead--Such of my aforesaid legatees as shall be entitled to the most valuable Lots of negroes shall pay to the other or others Such sum of money as shall make them all equal, according to the valuation made by my said friend. And in case a majority of my said friends whom I have appointed to value and divide my negroes shall neglect or refuse to act then the appraisers of my estate are authorized to perform the same duty—

Item I Will and bequeath to my daughter Mary Stevenson a negro girl named Milly and her daughter Mary, to my said daughter Mary Stevenson during her life and to her issue living at the time of her death.

Item. To my daughter Francis Dulin I will and bequeath a negro man named Lewis and a negro man named Abram to my Said daughter during her life and to her issue living at the time of her death--

Item. I Will and bequeath to My Son William Durham the sum of Three hundred Dollars and in case my Said son is now or shall be dead at the time of my decease then my executors are directed to pay the said sum to the Children of my said son William to be equally divided between them.

Item. I will and bequeath to my daughter Elizabeth Durham Two head of horses, and ten head of cattle to be chosen by her from all my horses & Stock at my death. And I do hereby confirm her in the right to two feather beds therefore give to her by me.

Item. I will and bequeath to my son George G. Durham One gun to be chosen by him from all my guns at my death.

Item. I Will and bequeath to my daughter Margaret Wallace the sum of Two hundred dollars to be held by my executors during the life of my said daughter Margaret in trust for her use and benefit by allowing her the interest thereof and at her death the said money to be equally divided between her children living at the time of her death—

Item. I do hereby direct my Executors to sell at public sale on a credit of Twelve months all my personal property of every kind and description capable of sale, and the proceeds of the sale I will and bequeath as follows one fourth part to Hugh Currence one fourth part to George G. Durham and one fourth part to Elizabeth Durham and one fourth part to the children of my deceased daughter Jane Stevenson to be equally divided between them.

Item. All my cash on hand outstanding debts, and all other of my property of every kind whatsoever not heretofore mentioned and bequeathed I do will and bequeath viz One fourth to my son George one fourth to my daughter Elizabeth, one fourth to Hugh Currence and one fourth to the children of my deceased daughter Jane Stevenson equally between them Lastly I nominate and appoint my dauhgter Elizabeth Executrix and George G. Durham and Hugh Currence Executors of this my last will and testament hereby revoking all other wills and ratifying and confirming this as my last Will and testament.

In testimony hereof I have hereunto set my hand and seal this nineteenth day of February in the year of our Lord One thousand and Eight hundred and Twenty nine—

Signed, Sealed published and declared as his last Will and testament by the testators, and signed by us and in his presence and in the presence of each other as witnesses at his request and we have also subscribed our names on the margin of the second and fourth pages on the annexed sheet.

Wm. Pressly   John Durham (LS)
Hugh Stevenson
W. R. Hill

    PROBATED APRIL 27, 1829.

WILL OF JOHN SPRINGS WILL BOOK "3" PAGE 263
CASE 24, FILE 1742
YORK COUNTY COURTHOUSE, S. C.
STATE OF SOUTH CAROLINA

Inventory and valuation of the Property and effects of John Springs 4 July 1853

Negroes

(Wheeler 53 years of age 400
(Jake 26. 600. Davice 20. 600 _____3 1600
(Alfred 18. 600. William 16. 600
(Tom 12. 375. John 10. 325 _____4 1900
(Rufus 8. 275. Charles 5. 225
(Joe 1 year old 125 _____3 625
(Nancey 39. 400. Lindsey 13. 375
(Margaret 3. 150 _____3 925   5050
                                                      ──   ──
                                                      13

Furniture
(Rockaway Carriage & blind horse_____ 100
(French Mahogany bed stead, Bed,
(Mattress & furniture _____80
(Mahogany ward robe 40. Do.
(Bureau marble slad & Glass 40 _____80
(Do. Wash stand & slab 20 Voltaire
(chair 15.4 office Do. 8 _____43
(Do. Tea table 30. 1 silver creamer
(25 Do. Soup spoon 10. 2 Do. cups 20 _____85   288
                                                        ──────
                                                        18044.49

Notes and debts due me as pr list
I have to my credit Bank Dividend
&C in Bank of Harisburg cash fund _____10150.
I have to my credit in
the Bank Republic N York _____ 1808.61
Cash in hand _____ 120.   30123
                                                             ─────
                                                             35561

I owe the Bank of Hamburg
Bank stock unpaid & other debts as pr. list _____ 33941
                                                             ─────
                                                             $ 1620

Cost
27425 . . 240 shares
U S Bank quoted now at 2% _____ 600
10600 . . 400 shares
Com Bank Columbia at 28 ea _____11 200
3000 . . 300 shares
Merchants Bank Cheraw at 120 ea _____3600
2000 . . . 200 shares
State Bank N Carolina at 120 ea _____2400
42580 . . 800 shares
Bank of Hamburg S. C. at 60 each _____4800
20113 . . 400 shares
Bank of Camden at 53 each _____21200
2000 . . 40. shares Graniteville
Mnftring Co. probably worth _____1800

10100 . . 100 shares
Camden Branch R Road worth _____10100
10800 . . 100 shares
S. C. R R and Bank now worth 125 _____**12500**
  5000 . . 50 shares
Charlotte & S. C R Road now worth 80 _____ 4000
10400 . . 100 shares
Georgia R R and Bank stock at 105 _____10500
10168 . . 480 shares
Com Insurance stock Charleston at 30 _____14400
20000 . . 200 shares
Atlanta & Legrange R R stock Par _____20000
13500 . . 15000
Man & Wilmington R R Bonds worth 95 _____14250
40000 . . Charlotte &
S. C. R R Bonds worth Par _____40000
10000 . . 200 shares
Bank of Charlotte Par _____10000
10625 . . 425 shares
Farmers & Exchange Bank Charleston Par _____10625
10100 . . 400 shares
Exchange Bank Columbia Par _____10000
10000 . . 400 shares
Bank of Chester 25 each Par _____10000   325375
331311 _____$326995
Add Negroes, Lands Cash &
effects, given off to my children
To Richard A Springs
see schedule in my old Merchants book _____24061
To Leroy Springs see schedule _____24196
                                                            _____
                                                            48257

Amount Total brot forward _____ 48257 $326.995
To Mary L Davidson see schedule _____ 17730
    Andrew B Springs _____27034
    Sophia C. Myers _____ 20196   113217
                                                            $440.212
The Inventory and valuation of 1852 or last year _____ 408 765
                                                            $ 31.447
Shewing an increase from the
valuation of last year of _____

   The above large increase is owing to large dividend and the increased value of the various stocks, still I am confident they are valued rather below the current rates _____

   A list of Property belonging to my Wife which I intend her or Heirs to have at my Dcease without let or hindrance
Negro man John 30 years of age _____ 800
24 Shares Bank of Cape Fear NC worth 115 _____ 2760

2 Shares State Bank New York at 106	212
Invested in Bond and Mortgage New York 7 per cent	1100
20 shares S. C. R. R. and Bank now worth Par or 125	2500
5000 dollars in Man & Wil. R. R. 7 pr. cent Bond (this included Harriots price) 95	4750

The stocks are in my name except the Bond & Mortgage and two shares in the State Bank N. Y. and is all that is my hand   John Springs

I hereby dispose of my estate and effects contained in the annexed schedule as my last Will and Testament in the following manned and form (Viz)

I leave to my beloved Wife all the property and effects named above that is to say Negro Man John. twenty four shares in the Bank of Cape Fear NC two shares in the State Bank of Nek York. eleven hundred dollars in Bond and Mortgage in New York, twenty shares S. C. R. R. and Bank, five thousand dollars of Manchester, and Wilmington. R. R. 7 pr cent Bond, I Will to her my silver creamer soup spoon, and two silver premium cups, Together with all rights credits hereditaments, and emoluments, she may now or hereafter be entitled to, forever at her own will and disposal—In addition it is my will and desire that she receive the dividends on one hundred shares of the S. Carolina R. road stock and Bank, and the dividends on two hundred shares of stock in the Bank of Charlotte now standing in my name, to be by her receiv'd and enjoyed by her during her natural life, and after that period said stocks to be equally divided between my five children, their Heirs Executors, Administrators and assigns.

I make the following special bequests (Viz) I leave to Unity the Church of my childhood, ten shares in the Charlotte and South Carolina R Road to be used by the constituted authorities of said Church, that is the dividends of said stocks, in the support of the ministry, repairs or building the Church, and especially so much as may be necessary for the Grave yard I leave to my beloved wife during her life my Portrait, at her death to Sophia C Myers, I leave to my Grandaughter Margaret Springs my Mahogany Ward robe my Voltaire chair, and four Office chairs. I leave to Julia Amanda Springs my Mahogany Bureau, slab and glass, and my large Tea Table, To Mary L Davidson I leave my French Mahogany Bed stead, Bed, Matrass, and all the bed clothes I at present own and my wash stand and Marble top, I leave to John S. Davidson my Negro Girl Lincey, my Gold watch and trimmings, I will to John S. Myers my small Negro girl Margaret, I leave to Eli B Springs Nanceys youngest Boy Joe, I give to Julia Amanda Springs Nancey's Boy Charles, The above bequests to my Grand children not to be taken into the account in the division.

I will and bequeath to my son Richard A Springs the whole of my lands on the west side of the Catawba river and which is more fully represented by a Plat of survey. made by William Campbell containing 1649 acres more or less, together with all the Negroes I have heretofore given him in possession and in addition I leave him my Negro Man Wheeler and boy William.

I will and bequeath to my son Leroy Springs the Brick corner House in Charlotte the Lots and appertainancies, which he now has in possession, and I leave him my Negro boys, Tom and John.

I will and bequeath to my Daughter Mary L Davidson have my brick House Dixon Plantation in Lincoln County containing 889 Acres more or less, and all the Negroes I gave off to her after her marriage, and in addition I give her my Negro Boy Alfred—I give and bequeath to my son Andrew B Springs, the whole of my lands in York District on the east side of the Catawba river, and which he now has in possession, containing in all 1658 acres more or less, and the whole of the Negroes, I have heretofore given him in possession, and in addition and in addition I leave him my Negro woman Nancey, and boy Davice,

I will and bequeath to my daughter Sophia C Myers, the whole of the Land I own on Sugar creek Lancaster District, containing twelve hundred and twenty six acres (1226) more or less, together with all the negroes I gave off to her after her marriage, and in addition I give her my Negro man Jake and boy Rufus.

And as it seems to be and has long been the custom of the Country to give the lands to the sons, it is my will and desire in the division of my estate that my sons have each, five thousand dollars ($5000) each more than my daughters, and my estate to be divided, by taking into count, what I have already given off to each at my own valuation, which will be found in schedules in my old Merchants book and the amounts sit forth in the annexed in ventory, and the debts they may owe me by. note or otherwise are to be taken into the account.

I will and bequeath to Margaret Springs (alias Bullinger) eight hundred dollars and to Adaline Springs (alias Flowers four hundred dollars (reputed daughter of Adam A Springs) and leave it in the hands of Leroy Springs as Trustee, with authority to appoint a Trustee or Trustees under him, and direct that the said Trustee or Trustees should pay them the interest yearly so long as they may live, and afterwards to their Heirs, whom it is my will should finally inherit the Principal, as it was obtained from the estate of their father in right of my children, and learning they are left destitute I make the above request.

It is my will and desire that the whole of my Public stocks of whatever description, mony, dues, rights and credits of every nature be equally divided between or among my five chilren, and should any of them die childless or without legal Heirs of their Body, in that case it is my will and desire, that the lands herein bequeathed should be sold, and that the proceeds together, with all the Public stocks, herein conveyed, be equally divided among my four other children or their Heirs and Assigns.

Deeming my unfortunate brother Richard C Springs, incompetent from his natural defects of transacting his business, and having at the particular request of his father acted as his agent for nearly twenty years, in the transaction of all his principal business, without commission or charge, It is now my will and desire that my son A B Springs will in like manner act as his Agent or Trustee, with permission to charge him a commission or not as he may choose or trouble may Justify.

And finally I hereby constitute and appoint Andrew B Springs and William R Myers, Executors to this my last will and Testament, but do not allow them to charge commissions, for merely giving off property or dividing my Public stocks, but am willing, but am willing they should be liberally paid for all money collected paid out, and expences incurred incurred.

In witness whereof I have hereunto set my hand and seal to this my last will and Testament, and hereby revoking all former ones this 19th July 1853.

Witnessed in presence of us and at the particular request of the Testator, as his last Will and Testament and in presence of each other, we subscribe our names to the due execution thereof.

Hugh M. White   John Springs (SEAL)
H. H. Coltharp
G. B. Withers
PROBATED NOV. 23, 1853.

WILL OF GEORGE PETTUS
STATE OF SOUTH CAROLINA

In the Name of God Amen I George Pettus being in my full & perfect sences, but Considering the uncertainty of this Mortol life and that it is appinted for all men once to die, and also the certenty of the same do make and publish this my last Will and Testament that is to say all former Wills, in manner & form following renounce—

Item I order that all my Lawful dets be fully discharg'd out of my Estate, and my Body decently interd. Second I leave unto my Lawful & well beloved Wife Jeane Pettus Eight Negroes Viz Frank, Cate, Sall, Jim, Dave, Barklet Jake Henry, dureing her life if she remanes a Widow after which as also her death the Sade Negroes with what Everelse I leave unto hir becomes the property of my Children Viz Five of them George Pettus Rebakah W. Pettus, Sarah Pettus Sinthay Pettus Susanna Pettus—my son George Pettus is to have Six Hundred Dollars more in the division then the Fore Girls a bove mensioned I also leave unto my sade wife all my Household Furniture & movables whatsoever with the halfe of the Cattle Hogs Hoses Sheeps & all the Gees 3 I also leave unto my son John D. O. K. Pettus one Hundred Dollars 4 I also leave unto my Daughter Ann D. Pettus now Clauson Jule Rose her Chile one Bead & covering to her & the Eirs of her body one gray mare named Molvow which she got all. 5 I also leave unto my Son Stephen Pettus one Hundred Dollars one bead & Covering 6 I also leave unto my Daughter Mary Pettus now Called Burton Negro Girl Named Jud & Horse Saddle & bed & Covering to her & the Ears of hir body which she has got 7 I also leave unto my daughter Jane Pettus now Colled Gudreds a Negro Girl Corled Luce & man named Suck saddle & bed & Covering to her & the Ears of her body which she has got—8 I also leave unto my daughter Elizebeth Pettus & Negro Girl named Suf & Horse Saddle & bed & Covering to her & the Ears of hir body her name is olted to Harres & she has all but the Horse that to be rated to Fifty Dollars 9 I also leave unto my daughter Rebakah W. Pettus a Negro boy named Ellick & Horse Saddle & bridle to be Valued to Sevety Dollars & bed & Covering to hir & the Ears of hir body 10 I leave unto my daughter Sarah Pettus a negro boy named bob a Horse Saddle & Bridle to be Valued to Seventy dollars & bed & Covering to hir & the Ears of hir body 11 I also leave unto my Son George Pettus Two Negroes Named Day & Mose & Horse Saddle & bridle to be Valued to one Hundred Dollars & bed & Covering & the Home Hous the Land belonging to it as fare as the branch that leads down this side of whare uncle Dillard lived by the spring that uncle made yuse of & that branch is to be the line including the Ole plase 12 I also leave unto my daughter Sintha Pettus & Negro Girl name lile & horse saddle & bridle to be Valued to Seventy Dollars & bed & Covering to hir & the Ears of hir body 13 I leave also unto my daughter Susanna Pettus a Negro Girl named dianna & Horse & Saddle & bridle to be valued to sevety Dollars & bed & Covering to hir & the Ears of hir body 14 I leave all lands & tennaments waggin & teams & michene to my beloved wife during hir widowhood that after hir death to be lefte to my sons my son George Pettus to have the home Hous & to the branch above mensoned 15 the upper peace & that little peace over the Creek the East side is to be Eaqually divided betwen John D. O. K. Pettus & Stephen Pettus John to have the upper & stepen next to the Creek 16 I also leave Ben to be solde & devided betwen my fore Dorters Ann Clossen Mary Burton Jane Gulrdge Elizebeth Harres.

I do Constitute & apoint my beloved wife & Stephen Pettus my son my Sole Executors to see this my last Will & Testament duly Executed & perform'd In Witness whereof I have heare unto set my hand & Seale this 26 of July in the Year of our Lord 1816.

Samuel B. hill   George Pettus (SEAL)
        his
William X Brown
     mark
Jos. Targert

PROBATED JULY 26, 1816. WILL BOOK "D" PAGE 162.
YORK COUNTY COURTHOUSE, YORK, S. C.

WILL OF ROBERT ELLIS
STATE OF SOUTH CAROLINA

South Carolina)
York District   )

In the Name of God amen I Robert Ellis of the State and District aforesaid being Sick and weak in body but of perfect Sound mind and Memory thanks be to God for the Same and being Disirous to dispose of all my woldly Substance in Which God hath blessed me do hereby Ordain the following Writing to be my last will and testament to wit my—will and pleasure is that I commit my body to the Earth to be buried Decently by my Executors hereinafter Named on My Own plantation the Spot of Ground to be pointed Out by my wife and my Soul I Recommend to God who gave it—and Who can and I believe will do Strict Justice to all men—

Item—In the first place I Will and Disire that all my Just debts be paid by My Executors out of my Estate.

Item—I will and bequeath unto my will beloved wife Mary Ellis all that property particularized in our Marriage Contract which is Recorded in Yorkvill to be hers in Exact Conformity as therein agreed Upon.

Item—I will and bequeath to My Well beloved Daughter Sally Sumner Ellis the following Negroes to wit one Negro fellow Named Stephen and one Negro boy Named Austin one feather bed and furniture one Spining Wheel one Woman Saddle one Chest which belonged to her Mother and also her Mothers apparel to be delivered to her at the Age of Eighteen or Marriage.

Item—I will and bequeath to My well beloved Son Benjamin Ellis the following Negroes to wit one Negro fellow Named Luke and one Child Named Esther to be delivered to him at the Age of Twenty One.

Item—I will and bequeath to my Will beloved Daughter Rebekah Ellis the following Negroes to wit one Negro woman Named Amy and one Negro woman Named Milly to be hers at the age of Eighteen.

Item—As to My Lands which I hold by Indian Lease not herein disposed of by Marriage Contract as above I will and bequeath to My Will beloved Daughter Salley Sumner Ellis together with that part of Said tract of Land Conveyed by Marriage Contract to be hers at the death or Marriage of My Said Wife Mary Ellis, to be hers at the age of Eighteen or Marriage.

Item—I will and bequeath My tract of Land lying on the Stony fork of Fishing Creek Containing one hundred and Ninety Nine Acres and a half to My Son Benjamin Ellis at the Age of twenty one Years the Said Land to be rented out by My Executors Untill that period and the Rents arising therefrom to be Applyed to his Support.

Item—If My Negro fellow George which is herein Disposed of to My well beloved wife by Marriage Contract during her Natural life or Widowhood Should be living after Either of the two Above Mentioned Events then the said fellow George to Descend to My Daughter Sally Sumner Ellis.

Item—My will is that all the Remainder of My property Viz't Horses, Cattle, hogs, houshold and Kitchen furniture and all property Not herein disposed of to be Sold by My Executors and after paying My Just Debts to be Equally divided among My three Children Share and Share alike.

Item—In case Any of My Children Should die before they come of Age to Inherit the part of My Estate allotted to them by this My last will and testamento or before Marriage then the Survivor or Survivors are to Inherit the Whole of the Others portion or portions that are dead and in case all My Children Should die before they come of Age to Inherit their Respective portions herein above allotted to them in that case My will is that the Male Children of My Brother Thomas Ellis of Northampton County and State of North Carolina Shall Inherit the Whole of My Childrens portions Share and Share alike to be theirs at the Respective ages of twenty One—

Item—and I do hereby Nominate and appoint John Workman and David Hutchison my Executor and Guardian of all my Children to this my last will and testament hereby Revoking all former wills by me Made—Signed Sealed declared and published as My last will and testament Oct. 3d 1814 The words (fellow Named Stephen) and the words (and Guardian of all My Children) Interlined before Signed—

In presence of us   Robt. Ellis (L. S.)
Tho. Robertson
William Reeves
Robert Workman

PROBATED DEC. 26, 1816. WILL BOOK "D" PAGE 142.
YORK COUNTY COURTHOUSE, YORK, S. C.

WILL OF WILLIAM WYLIE
STATE OF SOUTH CAROLINA

In the name of God Amen I William Wylie of York District South Carolina planter being of sound and disposing mind and memory but weak in body and calling to mind the uncertainty of life and being desirous of disposing of all such worldly property as it hath pleased God to bless me with do make and ordain this my last will and testament in manner following that is after my decease I allow all my just debts to be paid out of moneys arising from all debts due me on notes book accounts & otherwise together with the moneys arising from the sale of such of my personal property as is not hereinafter willed.

2nd. I leave and bequeath unto my son William Wylie the occupancy use and benefit during his natural life of all my land on the east side of Neelys Creek which originally was my father Wm Wylies except a small scrap of about one acre now closed by my fence together with a scrap of land conveyed to me from Henry F. White all of which lies on the said east side of the North fork of said Neely Creek and after his death it is my will that all the aforesaid land shall descend to all his bodily begotten heirs equally and to then and then heirs forever & further I will to my son William during his natural life the use & benefit of the following negroes and other personal property viz my negro Patsy and her three children Rachel Betsey & Leroy and also my negro man named Bob but the said negroes not to be removed from this State or be desposed of by him or any other person whomsoever But to remain exclusively for the annual support of my said son and family and also three head of horses now in his possession and also what stock of hogs and cattle is now in his possession to remain there in the way and for the same purpose and a certain mortgage which I hold on certain property of my said son William for three hundred dollars and duly recorded when the same is foreclosed I will the whole product arising from the same be given to my daughterinlaw Caroline wife of my said son William 3d. I will and bequeath to my daughter Elizabeth White my negro woman Mariah and her four children Ben Martha Taylor & Sam and their future issue and my negro woman Rhody and negro girl Becca and my negro girl Gean and their future issue for the use and benefit of my said Daughter during her life and at her death all the aforesaid negroes and their issue to descend equally to all my said daughters bodily begotten heirs to them & their heirs forever 4th I will and bequeath unto my son Thomas G. Wylie all the rest of my lands viz where I now live both in both York and Chester District (except what I have already before willed during his natural life and also my negro woman Harriet and her two children Carter & Green also my negro man Julius or Bug and George my negro boy about fifteen years old also my negro woman Silvey and Charlotte also my old negro woman Siby and all their future issue and at his death I will all the land and negroes as aforesaid to descend to all the heirs bodily begotten of said son Thomas G. Wylie and to them and their heirs forever But if it shall so happen that my said son Thomas G. shall die having no lawfully bodily heirs then it is my will that said land and negroes shall descend equally to my son William and daughter Elizabeth aforesaid and to their heirs forever in the same way that the other land & negroes is willed to them And will and bequeath unto said son Thomas G. Wylie two of my horses which ever he shall choose two cows & calves whichever he may choose Also four head of sheep which he may choose Also one half of my stock of hogs and also I will unto him my waggon and harness provided he my said son Thomas shall pay within two years after my decease to James & John Kenmore thirty dollars or bond himself so to do And I also give and bequeath unto him two bed steads & clothing my folding leaf table six sitting chairs a sugar stand one half of my delf china and cupboard ware and one half the kitchen utensels and my Shot gun also two plows and plow gears.

4th. It is my will that if the provision made in the first clause of my will for the payment of all my just debts and funeral expences should prove insufficient that each of my three children William Elizabeth & Thomas G. shall pay each one third of the sum wanting or in case either of them shall refuse to advance their respective shares then I allow the negroes willed to such one or for such ones benefit to be hired out until the required share or shares is made up.

5th. And lastly I constitute and appoint my son Thomas G. Wylie and Henry F. White (my soninlaw) to be executors of this my last will & testament Signed sealed published and declared to be my last will and testament this 3d of January 1845 in presence of
John Roddy   William Wylie (SEAL)
James Kenmore
John Kenmore

Whereas I Wm Wylie have duly made and executed my last will & testament bearing date the 3d day of January 1845 and in my said last will given & bequeathed to my son Wm Wylie all that part of my land lying on the east side of the North fork of Neelys Creek except a scrap of about an acre now under my fence during his natural life. I now revoke that part of my will and leave him my son only a living on the said lands and at his death to descend to his heirs as is directed in my will and further that a certain scrap of land on the east side of the Landsford Road conditionally by me sold to Augustus Parish I will that my executors shall execute titles for the same to him or any person he shall wish them to be executed to as soon as he shall pay the balance of the price of five dollars per acre that is twenty three dollars has been paid and interest on one half from this time till paid. And further if it shall so happen that I should not survive during this year I will that no alteration or disposition of my property take place this year but that all the negroes and stock be kept on the plantation and the present crop be made and that all the provision and corn fodder etc. be kept for the support of this year and the crop so raised to be desposed of towards the payment of my debts except the eighth part which is to go to the overseer and except one hundred bushells corn & three stacks fodder and two bales cotton that I allow shall be given to my son Thomas G. Wylie signed sealed and executed as and for a codicil and to be taken as part of my last will & testament this thirteenth day of January 1845.
John Roddy   William Wylie (L. S.)
Isaac McFadden
John Kenmore

WILL BOOK "3" PAGE 114.
YORK COUNTY COURTHOUSE, YORK, S. C.

COURT RECORDS
CLERK OF COURT'S OFFICE, PICKENS, S. C.
No. 3 Pack 162—RETAILING WITH LICENSE

On Sept. 11, 1852 Archibald Haley made oath that he is informed and believes that Jefferson Prichard has repeatedly retailed spiritious liquors in a less quantity than 3 gallons during the last 6 months at his own house in Pickens County. That he is informed by various respectable persons that they have bought it by the small. Noah Grant has bought it from the said Prichard by the quart, also by Anderson Prichard that he had seen Jefferson Prichard sell by the small, that he has good reason to believe that he sells without a license. A true bill was found.

No. 4 Pack. 162—ASSAULT & BTRY

On April 3, 1852 William J. or I? Van says that on the 3rd April 1852 in the road near Uriah Hembree in Pickens District, he met William Murray Junr. who ordered him to stop and on his refusal to do so Murray committed an assault & btry on him by striking him on the back of the head with a club, causing a severe wound . . . A lot of witness on behalf of Wm. Murray states that he is a very poor man, that his wife is a cripple, that he has 2 small children all dependent on him for support . . . He was sentenced to pay a fine of $10.00.

No. 5 Pack. 162—WARRANT FOR BASTRDY

On Oct. 19, 1852 Mary Phillips sworn says that she was delivered of a male child on the 22nd June 1852 and swears that it is Nathanial Reed and says he is the father of the said male child. Nathaniel Reed pled guilty in this case.

No. 6 Pack. 162—ASSAULT & BTRY

On Sept. 28, 1852 Nathaniel Reid sworn says that James Blakely did assault him on the 23rd of Sept. pushed his head up in his face & spit in his face and threatened to bea him and followed him all about Wm. Jones mill in a riotus manner. A true bill was found.

No. 4 Pack. 165—ASSAULT & BTRY

On Feb. 11, 1860 William A. Youngblood states that Timothy Queen, Frankling Queen & E. H. Russel did on the 10th of this inst did commit an assault on him & his family by using indecent language before them.

No. 5 Pack. 165—WARRANT OF ARREST

On Aug. 30, 1862 Jefferson L. Moore says that on Tuesday the 19th that in passing the public road from L. C. Youngs to his fathers that he was stopped by Nathaniel Day, Allen Day, Elias Day and assaulted & abused by them, they all using very abusive language & the said Allen Day did take me by the hair of the head & pulled me down in the road, beat & stomped me,

& when I got up he told me to take my hat & bucket and clear myself & I then made off in a run & he tried to set his dog upon me.

No. 6 Pack 165—ASSAULT & BTRY

On Nov. 14, 1879 James Peak made oath that in the town of Central on the 14th Nov. 1879 one William K. Powers did commit an assault with a base ball bat by striking Frank McCorkle on the head. John H. Ballentine says, Mrs. McCorkle was at his place of business. I heard the first lick and saw him fall. I saw the second lick, it was with a base ball bat. I do consider it a deadly weapon.

No. 7 Pack. 165—UNLAWFULLY MARKING HOG

On April 14, 1859 J. H. Beck states that James Nichols & John Nichols did without his knowledge or concent mark some of his hogs with their mark . . . James Nichols made oath that his three sons John Nichols, James Nichols & Alexander Nichols are all volunteers in the Confederate Service in the company organised in this district under the command of Capt. Johnson and are now at Lightwood Knot Springs. That they are material witnesses in his defense. That his daughter Mirra (who is the wife of Andrew Wilson a volunteer in the Confederate Service in the same company with (johnson) is living with him and must necessarily continue at his home during the absence of her husband in the war, that she is far gone in pregnancy and expects to be confined sometime between the middle and last of October next. That the absence of his sons and my location in the mountains renders it very important that he should be at home at the perilous crisis of his daughters confinement, especially so as he is the only person of the family who could be made available in procuring the necessary assistance for such an occasion. Also that Col. Orr my attorney is now & will be in the service of his country as officer in Commandment of "Orrs Regiment of Rifles and cannot be at court.

No. 8 Pack. 165—ASSAULT & BTRY

On Dec. 10, 1862 Jane Roberts made oath that on the 5th Dec. 1862 at the house of John Adairs in Pickens District, Andrew Carver did assault her by conversation he used, and by coming into the room, and coming twice to the bed where she lying, laying his hand upon her head and attempting to get into the bed, and that she has good reason to believe that Mary Jane Cobb is a material witness in behalf of the state.

No. 9 Pack. 165—UNLAWFUL DISTILLING

On Oct. 10, 1863 M. F. Mitchell state agent made oath that John Gossett & William Keith are material witnesses in evidence of a case the state Vs. G. W. Washington Fair for the unlawful distilling spiritious liquors from grain . . . Name also written Farr.

No. 1 Pack 166—UNLAWFUL DISTILLING

On Sept. 25, 1862 M. F. Mitchell state agent made oath that James Keith has been engaged in the distillation of spirtious liquors from grain contrary to the statute in that case made from information recd. John Sharp Magistrate commanded him to seize the still or stills & other apparatus used in the said distillery & to keep and take care of until discharged by the proper authority.

WILL OF WILLIAM ADAMS VOL. 1 PAGE 37
PROBATE JUDGES OFFICE, CHARLESTON, S. C.

In the Name of God Amen I William Adams of Charles Town in the s.d Province of South Carolina Glover being weak of body & of Sound & perfect Mind & Memory praise be there fore given to almighty god do make & ordaine this my present last will & Testament in manner and form following (that is to say) ffirst & principally I commend my Soul into the hand of Almight God hoping through the Merretts Death & passion of my Saviour Jesus Christ to have full & free Pardon & fforgiveness of all my Sins & To Inherit ever lasting Life & my body I Committ to the earth to be Decently buried And as touching the Disposition of all Such Temporall Estate as it hath pleased almighty God to bestow upon me I give & Dispose thereof as followeth ffirst I will my Debts & funeral Charges shall be paid & Discharged Item I give & bequeath to my Children William Adams John Adams Jane Adams & Lidiah Adams all my Estate both reall and personall after the charges Deducted for bring Said Children to be equally divided amongst them Share & Share alike and that Peter Guerard Esqr. & Mr. William Elliott be Executors of this my only will Item My will is that my son William Adams be bound out only ine till he be Twenty one years of age to Mr. William Elliott my Executor above named. Item my Will is that my Daughter Jane Adams live with her Sister Elizabeth Grimball wife of Mr. Tho. Grimball until she be Eighteen years of age & brought up to her needle Item My Will is that my Daughter Lydia Adams be brought to the age of Eighteen years of Age & put to Schoole to Learn by Mrs. Elizabeth Wetherick and that my Executors agree with the said Elizabeth Wetherick for the Same. Lastly I doe hereby make Void & Revoke all former & other wills by me heretofore made & that this be my Last will & Testament In Witness whereof I the Said William Adams have hereunto Sett my hand & Seal this Twenty first day of June Anno Domi 1707.

William Adams (SEAL)

The above Named Adams Did Sine Seale publish & Declare the above to be his Last Will & Testament in the Presence of us.
William Sadler
John Child
Timothy Bellomy
Tho. Scipworth

Recorded July 22, 1707.

WILL OF ELIZABETH WIGFALL ALLEN VOL. 1 PAGE 21
PROBATE JUDGES OFFICE, CHARLESTON, S. C.

In the Name of God, Amen, I Elizabeth Wigfall Allen of the Parish of Christ Church in South Carolina Widow being Sick of body but of Sound mind and Memory thanks be to God for it, Do Constitute and appoint this my Last Will and Testament in manner and form following, that is to Say, first

and Principally I recommend my Soul to God hopeing through the Merits of my Saviour Jesus Christ to Inherit Eternal Life my body to be decently Buried at the discretion of my Executor hereafter named and as to my Wordly Estate whereiwith it hath pleased God to bless me I dispose of in the manner & form following Imprimis I give and be. queath unto my Loving Brother Joseph Maybank a Negro Wench Nam'd Statira and also a Mare Colt to him and his heirs forever that is to Say, when he the Said Joseph Maybank shall arrive at the age of Eighteen Years till which time my will and pleasure is that they remain in the possession of My Executor hereafter named. Item I give unto my most Dear Sister Susanah Bond a Negro Man nam'd Bookey, and a Negro Woman named Rachell as also a Mare nam'd Pilot and the Third Part of the Household Goods left by my deceased husband Thomas Allen as also all my Poultry to her and to her heirs forever. Item I give unto my loveing Nephew George Paddon Bond a Negro Wench named Beck to him and to his heirs for ever. Item I give unto my Loveing Neice Elizabeth Bond a Negro Woman Named Deb and a Negro Girl named little Mary with all my trinkets to her and to her heirs for ever. Item I give unto my Son in Law James Allen a Negro Child the Son of the Negro Wench Named Deb and also an Iron pot which I will that he possess at that time at that time he possess and Enjoys the Estate given him by his deceased Father Thomas Allen and I also give him two mourning Rings and a pocket piece at the time aforesaid. Item I give unto my Son Thomas Allen the Mourning Ring which was his Mothers and to both my Sons in Law aforesaid I give my third part of the plantation tools provided they allow my Brother Jacob Bond the whipsaw Bought of Mr. Evliegh. Lastly I give unto my Loveing Brother Jacob Bond my horse Named Diamond and my Snuff Box and Seal ring together with my Share of the Crop made on the Rice house plantation and at home as also all my debts Bonds Notes Mortgages and what Else is appertaining to me Either in my Own Right or In my deceased Husband Thomas Allens' Right, and I do hereby appoint him the Said Jacob Bond Sole Executor of this my Last Will and Testament hereby revoking and Annulling all former Wills by me made or Constituted. In Witness whereof I have hereunto Set my hand and Seal this Twenty Eighth day of January in the Year of Our Lord One Thousand Seven hundred twenty and Two.
Sign'd Seal'd Published   Eliza. Wigfall Allen (SEAL)
& Declared in the Presence of Us the Subscribers.

John Pilgrim
William Watson
George Quelch
RECORDED FEBRY 7th, 1722.

WILL OF JOHN ALEXANDER VOL. 1 PAGE 12
PROBATE JUDGES OFFICE, CHARLESTON, S. C.

Carolina fs

In ye Name of God Amen I John Alexander of ye Province of Carolina Mercht. Considering of ye Certainty of Death & ye uncertainty of ye time of my death do make this my Last Will & Testamt. ffirst I commend my Soul to ye Mercy of God yt gave it & my Body I Comitt to ye Earth to be buried

in Such Place & wth Such Charges as my Execut. Shall think fitt & & for ye Wordly Estate wch God hath blessed me w.th I dispose of ye Same in Manner & form following vizt. Imp. I do give & bequeath to ye Ministery of ye Church at Charles Town Commonly Called ye presbyterian Church ye Sume of fifty Pounds to be delivered unto & left at ye Discretion & managemt. of John Jones gunsmity & robert ffenwick Item I Give & Bequeath unto Avid Adams liveing in Charles Town Widdo. Ten pounds Sterling Item I Give & Bequeath unto ye rt honorable Joseph Blake & George Logan Esqr. Executrs Ten Pounds each to Buy them Selves Mourning Item I Do Give, Grant, Devise & Bequeath to my beloved Wife Ann Alexander one full Moiety or half part of all & Singular my real & personal Estate whatsoever not already by this Will Bequeathed, to have & to hold ye sd full Moiety & half part of my sd real & Personal Estate in whatsoever part of ye world ye Same is or Shall be, unto my sd Wife Ann Alexander her heirs & assigns for ever Item I do Give, Grant, Devise & bequeath to my beloved daughter Ann Alexander ye other full Moiety or half part of all & Singular my real & personal Estate whatsoever not already by this will Bequeathed, to have & to hold ye said other full Moiety or half part of my sd real & Personal Estate in whatsoever part of ye worldly ye Same is, or shall be, unto my sd Daughter Ann Alexander her heirs & assigns for ever. Item My Will is yt in Case my sd daughter Ann should happen to dye before she Come of age yn I Give, Grant, Devise & bequeath, ye Moiety or half part of my real & Personal Estate, by this Will Bequeathed unto my sd daughter Ann unto my Beloved Wife Ann Alexander Item Also my Will is yt in Case my Beloved Wife ann alexander Should happen to dye now yt yn I Give, Grant, Devise & Bequeath my whole Estate real & personal by this Will bequeathed unto my sd Wife Ann Alexander & daughter Ann Alexander unto my loveing Brother Robert Alexander his Heirs & assigns for Ever Lastly I do make & ordain my sd Wife Ann & my friends ye rt honorable Joseph Blake & George Logan to be Executrs of this my Last Will & Testamt. requireing my sd Executrix & Executors to See ye Same Performed & I utterly revoke all former Wills & testamts. by me heretofore made & Declared In Witness whereof I have hereunto Sett my hand & Seal this twentieth & sixt day of September in ye year of our Lord one thousand Six hundred Ninety & Nine
Signed Sealed & Declared In the Presence of us

John Alexander (SEAL)

Abraham Eve
John Cock Senior
William Sadler
John Cock Junior

WILL OF EDWARD ARDEN VOL. 1 PAGE 54
PROBATE JUDGES OFFICE, CHARLESTON, S. C.

In the Name of God Amen. I Edward Arden in the Province of Carolina Considering of the certainty of death & the uncertainty of these do make this my last will & testament first I commend my soul to ye mercy of God that gave it, and my body I commit to the Earth to be buried in such place and with such charges as my Executrix shall think fitt & for the worldly estate which God hath blessed me with I dispose of as followeth my debts being first paid viz: Imprimis I do give grant devise & bequeath to my beloved wife Mary Arden one full moiety or half part of all and singular my real and personal estate in what soever part of the world the same is or shall be in to have and to hold the same to her and her heirs and assigns forever. Item. I do give grant devise and bequeath to my beloved daughter Margaret Arden one ful moiety or half part of all and singular my real and personal estate in whatsoever part of the world the same is or shall be in to have and to hold the same to her and her heirs and assigns forever and it is my will that if my daughter Margaret Arden should happen to dye before she comes to the age of twney one years that then the one full moiety or half part of my estate herein given to her shall go to my loving wife Mary Arden her heirs and assigns forever. Lastly I do make and ordain my said loving wife Mary Arden to be Executrix of this my last will and testament requiring my Executrix to see the same performed and to take the best care she can of my daughter to bring her up. and I utterly revoke all former wills & testaments by me heretofore made and declared. In witness whereof I have hereunto set my hand & seal this twentiety day of July in the year of our Lord one thousand seven hundred and twenty two.

(L)
Er: Arden (S)

Signed seal'd and delivered in
ye presence of us
Tho. Waring
John Stubley
John Borlan
Joseph Arden

Memorandum: On this 25th day of September 1722 Personally came and appeared before me Mr Thomas Waring Mr John Stubley and Mr Joseph Arden three of the witnesses to the with in will who being duely sworn on the holy Evangelist of all might God, declares that they were personally present and saw the within Testator Edward Arden sign seal publish and declare the within instrument of writing to be his last will and testament, and at the time of doing thereof he was of sound mind and memory to ye best of their knowledge and that they were likewise present and did see the within John Borlan sign his name as an evidence thereto. Sworn before me

ffr. Nicholson

And on 8 October 1722 at the Ponds plantation Mrs. Mary Arden was qualified Executrix.
Recorded October 24th 1722.

WILL OF JOHN ASH VOL. 1 PAGE 34
PROBATE JUDGES OFFICE, CHARLESTON, S. C.

I John Ash of Danho in the County of Colletion in South Carolina gent. doo constitute this my last will thereby revoking and anuling all former wills and that all former wills are hereby annulled y.t this is my last will is here by declared. Imprimis I make my beloved wife Mary the daughter of Samuell Batt late recor of Coulfon in Wiltshire in England my whole and sole Executrix in trust that she dispose of all my Estate as well reall as personal w.ch I hereby give her (except W.t is herein after otherwise bequeathed) for the maintenance of her self and children now born w.h may before ye twentieth of ffebruar next be born of her, as also that when either of the male children shall arrive to the age of twenty one years she shall to such child deliver than such part of the remains or improved product as divideing the same by the number of those children than liveing & her Self shall allow, and in like manner to the female Children as they shall arrive att the age of ffifteen To my son John my Martha Joy I give the product of 100 lb Tally payable to me or order with advantage of Survivorship out to the Exchequor as alsoo two ffiths of the dues on another tally for ffourteen p cent recompose for five hundred pounds dureing his life payable also out of the Exchequor to me or my order. To my Son William I give the recompence due on ye Survivorship fund 100 lb Tally for his life these tallys are all in the hands of sr. William Simpson, I also give to my said son William the advowfich of Colley vicarage bought of Mrff Mayne lying in the County of Devon. Lastly in case my Executrix herein mentioned dy before she know of my death it is my will that Landy l' Joseph Morton and the Lady Eliza. Blake be my Executors in trust she dispose of my Estate in like manoras has she lived she would have according to this my will have done

signed sealed and delivered my will
this ninth of Aprill Seventeen hundred
& three in PrSence off   John (SEAL(Ash
Edmnd. Bellinger
Ja Byres
James Kinloch

Before me the R.t Honble S.r Nathaniel Johnson Lut Governor Capt generall and admirall of South and & North Carolina and ordinary of the Same. Came and appeared on this present Nineteenth day of October an.o dni 1704 Mr. James Byres and Dandy r Edmund Bellinger two of the within Subscribing Evidentes who on their oaths on the holy Evangelists taken say that they and either of them were personally prsent and did see the within testator Mr. John Ash Sign seal Publish and declare the within Instrument to be his last will and testament and at ye time of his soo doing he was of Sound and Perfect mind and memory to ye best of their Judgm.ts and knowledges and that they saw James Kinloch ye other of the within subscribeing witnesses signye Same in Wittness thereto
Capt. et Jurat Coram me
die & anno Pr dict   N. Johnson

CORNELIUS KEITH PACK. 183 EQUITY
CLERK OF COURTS OFFICE, PICKENS, S. C.

Alfred Hester & Eady Hester his wife formerly Eady Keith sheweth that Cornelius Keith her father died owning considerable real estate. That a short time before his death he executed a paper purporting to be his last will and testament which paper he left unmarked at the time of his death, the paper bearing date May 19, 1820.

In the name of God Amen. I Cornelius Keith of Pickens District being sick in body but of sound mind and memory and knowing that it is appointed unto man to die, do make and ordain this my last will and testament—and first I recommend my soul unto the hands of God that gave it to me and body to be buried by my Executors and as for my worldly Estate that it hath pleased God to give me, I dispose of as follows to wit.

Item—I lend unto my beloved and lawful wife Mary all my land and Plantation whereon I now live during her natural life, at her decease to be equally divided between my eight youngest children to wit, James, Allen, Mary, Sarah, William, Rebecca, Eady, Cornelius, also I lend to my wife one negro girl named Chang during her natural life, after her death to be equally divided between all my ten children and her increase, also my sorrel mare one cow and calf and as many hogs as she thinks right to keep during her life and then to be divided amongst my ten children. I give my two negro men Andrew and Darby and all my money, debts, after my just debts be paid, two young sorrel mares, all my stock of cattle and the balance of my stock of hogs and sheep, all my household furniture, except two beds. one for Eady and one for William, and one I left for my wife, to be equally divided between all my ten children after my death—and I do hereby nominate and appoint my beloved sons John Keith and William L Keith to be my Executors of this my last will and testament, hereby disannulling all other will or wills by me made.

Mary Keith married Amos Sutherland, Sarah Keith married William Sutherland, Rebecca Keith married Joseph B. Reid, the heirs of George Keith who died since his father viz. Anderson Keith, John Keith, Matthew Keith, George Keith, Cornelius Keith, Mary Keith who married Robert McLure, Lucinda Keith who married Meredith Roper, Sarah Keith who married Abe? Roper, Margaret Keith who married Joseph Looper, Elizabeth Keith who married a Rembly all of whom reside without the limits of this state, and several of which are minors, which ones are unknown. . . .

Filed June 5, 1851.

WILLIAM CLEVELAND PACK. 184 EQUITY
CLERK OF COURTS OFFICE, PICKENS, S. C.

George Cleveland & his wife Nancy Cleveland, John O'Neal & his wife Mary O'Neal, Benjamin Laughridge & his wife Lucinda, Thomas Cleveland & his wife Elizabeth, all of the State of Georgia, states that William Cleveland of Pickens District, made a will bearing date on or about the 31st July stating, "To my daughter Fanny Wright formerly Fanny Cleveland I give a negro woman Milley now in her possession but with this condition, that should she die without lawful issue, the negro woman and all her issue to be equally divided among her surviving brothers and sisters." That the said Wm. Cleveland soon after making his will departed this life, leaving the same unrevoked and in full force and effect. That the said Fanny Wright the wife of James Wright recd. into her possession the said negro. William Cleveland died in 1839. James Wright died without leaving a will and admnr. of his estate was granted to Baylus Hix & Wm. E. Cleveland. The surviving brothers & sisters of Fanny Wright are, Wm. E. Cleveland, Jean wife of Baylus Hix, Martha Wright widow, Nancy wife of George Cleveland, Mary wife of Benjamin Laughridge, Elizabeth wife of Thomas Cleveland. Fanny Wright widow of James Wright died on or about the 28th April 1848 . . . Filed Jan. 28, 1851 . . . Nancy Harrison decd. was a sister of James Wright who intermarried with Robert Harrison . . . Martha Wright was the widow of Thomas Wright. Catharine Wright was the widow of Larkin Wright. John Wright & Charlton Wright were brothers of James Wright each supposed to be yet living though residing out of the state. The representatives of the following decd. brothers to wit, Heirs of David Wright to wit, Elizabeth Wright & two sons James & David Wright each long absent from the state. Heirs of Obedingo Wright to wit, J. C. Long & wife Pamelia, W. C. Wright, James W. Wright, W. Cains? & wife Hannah, Mary Wright, Nancy Wright, Thos. Wright, Rhoda Wright, Frances Wright. Heirs of Thos. Wright to wit, Wm. Wright, Robert Wright, Abednego Wright, , Saml. McJunkin? & wife Martha, Monroe Cleveland & wife Catharine and Lilburn Wright . . . Heirs of Larkin Wright who has departed this life since the death of the said James Wright to wit, his widow Catharine Wright and their 8 children viz. Frances wife of Milton Hix, Nancy Holland wife of Robert Holland, Lucinda Wright wife of Robert Isbell, Oliver Wright, James Wright, Martha Wright, Catharine Wright and the heirs of Julia Holland who had been the wife of William Holland viz her husband & 3 children, Robert Holland, Catharine Holland & Nancy Holland minors . . . Heirs of Nancy Harrison to wit, E. W. Harrison, Thomas Harrison, Larkin Harrison, James Harrison, Benjamin Holland & wife Lucinda, Jackson Lowry & wife Catharine, James W. Pickens? and wife Elizabeth and Harriet B. Harrison. These to gether with the widow Frances Wright of James Wright now residents of Georgia . . . Nancy Cleveland the widow of William Cleveland. . . .

MISCELLANEOUS RECORDS, PACK, 185
CLERK OF COURTS OFFICE, PICKENS, S. C.

No. 1 Alexander Bryce Jr., Writ of Habeas Corpus

On Oct. 19, 1867 Charles W. Hunt made oath that on the evening of the 12th Inst. Alexander Bryce Jr. passed by his house in company with his brother Wm. H. H. Hunt, halting without getting down long enough to make arrangements with him to go with them fox hunting, after the meetings of the debating society and Union League in that neighborhood have been attended as long as was agreeable to the parties. Bryce said he and William A. Lay were going to make speeches to the blacks at Hunnicutts Crossing. I followed Bryce and my brother very soon and found them at the school house where the Debating Society met. Bryce soon afterwards left said deponent and his brother aforesaid (who are his brotherinlaws) at the debating societys room as he said to make his speech to the blacks. Some two hours after this deponent was standing in the yard with a number of other persons and heard the negroes say in a loud excited manner, "take him dead or alive," and saw them charging up the hill not exactly in the direction of the schoolhouse, some 8 or 10 in front and many others scattered behind, they soon changed their direction towards the schoolhouse and then this deponenet ran off and concealed himself out of sight of the school house and so far off that he could not distinguish the noises made there. While running he heard a pistol fire in the direction of the school house which was the only one he recollects to have heard that night. After he ad been gone from the school house some quarter or half hour as well as he could in the excitement note the passage of time, and he and his brother who was with him returned there to get their horses, and mounted to start off when they were arrested and carried down to the League Room where they found their brotherinlaw Alexander Bryce Jr. aforesaid, who by interceding procured their release upon the giving of their names. The three then went off towards home, struck a track and a had a short race as they went. He left many, as he presumes all of the negroes in and about the league room and between their and the school house. Wm. H. H. Hunt made oath that he heard the negroes say "take him" as they were charging up, and said that Bryce went from his house that evening and went with him home that night and stayed until the next morning at 8 or 9 o'clock. That he saw nor heard any thing to connect Bryce in any way with the murder of the lad Hunnicut that night . . . James Keith, John Reid and Clark Cleveland made oath that they were present at the meeting of the Union League on Saturday the 12th Inst. at Hunnicutts Crossing. That Alexr. Bryce Jr. was present by invitation to address the meeting and was no officer in the League at all, that this was the first meeting and for the purpose of organizing a League there, that the officers in charge of the meeting were Clark Cleveland President, Jackson Henderson Vice President, George Wright, Treasurer, David Singleton, Secretary, Henderson McKinney, Sentald, James Keith, Marshall, Henry Jenkins alias Young, Chaplain, Issac Brown, Committee, Green Cleveland, Finance Committee, and the Guard consisting of December Gadsden, Sargant, Natt Frazier, Capt. Deans, Bob Brackenridge, John Keith, Wm. Munro, Jack Walker and Mark Adams. That during the meeting every member is subject to the order of the President. That while the meeting was in session, (these depnents and the said Alexr. Bryce Jr. being then in the house) heard a pistol fire and immediately afterwards the Sargent reported that the Guard was being crowded on and that Robert Smith was shooting at the crowd. Jackson Henderson the Vice President then ordered a reinforcement of the Guard which was done. The business of the meeting proceeded a few minutes when the report of another pistol was heard, then came the report that sombody was hurt, then business was suspended, most of the members rushing out to see what was the matter and James Keith says that he went out at that time and reached the place where the lad Miles M. N. Hunnicutt was killed and found that he had been shot. Clark Cleveland says he left the house about this time also by the advice of Alexr. Bryce Jr. to see what was the matter and stop the fuss and prevent any fighting. John Reid says he remained in the house until all escept the said Bryce & Elias Kennedy and Fed Garret had left the house after the firing of the second pistol. He then went towards where young Hunnicutt was killed and met Capt. R. L. Lewis coming away and was informed by him of the killing. They further state that they returned to the meeting house of their Union League about the same time and about half an hour after the firing of the second pistol and found the said Alexr. Bryce Jr. a prisoner, that they understood his arrest was made by order of Jackson Henderson Vice President. That said Bryce had not up to this time said anything except what has been above detailed in reference to the excitement outside. As far as these deponents heard nor did he do anything. James Keith says at the request of said Bryce before the transaction of any other business after the return of the deponents as aforesaid, had him released and he went off & was not seen again by them, that night or the next day until late in the evening about 12 or 2 hours by sun when James Keith saw him at Charles Hunts house after said Bryce left that night the meeting place of the League. The business of the League was resumed.

       John Reid
       James Keith
       Clark Cleveland

ESTATE OF JAMES MANSELL BOX 14 NO. 187
PROBATE JUDGES OFFICE, PICKENS, S. C.

Estate admnr. Feb. 10, 1846 by Mrs. Sarah Mansell, Joseph Mansell, Hulet Hunt, Henson Hunt, Lewis Hill who are bound unto William D. Steele Ordinary of Pickens District in the sum of $15,000.00 . . . On March 3, 1848 Frances Barratt recd. $200.00 on her part of the said estate . . . Left a widow & 12 children (Mrs. Sarah Mansell admnr. probably the widow) viz. Julia Ann Freeman, William Mansell, Mathew Mansell, Joshua Mansell, Joseph Mansell, Robert Mansell, Samuel Mansell, Lemuel Mansell, Judge G. Ferguson, Frances Barnett or Barratt (not positive). Other heirs mentioned were: Richard H. Mansell, John Mansell, Meredith Freeman.

WILL OF JOSHUA MANSELL BOX 32 NO. 371
PROBATE JUDGES OFFICE, PICKENS, S. C.

State of South Carolina
Pickens District. In the name of God Amen I Joshua Mansell being in a low State of health though of a sound and full disposing mind Also calling to mind the uncertainty of life and knowing the certainty of death also having a desire to dispose of my worldly goods & chattels to my satisfaction whilst I am now in proper sense doe ordain and make this my last Will & Testament. First After all my just Debts and funeral Expenses be Paid Doe will and bequeath to my wife Mahala Mansell one hundred acres of land to enclude my houses as follows Enduring her widow or natural life time the land marks commencing on a holly bush near above the Spring cald and known as my old Spring thence across the branch a westerdly course to a white oak on the bluff near the branch thence North down the spring branch leaving all the bottom land out within about three rods of Georges Creek near the mouth of said spring branch thence a straight line to the Rock corner on the table Mountain Road thence bounde by the said Road south to the Methodist Camp Ground thence to a gum corner of said Camp Ground thence along said line to the Greenville road as far as sufficient to have said hundred acres as near a Square as possible thence North a straight line as far as a field cald the Austain Day field thence taking all the enclosures runing along a hedge Roe to a hollow thence a straight line to the commencing holly bush leaving the said spring out I also will & bequeath one negro woman called Matilda & one negro boy called Laurense (Matilda & increase) to my beloved wife together with all my stock farming utensils household & kitchen furniture of Every Description with the exception of what is hereafter named to wit

one horse choice all the cattle hogs sheep &c with the corn bacon wheat fodder oats now on hand together with the privilege of the present years crop free of Rent on all of my lands all of which I will & bequeath to my beloved wife Enduring her natural life time or Widow after which I devise the same & increase to my six youngest children viz Camilla Jane, Tinsa Emmer, Thomas Fletcher, Abi, Baily, Malinda Allice Mansells to be sold & Equaly divided at the death or widow. I also will & bequeath to my beloved wife Enduring her natural life time or Widow after which I devise collect use and Distribute at her pleasure Also my one Horse wagon to said wife & harness. 2nd. I will & bequeath to oldest son John B Mansell & my third son Addison Mansell the Remainder of my land to be Divided at their pleasure After my wife takes choice of the horses the other horse I devise to said oldest son John B. Mansell also my Double Barreled shot gun & equippage also my Blacksmith tools to my before named son Adison Mansel my rifle gun and Equippage so concludes my will Respecting John and Addison. To my second son Westly Mansell I will and bequeath one negro girl named Ester the oldest daughter of Matilda To my Daughter Sarah Trotter & husband John R Trotter I will and bequeath one negro girl namemed Hannah 2nd daughter of Matilda To my second Daughter Anny Mansell I will and bequeath one negro girl Permelia youngest or third Daughter of Matilda Which includes all of my Real and personal property belonging to me at this time in witness whereof I doe here unto set my hand and afix my seal this the sixth day of March in the year of our lord one thousand Eight Hundred and fifty four and in the seventy Eighth year of the independence of the United States of America. Signed in the presence of

Joshua Jameson
Reuben Ellis   Joshua Mansel
Gideon Ellis

Codicil

Whereas I Joshua Mansell the Testator of the annexed Will still being in a low State of health though of still strong sound mind & Remembering that I have neglected to Appoint an Executor to the said will doe Appoint my Trusty Friend and brother in law Judge G. Ferguson my lawful Executor to this my last will & testament in witness whereof I doe hereunto set my hand and seal the 9 day of May in the year of our lord & saviour Jesus Christ 1854 And in the seventy Eighth year of the Independence of the United States of America. Signed in the presents of

Gideon Ellis   Joshua Mansell
John Ferguson
Reuben Ellis

On June 5, 1854 Gideon Ellis Sen'r states that he saw the other witnesses sign the will.

WILL OF GREEN MANSELL BOX 116 NO. 4
PROBATE JUDGES OFFICE, PICKENS, S. C.

The State of South Carolina
County of Pickens
The Last Will and Testament of Green Mancil In the Name of God

Amen. I Green Mancil Being of sound mind, viewing the uncertainty of this mortal life and the certainty of death do make and Publish this my last will and Testament 1st I Desire that all my just Debts Be Paid 2nd I Desire that all my Personal and Real Estate Be sold and Divided Between my six Children Equily, nameing Harriet Gordon, Amanda Johnson, Perry Mancil, Merida Mancil, James Mancil, Caroline Miller This Will to go Immediately into Effect at my Decease I here By appoint G. M. Lynch my Sole Executor of this my last will an Testament Given under my hand and Seal this the 14th Day of May in the year of our Lord one thousand Eight Hundred and Eighty Eight.

G. M. Lynch (Signed) Green Mancil
Ira T Roper
    his
M. R. X Chapman
    mark
Filed June 29, 1888.

WILL OF DOLLY FORD BOX 30 PACK. 30
PROBATES JUDGES OFFICE, SPARTANBURG, S. C.

State of South Carolina
Spartanburgh District

I Dolly Ford widow of Capt. Manly Ford De'd of the State and District afore Said, being of Sound and disposing mind memory and understanding praise be God for the Same. But being advanced in Years and calling to mind the uncertainty of life do make and declose this my last Will and Testament in Manner and form following

1st I give to the Mount Pleasant Church Five Dollars of which I am a member at present to be paid over unto the hands of Bowin Griffin.

2nd I devise that all my Just Debts and funeral Expenses be paid.

3rd. I give to my Brother William Chumner the One half of all my Estate of whatsoever Kind it may be.

4th. I give to my niece Nancy Inlow and the heirs of her boddy the One half of the Remaining half of my Estate not here to fore disposed of.

5 I Give to Dolly Young daughter of my Sister Sally Young the Residue of my Estate Remaining of what Soever Kind it may be hereby Revoking any and all wills here to fore made and decloses this to be my last Will and Testament. In Witness where of I the said Dolly Ford have hereunto Set my hand and Seal this the Twenty-fifth day of June in the Year of our Lord One Thousand Eight hundred and forty Nine.

DOLLY X FORD (L. S.)

Signed Sealed declared and acknowledged by the Said Dolly Ford for hir last Will and Testament in the presence of us who at hir request and in hir presence have subscribed our names at witnesses thereto.

John Poole
W. I. Brem
Y. J. Wingo
    Recorded March 8, 1854.

WILL OF DANIEL FORD BOX 3 FILE 164
PROBATE JUDGES OFFICE, GREENVILLE, S. C.

IN THE NAME OF GOD, AMEN. I DANIEL FORD of Greenville district and State of South Carolina being well of body and perfect sound of mind and memory, and calling to mind the mortality of my body and knowing that it is appointed for men once to die I make constitute and ordain this my last will and testament, viz, As for such worldly estate where with it has pleased God to bless me with in this life I give demise and bequeath in the following manner. Imprimis. I give bequeath unto Mary Ford my well beloved wife the whole of my estate both real and personal during her life or widowhood but in case of her marrying then I give bequeath to by well beloved daughter Elizabeth McElroy a negro man named Jack also two negro boys named Dick and Jatts on and the one half of my stock of goods and chattels to be equally divided between Mary Ford my wife and Elizabeth McElroy my daughter to divide between themselves as they think proper. And they cannot agree in their dividing then they may choose indifferent persons to make the divide between them and at the decease of Mary Ford my wife the whole or balance of any estate both real or personal to go unto Elizabth McElroy my beloved daughter. I also constiute and ordain Mary Ford my beloved wife my executrix with James McElroy my son-in-law my executor of this my last will and testament. And I do hereby disallow disannul and revoke all former wills legacies or bequeath heretofore willed or bequeathed ratifying and confirming this and no other to be my last will and testament. In witness whereof I have hereunto set my hand and seal this 13th day of December A. D. 1810 and the 35th year of the American Independency.

DANIEL FORD (SEAL)

Signed sealed Published & Pronounced in the presents of us
John McElroy
Micajah Berry
Hudson Berry
    Probated August 1, 1837.

WILL OF STEPHEN FORD BOX 3 NO. 168
PROBATE JUDGES OFFICE, GREENVILLE, S. C.

In the Name of God Amen
    I Stephen Ford of the State of South Carolina Greenville Dist. Being of sound and disposing mind and memory and cauling to mind the uncertainty of life, and being desirous to dispose of all such worldly estate as it haith pleased God to bless me with, do make and ordain this my last will and Testament in manner following, that is to say, I desire that immediately after my death all my Just Debts and funeral expenses be paid by my Executors hereafter named out of any money that I may leve or out of any other part of my estate, first I give to my Grand Daughter Polly Sullivan one bed and furnature, I then wish my executors to sell the whole of my estate both real and personal on such a credit as they think best for my heirs, and when the money is collected to divide it equally among my lawful heirs that is Milley & Thomas Owens John Ford Rebecca & Ananias Wallis Patsey Owens the

75

lawful heirs of Vicy & Charles Sullivan, Polly & Batey Chandler James Ford Stephen Ford Daniel Ford William Ford Sintha & Benjamin Brewer Keziah & William Thompson, lastly I do hereby constitute and appoint my Friend Micajah Berry and my Brother Daniel Ford Executors of this my last will and testament by me made, in Testimony whereof I have hereunto set my hand and affixed my seal this Tenth day of Dec'r A. D. 1829.

The word Polly Sullivan interlined before it was assigned. . . .

          his
        Stephen X Ford (L. S.)
          mark

Sign'd Seal'd Published and Declared as and for the last will and testament of the above named Stephen Ford in presents of us.

John McElroy
Hudson Berry, Jr.
Probated January 18, 1830.

ESTATE OF RUBEN MOORE BUNDLE 8 PACKAGE 2
BARNWELL COURTHOUSE, S. C.

Est. administrated June 11, 1805 by Zacharih Harrell, Edward Bush, and Alexander Shaw Newman bound unto Gideon Hagood Ord. Barnwell District in sum $2,000.00 . . . Citation published Dec. 1804 shows that Elizabeth Moore widow applied for Letters of Administration . . . James Maloan, Zachariah Harrell bought at sale. . . .

WILL OF WILLIAM MOORE BUNDLE 17 PACKAGE 5
BARNWELL COURTHOUSE, S. C.

The State of South Carolina
Barnwell District

In the name of God, Amen. I, William Moore being in a low state of health tho perfect Memory, do, constitute & Ordain this my last will & testament. first I desire that I may have a decent Burying & that all my funeral charges be paid after that, that all my Just Debts be paid and the residue of my worldly goods I Leave as follows viz. To my son William I give & bequeath the Plantation and tract of land where I now reside and fifty acres of Land Adjoining Sd. Land as above Mentioned of the Land that I purchased from Glynn & Forster (in one way looked like Foster) and the remainder of my Land more or less I give and bequeath to my son Thomas and the remaining part of my Property I Leave to Equally divided Between my wife Margaret & my three daughters Maria, Matilda & Margaret, Observing that my Sd. daughters as above mentioned is to have Reasonable Education of Sd. property to my daughters Matilda & Margaret I give & bequeath two cows & Calves Each Exclusive also to my son Thomas I give one negroe man named Mingo to be delivered to him, when my youngest daughter arrive of age & to my son William I give & bequeath one negroe Girl Namd Teresa to be delivered to him at the above term with all her issues from the present date and to my daughter Catherine I give six dollars cash and I do nominate and appoint Lewis Bryan and Joseph Bryan Exors. to Execute this my last will & testament.

his
William X Moore (L. S.)
mark

Sign'd Seal'd & delivered in Presence of us 30 Nov. 1810.
David Ewing
David Fitts
   Proven Dec. 13, 1810.

PROBATE JUDGES OFFICE, PICKENS, S. C.
BOX 44 NO. 487

L. G. BEACH to PHILIP YOUNG
Release for 700 Acres Land
State of South Carolina

   Pickens District. Know all men by these presents that I Laban G. Beach of Pickens District in consideration of the sum of Eight hundred dollars to me in hand paid by Philip Young of Pickens District have granted bargoned sold and Releast and by these presants do grant bargain sell and Release unto the Sd. Philip Young a tract of land containing seven hundred acres situate in Pickens District on Little Eastatoe Creek waters of Keowee River Reference being that to the annexed plat made by Thomas D Garvin on the twenty Seventh day of January Eighteen hundred and 41 will plainly show the bounds and Extent of the Sd. plantation or Tract of Land. Together with all and Singular the wrights mambers Heraditroments and apertainenses to the said premises belonging or in any wise incident or apertaining to have and to hold all and singular the premised before mentioned unto the said Philip Young his heares and assigns forever and I bind myself my heares and Executors and administrators to warent and forever defend all and singular the said premises unto the said Philip Young his heares and assigns against myself my heares and against all persons whomsoever lawfully claiming or to claim the same or aney part thereof. in witness whareof I have hereunto set my hand & seal this the twenty fifth day of March & in the Seventy third yeare of the Sovreingty & independence of the United States of America Assigned sealed & delivered in the preseants of

L. G. Beach

Enoch Chapman
Wm. B. Nix
South Carolina

   Pickens District. Before me personally appeared Enoch Chapman and made oath in due form of law and upon oath saith he was present and saw L. G. Beach sign seal and deliver the within DEED OF CONVEYANCE unto Philip Young for the use and purposes within mentioned and Wm. B. Nix was present with me and witness the same Deed. Sworn to and subscribed before me this the 5 day of August 1848.

Enoch Chapman

Rt. Srewart M. P. D.
   CERTIFIED Aug. 7, 1848.

WILL OF GORDON MOORE BOX 30 NO. 1246
PROBATE JUDGES OFFICE, YORK COUNTY, S. C.

STATE OF SOUTH CAROLINA, YORK

The last Will & Testament of Gordon Moore of York District.

State of South Carolina I Gordon Moore of York District & State of South Carolina do make ordain & Establish this writing to be my last will & Testament hereby revoking all others by me made & being of sound disposing Mind & memory at the time of executing the same do declare my will as follows) To wit) It is my will & desire that all my just debts & funeral Expenses be paid by my Executors hereafter named out of the money now on hand notes & book Accounts & the following Tracts of Land (To Wit) The Land lying & being in Union District & State aforesaid known by the names of Thomas Blacks plantation John Parker plantation & the Joseph Howell plantation as also the following tracts of Land in York District & State aforesaid One Tract of Land that I bought from John Darwin Senr. One Small Tract including the Spring that Joseph Logan makes use of that I bought from Amos Davis & if my Son John Gordon Moore will make a title from his to the Tract of Land that Joseph Logan now lives on to my Estate & let the Same be sold with the foregoing Tracts which I think will promote The sale of the adjoining Tracts Then my Executors Shall be bound to pay unto him the sum of One Hundred dollars if he agrees to the same in his own right Then I wish my Executors to lay of the adjoining Lands in small tracts to suit purchasers as my Executors as my Executors may think Best also my shares in the Howell plantation also a part of a tract that I bought from James Plexca Comencing one Chain on the North side on the Thompson line where it crosses the said Plexco Spring Branch Including the spring thence a straight line to the Howells Ferry line to the top point of the Stoney Hill Thence with Rhoda Smiths line Mabel Smith Line and said Thompsons line to the begining and if the fore going lands Monies Notes & Accounts & profits arising from my plantation is insufficient to settle my debts my Executors may sell the following Lands:

Beginning at Doctor Wrights North West Pine Corner from thence a straight line to Payton B. Darwins North East Dead Pine Corner Thence with Payton B. Darwins line & the said Doctor Wright lines to the first Mentioned Pine Corner on either tract that I Bought from Samuel Barkley the Two last tracts not sold untill it is ascertained that they others are not sufficient all the aforesaid Lands to be sold on a credit of one & two Years with lawful interest from said sales secured by Mortguage for the payment of the same my Executors to Execute titles to the Same as if I were personally present myself also all surplus property that can be spared from the use of my family & plantation I wish to be sold on a credit of twelve months it is my desire that they will proceed of the present Crop & the crops hereafter made after all necessary Expences of family & plantation are first paid go to the payment of my just debts Necessary if not the Same to be put at interest and that my Executors have the power to rent any of my lands if they it expedient & also to hire out my negroes yearly to the Carpenters trade & any other of the Negroes men if they think it would be more profitable than to work on a farm except my negro man Frank and all they hands that is now on the river plantation to remain there except said Frank & wish the Bottom Lands to be cleared up from the upper end of the field to the Mouth of the Goven Moore Creek & put in cultivation for the support of my family and the payments of my debts my negroe Frank and his Son Jerry & the negroes that is now on the plantation where my family now lives to remain there to work said plantation under the direction of my son John G. Moore & for his Services in Carrying on the same he shall receive Two Hundred dollars annually from my Executors and that my Daughters remain where they live now untill the youngest arrives at the age of Twenty one years or Marry by them attending to the domestic Concerns of the Household & when my youngest Daughter arrives at the age of Twenty one Years that all my property both real and personal except Specified Legacies hereafter mentioned shall b equally divided by lot amongst they then Surviving Heirs or representatives and it is my desire that my Negroes be valued & put in lots & drawn for by the Heirs & that the land not bequeathed to be sold or taken by any of the heirs at valuation & that my negroe Frank have his choice with any of the heirs to make choice to live with without being sold or divided I Bequeathe unto my son William Thompson Moore all that I have heretofore given him of my Estate which will be found charged to him on my Books also one note of hand from him to me also one tract of Land that I purchased from Jacob B. Moore in Union District on Broad River adjoining the lands of John Moore & Susan Parker also one good Bed sted but not to have possession of said Lands untill my youngest Child shall arrive at the age of Twenty one years.

I bequeath unto my son John Gordon Moore one negro Boy equal in value to the Boys that William Thompson Moore & Jacob Alexander Moore has already received from me also one good horse also one good Bed & Bedsted & Furniture for the Same Also I give & Bequeath unto my sons John G. Moore Jacob A. Moore (towit) the following tracts of Land the Tract of Land known by the name of the old plantation given to me by my father lying in York District & State aforesaid on the East side of Broad River Also on Tract of Land bounded by Mitchels lines & John Darwin Dec'd. landsuntill intersects with James Curriers grant at or near the Buffaloe stump Thence with said James Curriers grant untill it intersects with Daniel Smiths Land on the George Darwin Grant then with said grant the various lines untill it intersects with the old plantation also the part of Two other Tracts one that I Bought from Wilson Called the Henderson Place & was granted to Joshua Denton the other comencing on the Denton line on the East Side where said line will cross the South Fork of the Moores Branch running on the South west fork of Said Branch untill a due East line from Daniel Smiths post Oak Corner of the Tract Granted to George Darwin on the Ridge Road leading to Daniel Smiths will intersect the Branch or the head Hollows Thereof— Thence from Daniel Smiths Post Oak Corner with his lines the aforesaid Lands not to go into the possession of the Said John G. Moore & Jacob A. Moore untill my youngest Child shall arrive at the age of Twenty one years then to equally divided between in Quantity & Quality to Jacob A. Moore I give one good Bed Bedsted & Furniture I give & bequeath unto my Daughter Minerva Moore when she arrives at the age of eighteen years old one negroe Girl between the age of eight & twelve years one good Bureau one Good Bed & Bedstead & furniture for the same and requist that they may be sent

one year to some good Boarding School & that the expences of the same be paid by Executors out of my estate & when my Executors may think that she stand in need of a Saddle & bridle buy one for her pay for the same out of my estate I give & bequeath unto my Daughter Colnee when she arrives at the age of Eighteen Years one Negroe Girl between the age of eight twelve years one good Bureau One good Bed & Bedstead & furniture for the Same & request that she may be sent one year to some good Boarding School & the expences of the same be paid by my Executors out of my estate & when my Executors may think that she stands in need of a saddle & bridle to by one for her and pay for the same out of my estate & I also bequeath unto her my Gold Watch & it is my request that ever any of my Daughters may Marry that my Executors furnish each of them with a good Horse and my Will is that all the property I have given to my following Daughters Named (To Wit) Minerva Moore Temander Moore Diana Moore & Colenee Moore Either Specifically of by Division to them & the Natural Heirs of their body and my will is that if either of my sons or daughters shall die leaving no natural heirs of their body their share or shares shall return to my estate & be equally divided among the surviving heirs or their representatives It is further my will & desire that my aged Mother remain where she now is and that particular care attention be paid by my Executors to her ease & comfort & that she be decently supported during her life out of my estate & charge the same to my Mother and I do further give to my sons Jno G Moore & Jacob A Moore fifty acres of Land for which I have Daniel Smiths Bond to make me a title to the same lying between two Branches including my Negroe Quarter but to not go into possession of the same until my youngest child shall arrive at the age of twenty one years and lastly I do hereby Nominate and appoint my three sons William Thompson Moore John Gordon Moore & Jacob Alexander Moore Executors of this my last will & Testament and desire is that William Thompson Moore be acting Executor of this my last will & Testament and my sons John G Moore & Jacob A. Moore counsel & advise with him in all cases that may promote the interest of the estate & that my acting Executor make a regular return once in every year of all my estate & the number of deaths & births of all my slaves if any to be ordinary of said district in witness whereof I have hereunto set my hand & affixed my Seal this ninth day of November in the Year of our Lord Anno Dimoni one thousand Eight Hundred & thirty nine. Signed Sealed & Acknowledged)
in the presence of us.
James S. Hagan   Gordon Moore (L. S.)
Charles T. Murphey M. D.
James B Meek
Wm B. Meek
   Recorded in Will Book No. 2—P-97
   Case No. 30
   File No. 1246

ESTATE OF LINDSAY WHITTEN
PROBATE JUDGE OFFICE, LAURENS, S. C.

Settlement of the Estate of Lindsey Whitten dec'd made before the ordinary of Laurens District the 9th day of January 1846 present Marshall Duncan and Mrs. Nancy Whitten, Adm'r. James Dillard, & John Whitten & Col. Irby, Atty. for Isaac Jacks, Guardian of Alfred Whitten.

Amt. of sale bill		$4525.88
due 25 December 1845		75.42
amt. of Jno. Whitten note & int. $75.42		75.42
		$4601.30
Deduct comms. 2 pr. ct.		115.02
		$4486.28
Amt. paid out for debts and Expenses of Administration	$586	
add coms. 2 pr. ct.	14.65	600.83
		$3885.45
Deduct Comms. on 2-3 of Estate	$25.90	64.75
		$3820.70
Widow 1-3		1273.56
		$2547.14

Advancements

John Whitten		$725.00
1 Horse		50.00
200 ?		7.00
1 Bed & furniture		20.00
2 barrels flour		9.00
int.		72.53
		$883.53

James Dillard & Wife

1 Negroe girl		$ 150.00
1 Filley		40.00
1 bed & furniture		10.00
2 Bushels wheat		1.20
		$ 201.20
Interest		17.97
		$ 219.17
Advancements to Jno. Whitten		883.53
		$1102.70
Amt. of Estate coming to children		2547.14
Each share		1216.61
John Whitten, share		$1216.61

deduct advancements	883.53
	333.08
To bal. amt. of purchasers at sale and account against the estate	666.86
bal. due adm'r.	333.78
James Dillards share	$1261.61
Deduct advancements	219.17
deduct amt. of purchasers at sale	89.42
Bal. due 25 Dec. 1845	908.02
Sale of (Alpess?) Whitten	$1216.61
Paid R. B. Meaders for ?	3.09
Widows share	$1273.56
deduct com. at 174	15.91
	$1257.65
Deduct amt. purchased at sale	1004.83
	$ 252.82

Settlement of Lindsey Whitten
Recorded Page 246
COPY

WILL OF EDWARD HERING
PROBATE JUDGES OFFICE, SPARTANBURG, S. C.

In the name of God Amen—I Edward Herrin of the state of South Carolina and the District of Spartinburgh doth make this my last will and testament this twenty six day of July in the year 1811 my will and desire is that all my just debts be paid and that I may be deasently buried hoping that the lord may receive my sole my will and desire is that my loving wife Marian Herrin have my property Real and personal for her seport during her life and after her death to dispose of as she seas cause to divide amongst my children— I leave my Executor Morgan Herrin—I have set my hand the date above mentioned in presents of us.

Jesse Mathis   Edward Hering
William Cantrell
    her
Morning X Barnes
      mark
Recorded the 14th day of July 1813
Recorded in Will Book A Page 30
Box 14 Package 3

HENRY CANNON S. 8187—VIRGINIA
SPARTANBURG, S. C.

SERVED UNDER CAPT. McCLANAHAN, VIRGINIA
PENSIONED 1831—AGE 81. APRIL 11, 1752
BORN STAFFORD COUNTY, VIRGINIA, APRIL 11, 1752
LIVED IN CULPEPPER COUNTY, VA. WHEN HE VOLUNTEERED MOVED TO S. C. 1781 OR 1784? LIVED IN GREENVILLE DISTRICT ABOUT 22 YEARS. SERVED AT NORFOLK, DISCHARGED 1776. OLD JAMESTOWN, VA. SERVED 13 MONTHS. MENTIONED ELLIS CANNON A CLERGYMAN. ELLIS CANNON DID GET A PENSION.
(NOTE: COPIED FOR ME BY, MRS. LUCY McGHEE BOX 7213 APEX STATION, WASHINGTON, D. C.

LEWIS EATON PACK. 92 (EQUITY)
CLERK OF COURTS OFFICE, PICKENS, S. C.

Lewis Reese states that about 15 years since, Lewis Eaton his fatherinlaw moved from Pickens Dist. S. C. to the State of Kentucky and carried with him a family of negroes, his slaves to which he was very much attached. Sometime after his removal one Bailey Barton went on to the state where the said Lewis Eaton was then residing, and seized the said slaves under a pretended claim & brought them back to Pickens District, except one which he left to wait on the said Lewis Eaton & his wife, who were very old and feeble. Some short time after his return to this state, the said Bailey Barton died & the said Lewis Eaton brought his suit in Equity against the admnrs. of the said Bailey Barton for the slaves thus taken from him & which slaves were at that time in the possession of his said Admnrs. Jane Barton & Pleasant Alexander. The suit came to a hearing at June term 1848, the said slaves were ordered and decreed to be delivered to Lewis Eaton, which was done by the defendants Jane Barton & Pleasant Alexander. After the delivery of said slaves to the said Lewis Eaton, his Solicitors who had the management of the said suit, refused to let him carry off the said slaves till their counsel fees were paid. Consquently the said slaves were left in possession of Watson Collins a soninlaw of the said Lewis Eaton, residing in Pickens District, till the said Lewis Eaton could return to Kentucky & procure the money to pay the fees and charges of his Solicitors. This caused the old man one or two trips to the State of Kentucky. He finally succeeded in paying off the Solicitors. The said Watson Collins then refused to deliver up to the said Lewis Eaton one of the slaves a girl then about 5 or 6 years old, till he was paid $500.00 for his pretended services in assisting the said Lewis Eaton in his suit against the admnrs. of the said Bailey Barton for the said slaves. Not being able or willing to pay this unjust and groundless charge, the said Lewis Eaton was forved to leave the girl in the possession of the said Watson Collins, and shortly after his return to Kentucky with the other slaves, the said Lewis Eaton departed this life intestate, in the State of Indiana. Lewis Reese states that soon after he recd. the notice of his Lewis Eaton death thru a letter from one of the slaves, carried off, he applied to the Ord. of Pickens Distr. for letters of Admnr. on the personal estate of Lewis Eaton in South Carolina but the Ord. refused. Nothing more was done in the case till last year he renewed his application for Letters of Admnr. and they were granted to him by W. J. Parsons Ord. of Pickens Dist. In the meantime the said slave remained in the possession of the said Watson Collins till he sold her to James E. Hagood of Pickens Dist. for the sum of $800.00. Whether the deeds for the lands conveyed to Watson Collins by Lewis Eaton were not made to enable him to sell the same for the benefit of the said Eaton. Whether he ever paid any thing for the said lands? How much money he recd. for Lewis Eaton of Esquire Gillespie, of North Carolina, and whether he ever paid it over. That the said James E. Hagood do answer whether he did not know when he purchased the said girl slave of Collins, that Collins had no title to her, and that she was claimed as belonging to the estate of Lewis Eaton . . . Filed April 27, 1859.

JESSE CRENSHAW PACK. 120 (EQUITY)
CLERK OF COURTS OFFICE, PICKENS, S. C.

Jesse Crenshaw states that his fatherinlaw, Larkin Hendricks Esquire the father of his wife Jane Crenshaw departed this life some years since, leaving his will and that Dr. Andrew J. Anderson one of his Exors. advertised the lands & personal property for sale. When the sale came off, Jesse Crenshaw was absent in the army in Virginia. His wife was very anxious to purchase the home tract of land in partnership with her brother J. C. Hendricks. It was agreed that J. C. Hendricks should bid off the said tract of land containing about 212 acres and that it should be divided between himself and Jane Crenshaw. The land was in Pickens District and well known as the residence for many years of said Larkin Hendricks Esquire. His wife was put in possession of the house and a portion of the land purchased by her brother J. C. Hendricks with the understanding that the whole tract should be divided equally and that Jesse Crenshaw should pay what was right for the buildings on that portion assigned to him. J. C. Hendricks staked off a line, which he would answer for a dividing line. Jesse Crenshaw cultivated all the cleared land on one side of this line during the past year & the said J. C. Hendricks cultivated the other side of the said land. While in the army he recd. 2 letters from J. C. Hendricks as to the division of the land. In the last letter Hendricks urged very much the immediate division, said it must be and should be divided. Jesse wrote back that he was willing to a division & it should be made as soon as he returned from the army. The letters of the said J. C. Hendricks were destroyed but he could prove their contents by several persons who read them. Jesse states that he left $600.00 at home and he wrote to his wife to pay it over to Dr. Anderson in part payment of his share of the purchase money, for the said tract of land, which his wife did in the presence of witnesses. In the mean time the value of real estate thru out the country were one, two and three hundred per cent. Ascertaining that the land thus purchased could be sold for a great deal more than 6 hundred dollars, the purchase money, J. C. Hendricks then began to set up a claim to the whole tract, and deny that it was to be divided between Jesse and him. He went to Dr. Anderson after Jesse had signed the note already mentioned, and gave his own separate note with surety for the whole of the purchase money. Why the Exor. permitted this and took two notes each for the purchase money, he is at a loss to know, unless he wished to deprive him of his interest in the land. When the note became due he went to Dr. Anderson & tendered him the money for the share of the land which was refused on the ground that he had already recd. the whole amount of the purchase money from Joseph C. Hendricks. He then went to Hendricks & tendered him the one half of the purchase money, which herefused to receive & declaring that he should have no portion of the land.

Filed Jan. 6, 1864 . . . Charles J. Elford one of the Exors. of Larkin Hendricks just before the sale of the land went off to the war in command of a regiment. . . .

JAMES MANSEL PACK. 106 (EQUITY)
CLERK OF COURTS OFFICE, PICKENS, S. C.

Joseph Mansel states that James Mansel died in 184 . . . Owned 4 tracts of land . . . One tract known as the home tract situated on both sides of Doddy Creek waters of Saluda River. adjoining lands of Matthew Mansel, Lewis Hill & others containing 800 acres. Another tract known as the Widow Gorman tract containing 290 acres adjoining lands of A. Burdine, R. Bowen, William Gilstrap & others. Another tract known as the Flat Rock tract, adjoining lands of Joseph Young, John Higgin, Wm. Gilstrap containing 243 acres. Another tract known as the Davis tract situate on Little River adjoining lands of E. Lee, N. Gassaway, J. Norton & others containing 250 acres . . . Heirs, Widow, Sarah Mansell. 11 Children viz. Joshua Mansel, Matthew Mansel, Frances Barret formerly Frances Mansel widow of . . . Barrett, Jane Ferguson who intermarried with J. G. Ferguson, William Mansel, Lemuel Mansel who resides in Georgia, Juliet Freeman also written Julia who married Meredith Freeman of the state of North Carolina, Robert Mansel who resides in Georgia, John Mansel of Alabama, Richard H. Mansel a minor, Joseph Mansel & Samuel Mansel. Filed July 20, 1846 . . . Matthew Mansel was the guardian of Richard H. Mansel. . . .

POWER OF ATTORNEY
Lemuel Mansell
    to
Samuel Mansell
Georgia

Cherokee County) Know all men by these presents that I Lemuel Mansell of the State and County aforesaid for divers good causes & considerations me hereunto moving hav made constituted and appointed and do by these presents make constitute and appoint Samuel Mansell of said State and County my true and Lawful attorney in fact for me and in my name and for my own proper use to apply to Miles M. Norton Ordinary of Pickens District State of South Carolina and receiv from him any money in his hands and due me as one of the legatees or heirs of James Mansell late of the District last aforesaid deceased. also to apply as above and in my name as the legally appointed administrator of John Mansell deceased to receiv from the said ordinary the distributive share of the said John Mansell deceased of the estate of James Mansell Deceased, and the said Samuel Mansell is hereby fully authorized and empowered to giv receipts or other Sufficient acquitances in my name and in my name as administrator of John Mansell deceased & to Sign my name to the same hereby ratifying allowing whatsoever my said attorney may legally do in the premises as though I were personally present and did the same myself. In witness whereof I hav hereunto set my hand &

seal the Sixth day of March 1849.
Signed Sealed in presence of
J C Taylor   Lemuel Mansell (SEAL)
T H Satterfield J P (LS)
Georgia

Cherokee County) I, James Jordan Clerk of the Supreme Court of said County do hereby certify that Thedford H Satterfield whose name appears as a witness to the for going Power Attorney is an acting Justice of the peace in and for said county duly commissioned & authorized and that full faith & credit is due and ought to be given his official acts as such and that the Signature thereto purporting to be his genuine. Given under my hand & official Signature with the seal of said court annexed the Sixth day of March A. D. 1849.

James Jordan Clk

State of Georgia

Cherokee County) I John C. Maddox Clerk of the Court of Ordinary of said County do hereby certify that Lemuel Mansel is the administrator on the Estate of John Mansel of said County deceased. Given under my hand officially This 19th March 1849.

John C Maddox C. C. O.

JAMES COLLINS PACK. 125 (INQUEST)
CLERK OF COURTS OFFICE, PICKENS, S. C.

JAMES COLLINS NO. 1

An inquest was held Dec. 18, 1857 at Tunnel Hill in Pickens Dist. to view the body of James Collins of Tunnel Hill. The jury brought it out that he came to his death the 17th of Dec. 1857 at Tunnell Hill by a fall off of the bucket to the bottom of No. 2 shaft . . . William Holmes a witness said that he was a fireman at No. 2 shaft at Tunnell Hill. It was about 3 o'clock P. M. I was in the engine house looked out at the window and saw Henry Kelly standing as thought on the log as sailing around the shaft. I heard Kelly say "hoist away." I then heard the Engineer say, "There has been a man fell in the shaft . . . Thomas R. Bradley sworn says, "I am a labor at Tunnel Hill, have not been at work for 3 or 4 days however. I was at Mr. Fosters about 3 o'clock P. M. on the 17th Inst. 1857. I looked out and said something has happened at the shaft. Foster lived something over 100 yards from the shaft. I at once went up up to the shaft. When I got there I met Mr. McFarlen. He asked me to go down in the shaft and bring the men up. I went down into the shaft and found the dead body of James Collins lying in the water, sorter on his side. Henry Kelly was lying near him apparently lifeless, when I touched him he groaned. I said to Francis Makin? this man is not dead yet. I helped to put them in the bucket and Makin went up with them . . . John Foster sworn says, I was on duty at No. 2 shaft, with my back to Henry Kelly, I heard something like water falling in the shaft. I heard the engine driver say, a man fell in the shaft. I then looked in and saw a man on the bucket coming up 30 or 40 feet down. I asked what was the matter, he said he did not know, the name of that man was McFarlane, about this time a blast went off. Thos. R. Bradley, Francis Makin, Wm. Andright immediately went down in the shaft to see what was the matter, after going down there hollowed "hoist away," one of the men came back in the bucket with the dead body of James Collins & Henry Kelly. I am one of the banks man was at work with Henry Kelly and at the time I saw him as first stated with my back to him, he was coming out of one can into another. About dinner saw Kelly take a drink of whiskey, he had during the day a bottle of whiskey on the work. The shaft is about 220 feet deep . . . William McFarline said, "That he was Superintendent of No. 2 shaft at Tunnel Hill. At about 3 oclock had 3 holes charged in the bottom, went thru the regular forms, of hoist away. James Collins and myself was in the bucket. I heard a noise, did not know at the time whether it was below or above, about then something struck me on the arm and leg, I think the bucket was something about 100 feet from the bottom going at terrible speed, before I reached the top, I missed Collins, before I got out of the bucket I asked John Foster what he had let fall in the shaft, he looked around and missed Kelly and said he had fell in. I then said there is two men in the shaft. I then cried to the engine driver to hoist up. I then got Thomas Bradley to go down and bring them up. I then went home and sent William Miller my partner to the shaft, when the matches was set I was with one leg in the bucket, James Collins was in same position, a little time after I reached the top one of the blasts went off . . . Frederick Sharshal was the engine driver.

PETER SHARP NO. 2 INQUEST

An inquest was held Nov. 26, 1859 for Peter Sharp. The jury brought it out that he came to his death by conjestion of some vital caused by intemperance at the Cross Roads near Harvey Smiths old work shop . . . Lewis C. Smith sworn says, That he found Mr. Sharp a few minutes before he died lying in the road near Harvy Smiths old shop. He was lying on his right side rather quartering the right leg was crooked rather under him, his left leg was straight and lying on his right. His eyes were opened and set in his head and were red, his face was dark purple. I spoke to him 3 times, he made no answer. I went to see about him at the request of the family. Jeremiah Hinton said that he saw Mr. Sharp at the Muster Ground some 150 yards from where he was found dead. He left the muster grounds about 3 P. M. Thinks he went alone, he was drinking some, was not complaining any as I heard of.

WILSON McKINNEY NO. 3 INQUEST

An inquest was held at the grave yard at Mrs. Mary McKinneys in Pickens Dist. July 14, 1857, upon view of the body of Wilson McKinney there lying dead. The jury brought it out that he came to his death by drowning in the Keowee River about a quarter of a mile above the McKinneys Ford on sunday between the hours of 7 and 12 A. M. Held at the burial ground of Mrs. Mary McKinneys on Keowee River 13 miles above Pickens Court House on the Jocassee Road . . . Enoch Chapman states that he was the first person who found decd. in the river, was in swimming water, hands & feet in the position of a man swimming. He and Martin Hopkins and Thomas McKinney took decd. out of the river. He was perfectly naked. Saw no sign of violence on body. William Morgan states that decd. was drowned. Lived about a half a mile from where decd. was discovered. Decd. was floating on the water when found, the water was about 10 feet deep where decd. was found in what is called a turn hole in the river. Made no effort to take him out of the river when he first found him but went for Martin Hopkins to assist him and Martin Hopkins went to John McKinneys for help . . . Wm. Morgan said that he was coming down the river on last sunday morning about 7 oclock. Saw Wilson McKinney standing in the river near the bank holding to some bush on the east side of the river about a quarter of a mile above the McKinney Ford. I asked him could he swim and he said yes and waded into the river until it got up to his neck and then struck off swimming and swam pretty near to the bnak on the other side. He then turned his head right down stream & began to sink. The water was swift when he turned down stream. Saw him sink one time and then broke and ran after Enoch Chapman, it was 15 minutes or more before he and Enoch Chapman started back. Came on down to the river and found decd. near where he had left him in the river. . . .

EDWARD COLBER NO. 4 INQUEST

An inquest was held at Tunnel Hill over the dead body of Edward Colber. William Dunkley sworn says, He was working with Edward Colber in shaft No. 4 on the morning of July 8, 1857 at 3 o'clock when he suddenly observed that something fell near him, and after inquiring into the matter, he found Edward Colber lying senseless near him in the water, where upon he took hold of him and had him hoisted up to the surface where it was found that the skull was smashed. W. H. Frick says, that Edward Colber used to fill the water into the buckets and also to send tools up. On this morning however a bucket loaded with water and sundry tools was hoisted up out of which I took two shovels and 2 hammers and when the water ceased to make noise of this fall of about 120 feet, he supposes something fell to the bottom, when immediately after the bucket was sent down, his body was brought up . . . Franklin Belloo says that after taking out the 2 hammers and shovels, he felt in the bucket, but supposed that no tool was left in it. He thinks as the bucket is more than 3 ft. deep he could not ascertain whether there was any tool left in the bucket or not . . . Lucius Chambers says, That he was working together with Edward Colber on the shaft No. 4 when on the morning of July 8 at 3 o'clock, after a bucket with water was send up, he heard something strike above his head, and then saw Edward Colber falling near him and he intending to help him or to or to rescue him out of the water, found that blood was running from him, and he put the body in the bucket and Mr. Dunklin brought him to the surface, and then directly he found a hammer of which the handle was broke in an unusual manner, and he supposes that said hammer might have fallen from above and caused the death of Edward Colber, who used to load the water in the bucket and send tools up with the dirt or water . . . John Suit also was working with him and said that he heard something fall and at the same instance saw Edward Colber who stood about 2 feet from him and to whom he handed some drills, sink down whereupon he took hold of him and saw that he was hurt on the head, after which he called the other men to help up and that e believed he was dead, because he felt about his head and found that his skull was broken, whereupon Mr. Dunklin brought his body to the surface. Afterward he found the hammer and thinks that it might have fallen from the top . . . Willis Crow said that he was also working with him and that while he was charging for a blast he heard a blow like something and that he heard a blow like something striking against the shaft after which the other men called him for help, saying there was a man killed, whereupon he saw Edward Colber lie down on his hands and knees. . . .

ROBERT STUART NO. 5 (INQUEST)

An inquest was held at Jumping Off Rock in Pickens District Oct. 20, 1857 before Lenard Rodgers a Magistrate upon view of thee body of Robert Stuart. The jury brought it out that he came to his death by misfortune or accident. John Hancel sworn said, that the decd, was lying on his left side his gun lying across his neck. He did not see any appearance of any violence being used upon the body. He said that Elija Hinkel, Silas Hinkel, Isaac Stuart, Jackson Stuart, Thomas Stuart were present when the body was found. Dr. J. N. Lawrence said that he examined the body and found that his neck was broken. . . .

ANSEL GODFREY NO. 6 INQUEST

An inquest was held at William Stows in Pickens District Jan. 10, 1858 upon view of the body of Ansel Godfrey. The jury brought it out that he came to his death in the woods not far from the Seven Mile Port or Post on the road leading from Pickens Court House to Greenville Court House on or about the 23 Dec. 1857 from a dislocation of the neck produced probably from a fall while in a state of intoxication or by some other manner unknown to the jury . . . Mahaly Godfrey says that she saw the decd. 3 weeks ago. Ate breaksfast at home, left soon after saying he was going to Elijah Alexanders to get some money, and that he would be back soon as he could go there and back. HaveNt seen decd. since or heard of him until yesterday, when decd. left home. I never looked for him until he always came back home. Decd. was a drunkard, but went off sober. Was in the habit of hiding bottles out and thought she saw him have a bottle when he was leaving. When he was drinking he was very ill in his family and when sober very kind to his family. All was in harmony when he left home. He had no enemies as I know of. Never heard any one threaten or to do him any violence or injury. When ever he was drunk he was distracted and said that he remembered nothing while drunk. Was a dangerous man when drunk, and was afraid of him, he would get up and rave, stamp and throw axes at the family. Would have to leave home and stay until he was sober. Dont know how much money he went for, he family knew that he was going for money. Had been letting Mr. Alexander have cane, started with it and never recd. pay as I know of. Saw the bottles near the body, dont remember ever seeing them before Decd. came home under the influence of liquor the evening preceding his departure. There was no difficulty between the decd. and the boys before they went hunting that she knows of. which they did the night decd. came home. He was always given to going away and staying as long as he pleased some times a month or two, even when he promised to come back soon. Was always uneasy about him when he was absent. I told George Young to ask Cousin Ansel Godfrey if he had seen or heard any thing of him, this was about 2 weeks ago. When George Young returned he reported that Ansel had saw or heard nothing of decd. and I allowed that the decd. had gone to Spartanburg where he had children married. Ansel Godfrey lives at Mr. Smiths about 3 miles distant. Decd. frequently went to Spartanburg without letting me know and would some times stay 2 or 3 months and come back, just when the notion took him . . . Alfred Godfrey sworn says, that he is the son of said decd. and nearly 19 years old. Lived at home with the family, was there when decd. left home. Decd. left home 3 weeks ago today and said he was going to Elijah Alexanders to get what was owing to him. He had been to Bill Hunters the day before he left home and got a bottle of whiskey. Had been drinking when he returned from Bill Hunters. Did not see the bottle, decd. had hid it out. There had not been any late difficulty between decd. and family and never any except such as resulted from his drunkness. Decd. left home in a drinking spree, had done so over before when he lived near Cedar Rock & was gone a month or two. Decd. came home from Hunters about dark. I went hunting about an hour after he came home from Hunters, he was in a good humor. I returned from hunting the next morning before breakfast, he was there at home and left about an hour or two after breakfast. I had threatened decd. to the boys (John Gilham and Mrs. Youngs boys) I was the oldest son living at home, had a little quarrel with decd. near Cedar Rock. My father was trying to whip me. Mother and myself prevented him. Decd. generally passed along the path near where his body was found, when going to Balis Claytons and it would be his nearest way in returning home from Gilstraps . . . Robert W. Godfrey sworn says, He is a son of decd, lives at home and about 14 years of age. Was at home when father left there. Was with him the day before at Bill Hunters and came with him home. Father went to Bill Hunters and got him a quarter of whiskey and put it in 2 bottles. A black and a white bottle. The black bottle a pint bottle and the white held a little over. He drank most of the liquor as he came home from Hunters. About a pint and the rest after he came home. He hid the bottles out when he came home. I went hunting that night and returned home the next morning before sunrise. He was at home and left sober, as soon as he put on his clothes. I heard Alfred say that he would whip father if he whipped his mother, but he never did, but there was no difficulty between his father and Alfred when he left home. Father said that he was going to Mr. Howards when he left home. Asked me to go with him and said he would stay long if I went. He asked me this in the yard, no one was present. I and Alfred were at Mrs. Youngs the day he left. Stayed there nearly all day, then came home. The next day went to cut logs for Howard. Asked Mr. Howard about father and he said that father went by there and said he was going to Mr. Alexanders . . . John Gilham sworn says, He and Mrs. Youngs boys went by decd. house going possum hunting, last saturday night, 3 weeks ago. The old man was drinking some. Alfred said that his father whipped his mother when he was small and that he should not do it now . . . Isaac Chapman sworn says, he found the decd. about 3 oclock yesterday evening, saw him lying on the ground, thought perhaps it was some person drunk, that had layed down there, hollowed to him, approached and found him dead. . . .

WILLIAM WOODY NO. 7 INQUEST

An inquest was held at Jesse Chandlers on Aenas Hunters land Feb. 17, 1856 upon view of the body of Wm. Woody decd. . . . Mary Chandler sworn says, Wm. Woody died at my home in Pickens Dist. on land belonging to said Aenas Hunter lying on the waters of Goldens Creek on wednesday morning last about 6 oclock. He was taken sick about one oclock wednesday morning last. Had a fit. Has been subject to fits fits all his life time. When attacked with one he would go and lay down, appeared to drop off into a sleep. Would lie down some hour or more than would wake up and seem to be as well as ever, except that he would complain of being sore. When last attacked he had jerks, was beating himself on the ground at the end of the house in the yard, Did not speak, did not seem to be in his right mind. Neighboring men who were at my house picked him up, carried him into the house and laid him on the bed, where he was permited from hurting himself. Spoke once after being taken into the house. Asked to be raised up, which was done speedily. and some drops given him, he was then layed down. When he took another fit which did not last more than two minutes he then asked for his wife. She went to him and lay down by him. This was about half hour before day, he seemed to get easy and appeared to drop off into a dose of sleep. My family, Mr. Aenas Hunter and Mr. William Ray then down. I got up first about day break, went to him and felt of his hands then put her hand on his breast to see if she could feel the heart more. He seemed to be in a tremble, was warm. I called for Mr. Hunter to come to me, who said he is not dead. I replied that he had no pulse and that I could not hear him cetch his breath. I asked him to turn him on his back, then white froth ran out of his mouth, when it was found that he was gone. He had been living in my house about 2 months, was very disagreeable, was a drunkard, was quarrelsome, quarreled mostly with his wife, cursed her but never struck her. Had no fuss with the rest of the family. His wife would never speak back to him in anger, had treated him kindly in all respects, had been married 3 years last August, had one child. Had no enemies that I know of. Tues. night he took his child in the night and started to run away with it. Green Massingale & others followed him and brought him back. Decd. said he was going back to North Carolina, his wife refused to go to N. C. but was willing to stay with him on Hunters land, during the night of Wwdnesday he asked Aenas Hunter to see to the taking care of his wife and child. Tuesday morning last he said he would not stay with Enas Hunter, but that he would go back to N. C. He was jealous of his wife . . . Nancy Smith sworn says she was present when he was taken sick on Tues. night last about 8 or 9 oclock. Stayed there till about 12 oclock. at night, then I went home. He was powerful bad off from the beginning and continued to do so all the time. Enos Hunter gave him some kind of drops. He was in his senses most of the time, complained when he first came to Chandlers and afterwards 3 or 4 times that his wife would not live with him. I tried to get to and his wife said that if decd. would get house and do right she would go and live with him. I was present when he started off with the child and when he was brought back he gave the child to its mother. Heard nothing of him going back to N. C. decd. wanted his wife to stay with him on Enos Hunters land, a contract was made between them. Thinks that Hunter said there was launderman and brandy in the drops . . . Delilah Chandler sworn says, that decd. told Enas Hunter while in his last sickness during the night that he was going to die and he wanted him to take care of his wife & child . . . Milly Wood sworn says that she heard him complaining of a hurting in his breast about a day or so ago, lived agreeable as his wife, until he began to drank . . . William Ray says, that all the family were pretty attentive to him before he died . . . Green W. Massingale says, he was at the home of decd. on tuesday night last, got there about half an hour after dark. Mary Chandler, the decd. and his wife seemed to be in an uproar. Inquired what was the matter, it was a fuss about the child, he told me he wanted me to talk to his wife. Half hour after the decd. ran off with the child, came back and gave it to its mother. I talked to his wife and she said that she would not live with him here, but if he would go to her fathers she would live with him there. Old Mr. Chandler & wife threatened to have decd. taken with a warrant and sent to jail. The wife of decd. said that before he should take the child she would kill him or he would kill her. I was present when he was taken sick and carried into the house and put him in bed, where he layed about an hour. He then got up and sat by the fire. I asked him how he felt if he was sick, he said he was not, went and layed down and commenced crying. I asked him the cause and he said he troubled to death, said the family had threatened killing him. I then left and on Wed. morning went back to the home of decd. just after sun up. None of the family seemed affected by his death, not even his wife, who seemed to be in a very fine humor, all were packed up ready to mov. Decd. had not been out of the house exceeding 5 minutes before it was found out that he was sick . . . William John Smith said that he heard Mary Chandler say on sunday last that if decd. got to having fits about her she would knock him in the house, was laughing when she said so. Jesse Chandler ordered decd. out of the house the night he died.

JOHN NEWMAN NO. 8 INQUEST

An inquest was held at Tunnel Hill in Pickens Dist. the 19th Jan. 1859 upon view of the body of John Newman. The jury brought it out that he came to his death at Tunnel Hill on the 18th Jan. 1859 by effects of ardent spirits. James Newman said that Philip Shourdan came in my house last night between 9 and 10 oclock and told me that John Newman was in his house & said he felt mighty bad & I went and went for the doctor & he was not at home & when I returned I found him dead, he had been boarding with me, but left my house on monday the 17th inst, but had been complaining for some 2 or 3 days before he left my house. They both were friendly to each other and I have no opinion that he was hurt by any one that was there . . . Henry Johnson sworn says that he saw John Newman pass by No. 2 shaft about 9 oclock walking or staggering as he walked going in the direction of Philip Shourdans. After some time I heard some one crying at P. Shourdans and some on told that John Newman was dead. I went over about 10 oclock and found John Newman laying before the fire dead . . . Philip Farley said he was in Philip Shourdans house at the time the decd. came in. I remained with him until said Philip went after his brother James. I then up stairs to my bed, I left laying on the floor below, quiet and easy when Philip returned he came up stairs and told me he believed that John Newman was going to die. I went down and found him speechless, I felt of him and found him dead. . . .

JOHN McGRAW NO. 9 INQUEST

An inquest was held at Tunnel Hill in Pickens Dist. Jan. 21, 1858 upon view of the body of John McGraw of Tunnell Hill. The jury brought it out that he came to his death by falling into the shaft of No. 4 of Stump House Tunnel on the morning of Jan. 21, 1858 by misfortune or accident. John Knight said that was working between 3 & 4 oclock on the shaft with my back towards the shaft & I heard something sticke the bottom, John T. Williams asked if it was a rock fell in the shaft & he asked if any one was killed. James Cunningham looked around and saw no. I took up the lamp and looked around and said there is a man lying here & I found he was dead. J. T. Williams, James Cunningham & myself took him up and went put him in the barrel & went up with him. We did not know him. J. T. Williams said it was the dumper, was working one night before. Was not afraid to work under him with another good stead hand that knew his work . . . William Gassaway says that he was down in the bottom of the shaft, heard something fall & thought it was a rock and got out on the bench & some one said a man was killed & some said no body was hurt. The first thing I saw was the side of the skid knocked off. James Cunningham and myself raised him & put him in the barrel & he was dead. . . .

HENRY KELLY NO. 10 INQUEST

An inquest was held at Tunnel Hill in Pickens Dist. Dec. 18, 1857 upon view of the body of Henry Kelly of Tunnel Hill. The jury brought it out that he came to his death on Dec. 17, 1857 by falling into No. 2 shaft at the Stump House Tunnel, by misfortune or accident . . . Frederick Shershal says, that I am a Engine driver at No. 2 shaft Tunnel Hill. Henry Kelly hollowed out, are you alright Fred, I told him I was. Kelly looked into the shaft as if to listen to hear them below hollow out "hoist away" which is the rule in coming out of the shaft from a blast. Kelly immediately said hoist away. I then hoisted the bucket 15 or 16 feet slowly to steady the bucket. I then hooked on the engine and gave her steam and then looked up to see if the rope was steady. I then saw a man pitch into the shaft head foremost. I hollowed out at once boys there has has some body fell into the shaft. I continued to hoist, belt the bucket lighten, had to lessen the steam, thought some one had fallen off the bucket when the bucket reached the top. Wm. McFarland was on the bucket about that time a blast went off in the shoft, in about 2 minutes some one said hoist up the bucket some one is going down to see what is the matter. I at once let them down to see what was the matter. In about 5 minutes I then hoisted the bucke wih the dead bodies of Henry Kelly and James Collins or that I may say that Collins was lifeless and Kelly only drew a breath or two after being brought up. Henry Kelly was a bank man on my shift and I suppose that Kelly fell into the shaft.

CYRUS FELIX A SLAVE NO. 11 INQUEST

An inquest was held July 21, 1856 upon view of the body of Cyrus Felix late infant slave. The jury brought it out that he came to his death by misfortune and accident by drowning in the Keowee River near Fort George . . . Isaac Barron said that he was sent for yesterday of July 20 about 9 O'clock A. M. by William Alexander with notice that a black child had drowned. I came promptly to the place on Keowee River and when I arrived at the place found W. N. Craig, Davy Craig and William Alexander and others searching fot the body. I and others aided in the search and I found the body after considerable search and brought it out. Found him in a deep hole at the big bend of the river against the Fort field. Saw no marks of violence on the body. A negro woman calling herself the mother of the child was present and two other negroes a young woman and another younger still. Saw no other negroes but Craigs boy asked the mother how she lost her child, who said that she fell out of the Battiam & that when she ran she caught at the Battiam? and lost her child. The mother seemed to be making some little lamemtation. The Battiam? is very much like a canoe, easily turned aside so as to dipwater. I noticed the clothing of the mother and the two negro girls and the bodies of the dresses of said negroes appeared to be dry. To dry I think to have been all over the river. The lower portions of their clothing was wet and muddy. I did not feel the clothing. It must have been something over an hour after the drowning before I got there . . . W. N. Craig says, I saw Thomas Steeles Tom & 3 girls one of them carring the decd. I think an infant all going towards the Battiam? landing in Thomas Steeles field. I went directly home about 3-4 of a mile distant, had not been there more than 15 minutes before he heard of the drowning. I went promptly to the river, passed Tom a negro boy of Steels who was crying, asked him which one it was that was drowned, did not understand the answer. The decd. was drowned not at the landing of the canoe but above it some 2 or 3 hundred yards in a very deep hole in the bend of the river. Banks of the river steep, no landing there. When I got there I found Milly the mother of the child and 2 other negro girls crying. Milly was crying and said my child is right in there pointing to a place in the river near which it was found. I asked Milly what brought her there, she said Tom would take her there, that she tried to get Tom to take her to the landing but he would not. One of the girls was dry. The larger of the two who said that if it had not been for her Milly and the other girl we both would have been drowned and that Milly sunk 3 times and that she pulled them out. Isaac Barron found the decd. by diving in about 12 feet of water.

ISAIAH TROTTER TO JOSIAH TROTTER PACK. 124 DEED
CLERK OF COURTS OFFICE, PICKENS, S. C.

South Carolina

Pickens District) Know all men by these presents that I Isaiah Trotter of the State & District afore sd. for & in Consideration of the sum of four Hundred Dollars to me in hand paid by Josiah Trotter of the State & District afore sd. the Rect. whereof is hereby acknowledged Have Granted Bargained Sold & Releas'd & by these presents do grant Bargain Sell & Release unto Josiah Trotter one certain tract of Land Lying & being in the State & District afore sd. Begining on a poplar thence So. 65 E 6 Chains to a hickory thence 10 W 16 Chains to a stake, thence N 68 W 46 Chains & 50 Links to a stake thence S 16 to the Beginning corner Containing fifty acres be the same more or less—Also another tract containing ten acres be the same more or less Begining on James Fergusons poplar Corner on the N E Side of a Branch of Town Creek thence up sd. Branch to the mouth of a Small branch, thence up sd. small branch to a stake, thence N 68 W to a stake on Binums old Line on Muddy branch, thence S to the begining also Tract Containing one hundred acres be the same more or less begining on a B jack Corner thence along Perrys line to a Bl. gum corner on the Branch, thence up sd. Branch to a Conditional Corner on John Princes line Thence along the big Road to a P. ak Station on Nathaniel Perrys line thence along sd. line S 55 W to a P oak corner thence S 16 E 16 Chains to a pine knot corner, thence to the Beginning Corner—Together with all & Singular the Rights Members hereditraments & appertainances to the sd. premises be longing or in any wise incident or appertaining to have and to hold all & Singular the sd. lands above mentioned—unto the sd. Josiah Trotter his heirs & assigns for ever I do hereby bind myself my heirs Executors & administrators to warrant & forever Defend all & Singular the the sd. before mentioned Land unto the sd. Josiah Trotter his heirs & assigns & against all & Every other person or persons Lawfully Claiming the same or any part thereof In witness whereof I have hereunto set my hand & seal this 7th Day of October in the year of our Lord one thousand Eight hundred & forty two.

Sign'd Sealed & Delivered in presence of
A. S. Bird   Isaiah Trotter (SEAL)
Robt. Norris
South Carolina

Pickens District) personally appeared Robert Norris before me the subscribing Justis and maid oath in due forme of law and on oath saith that he did see the within named Isah Trotter Sine Seal and Execute the with in Deed for the use and purpose there in expressed and set forth and that A S Bird was with him him and in his presents· a subscribing witness to the Execution of the same. Sworn to and subscribed before me this 10th Oct. 1842.
Wm. Smith, M. P. D.   Robert Norris
Recorded in BOOK D PAGE 350. CERTIFIED OCT. 10, 1842.

WILLIAM JAMESON TO JOSIAH TROTTER PACK. 124
CLERK OF COURTS OFFICE, PICKENS, S. C.

South Carolina

Pickens District) Know all men by these presents that I William James on of the state and district for and in Consideration of the sum of twenty eight dollars to me in hand paid by Josiah Trotter of the same state and district I have granted bargained sold and Released and by these presents do grant bargin sell and Convey unto the said Josiah Trotter a certain tract or parcel of land Containing nine and a half acres be the same more or less aituated in the state and district afore said adjoining lands of the said Trotter on the

East and the said Wm. Jameson on the west Begining on a old stump in the Pickensville Road thence N 47 E. 9.95 to a (word) thence N 450 W 11.70 to a Rock thence N. 60 W 5.68 to Rock at the Road thence along sd. Road S 17 E 19 to the begining Together with all and singuler the Rights members heredataments and appertainances there unto belonging or in ane wise insadent or appertaining to have and to hold all and singular the premises before mentind unto the said Josiar Trotter his heirs and assigns and I do here by bind my self and Ech of my heirs Executors and administrators to warrant and for Ever defend the said premises unto the said Josiah Trotter his heirs and assigns against myself my heirs and asigns and all other person or persons whoomso Ever Lawfully Claming or to clame the same or aney part thereof given under my hand and seal this 23 day of June in the year of our Lord one thousand Eight hundred and forty nine signed sealed and delivered in the presents of us.

           William Jameson (LS)

B. J. Williams
Carrol Jameson
South Carolina

  Pickens District) B. J. Williams appears Personally Before me L. Hendricks an acting Magistrate in & for said District & after Being Duly sworn on the holy Evangetlist of almighty god sayeth he saw William Jameson Sen? sighn seal & Deliver the within Deede of Conveyance to Josiah Trotter for the use & Purpose there in mentioned & that Carroll Jamison was with himself a subscribing witness to the same. Sworn to & subscribed before me this the 8th day of August 1850.
L. Hendricks M. P. D.   B. J. Williams

ELIJAH & LEVI MURPHREE TO JOHN STANLEY PACK. 124
CLERK OF COURTS OFFICE, PICKENS, S. C. DEED

State of South Carolina
  Pendleton district) Know all men by these presents that we Elijah & levi Murphyree in the district and state afore said in consideration of the Sum of won hundred dollers to us paid by John Standly of the state and district aford Said have granted bargined sold and Released and by these presents do grant bargin and sell and Releas unto Said Standly all that tract of land it lying and being in the state and district aforesaid on (WORD) waters of twelve mile River it being part of a tract of land granted to Nathaniel Perry Begining on a black jack corner thence along perrys line to a black gum gum corner on the Branch thence up said branch to a conditional corner on John princes line thence along the big Road to a post oak station on Nathaniel perrys line thence along said line S 54.23 to a post oak corner thence W 19 chains 50 links to a stak corner thence S 16 E 16 chains to a pine not corner thence to the Begining corner be the same more or less to gather with all and singular the rites titles members Heredeterments and appertainances to the said premises Belonginr o in any wise incident or appertaining thereto to have and to hold all and singeler the afore said premises unto the said John Stanly his heirs and assigns and wee do hearby bind our selves overs heirs Exrs. and admnrs to warrant and for ever defend all and singelar the afore said premises unto the said John Stanly his heirs and assigns agains over

selves our heirs and assign and against all person or pursons what soever lawfully claiming or to Claim the same or any part thereof in witness I whereof we have hear unto set our hands and seals this twenty sixth day of febuwary in the year of our lord won thousand Eight hundred and Seventeen.

Signd seald and delivered in presents of us

test   Elijah Murphree (LS)

Jesse Sugg   Levi Murphree (LS)

      his

Robberd X Brown

      mark

State So. Carolina

Pendleton District) Personally came Jesse Sugs Before me one of subscribing Justices for Sd. Dst. and made oath in Due form of law that he saw Elijah Murphree and Levi Murphree sign seal and deliver the within Deed as ther act and Deed also Robert Brown was a subscribing witness with himself Sworn to and subscribed the 14th Day october AD 1817 Before me

Bailey Barton J. P.   Jesse Sugg

Recorded March 25, 1818.

ELIJAH MURPHREE TO LEWIS BROWN PACK. 124 DEED CLERK OF COURTS OFFICE, PICKENS, S. C.

South Carolina

Pendleton district) Know all men by these presents that I Elijah Murphree of the State and District afore said in consideration of the sum of fifty dollars to me in hand paid by Lewis Brown of the State and Destrict afore said have granted bargined and sold and Releast unto lewis brown all that tract of land lying and being Sd. state and destrict on the waters of town creek waters of twelve mile river begining on a stake thence south 40 to a pine corner thence S 55 to a red oak station thence W 59 to a post oak station thence to a post oak corner thence west 40.00 to a stake corner thence N 62 E 57.00 to a post oak thence W 15 E 42.00 to a stake corner thence South 73 E 7 to the beging Corner Containing won Hundred and Seventy fore aCres together with all and Singiler the rites members hereditamets and appertainances to the sd. premises belonging or in any wise incident or appertaining to hav and to hold all and Singiler the premises unto the Said lewis Brown his heirs and assigns I do hereby bind myself my heirs Exrs, admnrs and assigns and from all person or pursons lawfully claiming any part or part thereof inteste money hear of I have Set my hand and Seal this the 25 day of april in the year of our lord one thousand Eight hundred and and Seventeen and the fortifirst year of americian independentsce Signd Sealed and delivered in the presents of us

Test

Jesse Sugg   Elijah Murphree (SEAL)

Hugh tatum

South Carolina

                     Mr brown (this wriiten like this).

Pendleton Dist. Personally came Jesse Sugg Before me one of the Justis of Sd District and made oath in form of Law that he Saw Elijah Murphree

a sign seal & Deliver the with in as his act & deed all so saith that Hugh Tatum was a Subscribing witness with him Self Swoarn and Subscribed Before me this 25th April 1817.
Elijah Murphree   Jesse Sugg
    Recorded in BOOK E PAGE 531. Certified March 1, 1847.

JOHN FIELDS SR. TO JOSIAH TROTTER PACK. 124
DEED OF LAND FOR 50 ACRES
CLERK OF COURTS OFFICE, PICKENS, S. C.

State of South Carolina
    Pickens District) Know all men by these presents that I John Field Senr of the State and District afore said and for and in consideration of the sum of seventy five dollars to me in hand Paid by Josiah Trotter of the same State and destrict I have granted bargained sold and Relecd and by these Presents do grant bargin sell and convey unto the said Josiah Trotter his heirs and assigns a certain tract or parsel of Land containing fift yacres be the same more or less Situated in the State and Destrict afore said on branches of Georges Creek waters of Saluda River Begining on a Pine thence S 27 W 23 chains to a black oake fallen down thence N 1-2 W 32 chains to a Lite wood Stake thence N 16 E 20 chains to a white oak at the head of a branch thence St E to the begining corner To gether with all and Singular the Rights members hereditrements and appertainence there unto belonging or in any wise incident or appertaining to have and to hold all and singular the said premises unto the said Josiah Trotter his heirs and assigns forever and I do hereby Bind my self my heirs Executors and administrators to warrante and forever defende the same unto the said Josiah Trotter his heirs and assigns against my self my heirs and assigns and all other person or perons Lawfully claiming or to claim the same or aney part thereof given under my hand and Seal this Eighteenth day of May in the year of our Lord one thousand Eight hundred and Forty two Signed Seald and delivered in the presents of us
Benjamin J. Williams   John Field Sr. (SEAL)
Eli Watson
South Carolina
    Pickens disct) Before me J. M. Barton Esqr personally appeared Benjamin Williams and after being duly sworn saith on oath that he saw John Field sign seal and deliver the within deed to Josiah Trotter for the purposes within mentioned and that Eli Watson was with him self a Subscribing witness to the due execution of the same Sworn to and Subscribed this 26th Aug 1842.
J. M. Barton M. P. D.   B. J. Williams
    Recorded in BOOK D PAGE 520. CERTIFIED 29th Aug. 1842.

DAVID McCOLLUM TO JOHN STANLEY PACK. 124
CLERK OF COURTS OFFICE, PICKENS, S. C. DEED

State of South Carolina
    Know all men by these presents that I David McCollum of Pendleton District and State aforesaid for and in Consideration of the sum of Eighteen Dollars to me in hand paid by John stanley of the state and District aforesaid

the receipt whereof I do hereby acknowledge have Granted Bargained sold Conveyed & Confirmed & By these presents do grant Bargain sell Convey & Confirm unto the said John Stanley his heirs and assigns all my respective right Interest Claim or Demand of in or to a part of a Tract or parcel of Land Situate in Pendleton District aforesaid on Town Creek Being a Branch of Twelve mile River of which said part is computed by Estimation to contain Ten acres (be the same more or less) Beginning on a stake at Jas. Ferguson Poplar Corner on the N. E. side of a Branch of Town Creek Thence up sd. Branch to the mouth of a small Branch Thence up sd small Branch to a stake Thence N 68 W to a stake on Binums old line on the muddy Branch Thence south to the Beginning together with all and singular the rights Hereditriments or appeartainances Belonging or in any wise Incidents or appertaining there to with all the profits and Commodities woods waters water courses to have and to hold all and singular the premises above mentioned unto the sd John stanley his heirs and assigns for ever and I the sd. David McCollum do bind myself my heirs Executors & administrators to warrant & ever Defend the right and title to sd. premises against any person or persons whosoever laying any Lawful Claim to the same or any part thereof in witness whereof I have hereunto set my hand and affixed seal the seventeenth Day of February one thousand Eight hundred and sixteen.

David McCollum (SEAL)

Signed sealed & Delivered in presents of
James Ferguson
Hundley Evatt
South Carolina

Pendleton Dst.) personally appeared James Furgason before me the subscribing justice and made oath that he saw David McCollum Sign and Deliver the within Deed to John Stanly for the purposes therein mentioned and also that Hundley Avett was a Subscribing witness with himself sworn and subscribed before me this 28 of february 1817.
Elijah Murphree J. P.   James Ferguson

LETTER PACK. 124
CLERK OF COURTS OFFICE, PICKENS, S. C.

South Carolina
Pickens Dist) August the 29th 1856

Mr. R. A. Thompson Sir I Send you A few lines Shoeing you my Claims that I have upon A certain Tract of land belonging to the Estate of Josiah Trotter Decd. it is the tract No 1 containing 67 Acres the said Trotter Agreed that if I wold Pay for the house I Shold have the use of the house & lot Suposed to be one Acre & fire wood to Doe me my lifetime & A open Passway to & from my house for which I paid forty Dollars in cash this I Am able to prove by Different good responsable witnesses & more than this I have the chance of A Dowery on the land & I have bin in Posession of the house lone Enough to holde it by Peasable Posession therfore I for bid the Sale of the land on any other terms than the above Stated & if I Sold otherwise the

Purchaser may Exppect troble before he gets me of of the place.

Test J. R. Trotter
                                                                her
                                                    Rahab X Fields
                                                                mark

We The under Signed Lawfull heirs of Josiah Trotter Decd. being well acquainted with Above stated facts Doe Petition that the tract No 1 is Solde upon the conditions that the said Rehab Fields Has the use of he house & lot & fire wood & A open Passway to & from her house her lifetime as that is all she wants we think it nothing but Just & rite that She Shold have it we being all of age Except one the last & us all will vouch for her being Satisfied when she comes of age Given under our hand & seals this August the 29th 1856.

Josiah Trotter (L. S.)
J. R. Trotter (L. S.)
Clemintine Trotter (L. S.)
A. C. Trotter (L. S.)
Arminda Trotter (L. S.)

JAMES T. SIMPSON TO JOSIAH TROTTER PACK. 124
CLERK OF COURT'S OFFICE, PICKENS, S. C.

Pickens District) Know all men by these presents that I James T Simpson of state & District aforesd. for & in Consideration of the sum of two hundred Dollars to me in hand paid by Josiah Trotter of state & Dst. aforesd. have Granted Bargained sold & released & by these presents do grant bargain Sell and release unto to the said Josiah Trotter All that tract or parcel of Land Lying & being in the Dst aforsd. on the Waters of Georges Creek waters of saluda River containing Eighty Acres more or Less Begining on a forked Ash on the Branch running S 52¼ W 33.6 to a small Postoak by the road thence S 44½ E 27.28 L to a postoak thence N 42 E 12 C to A Stump thence N 54½ E 13 C to a sm. Gum on the branch thence up sd. Branch 26 C to the begining corner Together with all & singular the premises before mentioned belonging or in any wise incident or Appertaining to said premises to have & to hold all & singular the premises before mentioned & I do hereby Bind myself my heirs Executors & Administrators to warrant & Forever Defend All & singular the sd. premises unto the said Josiah Trotter his heirs & assigns Forever Against myself my heirs or assigns & Against Evry other person or persons whomsoever Lawfully Claiming or to claim the same or any part thereof. As Witness my hand & seal this the 3rd Day of February in the year of our Lord one thousand Eight hundred & Thirty eight 1838.

                                                    James T Simpson (SEAL)
Signed Sealed & Delivered In the presence of us
test Levi Allred
Benjamin Williams

W. L. KEITH TO JOSEPH TROTTER PACK. 124
CLERK OF COURTS OFFICE, PICKENS, S. C. (DEED)

State of South Carolina

Know all men by these presents that I William L. Keith qualified Executor of the last Will and Testament of Lewis Brown late of Pickens District and State aforesaid deceased for and in consideration of the sum of Ninety Two Dollars and Seventy three cents to me in hand secured to be paid by Joseph Trotter of the same place, Have granted bargained sold and released and by these presents do grant bargain sell and release unto the said Joseph Trotter a certain Tract of land situate in the State and District aforesaid and lying on the head branches of Town Creek containing one hundred and Seventy four acres more or less originally granted to Elijah Murphree on the 7th Mar. 1814 adjoining lands of Geo. Hendrick, J. Ferguson and others reference being had to the Plat & Grant will more fully appear. Together with all and singular the rights members Hereditaments and appurtenances to the same belonging or in any wise incident or appertaining To have and to hold all and singular the said premises unto the said Joseph Trotter his heirs and assigns forever And I do here by bind myself as Executor my Heirs Executors and administrators and assigns to warrant and forever defend all and singular the said premises against my self my Heirs and the Heirs of the said Lewis Brown decd. and against all persons whom so ever lawfully claiming or to claim the same or any part thereof Witness my hand and seal this Twenty fourth day of May in the year of our Lord one thousand eight hundred and Forty Seven and in the Seventy first year of Americian Independence Signed Sealed and delivered in the presenc of

Mils M. Norton   W. L. Keith, Executor (SEAL)
James Lawrence
South Carolina

Pickens District) Before me personally appeared Miles M. Norton and made oath that he was present and did see W. L. Keith (as Executor) sign seal and deliver the within deed for the uses and purposes therein mentioned and James Lawrence with himself witnessed the same Sworn to this 23 day of June 1847. Before E. M. Keith, Not Pub   Miles M. Norton

Recorded in BOOK F PAGE 13. Certified June 23, 1847.

BENJAMIN & ISAIAH TROTTER TO JOSIAH TROTTER PACK. 124
CLERK OF COURTS OFFICE, PICKENS, S. C.

State of South Carolina

Pickens District) Know all men by these presents that we Benjamin & Isaiah Trotters of the same State & Destrict a foard Sd. for and in consideration of the sum of three Hundred & twenty five Dollars to us paid by Josiah Trotter of the same state & district afore sd. we the Sd Benjamin & Isaiah Trotters have granted bargained sold & released & by these presents do grant bargain Sell & Release unto the Sd. J. Trotter a certain tract or parcel of land containing one hundred and fifty two acres & a half be the same more or less situated in the State & destrict afore Sd. Lying & being on the North Side of the South fork of Georges Creek called the pole Bridge forke waters of Saluda river in the State & Destrict afore Sd. Bounding as follows begining at Boyds old Stake near the big rock thence S ? to a Station in the branch Swamp thence down Sd branch to the mouth thence up the pole Bridge branch to the mouth of the second Branch to a maple thence up Sd branch to the head thence No. 13 W. to a red oake Saplin thence N. to a stake thence N. 40 E. 3 chains to a white oake thence S 60 E 40 chains to the begining corner together with all & Singular the rites members herediterments & appertainances to the Sd Premises belonging or in any wise incident or appertaining to have & to hold all & Singular the premises before mentioned to the Sd. J. Trotter his heirs & assigns & we do here By binde our selves & our heirs Executors administrators or assigns To warrant & for ever defend all & Singular the Sd. premises unto the Sd. J. Trotter his heirs & assigns against our selves & our heirs or any other person or persons claming the same or any part thereof in witness where of we have here unto Set our hands & Seals this first Day of April one thousand Eight hundred and thirty Seven. Signd Seald and delivered in the presents of

Test
Levi Allerd
        his
Regnold X Duckett
        mark

Benj Trotter (SEAL)
Isaiah Trotter (SEAL)

REBECCA THOMAS TO JOSIAH TROTTER PACK. 124
CLERK OF COURTS OFFICE, PICKENS, S. C. DEED

State of South Carolina

Pickens Destrict) Know all men by these presents that I Rebeca Thomas of the same state & destrict Afoarsd for & in consideration of the sum of three hundred and twenty Dollars to me in hand paid the receipt where of I here by acknledge I have bargained Sold & releast unto Josiah Trotter of the Sd. state and Destrict afoar Sd. a certain tract or parcel of Land whereon I now Live on the waters of Georges Creek waters of Saluda river containing one Hundred & Twenty acres be the same more or less bounding And runing as follows begining at a stake thence S 40 W 23.90 to A post oake stump at the road thence a long the Road S 5 W 17.33 to a Stake at the road thence N 80½ W 5.40 to a stake thence S 23 W 6.88 To a Dogwood at the creeke thence Down the Meanders of the creeke 45 to the mouth of a branch thence up the branch to the head And Nearly the same course to the begining corner together withe all & singular the premises herediterments & appertainances All & singular or in any wise incident & I do warrant & for Ever Defend the Sd premces to the Sd J. Trotter & his heirs Administrators & assigns to warrant & forever defend the same unto him & his heirs & assigns in witness hereof I Hereunto Set my hand & fixed my Seal this twentyeth day of December one thousand Eight hundred and thirty seven.

                         her
                Rebeca X Thomas (SEAL)
In the presents of us   mark
Attest. C. B. Harris
L. T. Barrett

JOSEPH TROTTER PACK. 124 (EQUITY)
CLERK OF COURTS OFFICE, PICKENS, S. C.

Micah Miller & his wife Martha Ann Rebecca Miller sheweth that many years ago Joseph Trotter of Pickens District died intestate, leaving as his heirs his wife Jane Trotter who is yet living, the said Martha Ann Rebecca Miller, John Reed Trotter, Clemtine Trotter, Andrew Trotter, Arminda Trotter of whom the said Andrew & Arminda Trotter are minors . . . Owned considerable property. Tract No. 1 situate on waters of Georges Creek in Pickens Dist. containing 67 acres, adjoining lands of G. W. Higgins, G. Ellis, David Duncan & others. Tract No. 2 situate on waters of Georges Creek containing 230 acres adjoining lands of G. W. Higgins, John Couch, B. J. Williams & others. No. 3 containing 88 acres on waters of Georges Creek waters of Saluda River adjoining lands of John Jamison, estate of Childers & others. No. 4 has been divided into 2 tracts viz Tract A situate on waters of Town Creek in Pickens District, containing 280 acres, adjoining lands of H. J. Anthony, James Ferguson, George Hendricks. Filed May 10, 1856.

JOSHUA CADY TO JOSIAH TROTTER PACK. 124
DEED. CLERK OF COURTS OFFICE, PICKENS, S. C.

South Carolina

Pickens District) Know all men to whom these presents shall come Greeting That I Joshua Cady of the same State and District aforesaid, for and in consideration of the sum of Nine Dollars & thirty seven cents, paid to me by Josiah Trotter of the same State and District aforesaid, have granted bargained sold and Released and by these presents do grant bargain sell and Release unto the sd Josiah Trotter, a certain piece of Land, Situated in Pickens District aforesaid, and lyeing about five miles North of Pickensville, on the Market Road, from pumpkin Town to Hamburg, and Augusta, Containing three acres, one Road and sixteen Rods of Land, be the same more or less, Bounded as follows (Viz) Beginning at a post oak, at the Northeast corner Joining Lands of Josiah Trotter and running in a Southeast direction to a point, at a Rock corner, Sixty six Rods, wanting six feet. From thence joining lands of William Gimerson West, to a Rock Corner in a North west direction; From the last mentioned Corner runing East, sixteen Rods and six feet; Joining Lands of Joshua Cady to the first mentioned Bouns, together with all the Rights & priviledges that appertains to the same; to have and to hold, all and singular the premises aforesaid unto the Said Josiah his heirs & assigns, against myself my heirs Executors administrators and assigns & against the claims of every other Person or persons claiming the sam or any part Thereof. In witness whereof I have hereunto set my hand and Seal this   day of February in the year of our Lord, one Thousand Eight hundred & forty five. Signed sealed & delivered In the presents of   Joshua Cady (LS)

B. J. Williams
John Williams
South Carolina

Pickens District) B. J. Williams appears Personally Before me L. Hendricks an acting Magestrate in & for said District & after Being Duley sworn on the holy Evengalist of Almighty god sayeth that he saw Joshua Cady sighn seal & Deliver the within Deede of Conveyance to Josiah Trotter for the use & Purpose therein mentioned & that John Williams was with him self a subscribing witness to the same. Sworn to & subscribed before me the 8th day of August 1850.

L. Hendricks M. P. D.   B. J. Williams

JAMES McKINNEY PACK. 102 (EQUITY)
CLERK OF COURT'S OFFICE, PICKENS, S. C.

James McKinney states that on Aug. 2, 1832 he purchased of John Corbin 2 tracts of land one of them containing 213 acres, the other 150 acres. That on the sale day in April 1833 the above tracts of land were sold by the Sheriff of Pickens District. That the said John Corbin with a view to purchasing the said tracts of land (word?) the sale of the same pretending that he had a title to the said lands better that that of James McKinney. Having previously procured one Tarlton Lewis to bid off the said land, further states that when the lands were exposed to sale by the Sheriff, that the said Tarlton Lewis, the agent of the said John bid off the lands for which your orator had paid $600.00 . . . Filed March 9, 1835.

FREDERICK N. GARVIN PACK. 122 (EQUITY)
CLERK OF COURTS OFFICE, PICKENS, S. C.

George W. Rankin assignee of the estate of Frederick N. Garvin of Pickens District. That said Frederick N. Garvin being seized in fee simple of a certain tract of land situate in said district and being desirous of selling said tract of land, and William Walsh of the same district, being anxious to purchase the same, he and Frederick Garvin on or about June 1, 1857 intered into a verbal agreement, respecting the sale and purchase of the said tract of land. The said William Walsh agreed to pay Frederick Garvin the sum of $400.00 for the said tract of land, and the said Frederick Garvin agreed to make it to the said William Walsh a good and sufficient warranty title to the said tract of land whenever the said purchase money was paid in full. The said tract was situated on the head waters of Chauga adjoining lands of George Seaborn, John West & others and contained 138 acres. William Walsh by permission of Frederick Garvin went into the immediate peaceable and quite enjoyment & possession of the said premises where he has remained up to this time, and that Garvin has always been ready and willing to perform his part of the said agreement, and being paid the purchase money to convey the said tract of land to William Walsh, and hoped that the said William Walsh would have performed his agreement in his part as in justice and equity he ought to have done. That on the day of the sale and purchase of said land, that Frederick Garvin at the special instance and request of the said William Walsh sold to him cattle, hogs and sheep for which Wm. Walsh promised and agreed to pay him the sum of $150.00. Your orator further shews that upon the day of the sale of the said land, Wm. Walsh paid to F. N. Garvin $242.00 for which Garvin gave Wm. Walsh a receipt and that some time after, the said Wm. Walsh paid F. N. Garvin the further sum of $120.00 and that there still is a balance due and owing to F. N. Garvin of $188.00 with interest from the 1st June 1857, which Wm. Walsh neglects and refuses to pay. That on Oct. 1, 1860 F. N. Garvin laboring under great pecuniary embarrassment & desirious of paying his just debts made an assignment of all his estate both real & personal to the said George W. Rankin . . . Filed May 14, 1861. . . .

SHERIFF HAYNES PACK. 123 (EQUITY)
CLERK OF COURTS OFFICE, PICKENS, S. C.

Nathaniel Haynes states that Sheriff Haynes of Pickens District died intestate on March 6, 1848 . . . That he owned 2 tracts of land. No. 1 The Home Tract lying on the waters of Wolf Creek containing 363 acres. No. 2 Lying on Town Creek containing 888 acres. That the lands are subject to division among his widow Mary Haynes and 10 children viz. Harrison Haynes, Jesse Haynes, Nancy Haynes, Harper Haynes a minor under 14 years, Rebecca Haynes a minor under 12 years, Andrew Haynes a minor over 14 years, Parthenia Haynes a minor over the age of 12 years, Mary Haynes and Dorcas Haynes minors under 12 years, and the said Nathaniel Haynes. Filed May 24, 1852 . . . Tract No. 2 was sold to James T. Ferguson for $2485.00.

SAMUEL JOHNSTON PACK. 121 (EQUITY)
CLERK OF COURTS OFFICE, PICKENS, S. C.

Mary H. Johnston states that her husband Samuel Johnston of Pickens District died in March 1850 intestate, leaving her as his widow, and seven children viz. James T. Johnston, William H. Johnston, Eliza J. Johnston, Elijah M. Johnston, Robert Johnston, Edward Johnston, Joseph W. Johnston all of whom except the first 2 are minors . . . Owned 1 tract of land originally granted to Samuel Johnston containing 118 acres situated in Pickens District on a branch of Big Beaver Dam Creek, waters of Tugaloor River & bounded by lands of Elias Earle, William Fraser & others . . . Another tract of 470 acres on Little Beaver Dam Creek, waters of Tugaloo River and on a branch of Conneross Creek & bounded by lands of James Harris, Ruth Pritchard, James Johns & others, it being comprised of 2 tracts of land one of which was purchased by Samuel Johnston decd. from William Honea, the other from the heirs of James Johnston decd. Filed April 20, 1855. . . .

WILLIAM HONEA   Release For 250 Acres Land.
    to
SAMUEL JOHNSON
State of So. Carolina

Pickens District) Know all men by these presents that I William Honea of the State & District aforesd. for & in consideration of the sum of four hundred dollars to me in hand paid by Samuel Johnston of the State & District aforesd. have granted bargained sold and released and by this presence do grant bargain sell & release unto the said Samuel Johnston a certain tract or parcel of land situate lying & being in Pickens District aforesd. on a branch of little Beverdam Creek & a branch of Conneross Creek adjoining Lands of Henry Johns, Margaret Johnston Alexr Bryce & William Honea containing two hundred & fifty acres Begn. at a Stake X 3 on Mrs. Johnstons line, running thence S 70 E 11.12 links to a hicky. x 3 ? N 11 E 51.50 to a PO x 3 A Bryces x 3 Th.s across the spring branch and through the old field to a stone x 3 on Henry Johns line. Th.s to the Beg.n Together with all & singular the rights members heredetaments & appertenances to the said premises belonging or in any wise incident or apertaining to sd. premises To have & to hold the sd. premises above mentioned unto the Samuel Johnston his heirs & assigns forever And I do hereby bind myself my heirs Executors to warrant & forever defend the said premises to the said Samuel Johnston his heirs Executors adms. & assigns against myself my heirs Exors. Admnrs & assigns and against every other person or persons whomsoever lawfully claiming or to claim the same or any part thereof. In witness whereof I have hereunto set my hand & seal this thirteenth day of August one thousand eight hundred & twenty Nine and In the 53rd year of Americian Independance.

               his
          William X Honea (SEAL)
               seal

Sign'd Seal'd & Deliver'd in presence of
J. C. Kilpatrick
Thomas Bryce
South Carolina

Pickens District) Personally appeared John C. Kilpatrick before me and made oath as the law directs that he saw William Honea sign seal & as his act and deed deliver the within deed of conveyance to Samuel Johnston for the uses within mentioned and also that he saw the said William Honea sign the receipt endorsed and also saw Thomas Bryce subscribe his name. Sworn to this 5th of August 1831.

As a witness hereto Before me   J. C. Kilpatrick
John Myers J. P.

Rec'd the day and date of the within deed of the within named Sam'l Johnston four hundred dollars it being the full consideration money within mentioned.

               his
$400   William X Honea
               mark
J. C. Kilpatrick
Thomas Bryce

Recorded in BOOK C PAGE 347. Certified March 20, 1837.

WILL OF DOLLY FORD
PROBATE JUDGES OFFICE, SPARTANBURG, S. C.

State of South Carolina Spartanburgh District—I Dolly Ford widow of. Capt. Manly Ford De'd of the State and District afore Said, being of Sound and disposing mind memory and understanding praise be God for the Same. But being advanced in Years and calling to mind the uncertainty of life do make and declose this my last Will and Testament in Manner and form following

1st I give to the Mount Pleasant Church Five Dollars of which I am a member at present to be paid over unto the hands of Bowin Griffin.

2nd I devise that all my Just Debts and funeral Expenses be paid.

3rd I give to my Brother William Chumner the One half of all my Estate of whatsoever Kind it may be.

4th I give to my niece Nancy Inlow and the heirs of her boddy the one half of the Remaining half of my Estate not here to fore disposed of.

5th I Give to Dolly Young daughter of my Sister Sally Young the Residue of my Estate Remaining of what Soever Kind it may be hereby Revoking any and all wills here to fore made and decloses this to be my last Will and Testament. In Witness where of I the said Dolly Ford have hereunto Set my hand and Seal this the Twenty-fifth day of June in the Year of our Lord One Thousand Eight hundred and forty Nine.

                                        Dolly X Ford (L. S.)

Signed Sealed declared and
acknowledged by the Said Dolly
Ford for his last Will and
Testament in the presence of us
who at his request and in his
presence have subscribed our
names as witnesses thereto—
John Poole
W. I. Brem
Y. J. Wingo
Recorded in Will Book D, Page 375
Box, Pkg. 30
Recorded 8th March 1854.

PROBATE JUDGES OFFICE, SPARTANBURG, S. C.
WILL OF SARAH BAGWELL

In the name of God Amen: I Sarah Bagwell of Spartanburg District & State of South Carolina, being of Sound & disposing mind and memory, but being weak in body, and of feeble health, as preparatory to the event that I may be soon called from time, and time's things—Do constitute, This instrument, by me solemnly executed, my last Will & Testament, from which it may be learned, how, & in what manner, I wish my property disposed of, after I am gone. My property, consists of the land on which I live, being that which I derived from the estate of my Deceased husband—I also have the following negros, Frank, Maria & her infant child, Cato, George Rufus, Mary, Susan, and Narcisa, nine in number, also some cattle, hogs, horses, & sheep—besides house hold & kitchen furniture, and plantation tools. I also have had nine children, who have lived to be grown, and have married—viz Allen, Simsford, Josiah, Rachael (who married I. D. Canon) Jas Madison, Nancy (who married Jas Gore)—William, John , & Winkfield. Of my above named nine children, three have died, leaving children viz—Allen, Rachael Canon, and Nancy Gore. Now it is my will, that all of my property of whatever kind, shall be sold by my Executors, and the proceeds of the sale to be equally divided among them all—share and share alike, the children of my above named children who are dead, to receive among themselves equally the portion to which their parent—would have been entitled if living. It is farthermore my will, that if any one of my grandchildren shall die, without heirs of their body begotten that the grandchildren shall die, without heirs of their body begotten that the surviving brothers & sisters, or brother or sister of such deceased grandchild—shall take the whole property from me derived by this my will, to the exclusion of their parent.

It is furthermore my will, that my executors, shall retain the management, of so much of my estate, as my grandchildren, may entitled to by this my will, and be by them put to interest and paid over to my grandchildren, each his share as he may become Twenty one years old, except—my female grandchildren, to whom it is my will, their share shall be paid, when they shall arrive at the age of Twenty one years or marry. In addition to the land on which I live, above described, I have purchased twenty five acres more or less—which I wish disposed of as—I have directed that this should be on which I live. I also have some money due me which is loaned out on notes—out which I want my funeral expences to be paid and the balance equally divided as above directed and I do hereby constitute & appoint, my sons Winkfield, Jas Madison & William Bagwell, the Executors of this my last will & Testament—Witness my hand & seal this Twentieth day of June A. D. 1851.

           her
        Sarah X Bagwell (Seal)
          mark

Executed before us, and witnessed
by us in presence of the Testatrix
& in the presence of each other,
Day & year above written—
John Simpson
Washington Poole
John Brook
Recorded in Will Book D, Page 316
Box 8, Pdg. 37
Recorded Oct. 6, 1851.

WILL OF JOHN WHITTEN SR.
LAURENS COURTHOUSE, S. C. PROBATE JUDGES OFFICE

 In the name of God Amen. I John Whitten Sr. of South Carolina Laurens District considering the uncertainty of this mortal life and being of Sound mind and memory (Blessed be Almighty God for the Same, do make and publish this my last will and Testament in manner and form following, that is to say. I desire to be decent buried and my debts paid, after which I give and bequeath all my personal property to my children, Lyndsey Whitten, John Whitten Jr., Sally Henly, Anne Jacks, Fanny Ray and Susannah Kennedy to be equally devided between them, Except my wearing apparel which I give and bequeath to my Sons Lyndsay Whitten and John Whitten Jr. to be equally divided between them, and Lastly all Gifts that I have made to my children during my Lifetime, whereof no notice has been taken of the Same by me shall not be bought in question at their division and I do hereby constitute and appoint my Son Lyndsey Whitten and Blaseton Ray Sole Executors of this my last will and Testament whereof hereby revoking all other will by me made, in Witness whereof I have hereunto set my hand and seal this Third day of July in the year of our Lord One Thousand Eight hundred and twenty eight.

                 John Whitten Sr.

 Signed, Sealed, published and declared by the Said testator as and for his last will and testament in our presence, who at his request in his presence and the presence of each other have Subscribed our names as Witnesses

thereto.
John F. Kern Jr.
Alfred A. Kern
John Fred'ick Kern Sr.

Memorandum

The within will of John Whitten Senr. Deceased was proven Before me in the Court of ordinary on the 2 day of January 1832 by the oath of John F. Kerne one of the subscribing witnesses to the same.

D. Anderson, Ordy.

John Whitten will deceased
Recorded Book F Page 381
(COPY)

RECORDED IN WILL BOOK "A" PAGE 220 & 221
STATE OF SOUTH CAROLINA
COUNTY OF EDGEFIELD

WILL OF RICHARD ALLISON

IN THE NAME OF GOD AMEN:

I, Richard Allison, of the County of Edgefield and State of South Carolina, being of sound mind and memory Blessed be God, do this twenty eight day of December in the year of our Lord one Thousand Seven Hundred and eighty seven, make and publish this my last will and testament in manner following.

FIRST: I commend my soul to Almighty God who gave it me, hoping through the merits of my Blessed redeemer to obtain forgiveness of all my sins, and as touching what it has pleased God in his goodness to bestow upon me I leave in the following.

FIRST: I desire that all my just debts be paid by my Executors hereinafter named and that my body be decesently buried by my Executors.

ITEM: I leave and bequeath to my son **James Allison, one hundred acres** of land whereon I now live, as also my negro wench called Beltor and my Mollatto boy named Cyrus or Mack, and one negro wench called Silvey, and one negro boy called Jack, and one other negro boy called Sanney, to be to him and his heirs and assigns forever. And further it is my will that if my said son James Allison should die before he attain the age of twenty one years or should die without, issue lawfully begotten of his body that then and in such case my will is that the land and negroes aforesaid shall return to the nearest heir on the right line of my brothers family, or nearest kin to me by my fathers side.

IMPRIMES: I leave and bequeath to my well beloved wife **Sarah Allison,** the one third part of my present dwelling plantation during her natural life as also the profits and labor of my negroes aforesaid until my son James should come of age or be married, as also one negro molatto girl called Hagor, and all my stock of horses and cattle, hogs and household furniture and plantation tools to be hers during her natural life, and after her decease to return to my said son James Allison his heir and assign forever.

IMPRIMIS: I leave and bequeath to Isaac Norrell, my negro boy called Cash and my negro girl called Rachel, to him his heirs and assigns forever, and I do hereby constitute and appoint my trusty and well beloved friends Thomas Anderson and William Hill and my wife, Executors of this my last will and testament, hereby ratifying and confirming this and no other to be my last will and testament and revoking all other wills by me heretofore made, in witness whereof, I have hereunto set my hand and seal the day and date above written.

Richard Allison (SEAL)

Signed, sealed, published and declared by the within named testator as and for his last will and testament in presence of us, who were present at the signing and sealing those of and in presence of each other.
William Anderson
Abney Mays
Samuel Thomas
Recorded: October 15, 1806
J. N. Simkins, O. E. D.
Box No. 33, Pkg. No. 85

LINDSEY WHITTEN
PROBATE JUDGES OFFICE, LAURENS, S. C.

South Carolina
Laurens District
To W. D. Watts Ordinary of said District

The Petition of Nancy Whitten and Marshall Duncan shewith that Lindsey Whitten late of the district aforesaid recently died intestate being seized and possessed of a considerable personal Estate which is liable to waste and that your Petitioners has taken out Administration on said estate and that said dec'd was indebted to sundry persons and in order to prevent waste pay debts and make distribution amongst the parties in interest prays that your would Grant them an order to sell the personal Estate of said Dec'd. on a credit of Twelve months and your petitioner will pray, etc. this 11th October 1844.

her
Nancy   X   Whitten
mark
Marshal Duncan

On hearing the above petition ordered that the administrators expose to public out cry at the late residence of said dec'd on the 6th day of November next on a credit of Twelve months all the personal Estate of said Dec'd taking notes and approved security for all sums of and above three dollars all sums under that amt. to be paid in cash. Given under my hand and seal this 11th Oct. 1844.

W. D. Watts (Seal)
O. L. D.

Order of Sale on the Estate of Lindsey Whitten, dec'd.
Filed 11 Oct. 1844.
(COPY)

Administration Bond on the Estate of Lindsey Whitten, Dec'd.
Bond dated 11th October 1844
Amount of bond $6,000.00

Bond signed by Nancy Whitten (Her mark)
               Marshal Duncan
               Henry S. Neele
Filed Oct. 1844
Recorded Page 128
Sale Bill of the effects of Lindsey Whitten, Dec'd. Nov. 6, 1844.
Names of purchasers:
    Jno. Whitten, Widow, Dr. Aiken, Mrs. Philson, Jas. Dillard, Wm. Abrams, Jas. Dillard, M. Duncan, Jno. Whitten, Jno. Poole, Col. Kern, John Horton,
    Jno. McCord, Thos. Craig, Widow Garrett, R. Adair, Jno. Miller, Wm. Kennedy, O. Beasley, H. Lindsey, Adam Bell, Capt. Whitmore, Isaac Jacks, Jno. Jacks, Isaac Jacks, Wm. Hendrix, Nancy Whitten, Robert Pitts, Elizabeth Philson, Robert Adair, Plesant Abraham, Thomas Wier, J. F. Kern, John Horton, Mary Garrett, Clark Beasley, Thos. Craig, Seborn Dillard.

- Place of sale not listed.

SOLOMON DOUTHIT PACK. 116 EQUITY
CLERK OF COURTS OFFICE, PICKENS, S. C.

Matthew Keith, Warren D. Keith, Crafton Keith states that their mother Rebecca eith formerly Rebecca Douthit died leaving the following children also, Rosa Hendricks, Margaret Edens who intermarried with Alexander Edens and Jane Keith. Their grand father Solomon Douthit died in 1830 owning a tract of 500 acres in In Pickens District, and a portion in Greenville District, lying on both sides of Saluda River, adjoining lands belonging to the estate of Joshua Burgess decd. Col. B. Hagood & others . . . That these lands are subject to division among the 10 children of Solomon Douthit, his wife having died some time since. viz. Davis Douthit, Eleanor who married Daniel McJunkin and who reside in Georgia, Robert & Silas Douthit who reside in the west, the heirs of John Douthit decd., Andrew Douthit who reside in Georgia, Mary Ann who married Benjamin Burgess who reside in Georgia, Margaret who married James McJunkin who reside in Georgia or Tennessee one, Lucy who married Samuel Erwin who have been separated for about 13 years, Lucy Erw in residing in North Carolina, and Samuel Erwin in parts unknown. The heirs of Rebecca Keith who are of full age. The heirs of Solomon Douthit decd. who reside in Alabama. Filed March 14, 1853. Roas Hendricks was the wife of Larkin Hendricks . . . John Douthit died in 1832. . . .

POWER OF ATTORNEY   From Lilly Ann Douthit to Robt. B. McClure
State of Georgia
Fannin County? Check county for sure not plain.

    Know all men by these presents that I Lilly Ann Douthart widow of John Douthart and guardian of the orphans of the said John Douthart to wit, John Douthart, Davis W Douthart, Rebecca J. Douthart Levica A Douthart & Samuel T Douthart of the county and state aforesaid for divers good causes and considerations me hereunto moving as guardian as aforesaid have made ordained and appointed and by these do make ordain and appoint Robert B. McClure of the County of Lumpkin in the state of Georgia my true and lawful attorney as aforesaid for me and in my name and for my own proper use and benefit as aforesaid to ask demand sue for recover and receive from Robert A. Thompson Commissioner in Equity in Pickens District State of South Carolina all such sums of money as may be due or coming to me as guardian as aforesaid from the estate of Solomon and Polly Douthart deceased in Greenville District in the State of South Carolina and to have all and take all lawful ways and means in my name or otherwise as Guardian as aforesaid and to compound and agree for the same and acquittances or other sufficient Receipts and discharges for the same for me and in my name as Guardian as aforesaid to make seal and deliver and to do all other lawful acts and things whatsoever concerning the premises as fully and in every respect as I myself as guardian as aforesaid might or could do were I personally present at the doing thereof ratifying and confirming and by these presents allowing whatsoever my said attorney shall in my name as guardian as aforesaid lawfully do or cause to be done in and about the premises by virtue of these presents in witness whereof I have as guardian aforsaid hereunto set my hand and seal as guardian as aforsaid this 11th day of October 1855.

John M. Johnston   LILLY Ann Douthit (L. S.)
Mahaley Smith
Levi Willson J. P.
State of Georgia

Fannin County) I William Franklin Clerk of the Superior Court for said County do hereby certify that Levi Willson whose name appears to the foregoing letter of attorney as a Subscribing witness is a Justice of the peace in and for said county and that full faith and credit ought to be had and given to his attestation as such and that the same is in due form Given under my hand and seal of office this 12th day of October 1855.

                                                    William Franklin C. S. C.

State of Georgia

Fannin County) I James H. Morris? of the justice of the Inferior Court for the county aforesaid do certify that William Franklin whose name appears to the above and foregoing certificate is clerk of the Superior Court for said county and that full faith and credit ought to be had and given to his attestation as such and that the same is due form. Given under my hand and private seal having no seal of office this 12th day of October 1855.

                                                    J. H. Morris J. I. C.

State of Georgia

Fannin County) I, James Kincade ordinary for said county do hereby certify that Lilly Ann Douthit widow of John Douthit of said county deceased has come forward to my office and given bond and security in terms of law as Guardian of the orphans of the said John Douthit Lavica Douthit & Samuel Douthit who is the orphans of said deceased. Given under my hand and seal of office this 12 day of October 1855.

                                                    James Kincaid ordinary

State of Georgia

Fannin County) I, William Franklin clerk of the Superior Court for said county do hereby that James Kincade whose name appears to the foregoing certificate is the Judge of the court of Ordinary for said County and that full faith and credit ought to be had and given to his attestation as such Given

under my hand and seal of office this 12th day of October 1855.
                              William Franklin C. S. C.
Georgia
   Fannin County) Before me personally came Reece J. McClure and Lavica S. Galloway who being duly sworn deposeth and saith that they saw John Douth and Lilly Ann McClure of Pickens District in the State of South Carolina married on the Sixth day of January 1828 and they was married by one Jacob Lewis who was a Minister of the Gospel Sworn to and Subscribed before me this 11th day of October 1855.
                              Reece J. McClure
                              Levissa S. Galloway

   $142.72. Received of Robert A. Thompson, Commissioner in Equity for Pickens District, So Ca. one Hundred & Forty two Dollars & Seventy two cents, on this Power of Attorney in full of the distributive share of the minors, John M Douthett, Davis W. Douthet, Rebecca J. Douthett, Levina A Douthett and Samuel T. Douthett, in the Real Estate of their Grand father Solomon Douthett deceased.
Oct. 15, 1855   Robt. B. McClure
The State of Alabama
   Jefferson County) Before me Hardy Hancock an acting Justice of the Peace in and for the county and state aforesaid personally appeared Mary Ann Bivens to me well known who being by me duly sworn deposeth and syeth that in the year 1831 she married one Solomon Douthitt—that the marriage took place in the said County of Jefferson—that the maiden name of affidavit was Mary Ann Linn—that the said Solomon Douthitt came to this state from Greenville District South Carolina—that after her marriage with affiant he lived several years in Jefferson County and from thence moved to County of Talladega & about the year 1835 he died. Affiant furthed deposeth and sayeth that the father of the said Solomon Douthitt lived in Greenville District South Carolina as she was informed—that his name was Solomon Douthitt and that he is now dead as she has been told. Affiant further swears that of the marriage of herself and the said Solomon Douthitt there was born James R Douthitt that he was born about the 4th day of March 1833, that he is the only child and heir of the said Solomon Douthitt that the said James R Douthitt left this country for Greenville District South Carolina about the month of October 1854, and that he was in said Greenville District on the 7th day of August last (1855) as appears from a letter written by him and dated then of that date. Affiant further swears that the said James R Douhitt is the identical same James R Douthitt who about the year 1839 received a legacy from the estate of Solomon Douthitt of Greenville District South Carolina through one James H Hewitt who went to Greenville after the money. Affiant further swears that since the death of Solomon Douthitt her first husband she intermarried with and is now the wife of Valentine Bivens of this county.
                                        her
                         Mary Anne   X   Bivens
                                       mark
   The above affidavit was made before me & signed by affiant in my presence this 29th day of September 1855.

Hardy Hancock
Justice of the peace
The State of Alabama

Jefferson County) Before me Hardy Hancock an acting Justice of the Peace in and for the County and State aforesaid personally appeared Marinda Linn to me well known who being duly sworn deposeth and sayeth that she is the step mother of Mary Ann Bivens—that she knew the said Mary Ann long before her first marriage—that she was well acquainted with Solomon Douthitt—that the marriage between the said Solomon Douthitt and the said Mary Ann took place in the County of Jefferson in this state about the year 1831 and after their marriage the said Solomon Douthitt lived in Jefferson County for several years and from thence moved to Talladega County when he died about the year 1835—the said Douthitt came as he said from Greenville District South Carolina—that his father resided in said District. Affiant further swears that of the marriage of the said Solomon Douthitt and the said Mary Ann there was born James R Douthitt who is the only child and heir of the said Solomon Douthitt—that the said James R Douthitt was born about the year 1833—that she has known him ever since his birth—that about the month of October 1854 he left this country for Greenville District South Carolina when she is informed he now is. Affiant further swears that he is the same identical James R Douthitt who about the year 1938 received a legacy from the estate of his grandfather in Greenville District South Carolina, the said legacy having been paid over to one James R Hewitt of this county who went to Greenville as was informed after the money.

The above affidavit was made before me & signed by affidavit in my presence this 29th day of September 1855.

her
Marinda   X   Linn
mark

Hardy Hancock
Justice of the peace
The State of Alabama

Jefferson County) I Joab Bagley? Judge of Probate for said County hereby certify that Hardy Hancock whose genuine signature is signed to the foregoing affidavit was at the date thereof an acting Justice of the Peace within and for said county duly commissioned and qualified as by law required that all his acts as such are entitled to full faith and credit. Given under my hand and seal of office this 4th day of October 1855.

J. Bagley? Judge of Probate

State of Georgia

Fannin County) Know all men by these presents that I Mary Ann Burgess wife of Benjamin Burgess both of the County and State aforesaid for divers good causes and considerations me here unto moving have made ordained and appointed and by these presents do make ordain and appoint said Benjamin E. Burgess of said County and state my true and lawful attorney for me and in my name and for my own proper use and benefit to receive and recept for my distributive share of the money arising from the sales of the real estate of Solomon Douthit and Mary Douthit deceased of Greenville District in the State of South Carolina. And to have use and take all lawful ways and means in my name or other wise that may be found necessary or proper in the executio ᵗof this power of attorney to do all lawful acts and things whatsoever concerning the premises as fully in every respect as I myself might as could do were I personally present at the doing thereof Ratifying and confirming and by these presents allowing whatsoever my said attorney shall in my name lawfully do or cause to be done in and about the premises. In witness whereof I have hereunto set my hand and affixed my seal this March 1857.

           Maryan Burgess (SEAL)

 Signed Sealed and delivered in presence of
Wm. Franklin
(Another name not plain)

State of Georgia
 Fannin County) Be it remembered before me P. D. Claiborn a Justice of the Inferior Court in and for said state and county duly commissioned and sworn this day came Mary Ann Burgess who acknowledged the above to be her act and deed. Given under my hand and seal this March 1857.

         P. D. Clairborn J. I. C. (SEAL)

State of Georgia
 Fannin County) I William Franklin Clerk of the Superior Court in and for said county and state hereby certify that P. D. Claiborn is and was at the time of taking the above acknowledgement a Justice of the Inferior Court in and for said county and state duly commissioned and sworn and authorized by law to take acknowledgement and that all his official acts or such are entitled to full faith and credit and that his Signature thereunto is genuine. In testimony whereof I have hereunto set my hand and affixed the seal of my office this March 17th 1857.

            Wm. Franklin C. S. C.

State of Georgia
 Fanin County) Know all men by these presents that we Andrew J. Douthert and Solomon M. Douthert of said County heirs of John Douthert deceased for divers good causes and considerations us hereunto moving have made ordained and appointed and by these presents do make ordain and appoint Robert B. McClure of the County of Lumpkin in the State of Georgia our true and lawful attorney for us and in our name and for our own proper use and benefit to ask demand sue for recover and receive of and from Robert A. Thompson Commissioner in Equity in Pickens District and State of South Carolina all such sums of money as may be due or coming to us from the Estate of Solomon and Polly Douthert deceased in Greenville District in the State of South Carolina and to have an and take all lawful ways and means in our names or otherwise and to compound and agree for the same and acquittances or other Sufficient receipts and discharges for the same for us and in our names to make seal and deliver and to do all other lawful acts and things, whatsoever might or could do were we personally present at the doing thereof ratifying and confirming and by these presents allowing whatsoever our said attorney shall in our names lawfully do or cause to be done in and about the premises by virtue of these presents. In witness whereof we have hereunto set our hands and affixed our seals this 11th day of October 1855.

John M. Johnston
Mahaley Smith
Levi Willson J. P.

         Solomon M. Douthit (L. S.)
         Andrew J. Douthit (LS,S,)

State of Georgia
  Fanin County) I, William Franklin Clerk of the Superior Court for said County do hereby certify that Levi Willson whose name appears to the foregoing letter of attorney as a Subscribing witness is a Justice of the peace in and for said county and that full faith and credit ought to be had and given to his attestation as such and that the same is in due form. Given under my hand and seal of office this 12th day of October 1855.
            William Franklin C. S. C.

State of Georgia
  Fanin County) I, James H. Morris? one of the Justices of the Inferior Court for said county do certify that William Franklin whose name appears to the above and foregoing certificate is clerk of the Inferior Court for said County and that full faith and credit ought to be had and given to his attestation asi such and that the same is due form. Given under my hand and private seal having no seal of office this 12th day of October 1855.
            J. H. Morris? J. C.

State of Georgia
  Fanin County) Before me personally came Reese J. McClure and Lavica S. Galloway who being duly sworn deposeth and saith that Andrew J. Douthart and Solomon M? Douthart who has executed the within letter of attorney to Robert B. McClure is the lawful heirs of John Douthart and Lilly Ann Douthart widow of said deceased. Sworn to and Subscribed before me this 11th day of October 1855.
Levi Willson J. P.

            R. J. McClure
            Levise S. Galloway

DAVIS DOUTHITT
  TO
MATTHEW KEITH (DEED)
State of South Carolina
  Pickens District) This indenture made and Entered into this tenth day of December in the year of our Lord one thousand eight hundred and forty five between Davis Douthit of the District of Greenville and State aforesaid of the one part & Matthew Keith of Pickens District of the other part. Witnesseth that I the said Davis Douthit have this day bargained sold released & delivered unto the aforesaid Matthew Keith all my interest in the estate of my Father Solomon Douthit deceased of Greenville District this is to say the Estate both real and personal for a consideration of the sum of one hundred and fifty dollars to me in hand paid by the said Matthew Keith at or before the sealing or delivery of these presents the rights whereof is hereby acknowledged to have and to hold from me my heirs assigns & executors and Administrators and all and any other person or persons what ever unto him the

said Matthew Keith his heirs and assigns for ever to his & proper use & benefit and by infirmities. In witness whereof I have hereunto set my hand and affixed my seal this day and year first written.

                D. Douthit (SEAL)

Allen Keith
   his
James X Keith
   mark

The State of South Carolina

Pickens District) Allen Keith this day personally appears Before me J. B. Reid Notary Public for said District and whom being duly sworn as the Law directs deposeth and Saith on oath that he saw the within named Davis Douthit Sign Seal and deliver the within deed of Conveyance for the use therein contained and also deposeth saith that Jane Keith with himself Subscribed there names to as witnesses to the same. Sworn to this 21st day of April 1853 before me.

J. B. Reid   Allen Keith
Notr. Publick for P. D.

Recorded the 13th May 1853.

"LAND WARRANTS," PACK. 114
CLERK OF COURTS OFFICE, PICKENS, S. C.

R. J. BALL NO. 3
So Ca.

Pickens Dst.) By Thomas Garvin Esq. Commissioner of Location for Sd District to any Lawful surveyor you are hereby required to admeasure and lay out unto R. J. or R. T.? Ball a tract of land not exceeding ten thousand acres observing the Surveyor Generals instructions in laying out the same and a true plat thereof return into my office within two months. Given under my hand seal this 31st day of July 1840.

              Thos. Garvin (SEAL)

Executed part of the within warrant Sept. 8, 1840.
              Robt. Fullerton D. S.

Recorded Oct. 30, 1843.

WILLIAM VAN WYCK NO. 175
State of South Carolina

Pickens District) By W. L. Keith clerk of the court and by virtue of office Commissioner of Location for the District aforesaid. To any lawful Surveyor you are hereby authorised to lay out unto William Van Wyck a tract of land not exceeding ten thousand acres observing the Surveyor Generals instructions in laying out the same and a true plat thereof return into my office within two months form the date hereof the above warrant is for the purpose of having certain lands regranted. Given under my hand and seal the 11th day of June A. D. 1853.

       W. L. Keith (SEAL) C. C. & C. L. P. D.

Executed on the within warrant 275 acres June 18, 1853.
              Thos. D. Garvin D. S.

Certified July 8, 1853.

EDMUND CAINEY OR CAIREY NO. 73
State of South Carolina

Pickens District) By W. L. Keith Clerk of the Court and by virtue of office Commissioner of Location in and for the District aforesaid. To any lawful Surveyor you are hereby authorised to lay out and admeasure unto Edmund Cainey or Cairey? a tract of land not exceeding ten thousand acres observing the Surveyor Generals instructions in laying out the same and a true plat of the same return into my office within two months from the date hereof. the above warrant is for the purpose of having the tract of land whereon the said E. Gainey? now lives on the Waters of Village Creek regranted and vacant land adjoining the same. Given under my hand and seal this 23 Octr. 1844.

W. L. Keith (SEAL) C. C. & C. L. P. D.

Executed the within warrant 80 acres Oct. 21, 1844.

John O. Grisham D. S.

Certified Nov. 8, 1844.

"LAND WARRANTS," PACK. 114
CLERK OF COURTS OFFICE, PICKENS, S. C.

JOHN C. GORDON NO. 42
South Carolina

Pickens District) To any lawful surveyor you are hereby authorized and required to lay out unto John C. Gordon a tract of land not exceeding ten thousand acres, observing the Surveyor Generals instructions in laying out the same and a true plat thereof return into my office within two months from this date given under my hand & seal this 24th day of October 1842.

W. L. Keith (SEAL) C. L. P. D.

Executed part of the within warrant Nov. 1, 1842.

Robt. Fullerton D. S.

Certified Dec. 5, 1842.

MILTON R. HUNNICUT NO. 33
State of South Carolina

Pickens District) By W. L. Keith Clerk of the Court and Ex officio Commissioner of Location for Pickens District. To any lawful Surveyor you are hereby authorized and required to lay out and admeasure a tract of land unto Milton R. Hunnicut not exceeding ten thousand acres, to include a certain tract of land lying on the waters of Conneross formerly owned by W. Hunnicutt adjoining lands of Col. J. C. Kilpatrick originally granted to . . . and such lands as may be vacant adjoining the same. You will observe the Surveyor Generals instructions in laying out the same and a true plat thereof return into my office within two months from the date hereof. Given under my hand and seal this 19th day of June A. D. 1842.

W. L. Keith (LS) C. L. P. D.

Executed for the within 212 acres July 8, 1842.

John O. Grisham D. S.

JOSEPH CHAPMAN NO NUMBER
State of South Carolina

Pickens County) Office of the Comsr of Locations I R. A. Bowen Clerk of the Court of Common Pleas and General Sessions and ex officio Commissioner of Locations for the County aforesaid. To J. B. Clayton or some other lawful Deputy Surveyor for the said County, you are hereby authorized and required with proper attention to the instructions of the Surveyor General to lay off and locate unto Joseph Chapman a tract of vacant land within the County aforesaid which has been entered by him, and will be shewn to you in his behalf, and to return this warrant when executed, together with a true and correct plat of the survey you make under it, certified by you, into this office within two calendar months from the date hereof. Given under my hand and seal of office at Pickens C. H. this 30th day of August 1861.

        R. A. Bowen C. C. P. & Ex Officio
        Commsr of Locations

CLERK OF COURTS OFFICE, PICKENS, S. C.

JOHN O. GRISHAM NO. 72
State of South Carolina

 Pickens District) I W. L. Keith Clerk of the Court and by virtue of office Commissioner of Location for the District aforesaid. To any lawful Surveyor you are hereby authorized to lay out and admeasure unto Jno O. Grisham a tract of land not exceeding ten thousand acres observing the Survelor Generals instructions in laying out the same and a true plat thereof return into my office within two months from this date hereof the above warrant is for the purpose of resurveying a tract of land that lies on branches of little River and was originally granted to Thos. Beard and such vacant land as may be adjoining the same. Given under my hand & seal this 9th day of Sept. Anno Domini 1844.

        W. L. Keith (LS) C. L. P. D.

Executed for the within 1475 acres Sept. 13, 1844.
Certified Oct. 22, 1844.

WILLIAM VAN WYCK NO. 176
State of South

 Pickens District) By W. L. Keith Clerk of the court and by virtute of office Commissioner of Location for the District aforesaid. To any lawful Surveyor you are hereby authorized to lay out and admeasure unto William Vanwick a tract of land not exceeding ten thousand acres observing the Surveyor Generals instructions in laying out the same and a true plat thereof return into my office within two months from the date hereof the above warrant is for the purpose of having certain lands regranted. Given under my hand and seal this 11th day of June A. D. 1853.

        W. L. Keith (SEAL) C. C. & C. L. P. D.

Executed on the within warrant 371 acres June 23, 1853.
        Thomas D. Garvin D. S.

 Certified July 8, 1853.

JOHN O. GRISHAM NO. 81
State of South Carolina

 Pickens District) By W. L. Keith Clerk of the Court & by virtue of office

Commissioner of Location for said District. To any Lawful Surveyor you are hereby authorized and commanded to lay out and admeasure unto John O. Grisham a tract of land he purchased of William Watson on Conneross Creek, for the purpose of regranting the same and also all vacant lands adjoining not exceeding ten thousand acres observing the Surveyor Generals instructions in laying out the same and a true plat thereof return into my office within two months from this date. Given
This 10th day of June A. D. 1845.
W. L. Keith 173 acres July 16, 1845. Recorded Aug. 4, 1845.

ALEXANDER BRYCE NO. 107
State of South Carolina

Pickens District) By William L. Keith Clerk of the Court for said District and by virtue of office a Commissioner of Location for said District. To any lawful Surveyor you are hereby authorized to lay out and admeasure unto Thomas A. Yow? and Alexander Bryce a tract of land not exceeding one thousand acres observing the Surveyor Generals instructions in laying out the same and a true plat thereof return into my office within two months from this date. Given under my hand and seal this the 5th day of March Anno Domini 1849.

W. L. Keith C. C. P. & C. L. P. D.

Executed part of the within warrant April 10th 1849.

Robt. Fullerton D. S.

Certified April 30, 1849.

LEONARD CAPEHART NO. 70
State of South Carolina

Pickens District) By W. L. Keith Clerk of the Court and by virtue of office Commissioner of Location in and for the District aforesaid. To any lawful Surveyor you are hereby authorised to lay out and admeasure unto

---

Leonard Capehart a tract of land not exceeding ten thousand acres observing the Surveyor Generals instructions in laying out the same and a true plat of the same return into my office within two months from the date hereof. The above warrant is for the purpose of regranting a tract of land lying on Little River and taking in such vacant land as may be joining the same. Given under my hand and seal this 2d day of Septr. A. D. 1844.

W. L. Keith (SEAL) C. L. P. D.

Executed of the within warrant 772 acres Sept. 18, 1844.

John O. Grisham D. S.

Certified Sept. 7, 1844. (NOTE: ON BACK OF WARRANT WAS WRITTEN REV. T. DAWSON BUT INSIDE WRITTEN LEONARD CAPEHART).

WILLIAM VAN WYCK NO. 196
State of South Carolina

Pickens District) By W. L. Keith clerk of the court and by virtue of office

Commissioner of Location for the District aforesaid. To any Lawful Surveyor you are hereby required and authorized to lay out and admeasure unto William Van Wyck a tract of land not exceeding ten thousand acres observing the Surveyor Generals instructions in laying out the same and a true plat thereof return into my office within two months from the date hereof the above warrant is for the purpose of having ceartain lands regranted. Given under my hand and seal this 11th Day of June A. D. 1853.

W. L. Keith (SEAL) C. C. & C. L. P. D.

Executed on the within warrant 220 acres June 21, 1853.

Thos. D. Garvin D. S.

Certified July 8, 1853.

SAMUEL MAVERICKK NO. 44

South Carolina By William L. Keith Esqr.

To any lawful Surveyor of Pickens District you are hereby Required to admeasure & lay out unto Samuel Maverick a tract of land not Exceeding ten thousand acres observing the Surveyor Generals instructions in Laying out the same & a true plat thereof Return into my office within two months For the Special purpose of Regranting a certain body of Land in the Neighborhood of Doble branches. Given under my hand and seal this 10th day of Dec. 1842.

W. L. Keith (SEAL) C. L. P. D.

Executed on the within warrant 1890 acres Dec. 17, 1842.

Thos. D. Garvin D. S.

Certified Jany. 11, 1843.

WILLIAM CANTRELL NO NUMBER

State of South Carolina

Pickens District) By W. L. Keith Clerk of the Court and by virtue of office Commissioner of Location for said District. To any lawful Surveyor you are hereby authorized to lay out and admeasure unto William Cantrell a tract of land not exceeding ten thousand acres observing the Surveyor Generals instructions in laying out the same and a true plat thereof return into my office within two months from the date hereof. Given under my hand and seal this 20th day of December 1847.

W. L. Keith (SEAL) C. L. P. D.

Executed of the within warrant 85 1-2 acres Dec. 27, 1847.

Alexander Edens D. S.

WILLIAM VAN WYCK NO. 172

State of South Carolina

Pickens District) By W. L. Keith Clerk of the Court and by virtue of office Commissioner of Location for the District aforesaid. To any lawful Surveyor you are hereby authorized to lay out and admeasure unto William Van Wyck a tract of land not exceeding ten thousand acres observing the Surveyor Generals instructions in laying out the same and a true plat thereof return into my office within two months from the date hereof. the above warrant is for the purpose of having certain lands regranted. Given under my hand and Seal this 27th day of May A. D. 1853.

W. L. Keith (SEAL) C. C. & C. L. P. D.
Executed on the within warrant 650 acres May 28, 1853.
Thomas D. Garvin D. S.
Certified July 8, 1853.

JOHN P. BENSON NO. 40
State of South Carolina

Pickens District) By William L. Keith Clerk of the Court and by virtue of office Commissioner of Location in and for the District aforesaid. To any lawful Surveyor you are hereby authorized to lay out and admeasure unto John P. Benson a tract of land not exceeding ten thousand acres observing the Surveyor Generals instructions in laying out the same and a true plat of the same return into my office within two months from the date hereof. Given under my hand and seal this 28th day of Octr. A. D. 1842.

W. L. Keith (SEAL) C. L. P. D.
Executed of the within warrant 481 acres Oct. 28, 1842.
Martin MCay D. S.
Certified Nov. 5, 1842.

WILLIAM VAN WYCK NO. 179
South Carolina

Pickens District) By W. L. Keith Esq. C. C. & by virtue of office Commismissioner of Locations in said District. To any Lawful Surveyor you are hereby authorized to admeasure and lay out untoWilliam Van Wyck a tract of land not exceeding one thousand acres observing the Surveyor Generals instructions in laying out the same and a true plat thereof return into my office within two months from the date hereoff it being for the purpose of having ceartain lands regranted. Given under my hand and seal the 11th day of July A. D. 1853.

W. L. Keith (SEAL) C. C. & EX OFF C. L.
Executed on the within warrant 521 acres July 11, 1853.
Thos. D. Garvin D. S.
Certified July 12, 1853.

WILLIAM VAN WYCK NO. 173
State of South Carolina

Pickens District) By William L. Keith Esqr. clerk of court by virtue of office Commissioner of Locations in said District. To any Lawful Surveyor you are hereby authorized to lay out unto William Van Wyck a tract of land not exceeding one thousand acres observing the Surveyor Generals instructions in laying out the same and a true plat thereoff return into my office within two months from the date hereof, this warrant for the purpose of having ceartain lands regranted. Given under my hand and seal the 11th of June A. D. 1853.

W. L. Keith (SEAL) C. C. & C. L. P. D.
Executed on the within warrant 207 acres July 6, 1853.
Thos. D. Garvin D. S.
Certified July 8, 1853.

EZRA HYDE NO. 43
State of South Carolina
  Pickens District) By W. L. Keith Clerk of the Court and by virtue of office Commissioner of Location for the District aforesaid. To any lawful Surveyor you are hereby authorized to lay out and admeasure a tract of land unto Ezra Hyde not exceeding ten thousand acres observing the Surveyor Generals instructions in laying out the same and a true plat of the same return into my office within two months from the date hereof. Given under my hand and seal this 9th day of Novr. Anno Domini 1842.
                                W. L. Keith (SEAL) C. L. P. D.
  Executed part of the within warrant Nov. 23, 1842.
                                                Robt. Fullerton D. S.
  Certified Jan. 2, 1843.

DAVID BARTON NO. 63
State of South Carolina
  Pickens District) By W. L. Keith Clerk of the Court and by virtue of office Commissioner of Location in and for the District aforesaid To any lawful Surveyor you are hereby authorized to lay out and admeasure a tract of Land unto David Barton the tract of land he now lives on and certain vacant lands adjoining the same for the purposes of obtaining a Grant for the whole not exceeding ten thousand acres observing the surveyor Generals instructions in laying out the same and a true plat of the same return into my office within two months from this date. Given under my hand and seal this 4th day of March Anno Domini 1844.
                                W. L. Keith (SEAL) C. L. P. D.
  Executed of the within warrant 307 acres Mar. 9, 1844.
                                                M. MCay D. S.
  Certified April 1, 1844.

WILLIAM S. GRISHAM NO. 114
South Carolina
  Pickens District) By W. L. Keith Clerk of the Court and by virtue of office Commissioner of Locations for Pickens District. To any lawful Surveyor you are hereby authorized to lay out and admeasure unto William S. Grisham a tract of land not exceeding ten thousand acres observing the Surveyor Generals instructions in laying out the same and a true plat thereof return into my office within two months from the date hereof. Given under my hand and seal this 1st Novr. 1849.
                                W. L. Keith (SEAL) C. L. P. D.
  Executed of the within 1,884 acres Nov. 14, 1849.
                                                Tyre B. Mauldin D. S.
  Certified Nov. 18, 1849.

"LAND WARRANTS," PACK. 114
CLERK OF COURTS OFFICE, PICKENS, S. C.

REVD. THOMAS DAWSON NO. 31
State of South Carolina

Pickens District) By W. L. Keith Clerk of the Court and by virtue of office Commissioner of Location for the District aforesaid. To any lawful Surveyor you are hereby authorized to lay out and admesure unto Revd. Thomas Dawson a tract of land not exceeding ten thousand acres observing the Surveyor Generals instructions in laying out the same and a true plat thereof return into my office within two months from the date hereof. Given under my hand and seal this 25 day of April 1842.

W. L. Keith (SEAL) C. L. P. D.

Executed for the within 526 acres April 26, 1842.

John O. Grisham D. S.

Certified May 13, 1845.

LOT KENNEMON NO. 65
South Carolina

Pickens DDistrict) To any Lawful Surveyor you are hereby required to admeasure and Lay out unto Lot Kennemon a tract of land not Exceeding one thousand Acres observing the surveyor Generals instructions in laying out the same and a true plot thereoff return into my office within two months. Given under my hand and seal this 4th May 1844.

W. L. Keith (SEAL) C. L. P. D.

Executed on the within 661 Acres May 4, 1844.

Thos. D. Garvin D. S.

COL. JOSEPH GRISHAM NO. 35
State of South Carolina

Pickens District) By William L. Keith Clerk of the Court and by virtue of office Commissioner of Location for the District aforesaid. To any Lawful Surveyor you are hereby authorized to lay out and Admeasure to Col. Joseph Grisham of West Union a tract of land not exceeding Ten Thousand acres including where Nathan Dodd lived and lands which he claims adjoining thereto Granted to A Huffman to D Rusk and any others of his Land adjoining thereto on Cane Creek and waters observing the Surveyor Generals instructions in laying out the same and a true plat thereof return unto my office within two months from this date. Given under my hand & seal this 24th Jany 1842.

W. L. Keith (SEAL) C. L. P. D.

Executed 1491 acres March 14, 1842. John O. Grisham D. S.
Recorded Sept. 5, 1842.

SAMUEL MAVERICK NO. 41
State of South Carolina

Pickens District) By W. L. Keith Clerk of the Court and by virtue of office Commissioner of Location for said District. To any lawful Surveyor you are hereby authorized to lay out and admeasure unto Samuel Maverick a tract of land not exceeding ten thousand acres observing the Surveyor Generals instructions in laying out the same and a true plat thereof return into my office within two months from the date hereof. Given under my hand & seal this 5 Decr. 1842.

W. L. (Keith (SEAL) C. L. P. D.
Executed the within warrant 4400 acres Dec. 5, 1842.
Thos. D. Garvin D. S.
Certified Decr. 5, 1842.

THOMAS H. LEGRAND & NATHAN M. BERRY NO. 34
State of South Carolina

Pickens District) By W. L. Keith Clerk of the Court and by virtue of office Commissioner of Location for Pickens District in the State aforesaid; To any lawful Surveyor you are hereby authorized to lay out and admeasure a tract of land unto Thomas H. Legrand and Nathan M. Berry not exceeding ten thousand acres, observing the Surveyor Generals instructions in laying out the same and a true plat thereof return into my office within two months from the date hereof. Given under my hand and seal this 21st day of July Anno Domini 1842.

W. L. Keith (SEAL) C. C. & C. L. P. D.
Executed of the within warrant 82 acres July 22, 1842.
M. MCay D. S.
Certified Sept. 13, 1842.

ISAAC BALDWIN NO. 30
State of South Carolina

Pickens District) By W. L. Keith Clerk of the Court and by virtue of office Commissioner of Location for the District aforesaid. To any lawful Surveyor you are hereby authorized to lay out and admeasure a tract of land unto Isaac Baldwin not exceeding ten thousand acres observing the Surveyor Generals instructions in laying out the same and a true plat thereof make and return into my office within two months from the date hereof. Given under my hand and Seal this 2nd April Anno Domini 1842.

W. L. Keith (LS) C. L. P. D.
Executed of the within warrant 27 acres May 11, 1842.
Martin MCay D. S.

Recorded May 13, 1842.

JESSE P. LODEN NO. 156
State of South Carolina

Pickens District) By W. L. Keith Clerk of the Court and by virtue of office Commissioner of Location for said District. To any lawful Surveyor you are hereby authorized to lay out and admeasure unto Jesse P. Loden a tract of land not exceeding ten thousand acres observing the Surveyor Generals instructions in laying out the same and a true Plat of the same return into my office within two months from the date hereof. Given under my hand and seal this 6th day of Octr. 1852.

W. L. Keith (SEAL) C. C. & C. L. P. D.
Executed of the within warrant 600 acres Oct. 9, 1852.
T. B. Mauldin D. S.

Certified Nov. 5, 1852.

JOSHUA HERRIN NO NUMBER
State of South Carolina
 Pickens District) By W. L. Keith Clerk of the Court and by virtue of office Commissioner of Location in and for the District aforesaid. To any lawful Surveyor you are hereby authorized to lay out and admeasure unto Joshua Herrin a tract of land not exceeding one thousand acres observing the Surveyor Generals instructions in laying out the same and a true plat thereof return into my office within two months from the date hereof.
 Given under my hand and seal this 4th day of Septr. 1848.
W. L. Keith (SEAL) C. C. & C. L. P. D.
 Executed of the within warrant 846 acres Oct. 13, 1848.
Tyre B. Mauldin D. S.

EBENEZER P. VERNER NO. 155
State of South Carolina
 Pickens District) By Wm. L. Keith Clerk of the court and by virtue of office Commissioner of Locations in and for the said district. To any lawful Surveyor. You are hereby authorized to lay out and admeasure unto Ebenezer P. Verner a tract of land not exceeding ten thousand acres, observing the Surveyor Generals instructions in laying out the same and a true plat of the same return into my office within two months from the date hereof. Given under my hand and seal this 20th day of December Anno Domini 1847?
W. L. Keith (SEAL) C. L. P. D.
 Recorded Sept. 29, 1852.

ELLEANOR PATTERSON NO. 101
The State of South Carolina
 Pickens District) By W. L. Keith Clerk of the Court and by virtue of office Commissioner of Location in and for the said District. To any lawful Surveyor you are hereby commanded and requested to admeasure and lay out unto Elleanor Patterson a tract of land not exceeding ten thousand acres, observing the Surveyor Generals instructions in laying out the same and a true plat thereof returned into my office within two months from the date hereof.
 Given under my hand & seal this 11th of March 1848.
W. L. Keith (SEAL) C. L. P. D.
 Received of the within warrant 351 acres March 16, 1848.
John Bowen D. S.
 Certified April 3, 1848.

JAMES W. HARRISON NO. 68
State of South Carolina
 Pickens District) By W. L. Keith Clerk of the Court and by virtue of office Commissioner of Location in and for the District of Pickens in the said State aforesaid. To any lawful Surveyor you are hereby authorized to lay out and admeasure unto James W. Harrison a tract of land not exceeding ten thousand acres, observing the Surveyor Generals instructions in laying out the same and a true plat of the same return into my office within two months from the date hereof the above warrant is for the purpose of surveying several tracts

of land that lies adjoining and having the same regranted all in the same grant. Given under my hand and seal 22nd April 1844.

           W. L. Keith (SEAL) C. L. P. D.

Executed part of the within warrant April 30, 1844.

              Robt. Fullerton D. S.

Certified May 18, 1845.

MAJOR ANDREW HAMILTON NO. 64
State of South Carolina

  Pickens District) By W. L. Keith Clerk of the Court and by virtue of office Commissioner of Location in and for the District aforesaid. To any lawful Surveyor you are hereby authorized to lay out and admeasure unto Maj. Andrew Hamilton a tract of land not exceeding ten thousand acres, observing the Surveyor Generals instructions in laying out the same and a true plat of the same return into my office within two months from the date hereof.

  Given under my hand and seal this 4th day of March A. D. 1844.

           W. L. Keith (LS) C. L. P. D.

Received of the within warrant 1400 acres of land April 6, 1844.

              John Bowen D. S.

Certified April 16, 1844.

EVAN NICHOLSON NO. 103
State of South Carolina

  Pickens District) By W. L. Keith Clerk of the Court and by virtue of office Commissioner of Location in and for the District aforesaid. To any lawful Surveyor you are hereby authorized to lay out and admeasure unto Evan Nicholson a tract of land not exceeding one thousand acres observing the Surveyor Generals instructions in laying out the same and a true plat thereof return into my office within two months from the date hereof. Given under my hand and seal this 4 day of Septr. 1848.

           W. L. Keith (SEAL) C. C. LP. D.

Executed the within warrant 316 acres Oct. 13, 1848.

             Tyre B. Mauldin D. S.

Certified Oct. 24, 1848.

JOHN C. CALHOUN NO. 18
State of South Carolina

  Pickens District) By W. L. Keith Clerk of the Court and by virtue of office Commissioner of Location for Pickens District. To any lawful Surveyor you are hereby authorized to admeasure and lay out unto John C. Calhoun a tract of land not exceeding ten thousand acres observing the Surveyor Generals instructions in laying out the same and a true Plat thereof return into my office within two months from this date. Given under my hand and seal this 28 day of Nov. 1841.

           W. L. Keith (SEAL) C. L. P. D.

Executed of the within warrant 791 acres. Nov. 30th 1841.

             Martin MCay D. S.

Recorded Jan. 5, 1842.

T. C. CARSON NO. 178
State of South Carolina

Pickens District) By W. L. Keith Clerk of the Court and by virtue of office Commissioner of Location in and for the District aforesaid. To any lawful Surveyor you are hereby authorized to lay out and admeasure unto T. C. Carson a tract of land not exceeding ten thousand acres, observing the Surveyor Generals instructions in laying out the same and a true plat thereof return into my office within two months from the date hereof, the above warrant is for the purpose of regranting several tracts and parts of tracts, and such pieces of Vacant lands that may be adjoining the same. Given under my hand and seal this 10th day of May Anno Domini 1853.

W. L. Keith (SEAL) C. C. C. L. P. D.

Certified July 8, 1853.

ELAM SHARP NO. 164
State of South Carolina

Pickens District) By W. L. Keith Clerk of the Court and by virtue of office Commissioner of Location for the District aforesaid. To any lawful Surveyor you are hereby authorized to lay out and admeasure unto Elam Sharp a tract of land not exceeding ten thousand acres observing the Surveyor Generals instructions in laying out the same and a true plat thereof return into my office within two months from the date hereof. The above warrant is for the purpose of regranting several tracts of land and such vacant lands as may be adjoining the same. Given under my hand and seal this 22d day of January A. D. 1853.

W. L. Keith (SEAL) C. C. & C. L. P. D.

Executed the within warrant 2735 acres Jan. 22, 1853.

M. MCay D. S.

Certified March 19, 1853.

TYRE B. MAULDIN NO. 165
South Carolina

Pickens District) By William L. Keith Esqr Clerk of the Court & By virtue of Office Commissioner of Locations for Pickens District. To any Lawful surveyor you are hereby authorized to Lay out unto Tyre B. Mauldin a tract of land not exceeding one thousand acres observing the Surveyor Generals instructions in Laying out the same and a true plat thereof make and return into my office within two months from the date hereof. Given under my hand & seal this 20th day of November 1852.

W. L. Keith (SEAL) C. C. & C. L. P. D.

Executed of the within warrant 82 acres Nov. 23, 1852.

Tyre B. Mauldin D. S.

Certified March 17, 1853.

SAMUEL E. MAXWELL NO. 162
South Carolina

Pickens District) By W. L. Keith Clerk of the Court & Ex off Commissioner of Locations for Pickens District. To any lawful surveyor of said District you are hereby authorized and required to admeasure and lay out unto Samuel E.

Maxwell a tract of land not exceeding ten thousand acres observing the Suryevor Generals instructions in laying out the same and a true plat thereof return into my office within two months from this date. Given under my hand and seal this 15th day of February 1853.
        W. L. Keith (LS) C. C. & C. L. P. D.
 Executed of the within warrant 344 acres Feb. 16, 1853.
             M. MCay D. S.
 Certified Feb. 24, 1853.

JOHN GRISSOP NO. 158
South Carolina
 Pickens District) By William L. Keith Clerk of the Court & by virtue of Office Commissioner of Locations for Pickens District. To any lawful surveyor you are hereby authorized to lay out unto John Grissop a tract of land not exceeding one thousand acres observing the Surveyor Generals instructions in laying out the same and a true plat thereof make and return into my office within two months from the date hereof. Given under my hand & seal this 1st day of October 1852.
        W. L. Keith (SEAL) C. C. & C. L. P. D.
 Executed the within warrant 23 acres Oct. 2, 1852.
            T. B. Mauldin D. S.
 Certified Nov. 20, 1852.

DELILAH M. LEWIS NO. 83
State of South Carolina
 Pickens District) By William L. Keith Clerk of the Court and by virtue of office Commissioner of Location for said District. To any Lawful Surveyor you are hereby authorized and commanded to lay out and admeasure unto Delilah M? Lewis a tract of land not exceeding ten thousand acres observing the Surveyor Generals instructions in laying out the same and a true plat thereof return to my office within two months from this date. Given under my hand and seal this 6th day of June AD 1845.
        W. L. Keith (SEAL) C. C. & C. L. P. D.
 Executed an island in Keowee River containing 2 acres Aug. 6, 1845.
           John O. Grisham D. S.
 Certified Sept. 1, 1845.

WM. VAN WYCK NO. 171
State of South Carolina
 Pickens District) By W. L. Keith Clerk of the Court and by virtue of office Commissioner of Location for the District aforesaid. To any lawful surveyor you are hereby authorized to lay out and admeasure unto William Van Wyck a tract of land not exceeding ten thousand acres observing the Surveyor Generals instructions in laying out the same and a true plat thereof return into my office within two months the date hereof the above warrant is for the purpose of having certain lands regranted.
 Given under my hand and seal this 11th day of June AD 1853.
        W. L. Keith (SEAL) C. C. & C. L. P. D.

Executed on the within warrant 130 acres June 29, 1853.
Thomas D. Garvin D. S.
Certified July 8, 1853.

SAMUEL ALBERTSON NO. 145
South Carolina

Pickens District) By William L. Keith Clerk of the Court & by virtue of office Commissioner of Location for Pickens District. To any lawful Surveyor you are hereby authorized to lay out unto Samuel Albertson a tract of Land not exceeding one thousand acres observing the Surveyor Generals instructions in laying out the same and a true plat thereof make and return into my office within two months from the date hereof. Given under my hand and seal this 25th August 1851.
W. L. Keith (SEAL) C. L. P. D.

Executed of the within 19 acres Sept. 13, 1851.
Certified Oct. 25, 1851.

TYRE B. MAULDIN NO. 84
State of South Carolina

Pickens Dist.) By William L. Keith Clerk of the Court and by virtue of office Commissioner of Location in and for said District. To any lawful Surveyor you are hereby authorized to lay out and admeasure unto Tyre B. Mauldin a Tract of Land whereon Joseph Barton now lives for the purpose of obtaining a new grant and also vacant land not exceeding ten thousand acres observing the Surveyors Generals instructions in laying out the same and a true plat thereof return into my office within two months from the date hereof. Given under my hand & Seal this the 13 Oct. Anno Domini 1845.
W. L. Keith (SEAL) C. L. P. D.

Certified Oct. 29, 1845.

SAMUEL ALBERTSON NO. 146
South Carolina

Pickens District) By William L. Keith Clerk of the Court and by virtue of office Commissioner of Locations for Pickens District. To any lawful Surveyor you are hereby authorized to Lay out unto Samuel Albertson a tract of land not exceeding one thousand acres observing the Surveyor Generals instructions in laying out the same and a true plat thereof make and return into my office within two months from the date hereof. Given under my hand & seal this 25th August 1851.
W. L. Keith (SEAL) C. L. P. D.

Executed 82 acres Sept. 12, 1851.
Certified Oct. 25, 1851.

SPENCER CHAMBERS NO. 66
State of South Carolina

Pickens District) By W. L. Keith Clerk of the Court and by virtueofoffice Commissioner of Location in and for the District aforesaid. To any lawful Surveyor you are hereby authorized to lay out and admeasure unto Spencer

Chambers a tract of Land not exceeding ten thousand acres, observing the Surveyor Generals instructions in laying out the same and a true plat of the same return into my office within two months from the date hereof.

Given under my hand & seal this 13 March Anno Domini 1844.

W. L. Keith (LS) C. L. P. D.

Executed part of the within warrant May 7, 1844.

Robt. Fullerton D. S.

Certified May 18, 1844.

JOHN HAMMETT NO. 32
State of South Carolina

Pickens District) By W. L. Keith Clerk of the Court and by virtue of office Commissioner of Location in and for the District aforesaid. To any lawful Surveyor you are hereby authorized to lay out and admeasure unto John Hammett a tract of land not exceeding ten thousand acres observing the Surveyor Generals instructions in laying out the same and a true plat thereof return into my office within two months from this date. The above warrant is taken for the purpose of runing round a part of a tract I purchased of P. Kelly and to take in a small piece of vacant land lying joining the same to have a new grant for the same. Given under my hand & seal this 3d day of June 1842.

W. L. Keith (LS) C. L. P. D.

Executed 44 acres on branches of waters of Little River June 10, 1842.

John O. Grisham D. S.

Certified July 19, 1842.

JOSEPH V. SHANKLIN NO. 110
State of South Carolina

Pickens District) By W. L. Keith Clerk of the Court and by virtue of office Commissioner of Location in and for the District aforesaid. To any lawful Surveyor you are hereby authorized to lay out and admeasure unto Joseph V. Shanklin a tract of land not exceeding ten thousand acres, observing the Surveyor Generals instructions in laying out the same and a true plat thereof return into my office within two months from the date hereof.

Given under my hand and seal this 4th day of Septr. Anno Domini 1849.

W. L. Keith (SEAL) C. L. P. D.

Executed 640 acres Oct. 5, 1849.

M. MCay D. S.

Certified Oct. 30, 1849.

EBENEZER P. VERNER NO. 98
State of South Carolina

Pickens District) By W. L. Keith Clerk of the Court and by virtue of office Commissioner of Location in and for the District aforesaid. To any lawful Surveyor. You are hereby authorized to lay out and admeasure unto Ebenezer P. Verner a tract of land not exceeding ten thousand acres, observing the Surveyor Generals instructions in laying out the same and a true plat of the same return into my office within two months from the date hereof.

Given under my hand and seal this 22nd day of September Anno Domini 1847.

            W. L. Keith (SEAL) C. L. P. D.

Executed part of the within warrant Sept. 24, 1847.

                Robt. Fullerton D. S.

Certified Nov. 2, 1847.

MILES M. NORTON NO. 97
State of South Carolina

Pickens District) By W. L. Keith Clerk of the Court & Ex officio Commissioner of Location for the District aforesaid. To any lawful Surveyor you are hereby authorized to lay out and admeasure unto Miles M. Norton a tract of Land not exceeding ten thousand acres, observing the Surveyor Generals instructions in laying out the same and a true plat thereof make and return into my office within two months hereof.

Given under my hand and Seal this 17th day of August 1847.

            W. L. Keith (SEAL) C. L. P. D.

Executed 48 acres Aug. 18, 1847.

                Tyre B. Mauldin D. S.

Certified Aug. 20, 1847.

BRYAN FRETWELL NO. 69
South Carolina

Pickens District) By W. L. Keith Clerk of the Court and by virtue of office Commissioner of Location in and for the said District. To any lawful Surveyor you are hereby authorized to lay out and admeasure unto Bryan Fretwell a tract of land not exceeding ten thousand acres observing the Surveyor Generals instructions in laying out the same and a true plat of the same return into my office within two months from the date hereof. Given under my hand and seal this 16th day of May Anno Domini 1844.

            W. L. Keith (SEAL) C. L. P. D.

Certified June 10, 1844.

BENNETT HYDE NO. 78
State of South Carolina

Pickens District) By W. L. Keith Clerk of the Court and by virtue of office Commissioner of Location in and for the District aforesaid. To any lawful Surveyor you are hereby authorized to lay out and admeasure unto Bennett Hyde a tract of land not exceeding ten thousand acres observing the Surveyor Generals instructions in laying out the same and a true plat thereof return into my office within two months from the date hereof. Given under my hand and seal this 8 Feby. 1845.

            W. L. Keith (SEAL) C. L. P. D.

Executed the within warrant 69 acres Feb. 18, 1845.

                M. MCay D. S.

Certified April 1, 1845.

SAMUEL MOSELEY NO. 77
South Carolina

Pickens District) By W. L. Keith Clerk of the Court and by virtue of office Commissioner of locations for sd. district. To any lawful Surveyor you are hereby required to admeasure and lay out unto Saml. Mosley Esq. a tract of land not exceeding ten thousand acres observing the surveyor generals instructions in laying out the same and a true plat thereof return into my office within two months from the date hereof. Given under my hand & seal this 27th day of January 1845.

W. L. Keith (SEAL) C. C. & C. L. P. D.

Certified April 1, 1845.

BIRD W. ABBOTT NO. 123
South Carolina

Pickens District) By William L. Keith Clerk of the Court and by virtue of office Commissioner of Locations for Pickens District. To any lawful Surveyor you are hereby authorized to lay out and admeasure unto Bird W. Abbott a tract of land not exceeding one thousand acres observing the Surveyor Generals instructions in laying out the same and a true plat thereof make and return into my office within two months from the date hereof. Given under my hand & seal this 10th day of Feby. 1850.

W. L. Keith (SEAL) C. L. P. D.

Executed of the within warrant 13 acres Feb. 10, 1850.

Tyre B. Mauldin D. S.

Certified March 18, 1850.

THOMAS HALLUM NO. 112
State of South Carolina

Pickens District) By W. L. Keith Clerk of the Court and by virtue of office Commissioner of Location for the District aforesaid. To any lawful Surveyor you are hereby authorized to lay out and admeasure unto Thomas Hallum a tract of land not exceeding ten thousand acres observing the Surveyor Generals instructions in laying out the same and a true plat of the same return into my office within two months from the date hereof. Given under my hand and seal this 3rd day of Septr. 1849.

W. L. Keith (SEAL) C. L. P. D.

Received of the within warrant 950 acres Sept. 26, 1849.

John Bowen D. S.

Certified Oct. 30, 1849.

ABRAHAM MEREDITH NO. 76
State of South Carolina

Pickens District) By W. L. Keith Clerk of the Court and by virtue of office Commissioner of Location in and for the District aforesaid. To any lawful Surveyor you are hereby authorized to lay out and admeasure unto Abraham Meredith a tract of land not exceeding ten thousand acres observing the Surveyor Generals instructions in laying out the same and a true plat hereof.

Given under my hand and seal this 28th March, 1845.
                                    W. L. Keith (SEAL) C. L. P. D.
Executed the within warrant 226 acres March 29, 1845.
                                                M. MCay D. S.
Certified April 1, 1845.

WILLIAM CANTRELL NO. 99
State of South Carolina

Pickens District) By W. L. Keith Clerk of the Court and by virtue of office Commissioner of Location for said District. To any lawful Surveyor you are hereby authorized to lay out and admeasure unto William Cantrell a tract of land not exceeding ten thousand acres observing the Surveyors instructions in laying out the same and a true plat thereof return into my office within two months from the date hereof. Given under my hand and seal this 2nd Nov. 1847.
                                    W. L. Keith (SEAL) C. L. P. D.
Executed the within warrant 85¼ acres Nov. 4, 1847.
                                            Alexander Edens D. S.
Certified Nov. 4, 1847.

STEPHEN BALDWIN NO. 108
State of South Carolina

Pickens District) By W. L. Keith Clerk of the Court and by virtue of office Commissioner of Location in and for the district aforesaid. To any lawful Surveyor you are hereby authorized to lay out and admeasure unto Stephen Baldwin a tract of land not exceeding one thousand acres, observing the Surveyor Generals instructions in laying out the same, and a true plat of the same return into my office within two months from the date hereof.
Given under my hand and seal this 2nd day of July Anno Domini 1849.
                                    W. L. Keith (SEAL) C. L. P. D.
Executed part of the within warrant the 9th July 1849.
                                                Robt. Fullerton D. S.
Certified August 5, 1849.

JOEL MASON NO. 96
State of South Carolina

Pickens District) By Wm. L. Keith Clerk of the Court and by virtue of office Commissioner of Location in and for the District aforesaid. To any lawful Surveyor you are hereby authorized to lay out and admeasure unto Joel Mason a tract of land not exceeding ten thousand acres observing the Surveyor Generals instructions in laying out the same and a true plat of the same return into my office within two months from the date hereof. Given under my hand and seal this 24th day of July A. D. 1847.
                                    W. L. Keith (SEAL) C. L. P. D.
Executed part of the within warrant July 26, 1847.
                                                Robt. Fullerton D. S.
Certified Aug. 5, 1847.

GEORGE SIMS NO. 100
State of South Carolina

Pickens District) By W. L. Keith Clerk of the Court and by virtue of office Commissioner of Location for said District. To any lawful Surveyor you are hereby authorized to lay out and admeasure unto George Sims a tract of land not exceeding ten thousand acres observing the Surveyor Generals instructions in laying out the same and a true plat thereof return into my office within two months from the date hereof. Given under my hand & seal this 24 day of Jany. 1848.

W. L. Keith (SEAL) C. L. P. D.

Executed the within warrant 251 acres the 4th Feb. 1848.

Tyre B. Mauldin Dep. Sur.

Certified March 6, 1848.

DR. F. W. SYMMES NO. 75
State of South Carolina

Pickens District) By W. L. Keith Clerk of the Court and by virtue of office Commissioner of Location in and for the District aforesaid. To any lawful Surveyor you are hereby authorized to lay out and admeasure unto Dr. F. W. Symmes a tract of land not exceeding ten thousand acres observing the Suryevor Generals instructions in laying out the same and a true plat thereof return into my office within two months from the date hereof, the above warrant is for the special purpose of regranting several tracts of land adjoining and vacant land. Given under my hand and seal this 6th Novr. Anno Domini 1844.

W. L. Keith (SEAL) C. L. P. D.

Executed on the within warrant 839 acres Nov. 9, 1844.

T. D. Garvin D. S.

Certified Jan. 6, 1845.

EDWARD RANKINS NO. 74
State of South Carolina

Pickens District) By W. L. Keith Clerk of the Court and by virtue of office Commissioner of Location in and for the District aforesaid. To any lawful Surveyor you are hereby authorized to lay out and admeasure unto Edward Rankins a tract of land not exceeding ten thousand acres observing the Surveyor Generals instructions in laying out the same and a true plat of the same return into my office within two months from the date hereof. The above warrant is for the purpose of having several tracts of land lying on Oconey Creek and its branches whereon I now live surveyed and regranted and such vacant land as may be adjoining the same.

Given under my hand and seal this 11 day of Decr. Anno Domini 1844.

W. L. Keith (SEAL) C. L. P. D.

Executed Dec. 13, 1844 2,026 acres for the within.

John O. Grisham.

Certified Jan. 6, 1845.

JAMES A. NEVELL NO. 71
State of South Carolina

Pickens District) By W. L. Keith Clerk of the Court and by virtue of office Commissioner of Location in and for the District aforesaid. To any lawful Surveyor you are hereby authorized to lay out and admeasure unto James A. Nevell a tract of land not exceeding ten thousand acres observing the Surveyor Generals instructions in laying out the same and a true plat thereof return into my office within two months from the date hereof. The above warrant is for the purpose of regranting a certain tract of land lying on the South fork of Cane Creek and such vacant land that may be adjoining the same. Given under my hand and seal this 7th day of October A. D. 1844.

W. L. Keith (SEAL) C. L. P. D.

Executed Oct. 9, 1844 one thousand 150 acres.

John O. Grisham.

Certified Oct. 22, 1844.

MILTON R. HUNNICUT NO. 37
State of South Carolina

Pickens Dist.) By William L. Keith Clerk of the Court and by virtue of office Commissioner of Location in and for the Dist. aforesaid. To any lawful Surveyor you are hereby authorized to lay out and admeasure unto Milton R. Hunnicut a tract of land originally granted to E. Young and vacant land adjoining not exceeding ten thousand acres observing the Survey Genl. instructions in laying out the same and a true plat thereof return into my office within two months from the date hereof. Given under my hand & Seal this Eleventh day of Oct. 1842.

W. L. Keith (SEAL) C. L. P. D.

Executed 292 acres Oct. 13, 1842.

John O. Grisham D. S.

Certified Oct. 18, 1842.

JOHN GRAVELEY JR. NO. 154
State of South Carolina

Pickens District) I W. L. Keeith Clerk of the Court & by virtue of office Commissioner of Location for the District aforesaid. To any lawful Surveyor you are hereby authorized to lay out and admeasure unto John Graveley Jr. a tract of land not exceeding ten thousand acres observing the Surveyor Generals instructions in laying out the same and a true plat of the same return into my office within two months from the date hereof. Given under my hand and seal this 26 Augt. A. D. 1852.

W. L. Keith (SEAL) C. C. & C. L. P. D.

Executed of the within 220 acres Sept. 20, 1852.

Alexander Edens D. Sur.

Certified Sept. 27, 1852.

ALEANDER E. RAMSEY NO. 67
State of South Carolina

Pickens District) By W. L. Keith Vlerk of the Court and by virtue of office

Commissioner of Location for Pickens District. To any lawful Surveyor you are hereby authorized to lay out and admeasure unto Alexander E. Ramsey a tract of land not exceeding ten thousand acres observing the Surveyor Generals instructions in laying out the same and a true plat of the same return into my office within two months from the date hereof the above warrant is for the purpose of regranting several tracts and taking in all vacant land adjoining. Given under my hand and seal this 14th day of May Anno Domini 1844.

        W. L. Keith (SEAL) C. L. P. D.

 Executed 865 acres May 15, 1844.

          John O. Grisham D. S.

 Certified May 20, 1844.

BIRD W. ABBOTT NO. 123
South Carolina

 Pickens District) By William L. Keith Clerk of Court and by virtue of office commissioner of Locations for Pickens District. To any Lawful surveyor you are hereby authorized to lay out unto Bird W. Abbott a tract of land not exceeding one thousand acres, Observing the surveyor generals instructions in laying out the same and a true Plat thereof make and return to my office within two months from the date thereof. Given under my hand and seal the 10th day of Febry. 1850.

        W. L. Keith (SEAL) C. S. P. D.

 Certified 18th March 1850.

JOHN JACKSON HOWARD NO. 80
State of South Carolina

 Pickens District) By William L. Keith Clerk of the Court and Commissioner of Locations for the said District. To any lawful Surveyor you are hereby authorized and commanded to lay out and admeasure a tract of land unto John Jackson Howard whereon his father now lives all other tracts adjoining for the purpose of obtaining a regrant and vacant land adjoining, not exceeding ten thousand acres observing the Surveyor Generals instructions and a true plat of the same return into my office within two months from this date. Given under my hand and seal this the 17th day July 1845.

        William L. Keith C. C. & C. L. P. D.

 Executed for the within 350 acres July 17, 1845.

          John O. Grisham D. S.

 Certified July 25, 1845.

WILLIAM STEELE NO. 153
South Carolina

 Pickens District) By Wm. L. Keith Clerk of the Court and by virtue of office Commissioner of Locations for Pickens District. To any lawful Surveyor you are hereby authorized to lay out unto Wm. Steele a tract of land not exceeding one thousand acres observing the Surveyor Generals instructions in laying out the same and a true plat thereof make and return into my office within two months from the date hereof. Given under my hand and seal this 8th day of September 1852.

        W. L. Keith (SEAL) C. L. P. D.

Executed of the within 214 acres Sept. 13, 1852.

            Tyre B. Mauldin D. S.

Certified Sept. 18, 1852.

A. TODD AND A. B. SEARGENT NO. 150
State of South Carolina

Pickens District) By W. L. Keith Clerk of the Court and by virtue of office Commissioner of Locations for said District. To any lawful Surveyor you are hereby authorized to lay out and admeasure unto A. Todd and A. B. Seargent a tract of land not exceeding one thousand acres observing the Surveyor Generals instructions in laying out the same and a true plat of the same return into my office within two months from the date hereof.

Given under my hand and seal this 29th day of Octr. A. D. 1852.

      W. L. Keith (SEAL) C. C. & C. L. P. D.

Executed the within 59 acres Dec. 15, 1851.

        Tyre B. Mauldin DEPUTY SUR.

Certified Decr. 26, 1852.

WILLIAM BOATWRIGHT NO. 86
State of South Carolina

Pickens District) By W. L. Keith Clerk of the Court and by virtue of office Commissioner of Location in and for the District aforesaid. To any lawful Surveyor you are hereby authorized to lay out and admeasure unto William Boatwright a tract of land not exceeding ten thousand acres observing the Surveyor Generals instructions in laying out the same and a true plat thereof return into my office within two months from the date hereof.

Given under my hand and seal this 6 day of Nov. A. D. 1845.

        W. L. Keith (SEAL) C. L. P. D.

Executed the within warrant 552 acres Dec. 3, 1845.

            M. MCay D. S.

Certified Dec. 19, 1845.

JOHN MAXWELL NO. 53
State of South Carolina

Pickens District) I W. L. Keith Clerk of the Court and by virtue of office Commissioner of Location for said District. To any lawful Surveyor you are hereby authorized to lay out and admeasure unto John Maxwell a tract of land not exceeding ten thousand acres observing the Surveyor Generals instructions in laying out the same and a true plat thereof return into my office within two months from the date hereof. Given under my hand and seal this 27 day of Febry. 1843.

        W. L. Keith (SEAL) C. L. P. D.

Executed of the within warrant 1000 acres April 22, 1843.

            M. MCay D. S.

Certified April 23, 1843.

WILLIAM D. STEELE & EPHRAIM COBB NO. 54
The State of South Carolina

Pickens District) By W. L. Keith Clerk of the Court and by virtue of office Commissioner of Location in and for the said District. To any lawful Surveyor you are hereby authorized to lay out and admeasure unto William D. Steele Esqr. and Ephrian Cobb a tract of land not exceeding ten thousand acres observing the Surveyor Generals instructions in laying out the same and a true plat of the same return into my office within two months from the date hereof. Given under my hand and seal this 15th day of May Anno Domini 1843.

W. L. Keith (SEAL) C. L. P. D.

Executed 1065 acres on Bone Camp Creek May 17, 1843.

John O. Grisham D. S.

Certified May 22, 1843.

MRS. MARTHA LAWRENCE NO. 59
State of South Carolina

Pickens District) By W. L. Keith Clerk of the Court and by virtue of office Commissioner of Location in and for the District aforesaid. To any lawful Surveyor you are hereby authorized to lay out and admeasure unto Mrs. Martha Lawrence a tract of land not exceeding ten thousand acres observing the Surveyor Generals instructions in laying out the same and a true plat thereof return into my office within two months from the date hereof.

Given under my hand and seal this 8th day of January A. D. 1844.

W. L. Keith (LS) C. L. P. D.

Executed 67 acres Jan. 19, 1844.

John O. Grisham D. S.

Certified Feb. 4, 1844.

NIMROD LEATHERS NO. 58
State of South Carolina

Pickens District) By W. L. Keith Clerk of the Court and by virtue of office Commissioner of Location in and for said District. To any lawful Surveyor you are hereby authorized to lay out and admeasure unto Nimrod Leathers Senr. a tract of land not exceeding ten thousand acres observing the Surveyor Generals instructions in laying out the same and a true plat thereof return into my office within two months from the date hereof. Given under my hand and seal this 5 day of December Anno Domini 1843.

W. L. Keith (SEAL) C. L. P. D.

Executed the within warrant 134 acres Dec. 23, 1843.

Martin MCay D. S.

Certified Jan. 22, 1844.

CAPT. JOHN W. SMITH NO. 57
State of South Carolina

Pickens District) By W. L. Keith Clerk of the Court and by virtue of office Commissioner of Location for the District aforesaid. To any lawful Surveyor you are hereby authorized to lay out and admeasure unto Capt. John W. Smith a tract of land not exceeding ten thousand acres observing the Surveyor Generals instructions in laying out the same and a true plat thereof return into my office within two months from the date hereof. Given under my hand & seal this 20th Nov. Anno Domini 1843.

           W. L. Keith (SEAL) C. L. P. D.
 Received of the within warrant 640 acres Nov. 23, 1843.
                John Bowen D. S.
 Certified Jan. 17, 1844.

SAMUEL A. MAVERICK NO. 55
State of South Carolina

 Pickens District) By William L. Keith Clerk of the Court and by virtue of office Commissioner of Location in and for the District aforesaid. To any Lawful Surveyor you are hereby authorized and commanded to lay out and admeasure unto Samuel Augustus Maverick a tract of land not exceeding ten thousand acres observing the Surveyor Generals instructions in laying out the same and a true plat thereof return into my office within two months from this date. Given under my hand and seal this the twenty first day of October in the year of our Lord 1843.

           W. L. Keith (SEAL) C. L. P. D.
 Executed of the within warrant 565 acres Oct. 28, 1843.
                Martin MCay D. S.
 Certified Nov. 4, 1843.

WILLIAM W. LEATHERS NO. 60
State of South Carolina

 Pickens District) I William L. Keith Clerk of the Court and by virtue of office Commissioner of Location for Pickens District. To any lawful surveyor you are hereby authorized and commanded to lay out and admeasure unto William W. Leathers a tract of land not exceeding ten thousand acres and a true plat thereof return to my office within two months from this date. Given under my hand and seal this 31st October AD 1843.

           W. L. Keith (SEAL) C. L. P. D.
 Executed the within warrant 29 acres the 23rd Dec. 1843.
                Martin MCay D. S.
 Certified Dec. 25, 1843.

SAMUEL MAVERICK NO. 61
The State of South Carolina

 Pickens District) By William L. Keith Clerk of the Court and by virtue of office Commissioner of Location in and for the District aforesaid. To any lawful Surveyor you are hereby authorized and command to lay out and admeasure unto Samuel Maverick a tract of land not exceeding ten thousand acres and a true plat thereof return into my office within two months from this date.

Given under my hand and seal this the twenty first day of January the year of our Lord 1844.
W. L. Keith (SEAL) C. L. P. D.

Executed the within warrant 680 acres Feb. 4, 1844.
Martin MCay D. S.

Certified Feb. 12, 1844.

ABRAHAM MERADITH NO. 62
State of South Carolina

Pickens District) By W. L. Keith Clerk of the Court and by virtue of office Commissioner of Location in and for the District aforesaid. To any lawful Surveyor you are hereby authorized to lay out and admeasure unto Abraham Meradith a tract of Land not exceeding ten thousand acres observing the Surveyor Generals instructions in laying out the same and a true plat thereof return into my office within two months from the date hereof.

Given under my hand and seal this 1st day of January A. D. 1844.
W. L. Keith (LS) C. L. P. D.

Executed the within warrant 838 acres Feb. 15, 1844.
Martin MCay

JOHN R. M. CANNON NO. 122
South Carolina

Pickens District) By Wm. L. Keith Clerk of the Court and by virtue of office commissioner of Locations for Pickens District. To any lawful surveyor you are hereby authorized to lay out unto John R. M. Cannon a tract of land not exceeding one thousand acres observing the Surveyor Generals instructions in laying out the same and a true plat thereof make and return into my office within two months from the date hereof. Given under my hand and seal this 1st day of March 1850.
W. L. Keith (SEAL) C. L. P. D.

Executed the within warrant 215 acres the 9th March 1850.
Tyre B. Mauldin Dep. Sur.

Certified March 18, 1850.

WILLIAM CAPE NO. 140
State of South Carolina

Pickens District) By W. L. Keith Clerk of the Court and by virtue of office Commissioner of Locations in and for the District aforesaid. To any lawful Surveyor you are hereby authorized to lay out and admeasure unto William Cape a tract of land not exceeding ten thousand acres, observing the Surveyor Generals instructions in laying out the same, and a true plat of the same return into my office within two months from the date hereof. Given under my hand and seal this 8th day of April Anno Domini 1851.
W. L. Keith (SEAL) C. L. P. D.

Executed part of the within warrant April 14, 1851.
Robt. Fullerton D. S.

Certified May 19, 1851.

DAVID CHERRY NO NUMBER
State of South Carolina

Pickens District) By W. L. Keith Clerk of the Court and by virtue of office Commissioner of Location for said District. To any lawful Surveyor you are hereby authorized to lay out and admeasure a tract of land unto David Cherry not exceeding ten thousand acres observing the Surveyor Generals instructions in laying out the same and a true plat thereof return unto my office within two months from the date hereof. Given under my hand and seal this 24th day of June Anno Domini 1841.

W. L. Keith (LS) C. L. P. D.

"LAND WARRANTS," PACK. 114
CLERK OF COURTS OFFICE, PICKENS, S. C.

STEPHEN BALDWIN NO. 48
State of South Carolina

Pickens District) By W. L. Keith Clerk of the Court and by virtue of office commissioner of location for said district to any lawful surveyor you are hereby authorized to lay out and admeasure unto Stephen Baldwin a tract of land not exceeding ten thousand acres observing the Surveyor Generals instructions in laying out the same and a true plat thereof return into my office within two months from the date hereof. Given under my hand and seal this 14th Jany 1843.

W. L. Keith (SEAL) C. L. P. D.

Executed the within warrant 136 acres Jany 25, 1843.

Martin MCay D. S.

Certified March 9, 1843. W. L. Keith.

E. D. HOLLAND NO. 88
State of South Carolina

Pickens District) By W. L. Keith Clerk of the Court and by virtue of office Commissioner of Location of in and for the District aforesaid. To any lawful Surveyor you are hereby authorized to lay out and admeasure unto E. D. Holland a tract of land not exceeding ten thousand acres observing the Surveyor Generals instructions in laying out the same and a true plat of the same return into my office within two months from the date hereof.

Given under my hand & seal this 17th Decr. 1845.

W. L. Keith (LS) C. L. P. D.

Executed of the within warrant 41 acres Decr. 22, 1845.

M. MCay D. S.

Certified Decr. 27, 1845. W. L. Keith.

REVD. JOHN BURDINE NO. 89
State of South Carolina

Pickens District) By W. L. Keith Clerk of the Court and by virtue of office Commissioner of Locations in and for the District aforesaid. To any lawful Surveyor you are hereby authorized to lay out and admeasure unto Revd. John Burdine a tract of land not exceeding ten thousand acres observing the Surveyor Generals instructions in laying out the same and a true plat thereof

return into my office within two months from the date hereof.
Given under my hand and seal this 17 day of Jany A. D. 1846.
W. L. Keith (SEAL) C. L. P. D.
Received of the within warrant 15 1-2 acres Jany. 20, 1846.
John Bowen D. S.
Certified Feb. 2, 1846. W. L. Keith.

DUDLEY JONES NO. 87
The State of South Carolina

Pickens District) By W. L. Keith Clerk of the Court and by virtue of office Commissioner of Location in and for the District aforesaid. To any lawful Surveyor you are hereby authorized to lay out and admeasure a tract of land unto Edley Jones not exceeding ten thousand acres observing the Surveyor Generals instructions in laying out the same and a true Plat of the same return into my office within two months from the date hereof.
Given under my hand and Seal this 5th day of Nov. A. D. 1845.
W. L. Keith (SEAL) C. L. P. D.
Executed of the within warrant 68 acres Dec. 9, 1845.
Alexander Edens Dept. Suvr.
Certified Dec. 27, 1845. W. L. Keith.
On back of warrant was written Dudley Jones but inside was written Edley Jones.

JOEL JONES NO. 52
State of South Carolina

Pickens District) By W. L. Keith Clerk of the Court and by virtue of office Commissioner of Location in and for the District aforesaid. To any lawful Surveyor you are hereby authorized to lay out and admeasure unto Joel Jones a tract of land whereon he now lives and other lands adjoining the same and vacant land not exceeding ten thousand acres observing the Surveyor Generals instructions in laying out the same and a true plat thereof return into my office within two months from the date hereof.
Given under my hand and seal this 24 day of Febry 1843.
W. L. Keith (SEAL) C. L. P. D.
Executed of the within warrant 527 acres Feb. 27, 1843.
Jno. Bowen D. S.
Certified April 4, 1843. W. L. Keith.

JOHN CRAWFORD NO. 2
South Carolina

Pickens District) By Thos. Garvin Commissioner of Location for sd District to any lawful surveyor you are hereby required to admeasure and lay out unto John Crawford a tract of land not exceeding ten thousand acres observing the Surveyor Generals instructions in laying out the same & a true plat thereof return into my office within three months given under my hand & seal this 27th day of June 1840.

Tho. Garvin D. S. (SEAL)
Executed of the within warrant 509 acres July 11, 1840.
Martin MCay D. S.
Recorded Oct. 11, 1840. W. L. KEith.

NIMROD LEATHERS NO. 91
State of South Carolina

Pickens District) By William L. Keith clerk of the court and by virtue of Office Commissioner of Location in and for the District aforesaid. To any lawful Surveyor you are hereby authorized to lay and admeasure unto Nimrod Leathers a tract of land not exceeding ten thousand acres observing the Surveyor Generals instructions in laying out the same and a true plat of the same return into my office within two months from the date hereof.

Given unto my hand and seal this 10th day of July A. D. 1845.
W. L. Keith (SEAL) C. L. P. D.
Executed part of the within warrant July 11th 1845.
Robt. Fullerton D. S.

WILLIAM S. WILLIAMS NO. 90
State of South Carolina

Pickens District) By W. L. Keith Clerk of the Court and by virtue of office Commissioner of Location in and for the District aforesaid. To any lawful Surveyor you are hereby authorized to lay out and admeasure unto W. S. Williams a tract of land not exceeding ten thousand acres observing the Surveyor Generals instructions in laying out the same and a true plat thereof return into my office within two months from the date hereof. Given under my hand & seal this 5 Jany 1846.
W. L. Keith (SEAL) C. L. P. D.
Executed on the within warrant 24 acres the 26th Feby 1846.
Tho. D. Garvin D. S.
Certified March 20, 1846. W. L. Keith.

AARON TERRELL NO. 51
State of South Carolina

Pickens District) By W. L. Keith clerk of the court and by virtue of office Commissioner of Location for the district aforesaid. To any lawful Surveyor you are hereby authorized to admeasure and lay out unto Aaron Terrell a tract of land not exceeding ten thousand acres observing the Surveyor Generals instructions in laying out the same and a true Plat thereof return into my office within two months from the date hereof. Given under my hand and seal this 9th day of February 1843.
W. L. Keith (SEAL) C. L. P. D.
Executed the within warrant 385 acres Feb. 11, 1843.
James Gilmer D. S.
Certified April 4, 1843. W. L. Keith.

A. G. FIELD NO. 93
State of South Carolina

By Wm. L. Keith Esq. commissioner of Location for Pickens District. To any lawful Surveyor of said Dist. you are hereby required to admeasure and lay out unto G. Field a tract of land not Exceeding one thousand acres observing the Surveyor Generals instructions in laying out the same and a true plat thereof return into my office within two months from this date.

Given under my hand and seal the 22d of Sept. 1846.

W. L. Keith (SEAL) C. L. P. D.

Certified Oct. 20, 1846. W. L. Keith. (Number of acres not given).

JAMES KING NO. 95
State of South Carolina

Pickens District) By W. L. Keith Clerk of the Court & by virtue of office Commissioner of Location for the said District. To any lawful Surveyor you are hereby authorized to lay out & admeasure unto James King a tract of land not Exceeding ten thousand acres observing the Surveyor Generals instructions in laying out the same and a true plat thereof make & return into my office within two months thereof. Given under my hand & seal this 21st day of June 1847.

W. L. Keith (SEAL) C. L. P. D.

Executed of the within warrant 117 acres June 23, 1847.

Tyre B. Mauldin D. S.

Certified July 10, 1847. W. L. Keith.

W. L. KEITH NO. 92
State of South Carolina

Pickens District) By W. L. Keith Clerk of the Court and by virtue of office Commissioner of Location for the said District. To any lawful Surveyor you are hereby authorized to lay out and admeasure unto W. L. Keith a tract of land not exceeding ten thousand acres observing the Surveyor Generals instructions in laying out the same and a true plat thereof return into my office within two months from the date hereof. The above warrant is for the express purpose of having a tract of land situate in said District and lying on Six mile Creek regranted the same whereon E. Alexander now lives. Given under my hand and seal this 20 day of March A. D. 1846.

W. L. Keith (SEAL) C. L. P. D.
Robt. Fullerton D. S.

Executed of the within warrant 338 acres May 10, 1846.
Certified May 10, 1846. W. L. Keith.

JOHN MOORE NO. 47
State of South Carolina

Pickens District) I W. L. Keith Clerk of the Court and by virtue of Office Commissioner of Location for said Dist. To any lawful Surveyor you are hereby authorized to lay out and admeasure unto John Moon a tract of land whereon he lives & vacant land adjoining same not exceeding ten thousand acres observing the Surveyor Generals instructions in laying out the same and a true plat thereof return into my office within two months from the date hereof. Given under my hand and seal this 6h day of Feby. Anno Domini 1843.

W. L. Keith (SEAL) C. L. P. D.

Executed 372 acres on North Cane Creek Feb. 13, 1843.

John O. Grisham D. S.

Certified Feb. 15, 1843. W. L. Keith.

(NOTE) On back of warrant was written John Moore but inside was written John Moon).

MAJOR JAMES W. HARRISON & JAMES ATKINS NO. 46
State of South Carolina

Pickens District) By W. L. Keith Clerk of the Court and by virtue of office Commissioner of Location for the District aforesaid. To any lawful Surveyor you are hereby authorized to admeasure and lay out unto Maj. James W. Harrison and James Atkins a tract of land not exceeding ten thousand acres observing the Surveyor Generals instructions in laying out the same and a true plat thereof return into my office within two months from the date hereof. Given under my hand and seal this 18 day of January A. D. 1843.

W. L. Keith (SEAL) C. L. P. D.

Executed 607 acres for the within 24th Jany. 1843.

John O. Grisham D. S.

Certified Feb. 10, 1843. W. L. Keith.

E. H. GRIFFIN NO. 94
State of South Carolina

Pickens District) By W. L. Keith Clerk of the Court and by virtue of Office Commissioner of Location for said Dist. To any lawful Surveyor you are hereby authorized to lay out and admeasure unto E. H. Griffin a tract of land not exceeding ten thousand acres observing the Surveyor Generals instructions in laying out the same and a true plat thereof return into my office within two months from the date hereof the above warrant is for the purpose of regranting the tract he lives on and such vacant land as may be adjoining.

Given under my hand and seal this 26 Octr. 1846.

W. L. Keith (SEAL) C. L. P. D.

Executed the within warrant 434 acres Nov. 7, 1846.

Tyre B. Mauldin D. S.

Certified Nov. 10, 1846. W. L. Keith.

STEPHEN CLAYTON NO. 17
State of South Carolina

Pickens District) By W. L. Keith Clerk of the Court and virtue of office Commissioner of Location for the District aforesaid. To any lawful Surveyor you are hereby authorized to lay out and admeasure unto Stephen Clayton a tract of land not exceeding ten thousand acres observing the Surveyor Generals instructions in laying out the same and a true Plat thereof return into my office within two months from the date thereof. Given under my hand and Seal this 12 day of Octr. 1841.

W. L. Keith (SEAL) C. L. P. D.

Executed of the within warrant 1313 acres the 12th Oct. 1841.

Tho. D. Garvin D. S.

Recorded 26th Oct. 1841.

OWEN BUCHANAN NO. 16
State of South Carolina
   Pickens District) By W. L. Keith Ex officio Commissioner of Location for the District aforesaid. To any lawful Surveyor you are hereby authorized to lay out and admeasure unto Owen Buchanan a tract of land not exceeding ten thousand acres observing the Surveyors Generals instructions in laying out the same and a true plat thereof make and return the same into my office within Two months from the date thereof. Given under my hand and seal this 16 day of Octr Anno Domini 1841.
                           W. L. Keith (SEAL) C. L. P. D.

   Executed the 18th Oct. 330 acres.
                                   John O. Grisham D. S.

   Recorded Oct. 26, 1841. W. L. Keith.

JOHN ROHLEDDER NO. 142
South Carolina
   Pickens District) By W. L. Keith Esqr. Clerk of the Court & by virtue of office Commissioner of Locations for the said District. To any lawful Surveyor you are hereby authorized to lay out unto John Rohledder a tract of land not exceeding one thousand acres observing the Surveyor Generals instructions in laying out the same and a true plat thereof make and return into my office within two months from the date hereof. Given under my hand and seal this 2nd day May 1851.
                        W. L. Keith (SEAL) C. C. & C. L. P. D.
   Executed of the within warrant 125 acres, May 9, 1851.
                                        Tyre B. Mauldin

   Certified May 23, 1851.

DICKINSON M. OR A? LUMPKIN NO. 49
State of South Carolina
   Pickens District) By W. L. Keith Clerk of the Court and by virtue of office Commissioner of Location for the said Dist. in the said State. To any lawful Surveyor you are hereby authorized to lay out and admeasure unto Dickinson M. or A? Lumpkin a tract of land not exceeding ten thousand acres observing the Surveyor Generals instructions in laying out the same and a true plat thereof return into my office within two months from the date hereof. Given under my hand and seal this Seventh day of February A. D. 1843.
                           W. L. Keith (SEAL) C. L. P. D.
   Executed of the within warrant 178 acres Feb. 8th, 1843.
                                        Martin S. or L. MCay
   Certified March 9, 1843. W. L. Keith C. L. P. D.

ROBERT ISBELL NO. 21
State of South Carolina
   Pickens District) By W. L. Keith Clerk of the Court and by virtue of office Commissioner of Location for the District aforesaid. To any lawful Surveyor you are hereby authorized to lay out and admeasure unto the Heirs of Robt. Isbell a tract of land not exceeding ten thousand acres observing the Surveyor Generals instructions in laying out the same and a true plat thereof return into

my office within two months from the date hereof. Given under my hand and seal this 7th day of March 1842.

W. L. Keith (SEAL) C. L. P. D.

Executed of the within warrant 1,596 acres March 8th 1842.

Martin MCay. D. S.

Recorded March 22, 1842.

JAMES CHANDLER NO. 20
South Carolina

Pickens District) By W. L. Keith Clerk of the Court and by virtue of office Commissioner of Location for the District aforesaid. To any lawful surveyor you are hereby authorized to lay out and Admeasure unto James Chandler a tract of land not exceeding ten thousand acres observing the Surveyor Generals instructions in laying out the same and a true plat thereof return into my office within two months from this date. Given under my hand and seal this 24th Jany 1842.

W. L. Keith (SEAL) C. L. P. D.

Executed of the within warrant 185 acres. Alexander Edens D. S.
Recorded March 23, 1842.

MATTHIAS FRICKS NO. 149
South Carolina

Pickens District) By W. L. Keith Clerk of the Court and by virtue of office Commissioner of Locations for Pickens District. To any lawful surveyor you are hereby authorized to lay out unto Matthias Fricks a tract of land not exceeding one thousand acres observing the Surveyor Generals instructions in laying out the same and a true plat thereof make and return into my office within two months from the date hereof. Given under my hand and seal this 22nd day of March 1852.

W. L. Keith (SEAL) C. C. & C. L. P. D.

Executed of the within warrant 824 acres March 26, 1852.

Tyre B. Mauldin D. S.

Recorded March 29, 1852. W. L. Keith.

LEVI N. ROBBINS NO. 148
South Carolina

Pickens District) By W. L. Keith Clerk of the Court and by virtue of office Commissioner of Locations for Pickens District. To any lawful Surveyor you are hereby authorized to lay out unto Capt. L. N. Robins a tract of land not exceeding ten thousand acres observing the surveyor Generals instructions in laying out the same and a true plat thereof make and return into this office within two months from the date hereof. Given under my hand and seal this 15th day of March 1852.

W. L. Keith (SEAL) C. C. & C. L. P. D.

Executed of the within warrant 2,920 acres March 18, 1852.

T. B. Mauldin D. S.

Certified March 29, 1852. W. L. Keith.

TYRE B. MAULDIN & JOSEPH FRICKS NO. 147
South Carolina

Pickens District) By W. L. Keith Clerk of the Court and by virtue of office Commissioner of Locations for Pickens District. To any lawful Surveyor you are hereby authorized to lay out unto Tyre B. Mauldin & Joseph Fricks a tract of land not exceeding one thousand acres observing the Surveyor Generals instructions in laying out the same and a true plat thereof make and return into my office within two months from the date hereof. Given under my hand and seal this 22nd day of March 1852.

W. L. Keith (SEAL) C. C. & C. L. P. D.

Executed of the within warrant 88 acres March 26, 1852.

T. B. Mauldin D. S.

Certified March 29, 1852. W. L. Keith.

JACOB FREDERICK NO. 168
State of South Carolina

Pickens District) By W. L. Keith Clerk of the Court and by virtue of office Commissioner of Location in and for the District aforesaid. To any lawful Surveyor you are hereby authorized to lay out and admeasure unto Jacob Frederick a tract of land not exceeding Ten thousand acres observing the Surveyor Generals instructions in laying out the same and a true plat thereof return into my office within two months from the date hereof.

Given under my hand and seal this 21 June 1853.

W. L. Keith (SEAL) C. C. & C. L. P. D.

Executed of the within warrant 13 acres June 24, 1853.

M. S. McCay D. S.

Recorded 29th June 1853. W. L. Keith.

MAJOR WILLIAM S. GRISHAM NO. 180
South Carolina

Pickens District) By William L. Keith Clerk of the Court & Ex officio Commissioner of Locations for Pickens District. To any lawful surveyor you are hereby authorized to lay out unto Maj. William S. Grisham a tract of land not exceeding one thousand acres observing the Surveyor Generals instructions in laying out the same and a true plat thereof make and return into my office within two months from the date hereof. Given under my hand & seal this 20 July 1853.

W. L. Keith (SEAL) C. C. & C. L. P. D.

Executed of the within warrant 540 acres 29th July 1853.

Tyre B. Mauldin D. S.

Recorded Aug. 1, 1853. W. L. Keith.

THOMAS BARTON NO. 141
State of South Carolina

Pickens District) By W. L. Keith Clerk of the Court and by virtue of office Commissioner of Location in and for the district aforesaid. To any lawful Surveyor you are hereby authorized to lay out and admeasure unto Thomas Barton a tract of land not exceeding ten thousand acres, observing the Surveyor Generals instructions in laying out the same and a true plat of the same return into my office within two months from the date hereof.

Given under my hand and seal this 8th day of April Anno Domini 1851.

W. L. Keith (SEAL) C. L. P. D.

Executed part of the within warrant April 9th 1851.

Robt. Fullerton D. S.

Certified May 19, 1851. W. L. Keith.

JACOB R. COX NO. 23
State of South Carolina

Pickens District) By W. L. Keith Clerk of the Court and by virtue of office Commissioner of Location for the District aforesaid. To any lawful Surveyor you are hereby authorized to admeasure and lay out unto Jacob R. Cox a tract of land not exceeding ten thousand acres observing the Surveyor Generals instructions in laying out the same and a true plat thereof return into my office within two months from the date thereof. Given under my hand and Seal this 19th day of February Anno Domini 1842.

W. L. Keith (SEAL) C. L. P. D.

Executed of the within warrant 213 acres Feb. 26, 1842.

Martin L. MCay D. S.

Recorded 22nd March 1842. W. L. Keith C. L. P. D.

EDWARD H. EDGAR & DANIEL BALDWIN NO. 24
State of South Carolina

Pickens District) By W. L. Keith Clerk of the Court and by virtue of office Commissioner of Location for the District aforesaid. To any lawful Surveyor you are hereby authorized to admeasure and lay out unto Edward H. Edgar and Daniel Baldwin a tract of land not exceeding ten thousand acres observing the Surveyor Generals instructions in laying out the same and a true Plat thereof return into my office within two months from the date thereof. Given under my hand and seal this 2nd Feb. 1842.

W. L. Keith (SEAL) C. L. P. D.

Executed of the within warrant 234 acres Feb. 14th 1842.

Martin L. MCay D. S.

Recorded April 2, 1842. W. L. Keith C. L. P. D.

JOHN W. GASSAWAY NO. 22
State of South Carolina

Pickens District) By W. L. Keith Clerk of the Court and by virtue of office Commissioner of Location for the District aforesaid. To any lawful Surveyor you are hereby authorized to lay out and admeasure unto John W. Gassaway a tract of land not exceeding ten thousand acres observing the Surveyor Generals instructions in laying out the same and a true Plat thereof return into my office within two months from the date hereof. Given under my hand and seal this 22nd day of Jany. 1842.

W. L. Keith C. L. P. D.

Executed part of the within warrant the 25th Jan. 1842.

Robt. Fullerton

Recorded the 22nd March 1842. W. L. Keith.

JOHN McCRACKIN NO. 109
The State of South Carolina

Pickens District) By W. L. Keith Clerk of the Court and by virtue of office Commissioner of Location in and for the District aforesaid. To any lawful Surveyor you are hereby authorized to lay out and admeasure unto John McCrackin a tract of land not exceeding ten thousand acres observing the Surveyor you are hereby commanded and required to admesur and lay out unto return into my office within two months from the date hereof. Given under my hand and seal this 27th day of June Anno Domini 1849.

W. L. Keith (SEAL) C. L. P. D.

Executed of the within one thousand and 10 acres 5th July 1849.

Tyre B. Mauldin D. S.

Certified August 15, 1849. W. L. Keith.

SAMUEL ALBERTSON NO. 144
South Carolina

Pickens District) By William L. Keith Clerk of the Court & By virtue of office Commissioner of Locations for Pickens District. To any Lawful Surveyor you are hereby authorized to lay out unto Samuel Albertson a tract of land not exceeding one thousand acres, observing the surveyor Generals instructions in Laying out the same and a true plat thereof make and return into my office within two months from the date hereof. Given under my hand & seal this 25th day of August 1851.

W. L. Keith (SEAL) C. L. P. D.

Executed of the within 203 acres the 11th September 1851.

Tyre B. Mauldin Dept. Sur.

Certified 25th Oct. 1851. W. L. Keith C. L. P. D.

H. J. ANTHONY (NO NUMBER GIVEN)
The State of South Carolina

Pickens District) By W. L. Keith Clerk of the court and by virtue of offis Commissioner of Location in and for the said District. To any Lawful Surveyor you are hereby commanded and required to admesur and lay out unto H. J. Anthony a tract of land not exceeding ten thousand acres observing the surveyors generals instruckions in laying out the same and a tru plat thare off returned in my office within two months from the date hereof. Given under my hand and seal this first day of february 1848.

W. L. Keith C. L. P. D.

Received of the within warrant 275 acres the 2nd February 1848.

John Bowen D. S.

JEPTHA NORTON NO. 9
State of South Carolina

Pickens District) By William L. Keith Clerk of the Court and Ex officio Commissioner of Locations for Pickens District. To any Lawful Surveyor of the District aforesaid. You are hereby authorized and required to lay out unto or for Col. Jeptha Norton a tract of land not exceeding ten thousand acres to include the plantation whereon he now lives & claims and vacant lands adjoining. You will observe the Surveyor Generals instructions in laying out the same and a true plat thereof return into my office within two months from the date. Given under my hand & seal this 16 day of March 1841.

W. L. Keith (SEAL)
CLERK OF the court & Ex officio Commr. of Locations P. D.
Executed the 18th March 539 acres. J. O. Grisham D. S.
Recorded the 30th March 1841.

JESSE JENKINS NO. 29
State of South Carolina

Pickens District) By W. L. Keith Clerk of the Court and by virtue of office Commissioner of Location for the District aforesaid. To any lawful Surveyor you are hereby authorized to lay out and admeasure a tract of land unto Jesse Jenkins not exceeding ten thousand acres observing the Surveyor Generals instructions in laying out the same and a true plat thereof return into my office within two months from the date hereof. Given under my hand & seal this 25th day of March 1842.

W. L. Keith (LS) C. L. P. D.
Executed part of the within warrant March 28th 1842.

Robt. Fullerton
Recorded the 2nd May 1842. W. L. Keith C. L. P. D.

EDWARD RANKINS NO. 10
South Carolina

Pickens District) By William L. Keith Commissioner of Location for Pickens District. To any lawful Surveyor you are hereby required to admeasure and lay out unto Edward Rankins a tract of land not exceeding ten thousand acres observing the Surveyor Generals instructions in laying out the same and a true plat thereof return into my office within two months. Given under my hand and seal this 1st day of April 1841.

W. L. Keith (SEAL) C. L. P. D.
Executed of the within warrant 155 acres April 1st 1841.

Martin S. MCay D. S.
Recorded the 7th April 1841. W. L. Keith C. L. P. D.

A. P. REEDER NO. 6
South Carolina

Pickens District) By W. L. Keith Commissioner of Location for said District. To any lawful Surveyor you are hereby required to admeasure and lay out unto A. P. Reeder a tract of land not exceeding ten thousand acres observing the Surveyor Generals instructions in laying out the same and a true plat thereof return into my office within three months from this date. Given under my hand and seal 30 Jan. A. D. 1841.

W. L. Keith (LS) C. L. P. D.
Executed of the within warrant 404 acres Feb. 1, 1841.

Martin L. MCay D. S.
Recorded the 15th March 1841. W. L. Keith C. L. P. D.

JOHN MARET NO. 26
State of South Carolina

Pickens District) By W. L. Keith Clerk of the Court and by virtue of office Commissioner of Location for the District aforesaid. To any lawful Surveyor you are hereby authorized to lay out and admeasure unto John Maret a tract of land not exceeding ten thousand acres observing the Surveyor Generals instructions in laying out the same and a true plat thereof return into my office within two months from the date hereof. Given under my hand and seal this 21st day of March A. D. 1842.

W. L. Keith C. L. P. D.

Executed of the within warrant 280 acres March 29th 1842.

M. L. MCay D. S.

Recorded April 23, 1842. W. L. Keith C. L. P. D.

JEFFERSON DALTON NO. 28
South Carolina

Pickens District) By William L. Keith Clerk of the Court and by virtue of office Commissioner of Location for said District. To any lawful Surveyor you are hereby authorized to lay out and admeasure to Jefferson Dalton a tract of land not exceeding ten thousand acres observing the Surveyor Generals instructions in laying out the same and a true plat thereof return to my office within two months from this date. Given under my hand and seal this 7th March 1842.

W. L. Keith (SEAL) C. L. P. D.

Executed part of the within warrant the 20th April 1842.

Robt. Fullerton D. S.

Recorded May 2, 1842. W. L. Keith.

DAVID CHERRY (NO NUMBER GIVEN)
State of South Carolina

Pickens District) By W. L. Keith Clerk of the Court and by virtue of office Commissioner of Location for Pickens District. To any lawful Surveyor you are hereby authorized to admeasure and lay out unto David Cherry a tract of land not exceeding ten thousand acres observing the Surveyor Generals instructions in laying out the same and a true plat thereof return into my office within Two months from this date. Given under my hand and seal this 28th Nov. 1841.

W. L. Keith (SEAL) C. L. P. D.

DAVID ALEXANDER NO. 13
State of South Carolina

Pickens District) By W. L. Keith Clerk of the Court and Ex officio Commissioner of Location in and for the District in the said state. To any lawful Surveyor you are hereby authorized to lay out and admeasure unto David Alexander a tract of land not exceeding ten thousand acres, observing the Surveyor Generals instructions in laying out the same and a true plat thereof return into my office within two months from the date thereof.

Given under my hand and seal this 26th day of April A. D. 1841.

W. L. Keith (SEAL) C. L. P. D.

Executed for the within 221 acres the 27th day of April 1841.

John O. Grisham D. S.

Recorded the 11th May 1843. W. L. Keith C. L. P. D.

EDWARD HUGHES NO. 14
State of South Carolina
Pickens District) By William L. Keith Clerk of the Court and by virtue of office Commissioner of Location for said District. To any lawful Surveyor you are hereby authorized to admeasure and lay out unto Edward Hughes a tract of land not exceeding ten thousand acres observing the Surveyor Generals instructions in laying out the same and a true plat thereof return into my office within two months from the date thereof. Given under my hand and seal this 23d June Anno Domini 1841.

W. L. Keith (LS) C. L. P. D.

Executed part of the within warrant July 17th 1841.

Robt. Fullerton D. S.

Recorded Aug. 2, 1843. W. L. Keith.

WILLIAM VAN WYCK NO. 167
The State of South Carolina
Pickens District) By William L. Keith Clerk of the Court and by virtue of office Commissioner of Location in said District. To any Lawful Surveyor you are hereby authorized to lay out unto William Van Wyck a Tract of Land not Exceeding one thousand Acres observing the Surveyor Generals instructions in Laying out the same and a true Plat thereof return into my office within two months from the date hereof this warrant for the purpose of having ceartain Lands regranted. Given under my hand and Seal the 11th Day of Jan. A. D. 1853.

W. L. Keith (SEAL) C. C. & C. L. P. D.

Executed on the within warrant 650 acres July 7th 1853.

Thomas D. Garvin

Certified the 29th May 1853.

WILLIAM D. STEELE NO. 169
South Carolina
Pickens District) By Wm. L. Keith Esqr. Clerk of the Court & Exofficio Commissioner of Locations for Pickens District. To any lawful Surveyor you are hereby authorized to lay out unto William D. Steele Esqr. a tract of land not exceeding ten thousand acres observing the Surveyor Generals instructions in laying out the same and a true plat make and return into this office within two months from the date hereof. Given under my hand & seal this 1st day of June 1853.

W. L. Keith (SEAL) C. C. & C. L. P. D.

Executed the within warrant 2550 acres 29th June 1853.

Tyre B. Mauldin

Certified the 4th July 1853.

DAVID GILLILAND NO. 12
State of South Carolina
Pickens District) By W. L. Keith Commissioner of Location for Pickens District. To any lawful Surveyor you are hereby authorized to admeasure and

lay out David Gilliland a tract of land not exceeding ten thousand acres observing the Surveyor Generals instructions in laying out the same and a true plat of the same make and return the same into my office within Two months from the date thereoff. Given under my hand and seal this 3d Feby. A. D. 1841.
W. L. Keith (LS) C. L. P. D.

Executed of the within warrant 22 acres. Alexander Edens D. S.

Certified the 24th April 1841.

AARON CAIN NO. 160
South Carolina

Pickens District) By me W. L. Keith Clerk of the Court and by virtue of office Commissioner of Location in and for said District. To any lawful Surveyor you are hereby commanded to lay out and admeasure unto Aaron Cain a tract of Land not exceeding ten thousand acres observing the Surveyor Generals instructions in laying out the same and a true Plat of the same return into my office within two months from the date hereof. Given under my hand and seal this 3d Novr. A. D. 1852.
W. L. Keith (SEAL) C. C. & C. L. P. D.

Executed part of the within warrant the 29th Decr. 1852.
Robt. Fullerton D. S.

Certified the 1st Jan. 1853.

SAMUEL E. MAXWELL NO. 161
South Carolina

Pickens District) By W. L. Keith Clerk of the Court & Ex Off. Commissioner of Location for said District. To any lawful Surveyor of Location for said District. To any lawful Surveyor you are hereby authorized and required to admeasure and lay out unto Samuel E. Maxwell a tract of land not exceeding ten thousand acres observing the Surveyor Generals instructions in laying out the same and a true plat thereof return into my office within two months from this date. Given under my hand and seal this 15th day of February 1853.
W. L. Keith (SEAL) C. C. & C. L. P. D.

Executed of the within warrant 6 acres Feb. M. L. MCay D. S.

Certified the 24th Feb. 1853.

G. W. PHILLIPS NO. 166
South Carolina

Pickens District) By W. L. Keith Clerk of the Court & by virtue of office Commissioner of Locations for Pickens District. To any lawful Surveyor you are hereby authorized to lay off unto G. W. Phillips a tract of land not exceeding ten thousand acres observing the Surveyor Generals instructions in Laying out the same and a true plat thereof make and return into my office within two months from the date hereof. Given under my hand and seal this the first day of April 1853.
W. L. Keith (SEAL) C. C. & C. L. P. D.

Executed of the within warrant 650 acres the 21st April 1853.
Tyre B. Mauldin Dep. Sur.

Certified the 20th May 1853.

LEONARD MOSELEY NO. 116
South Carolina

Pickens District) By Wm. L. Keith Clerk of the Court and by virtue of office Commissioner of Locations for said District. To any lawful Surveyor you are hereby authorized to lay out and admeasure unto Leonard Moseley a tract of land not exceeding ten thousand acres observing the Surveyor Generals instructions in laying out the same and a true plat thereof make and return into my office within two months from the date thereof. Given under my hand and seal this 26 day of Decr. 1849.

W. L. Keith (SEAL) C. C. & C. L. P. D.

Executed of the within warrant 68 acres.

Tyre B. Mauldin Depty Surveyor

Certified the 2nd Jany. 1850. W. L. Keith C. L. P. D.

JOHN GRISSOP NO. 157
South Carolina

Pickens District) By William L. Keith Clerk of the Court & by virtue of office Commissioner of Locations for Pickens District. To any lawful Surveyor you are hereby authorized to lay out unto John Grissop a tract of land not exceeding one thousand acres observing the Surveyor Generals instructions in laying out the same and a true plat thereof make and return into my office within two months from the date hereof. Given under my hand & seal this 1st day of October 1852.

W. L. Keith (SEAL) C. C. & C. L. P. D.

Executed of the within warrant 54 acres 2nd Oct. 1852.

T. B. Mauldin D. S.

Certified the 20th Nov. 1852. W. L. Keith C. C. & C. L. P. D.

JOEL PATTERSON NO. 159
State of South Carolina

Pickens District) By W. L. Keith Clerk of the Court and by virtue of office Commissioner of Location in and for the District aforesaid. To any lawful Surveyor you are hereby authorized to lay out and admeasure unto Joel Patterson a tract of land not exceeding ten thousand acres observing the Surveyor Generals instructions in laying out the same and a true Plat of the same return into my office within two months from the date hereof. Given under my hand and seal this 1st day of Augt. A. D. 1852.

W. L. Keith (SEAL) C. C. & C. L. P. D.

Executed of the within warrant 13 acres August 19th 1852.

M. L. MCay D. S.

Certified Nov. 29, 1852.

JOHN CAPEHART NO. 119
State of South Carolina

Pickens District) By W. L. Keith Clerk of the Court and by virtue of office Commissioner of Location for said District. To any lawful surveyor you are hereby commanded to admeasure and lay out unto John Capehart a tract of land no exceeding one thousand acres and true plat thereof return into my office within two months from the date hereof. Given under my hand and

seal this 11th day of Feby. A. D. 1850.
                              W. L. Keith (SEAL) C. L. P. D.
   Executed of the within warrant 638 acres 20th Feb. 1850.
                              Tyre B. Mauldin Dep. Sur.
   Certified 22nd Febry. 1850. W. L. Keith C. L. P. D.

   DAVID S. STRIBLING NO. 118
   State of South Carolina
      Pickens District) By W. L. Keith Clerk of the Court and by virtue of office Commissioner of Location for said District. To any lawful Survey you are hereby authorized to lay out and admeasure unto Maj. David S. Stribling a tract of land not exceeding ten thousand acres observing the Suveyors Generals instructions in laying out the same and a true copy thereof return into my office within two months from the date hereof.
      Given under my hand and seal this 23d Novr. 1849.
                              W. L. Keith C. C. & C. L. P. D.
      Executed of the within warrant 6¼ acres. Nov. 27, 1849.
                              M. L. MCay D. S.
      Certified the 27th Jan. 1850. W. L. Keith C. L. P. D.

   JOHN S. YOUNG NO. 117
   State of South Carolina
      Pickens District) By W. L. Keith Clerk of the Court and by virtue of office Commissioner of Location for the District aforesaid. To any lawful Survey you are hereby authorized to lay out and admeasure unto John S. Young a tract of land not exceeding one thousand acres observing the surveyor Generals instructions in laying out the same and a true plat thereof return into my office within two months from the date hereof.
      Given under my hand and seal this 5th day of October Anno Domini 1849.
                              W. L. Keith C. L. P. D.
      Executed of the within warrant 609   acres.
                              Tyre B. Mauldin Depty Sur.
      Certified the 23rd Decr. 1849. W. L. Keith C. L. P. D.

   MAJOR MORGAN HARBIN NO. 137
   State of South Carolina
      Pickens District) By W. L. Keith Clerk of the Court and by virtue of office Commissioner of Location in and for the District aforesaid. To any lawful Surveyor you are hereby authorized to lay out and admeasure unto Maj. Morgan Harbin a tract of land not exceeding ten thousand acres observing the Surveyor Generals instructions in laying out the same and a true plat of the same return into my office within two months from the date hereof. Given under my hand and seal this 5th day of February AD 1851.
                              W. L. Keith (SEAL) C. C. & C. L. P. D.
      Executed of the within warrant 100 acres Feb. 14, 1851.
                              M. L. MCay D. S.
      Certified 25th Febry 1851. W. L. Keith C. L. P. D.

THOMAS AND JAMES W. VISAGE NO. 139
South Carolina

Pickens District) By William L. Keith Clerk of the Court and by virtue of office Commissioner of Locations for Pickens Dist. To any lawful surveyor you are hereby authorized to lay out unto Thomas Visage and James W. Visage a tract of land not exceeding one thousand acres observing the Surveyor Generals instructions in laying out the same and a true plat threof make and return into my office within two months from the date hereof. Given under my hand & seal this 1st day of March 1851.

W. L. Keith (SEAL)

Executed of the within warrant 652 acres. 20th March 1851.

Tyre B. Mauldin Dep. Sur.

Certified the 1st April 1851. W. L. Keith C. L. P. D.

HENRY R. HUGHS NO. 121
State of South Carolina

Pickens District) By W. L. Keith Clerk of the Court, and by virtue of office Commissioner of Location in and for the District aforesaid. To any lawful Surveyor you are hereby authorized to lay out and admeasure unto Henry R. Hughs a tract of land not exceeding ten thousand acres observing the Surveyor Generals instructions in laying out the same, and a true plat of the same return into my office within two months from the date hereof. Given under my hand and Seal this 31st day of January Anno Domini 1850.

W. L. Keith (SEAL) C. L. P. D.

Executed part of the within warrant the 1st day of Febry. 1850.

Robt. Fullerton Dep. Sur.

Certified the 4th March 1850. W. L. Keith C. L. P. D.

JOSIAH BARKER NO. 135
South Carolina

Pickens District) By W. L. Keith Clerk of the Court and by virtue of office Commissioner of Locations for Pickens District. To any Lawful Surveyor you are hereby authorized to lay out unto Josiah Barker a tract of land not exceeding one thousand acres observing the Surveyor General Instructions in laying out the same and a true plat thereof make and return into my office within two months from the date hereof. Given under my hand and seal the 15th day of October 1850.

W. L. Keith (SEAL) C. L. P. D.

Executed of the within 329 acres 23rd October 1850.

Tyre B. Mauldin, Dep. Sur.

Certified 23rd October 1850.

WILLIAM KING NO. 134
South Carolina

Pickens District) By W. L. Keith Clerk of the Court and by virtue of office Commissioner of Locations for Pickens District. To any lawful Surveyor you are hereby authorized to lay out unto William King a tract of land not exceeding ten thousand acres observing the Surveyors Generals instructions in laying out the same and a true plat thereof make and return into my office within two months from the date hereof. Given under my hand & seal this 15th day of August 1850.

No name signed (SEAL)

Executed of the within one thousand four hundred and fifty five acres. Certified 3rd Oct. 1850. W. L. Keith C. L. P. D.

ARCHIBALD TODD NO. 136
State of South Carolina

Pickens District) By W. L. Keith Clerk of the Court and by virtue of office Commissioner of Location for the District aforesaid. To any lawful Surveyor you are hereby authorized to lay out and admeasure unto Archibald Todd a tract of land not exceeding ten thousand acres observing the Surveyor Generals instructions in laying out the same and a true plat of the same return into my office within two months from the date hereof. Given under my hand & seal this 30 Septr. 1850.

W. L. Keith (SEAL) C. L. P. D.

Executed of the within warrant 724 acres 1st October 1850.

Tyre B. Mauldin Dep. Sur.

Certified the 4th Noc. 1850. W. L. Keith. C. L. P. D.

JAMES EATON NO. 130
State of South Carolina

Pickens District) By W. L. Keith Clerk of the Court, and by virtue of office Commissioner of Location in and for the District aforesaid. To any lawful Surveyor you are hereby authorized to lay out and admeasure unto James Eaton a tract of land not exceeding Ten thousand acres, observing the Surveyor Generals instructions in laying out the same, and a true plat of the same return into my office within two months from the date hereof. Given under my hand and Seal this 1st day of April Anno Domini 1850.

W. L. Keith (SEAL) C. L. P. D.

Executed part of the within warrant the 2nd day of April 1850.

Robt. Fullerton D. S.

Certified the 20th May 1850.

PHILIP CHAMBERS NO. 132
South Carolina

Pickens District) By Wm. L. Keith Clerk of the Court and by virtue of office Commissioner of Locations for said District. To any lawful Surveyor you are hereby authorized to Lay out unto Phillip Chambers a tract of Land not exceeding ten thousand acres observing the Surveyor Generals instructions in laying out the same, and a true plat thereof make and return into my office within two months from the date hereof. Given under my hand and seal this 25 Feby 1850.

W. L. Keith (SEAL) C. L. P. D.

Executed of the within 453 acres 16th April 1850.

Tyre B. Mauldin D. S.

Certified 3rd June 1850.

REVD. JOSEPH GRISHAM NO. 131
State of South Carolina

Pickens District) By William L. Keith Clerk of the Court and by virtue of office Commissioner of Location for said District. To any lawful Surveyor, you are hereby authorized to lay out and admeasure unto Revd. Jos Grisham a tract of land not exceeding ten thousand acres, observing the surveyor Generals instructions in laying out the same and a true plat thereof return into my office within two months from this date. Given under my hand and seal this the Sixth day of May AD 1850.

       W. L. Keith (SEAL) C. C. & C. L. P. D.

Executed of the within warrant 2342 acres 22nd May 1850.

       Tyre B. Mauldin Dep. Sur.

Certified 3rd June 1850.

WILLIAM H. STRIBLING NO. 120
State of South Carolina

Pickens District) By W. L. Keith Clerk of the Court and by virtue of office Commissioner of Location in and for the District aforesaid. To any lawful Surveyor you are hereby authorized to lay out and admeasure unto William H. Stribling a tract of land not exceeding ten thousand acres, observing the Surveyor Generals instructions in laying out the same and a true plat of the Same return into my office within two months from the date hereof. Given under my hand and Seal this 18th day of February Anno Domini 1850.

       W. L. Keith (SEAL) C. L. P. D.

Executed part of the within warrant the 19th day of Febr. 1850.

       Robt. Fullerton Dep. Sur.

Certified 2nd March 1850.

PHILIP SNEAD NO. 125
South Carolina

Pickens District) By Wm. L. Keith Clerk of the Court and by virtue of office Commissioner of Locations for Pickens District. To any Lawful Surveyor you are hereby authorized to lay out unto Phillip Snead Senr. a tract of land not Exceeding one thousand acres. Observing the surveyor General Instructions in Laying out the same and a true plat make of the same and return into my office within two months from the date hereof. Given under my hand and seal this 18 day of January 1850.

       W. L. Keith (SEAL) C. L. P. D.

Executed of the within warrant 99 acres 19th January 1850.

       Tyre B. Mauldin Dep. Sur.

Certified 18 of March 1850.

TYYRE B. MAULDIN NO. 126
South Carolina

Pickens District) By Wm. L. Keith Clerk of the Court and by virtue of office Commissioner of Locations for Pickens District To any lawful Surveyor you are hereby authorized to lay out unto Tyre B. Mauldin a tract of land not exceeding one thousand acres observing the Surveyor Generals instructions in Laying out the same and a true plat thereof make and return into my office within two months from the date hereof. Given under my hand and seal this 10 day of March 1850.

           W. L. Keith (SEAL) C. L. P. D.

Executed of the within 289 acres 14th March 1850.

            Tyre B. Mauldin Dep. Sur.

JOHN HOWARD NO. 50
State of South Carolina

 Pickens District) By W. L. Keith Clerk of the Court and by virtue of office Commissioner of Location in and for the District aforesaid. To any lawful Surveyor you are hereby authorized to lay out and admeasure unto John Howard a tract of land not exceeding ten thousand acres observing the Surveyor Generals instructions in laying out the same and a true plat thereof return into my office within two months from the date hereof.

 Given under my hand and seal this 10th day of Feby. 1843.

           W. L. Keith (SEAL) C. L. P. D.

Recieved of the within warrant 53 acres Feb. 4, 1843.

            John Bowen D. S.

Certified April 4, 1843. W. L. Keith.

JAMES COX AND TYRE B. MAULDIN NO. 113
State of South Carolina.

 Pickens District) By W. L. Keith Clerk of the Court and by virtue of office Commissioner of Locations for the District aforesaid. To any lawful Surveyor you are hereby authorized to admeasure and lay out unto James Cox and Tyre B. Mauldin a tract of land not exceeding one thousand acres observing the Surveyor Generals instructions in laying out the same and a true plat thereof return into my office within two months from the date hereof. Given under my hand and seal this 5th day of October 1849.

           W. L. Keith C. C. & C. L. P. D.

Executed of the within warrant 503 acres.

            Tyre B. Mauldin D. S.

Certified the 17th Nov. 1849.

NEHEMIAH DUNN NO. 115
State of South Carolina

 Pickens District) By W. L. Keith Clerk of the Court and by virtue of office Commissioner of Location in and for the District aforesaid. To any lawful Surveyor you are hereby authorized to lay out and admeasure unto Mehemiah Dunn a tract of land not exceeding ten thousand acres observing the Surveyor Generals instructions in laying out the same and a true plat of the same return into my office within two months from the date hereof. Given under my hand and seal this 18th day of Decr. A. D. 1849.

           W. L. Keith (SEAL) C. C. & C. L. P. D.

Executed of the within 465 acres.

            Tyre B. Mauldin Dep. Sur.

Certified Jan. 2, 1850.

    "INQUEST PAPERS," PACK. 115
   CLERK OF COURTS OFFICE, PICKENS, S. C.

EDWARD NORRIS NO. 1

An inquest was taken at Farrs still house in Pickens District, the 7th July 1861 before John R. Gossett Magistrate, acting as coroner for said district, upon the view of the body of Edward Norris of Pickens, then and there being dead by the oaths of R. E. Bowen, Wm. Watkins, Pinkney Gossett, John T. Gossett, Tillman Miller, Abel Bishop, Henry Wade, Charles Roper, Henry Lark, M. Cothran, Washington Farr, Wm. Haynes being a lawful jury of inquest, who being charged and sworn do say that decd. came to his death by a wound inflicted by a knife in the hands of George Trannum at Farrs Still House on the 6th July 1861.

W. N. Turner sworn sayeth, "The decd. was lying on the ground near the still house. Both decd, and prisoner came near the witness in an angry humor. Prisoner had his knife in his hand and cursing and swearing and threating to stick it in decd. The decd. told prisoner that if he did not go off and let him alone, he would slap him. Decd. did slap him, when prisoner stabbed him. Both were drinking but not so much so but that they knew what they were about. After the prisoner stabbed him he said "now dam you, you will not come against me any more," and immediately walked off up the road. Witness followed the prisoner and found him laying up in the woods between two logs, flat down on his stomach. Witness said to prisoner, "George what did you do this for," and prisoner said, "Lord, I am sorry for what I have done. Prisoner still had his knife open in his hand, and there was blood on the blade. Witness said to prisoner, "Give up this knife or I will kill you." Prisoner seemed to be reluctant to give up the knife. Witness saw no weapon in decd. hands, and saw both licks struck. Witness saw the knife in the hand of prisoner at the time he made the blow. Decd. followed prisoner some 8 or 10 steps. Wilson N. Turner.

H. C. Hunt swirn sayeth, "There was to be a shooting match at the still house the day the murder was committed. I was present at the still house, all semmed to be romancing together. I paid very little attention to what, was transpiring. There may have been angry words passed between both men, but I did not hear any, and I did not see the blow struck, and knew nothing untill he saw Mr. John Tranham taking decd. up off the ground, his intestines was out, and tried to put them back, but could not do so. I put a bandage around the decd. H. C. Hunt.

Dr. W. R. Jones sworn sayeth, "Last evening avout dark two men called at my office and said they wanted me to go over to Pickens, that there was a man stabbed there. I asked who it was, and was told that it was Edward Norris. The person speaking said he generally called him Uncle Ned. I ordered my horse and came on as soon soon as I could. When I arrived at the spot I found the decd. cold, and pulseless in a dying condition. Remarked at the time he would do what he could for decd. but that it would not avail him anything. Dressed the wound to make him as comfortable as possible. At hald past 11 oclock P. M. he died. He died from the wound. W. R. Jones.

Jerry M. Clements sworn, "Decd. was lying on the ground. Both cursed each other and decd. said he would slap prisoner. Prisoner said he would "slap a rough sonag," or words to that amount. Decd. did slap prisoner, when he struck him a blow. I did not see the knife in the prisoners hands until after he made the blow at decd. Both appeared to be drinking but cant say whether they were so drunk as not to know what they were about. Decd. commenced throwing out jokes, I thought at himself, but the prisoner seemed to get offended at it. Decd. was a man who said what he pleased, in a romancing way to any and every person. J. M. Clements.

INQUEST OF JOSEPH B. McGUFFIN PACK. 115 NO. 3

An inquest was held at the house of Joseph B. McGuffin in Pickens District Dec. 14, 1864 to view the dead body of said Joseph B. McGuffin. The jury brought it out that the decd. came to his death by a wound inflicted by a knife in the hands of a man supposed by evidence to be Peter L. Barton of the Town of (in) Walhalla on the 6th Dec. 1864. Capt. C. H. Taylor sworn sayeth, I was present in the town of Walhalla on Dec. 6th and saw a man called Peter Barton and J. B. McGuffin have a fist fight. McGuffin wanted to borrow 50 dollars from Barton. Barton told him he did not have it. McGuffin swore he did have it. Then he chased Barton. Barton drew his knife and made at McGuffin with it open. McGuffin broke ti run. Barton stabbed him in the back and then in the side and shoulder. They were then parted by the former Sheriff of the District (W. N. Craig). On cross examination he stated that McGuffin pulled Barton off his horse, pushed him up against a shady tree with violence. McGuffin called him a God damned liar and scoundel and that he was not worth a dogs notice, and swore he would whip him before he left the place. Barton did not abuse him with his tongue. Both were drinking to some extent. C. H. Taylor.

JOHN HICKS NO. 4

An inquest was taken at Aaron Thomases in Pickens District Oct. 25, 1866 to view the dead body of John Hicks. The jury brought it out that John Hix came to his death from gunshot wounds on or about the 16th Oct. 1866 and that he was killed & murdered by some person or persons unknown to the jury. . . . Miss Sarah L. Boggs sworn sayeth, "I was coming from the spring seeing some buzzards down in the corn field. I said to my Aunt Bet lets go down there and see what is dead there, she said well, then we started. She looked in the ditch or gully and said, Ah, Ah Lord, there is John. I did not look in the ditch, then we started home. Then I went to the spring and told mother. The last time I saw John he was standing near the smoke house. I was going to the spring. While going to the spring I heard a gun or pistol after dipping up the water & starting home I heard another gun. The second was lounder than the first. Sarah L. Boggs.

Mrs. D. Ann Thomas sworn sayeth, "I saw John Hix on the morning of Oct. 16th 1866. He was well and in good health, he ate breaksfast at my house, he then went towards the crib, the crib and smoke house are near each other. I went to my fathers as he went out of the yard. I went about 150 yards when I heard the report of a gun. After going about the same distance I heard another the second was lounder than the first. The second seemed to be more in the hollow. I heard no hollowing nor did I see any one. I breaksfasted by sun up. I heard the guns about 1½ hours after sun rise. On the 24th of Oct. my daughter Sarah came to me & said Uncle John was dead down there in the gully. I went down and saw him. I heard Mr. R. W. Linderman say, "He intended to kill him the first time on sight, he saw of him."

I heard Mr. Balis Hendrix say, "Yes we will," that was one night at my house. This was before the day on which John Hix whipped Mr. Linderman. I never heard John Hix threaten to take his own life.

Test J. C. C. Parsons   Mrs. D. Ann Thomas

Mrs. Elizabeth Hix sworn saith, "I was twisting thread at the house when my niece came from the spring & said come Aunt Bet and let us go down yonder and see what those buzzards are after. I went and saw Mr. John Hix lying in the gully & I said, "Lord here lies your Uncle John." I told her to go to the branch & tell her mother to come and also her Aunt Adeline. We came back to the house & I asked my sister Dilly Ann to go down and put something over him. I never heard any one threaten his life.

S. E. Hix

Mrs. M. M. Durham saith, "The last time I saw John Hix was the evening he whipped Mr. Linderman as he was passing B. Durhams house. I saw Mr. R. W. Linderman on the evening John Hix whipped him both before & after that occured. After he had him whipped he said, "All he wanted was the sight of John Hix, if it was one hundred yards.   M. M. Durham

Mrs. W. A. McWhorter saith, "I saw John Hix on Oct. 13th near 11 Oclock at the place he usually staid near Mrs. D. A. Thomas. He was well and in good health. Since then I have not seen him, till the time we found him in the gully. I heard Mr. R. W. Linderman says, "the very first time I see of John Hix, I will kill him. Mr. Balis Hendrix said in reply, "Yes we will. This was about fodder pulling time on a thursday night. One day when I was carring Mr. John Hix provisions at his shelter in the woods he said, "Adeline I attempted to do several days ago what I neved did before." I said what was it John. Why I put the pistol to my forehead & thought I would kill myself & I could not pull the trigger to save my life. After that I said never to do that. He made no answer, but went to eating his dinner.

W. A. McWhorter

JAMES PELFREY NO. 5

An inquest was taken near Henry Crenshaws in the woods March 10, 1858 to view the body of said James Pelfrey of Pickens District. The jury brought it out that on Sun. March 7, from the best information we can arrive at, "that Pelfrey left Crenshaws at 9 P. M. with a quart of whiskey which is about half gone. It appears that he being in a state of intoxication the decd. came to his death by misfortune, being a very cold night. . . .

JOHN MARTIN NO. 6

An inquest was taken at W. T. Hollands plantation near Warsaw Post Office in Pickens Dist. July 24, 1859 to view the body of John Martin. The jury brought it out that John Martin came to his death by hanging himself with a rope tied to a piece of lumber and placed across the joint in a shuck house on the plantation of Dr. W. T. Holland near the house in which decd. & his family resided on the 23 July 1859. . . . Elizabeth Martin sworn says, "Decd. went to the mill yesterday. Returned about 12 oclock. When dinner was ready, sent her children as usual to call him to dinner. They went to the shuckhouse when they saw decd. hanging. They gave the alarm to me and I went immediately to the shuck house and saw him hanging to a stick of timber by a rope. I let him down and saw that he was gone, and I went immediately for Mrs. Holland and Mrs. King hollowing for them as I went. They met me at the branch and came to the house with me. They refused to go with me to draw the body down. Then I went for Mr. Lumpkins who came. I do not know what was afterwards. The decd. was my husband. Elizabeth Martin. . . .

Janette Holland says, "Knows nothing of the case except what decd. wife told her, who came hollowing towrads my house, and whom I met near the branch between the two houses, who told me that her husband was dead, said he had hung himself. I came on to the house with her, who begged me and Mrs. King who was in company to go and cut him down. I told her that I could not do so. While I was making arrangements to send her little boys for some one, she started off and went to Mr. Lumpkins. Then I told her little boy to go to Mr. Archey McDaniels who was nearest and ask them to send for Mr. Gillison. We then followed Mrs. Martin who went screaming on in sight of Mr. Lumpkins. J. E. Holland.

D. L. Lumpkin sworns says Decd. came to my house yesterday morning of July 23, 1859 to borrow a horse to go to the mill. He looked very sulkey. I lent him a horse. When my little boy was gone to catch the horse Mrs. Emory was at my house said to Mr. Martin, you have the advantage of us, in having new flour. He said Yes who ever ate it or lived to eat it dont remember exact words. Knew nothing more until Mrs. Martin came hollowing about 1 oclock, saying, O Uncle, Uncle, go and cut my husband down for he has hung himself in the shuck house. I went to the shuck house, saw the condition he was in, thought he would not be justifiable in taking Mr. Martin down. Made no such attempt. He was perfectly dead. I knew the family well and was frequently with them. There was never any difficulty between any of them, they lived in perfect harmony. I think that Mr. Martins mind was some what deranged. Had no enemies that I know of. D. Lumpkin.

Z. Hall Jr. sworn says, Saw decd. about 9 oclock A. M. Had nothing to say, except what was dragged out of him. Would have nothing to say voluntarily at all. I asked him if he had raised the wheat he had at his mill, he said no, that he had sweatted for it. Before the decd. left the mill, I observed something strange in conduct of decd. Asked him if he was sick. He replied that he could not say that he was but that he did not feel right. When in the act of leaving he asked me ifhe thought he could ground hima turn of corn, if he would bring it. I said that I could. Z. Hall Jr.

FANNY ALEXANDER NO. 7 (COLORED)

An inquest was held near Watson Stewarts in Pickens Co. Oct. 30, 1866, upon view of the supposed body of Fanny Alexander. The jury brought it out that she came to her death by misfortune and strvation or accident . . . Adam Evett said that he was passing thru the woods on the 28th Oct. and saw the frame of bones lying in the woods. . . .

THOMAS O'BRIANT NO. 8

An inquest was held Feb. 26, 1859 to view the body of Thomas O'Briant the infant son of Carr OBriant. The jury brought it out that Thomas O'Brianr came to his death in bed at his fathers house in Pickens District on the night of Feb. 24, 1859 by the visitation of God. Thomas Stone sworn says, "Was here yesterday morning about day break when the child was found. Mrs. O'Briant first discovered the that the child was dead, she was in bed when the made the discovery. Told Mr. O&Briant who was up by the fire, he went to her. They were taking on about it. I told them maybe the child was not dead. Mr. O'Briant took the child out of the arms of his wife. Took it to the fire and sat down with it, the child was warm when taken up, the hands clutched tight. I then went after Mr. Rigdon and his wife at the request of Mr. O'Briant. I was not here during the night the child died. Thomas Stone. . .

William Evett sworn says, "Was at Carr O'Briants the night the child died till near 12 o'clock. Did not notice the child at all. Mrs. O'Briant put the child to bed to sleep. William Evett.

Carr O'Briant sworn says, "The child had not been well, was bad off from the sunday before. It was about midnight when I went to bed the night the child died, it was lying in its mothers arms, sleeping sound a little hoarse. I went to sleep, knew nothing except what Thomas Stone has told, with which I agree. Carr O'Briant.

Lucy Evans says, "The child has never been right healthy, since it was born. Sucked it several times, Did not suck like other children. Lucy Evans.

Dr. Lawrence says, "Thinks the child probably died of a fit, produced by hives. Dr. Lawrence.

JOHN COYLE NO. 9

An inquest was held at Tunnel Hill in Pickens Dist. Sept. 29, 1858 to view the body of John Coyle of Tunnell Hill. The jury brought it out that John Coyle came to his death at Shaft No. 4 Stump House Tunnell Sept. 29 by falling from the cage in said shaft. . . . Patrick O'Harra says, "That the body before him is the body of John Coyle. As i was coming off the night shift at 6 O'clock this morning I heard a man say let me off this cage. I thought it was John Coyle but it was not he. There was not more than 9 or 10 on the cage. I heard a man scream 2 or 3 times but did not know who it was. I knew there was something the matter and called out hold on, you are a thousand feet from the bottom. . . . Edward Curlay says, "After the cage left the bottom of shaft No. 4 about 20 feet I heard a man scream. When the cage was about half way up we stopped. I heard a man strike the scantling & afterwards heard a man scream. There were 10 or 12 on the cage at the time. 12 can come up on the cage with out any danger. Some man said let me off just as the cage left the bottom. When the man screamed I could not understand what he said. There was no confusion among the men on the cage. There was no disagreement between John Coyle and any man on the cage that I know of. . . . John Mul Vannay says, "I was one of the first on the cage. After we were about 30 feet up I heard a man scream below. He screamed twice afterwards. I heard him distinctly strike the bottom. I had blown out my lamp after I got on the cage. I did not see John Coyle on the cage when we left the bottom. I am acquainted with John Coyle. He worked on the opposite heading to me, I work at Shaft No. 4 Stump House Tunnell. . . . Dennis Slattery says, "I attend the jump and ringing of the bell at shaft No. 4 Stump House Tunnell. I knew of no danger till I heard a man scream. I immediately rang the bell once, the signal for the cage to stop. About 4 or 5 seconds after I rang a man dropped below. The smoke was so thick I could see very little.

The man fell on the turning and then into the stump? The man did not speak after he struck the turning table or after he commenced falling. He screamed 3 times. There was no man hanging to the cage as it hoisted away. I saw no more confusion as the cage left the stump? than usual. I am not acquainted with John Coyle. . . . Edward Foley says, "I am foreman in Shaft No. 4 east heading. Stump House Tunnell. John Coyle worked under me at my heading. I was in the heading when I heard a man fall & immediately left my work & when I got to the sump I saw a man lying there, whom I knew to be John Coyle. He was a peaceable man, so far as I know. There was no chance for Coyle to have been drinking, as he had been at work all night. If a man is not secure when the cage leaves the bottom, he may easily drop off, they probably secure themselves at the bottom.

JAMES HORAN NO. 10

An inquest was taken at Tunnell Hill in Pickens Dist. Feb. 18, 1859 to view the body of James Horan. The jury brought it out that James Horan came to his death, that he was killed at No. 3 shaft by the water bucket falling into the shaft and striking him on the head on the night of the 17th about 8 oclock. William Toy says, I was down 15 or 20 minutes before the accident about 8 oclock. The uel? was coming up full of water the clevis or links next to the clevis broke when the bucket was about 5 feet from the top and let the bucket back into the shaft. It struck the tank below and then fell into the shaft. The tank is about 40 feet from he bottom. I went down immediately and found him sitting. Mike Sullivan and myself put him in the skip and brought him up, he never spoke in my hearing we know of, he was badly hurt, we brought him here before he died. He was hurt in No. 3 Stump House Tunnell. . . . Michael Sullivan says, "I was working in No. 3 shaft with James Horan on the night of the 17th. We were working together, the steel? broke in the hole & he took the tongs to take it out but could not get it out, he told Jim Burns to come and try if he could get it, while he was trying to get it out James Horan took a kig and set down by the side of him about 10 minutes. When we heard the noise coming down the shaft we run under the tank. We were under there until it was all over, the wind and water blew our lights out: I called for Wm. Fall he answered. I then called for James Horan, he did not answer, we knew then that he was hurt. I went round then and felt around for him. I felt his leg, part of the barrel was lying on him, I pulled him out and called for help to get him out. James Burns came and we took him up, we set him up, Wm. Tall went up, first thing was Wm. Toy coming down with a light in the skip, we put him in the skip & went on top with him, put him on a part of a door and brought him home. He never spoke in my hearing. I heard him grown under the barrel once before we got him. (The name Wm. Tall may be Wm. Fall, writing not good.)

MARY A. HIETT NO. 11

An inquest was taken at Fair Play, Pickens District March 5, 1865 to view the body of Mrs. Mary Ann Hiett of Talladega, Ala. The jury brought it out that she came to her death by hanging herself by the neck with the hem of a dress twisted into a rope, in the house of G. T. Campbell to a joist of a back room, at Fair Play on the evening of March 4, 1865. . . . Mrs. E. Campbell said that the decd. appeared wrong the morning before her death. She kep her room and when visited said she wished she was dead. She was so distressed after a while she heard a struggling noise and gave the alarm, when the door was opened she was found hanging by the neck from one of the Joist. . . . Mrs. Mary Stephens says, "Mrs. Campbell came running to me greatly excited, saying that the decd. had had a fit and was trying to destroy herself. When I entered she was hanging by her neck & I called a negro man, who lifted her, while Miss Rebecca Whitfield cut the rope. She seemed quite dead. . . . Rebecca Whitfield says, "Hearing a noise I went to Mr. Campbells house & when I arrived found Mrs. M. A. Hiett hanging, and was requested to cut her down, while the negro boy Charles lifted her up. . . .

MICHAEL FITZPATRICK NO. 12

An inquest was taken at Patseys Creek in Pickens District July 1, 1861 to view the body of Michael Fitzpatrick. The jury brought it out that he came to his death by the visitation of God. . . . James J. Hunter says, "I was passing by Michael Fitzpatricks place and thought that he would turn in and ask him, if his apples was ripe and saw the door standing open. I step to the door and saw him lying on the floor in the same way the jurors found him, and knew from the way that he was lying, that he was dead. I went straight home and told my father about it. This was on the evening of June 30. . . . Frederick O. Herrin says, "That he was with James J. Hunter, they went to the decd. house to ask for apples and saw the door standing open. Stepped to the same and saw him lying on the floor dead. I went to Mr. Cooks and told him what he had saw. That was on the evening of June 30 just before sunset. . . . John R. Cook says, "That F. O. Herrin came to his house and told him that Michael Fitzpatrick was laying in his house dead and he Cook in the company of his father and David Hunter came to the decd. house and found it was so. Had never heard any threat made against the decd. . . . Enoc R. Cook says, "He saw the decd. on last monday evening and he complained being unwell. Said that he had gotten over heated after his cow on the day before. . . . John Morton says, "That decd. told him that Mr. William Welch had told him that he (Welch) would kill him, that if he was found dead any where on the premises that he wanted him to settle up his business. That if the law did not hurt Fitzpatrick, that he (Welch) would learhima lesson, that he would remember the longest day that he lived . . . Thinks that this conversation took place either in Feby. or March. A. West says, "That about a month ago he got in conversation with Welch and told him that he and Fitzpatrick should live to gether. Welch said that he and Fitzpatrick had but little correspondence, and that if he ever did find out that Fitzpatrick was to blame, he would use him ruefly, but nothing like taking his life.

JONATHAN S. HOLCOMBE NO. 13

An inquest was held at Pickensville Feb. 14, 1861 to view the dead body of Jonathan S. Holcombe. The jury brought it out that he came to his death at the residence of Wm. Slatten in Pickensville about 3 oclock P. M. on the 14th by cutting his throat with a razor.

THOMAS MONTGOMERY NO. 14

An inquest was held July 2, 1859 to view the body of Thomas Montgomery. The jury brought it out that he came to his death by an act of Providence. . . .

JIM (A SLAVE) NO. 15

An inquest was held Jan. 30, 1862 over the dead body of Jim a slave of Miss Matilda Walker, who was found dead on the plantation of Mr. C. M. Lay. . . . Mr. S. T. Knight says, "Was going from Mr. Lays on the morning of the present day, saw him lying on the side of the road. I hollowee to him but recd. no answer. I dismounted and went to the decd. and shook him until I became satisfied that he was dead. I saw no signs of any violence having beenused on or about him. . . . The jury brought it out that the decd. came to his death on the plantation of Mr. C. M. Lay by the visitation of God. . . .

JOHN SMITH NO. 16

An inquest was taken at Tunnell Hill in Pickens District August the 15, 1858 to view the dead body of John Smith. The jury brought it out that he came to his death by a blow inflicted with a stone thrown by John McGinnis and a shot fired by Charles O'Hara, together with wounds inflicted by other parties unknown. John Couch says, "I was at Mr. Jolleys, the decd. came running by, was followed by a crown, was fired at 3 times, think Pat Fallew fired, is not postive, decd. was drunk, heard "Kahoo" tell decd. to hand back or he would shoot him. Decd. then returned when he was followed by John Kahoe and another party, was followed to where he was killed by a large party. . . . Rachel Pitts says, "Saw decd. running toward Mr. Beards, followed by two men and a boy, heard decd. tell them that he had done nothing to insult them, they were then throwing stones at him. Decd. and Dowdle came to my house and then went into the town, then came back followed by a crowd. Ordered Dowdle out of the house, a portion of the crown followed John Smith, and a portion followed Dowdle fireing and throwing stones at both. Do not know the names of any of the parties, know the faces of some of them. The crowd came to my house swearing they would kill me if I did not tell them where Dowdle was. This was after John Smith was killed, heard one man swear they had slain one man and would slay another before dark. . . . Jeremiah C. Brown says, "That there was a disturbance at No. 2 shaft. John Smith started from there and was followed by a crowd and caught at the place found, the party following were armed and fired at him. Saw the party with stones and sticks. Do not think any of the party fired untill he commenced returning. John Smith with a man named Dowdle came by where I was sitting and commenced a conversation with Charles O'Hara and then passed on when they were followed by Charles O'Hara and another. I followed after being afraid there would be a disturbance and wished to prevent it. Young Costello a boy commenced throwing stones at him and Dowdle. Stones were thrown also by O'Hara and Kahoe, two men came from the bush and commenced firing at O'Hara and Kahoe, think they were Frank Tatum and William Allgood am not postive in regard to Allgood. Dowdle threated to shoot and used my name, think he intended to shoot me, the decd. said nothing to myself or any one else in my hearing. Think

Dowdle and Smith had been drinking at this time the crowd came on both. John told Dowdle to shoot, think the crowd fired at them before Dowdle fired. Dowdle told the crows to come on he was not afraid of his life. John urged Dowdle to come away. . . . William Beard says, "Was in Mr. Goldens house when the decd. came there followed bt the crowd who was throwing stones and firing at him, saw John McGinnis hit decd. with a rock after he was down was shot by a person. Decd. was shot after having fallen was not more than 5 feet from decd. when he fired, think there were about 20 men after him, think the party who fired the shot was Charles O'Hara. I was in house and saw it thru a crack in the wall. James Bynum was in the yard at the time, James Broom and James Gillespie was in the house. James Gillespie said that the man who fired had a red shirt on. . . .

JAMES BENNETT alias JAMES MARTIN NO. 17

An inquest was taken at the residence of James Bennett alias James Martin the 28th Dec. 1860 to view the dead body of said James Bennett. The jury brought it out that the decd. came to his death by gunshot wounds at his own house in Pickens District on the 27th Dec. 1860 early in the morning, by a revolver in the hands of Joel Buckhuster in discharge of his duty as an officer. . . . Miles Galloway says, "Jere? Buckhuster came yesterday morning of the 27th to Davis? where he boards and ask him to assist him in taking the said decd. I asked him was it necessary to take any weapons. He said no. We went on untill we got near the dwelling of said decd. then separated some 100 yards apart from the house. Buckhuster came up on one side of the house and I on the other. Buckhuster told me to come up in front of the house and stop. I did so. He entered the house of said decd. by the door on the opposite side to that on which I stood. After he entered the house, I also entered it. Buckhuster went into the entry between the rooms and called me to come around there. I slipped out of the same door thru which he entered the house and as he entered the yard the shooting took place. I remained in the yard a short space of time then reentered into the house at the same door. Then I went into the room where the decd. was leaning over on the bed prettu much on his face. I remained in the house with decd. a very short time and then came out with Buckhuster and got on Buckhusters horse to leave. Had rode about 10 steps when Buckhuster called to me to return and said he wanted me to help him take take decd. I came back and went with him into the room where decd. was. He told me to help him take decd. out. I did so, and when they gotten him out of the house I told Buckhuster that it was useless to take decd. any farther for that he believed he had killed him. Buckhuster would not stop with decd. but pressed me to to take him on into the road. When we got to the road found that he was mortally wounded. Buckhuster then got on his horse and rode off. I remained about an half an hour then left for Capeharts to get some one to come and assist me to get him back into the house. I think that I was gone about 15 minutes and when I returned Bennett was dead. Buckhuster made no threats as to what he intended to do. I do not know whether there was any unkind feeling between them. I heard several reports of gun arms, cant tell which was fired first the gun or pustol. They were in pretty quick succession, I heard no words between them. There was no shot fired after Buckhuster came out of the house. I heard Mrs. Bennett say something to him loud. I saw Buckhuster point his pistol at one of Mr. Bennetts boys. . . . Rhoda Bennett says, "That Buckhuster came with a warrant to arrest the decd. on Monday the 24th to the house of decd. The decd. was not at home. I sent for him, he came and when he came into the house, he told Buckhuster that he had no (word) with that warrant, and that if he put his hands on him, he would kill him. They talked some time. Both seemed to get mad. After a few minutes decd. said but if it will satisfy you, we will go to Green Hudsons to give security, but dont put your hands on me. Both left. decd. taking with him a walking stick, no other weapon. The next night Tuesday of the 25th Buckhuster came back to the house and said to decd. I am going to Capeharts, that he would be back in a few minutes and that if decd. who was about came in to stay till he came back and let him take him, that he wanted to take him, and to say to decd. to let him Buckhuster take him and that he would (word) by himself. I said to Buckhuster that decd. would let him take him and that as soon as the securities came I would let him know. Yesterday Buckhuster came back. I said to Jim yonder is Buckhuster coming and when he comes you can come out and talk to him. When I came out of the room where Bennett was, met Buckhuster, gave him my hand and asked him to sit by the fire. He still had hold of my hand and gave me a shove and made for the door of the room in which Bennett was and said, "God dam him I will take him or kill him, waving the pistol in his hand. I grabbed to Buckhuster and held on to him as long as strength would permit, he shoved me off and struck Bennetts door 3 times. I called on my children to get out of the way and left the house. I think I heard him break open the door of the room where decd. was. I fell insensible and when I came to my self, I asked the children, where their daddy was. one of them replied Mud he is not killed, he is in. I went into the room where he was, found him leaning over on the bed, did not know that he was hurt. I turned around directly after entering the room and saw Buckhuster and Galloway standing near decd. who by this time was off the bed. Buckhuster ordered Galloway to take hold of him 3 times before he Galloway touched him. The last time he said to Galloway, take hold of him or I will blow you thru, having the pistol still in his hands. Both took hold of him and started out of the door with him and I saw no more of him until he was in the road where he was laying on his back. I ran towards him, got as far as the gate, and saw that decd. was as thought dead, and turned back to the house. Decd. has been taken several times under statewarrants. He was killed the 27th Dec. 1860 at his own house in Pickens District early in the morning. I had fainted and did not hear the shooting at all. . . . Mary Jane Martin says, "I was lying in the bed in the entry. Buckhuster commenced knocking at the door. I got out ofthe bed and went to the other side. Buckhuster had the door open by that time. Buckhuster shot. Then daddy shot, then Buckhuster kept getting closer till he shot five times. Then Buckhuster broke out of the door, then daddy got hold of the bed post and turned round and fell with his face on the bed. Daddy shot with a rifle, Buckhuster with a revolver. I started then to my mother, met brother Ben going into daddy. Ben was this side of daddy. Buckhuster ran back into the room, got the other side of daddy, pointer the revolver in Bens face and threattened to shoot him.

I then left after the first 2 shots. . . . J. E. Coffe sworn says, "I was at Mt. Capeharts near a quarter of a mile off. Had been there a few minutes when he first heard gun fire. About 20 minutes afterwards Buckhuster came to Capeharts and wanted him to come to Bennetts, saying that he had killed Bennett, but that Bennett shot first and showed him the hole in his coat. I asked him was he hurt and he said yes, showed his clothing thru which the bullett passed, also the i njury on his side. He still insisted on going back to Bennetts. I told him that if he had killed Buckhuster he ought to to go to Pickens. Both of us went to Pickens. He gave himself up to the Sheriff of the District and then down to Dr. Greens as they went to Pickens. Buckhuster said that he would not resist the laws, that if they wanted to put him in jail he waned me to bring his horse back and give him to his wife and tell her to sell him.

JAMES T. JENKINS NO. 18

An inquest was held Oct. 14, 1864 to view the dead body of James T. Jenkins. The jury brought it out that the decd. came to his death by misfortune or accident by attempting to swim the Tugaloo River in time of high water. . . .

CHARLOTTE (A SLAVE) NO. 19

An inquest was taken near Robert E. Steels place in Pickens District Nov. 18, 1865 to view the body of Charlotte a freed woman of color. The jury brought it out that she came to her death by the visitation of God. . . .

COLORED INFANT NO. 20

An inquest was held at Cain Creek and Walhalla in Pickens Dist. June 14, 16, 1860 to view the body of an infant child being dead who came to her death by violence by the hands of Sarah Callhoon and a free man named Floid. . . .

INQUEST OF ALMON POWELL PACK. 111 NO. 5
CLERK OF COURTS OFFICE, PICKENS, S. C.

An inquest was held at the house of Almon Powell in Pickens Dist. the 2nd Nov. 1857 that the decd. was found lying dead in bed at about 5 O'clock on the first of Nov. died thru a dispensation of Providence, the cause being unknown. Mistress Powell sworn says that the decd. ate his supper as harty as usual, went to bed at usual bedtime, heard no complaint nore than bad coles and cough. She thought about five oclock he got up out of bed, went out of doors and came in, was gone but a few moments. She lay in bed awake and as he got in bed she turned over with her face to the wall, heard him say something, did not under stand what it was supposed it was some remark he was making about the weather as he was accustomed or usually done when getting up in the night she heard no mourn or struggle after day light he appeared to ly so still she thought he had got into a sound sleep & that she lay sometime thought that she would not disturb him, let him get his nap out and lying still as she did she could not hear him breathing. The sun was up by this time, she raised up in the bed pulled the cover from over his face and found that he was dead. The question was then asked if any other person lay in the same room that night she answered that her daughter with some little children lay in the same room to wit Mrs. McIntire she being cawld on stated that she was awake when her father got up went out and came in heard him say something to her mother could not understand what it was her child was freting so she heard her father grown or moan after he lay down she heard nothing more untill her mother made the alarm which was about sun up there was no person there that night but the family.

CORNELIUS KEITH PACK. 117 EQUITY
CLERK OF COURTS OFFICE, PICKENS, S. C.
WILL OF CORNELIUS KEITH

in the Name of god amen the ninth day of february one thousand and eighteen hundred and forty six pickings District I Cornelius Keith Now Being in helth of Body and Sound Mind and Memory do make this my last will and testament at the same time utterly Revokin all former wills made By me Declaring this to Be my last will and testament first I give to my wife Nancy Keith my two tracts of land that I live on and my mill tract Dureing hir life time to Doe as She pleases with also I give to hir one Sorrel Mare also I give to hir what of my Cattle and hogs she wants for hir Seport and after hir Death I give to my oldest Sun Allen Keith my mill track of land and all prophets therof for his Maintainance and after his Death to fall Back to the other Children also I give to my Son Stephen De Keith 160 acres of land lying in greenville over and Bove an Equill part at the Same time I Do appoint my two Sons John D. Keith and Willis J. Keith joint executors of this my Las will and testament to whitch I have hear unto Set my hand and Seal this Ninth of february in the year of hour Lord one thousand Eight hundred and forty Six inter Lind Before assignd.

Conelius Keith Senior (LS)

Test
Wilis J Keith
Lemuel S Keith
Stephen D Keith
Marquis D Keith

James M. Keith states that his father Cornelius Keith a citizen of Pickens County died many years ago. His widow Nancy Keith who lived with most of her children on the tract of land, continued to reside there and enjoy all the rents and profits of the same. Seaborn Keith, Willis Keith, Marquis Keith took charge of the said estate and managed the same for their mother during her lifetime. Tgeir mother died during the past year and the estate is liable to partition amongest the heirs at law of the said Cornelius Keith. The property which she was permitted to continue in possession of during her life time, consisted of a valuable tract of land in Pickens District, whereon Cornelius Keith died. A portion of the live stock was sold in the lifetime of Nancy Keith by Marquis Keith, Seaborn Keith & Willis Keith who all lived with their mother. Seaborn Keith & Willis Keith are now dead, and Marquis Keith and the other defendants are still in possession of the lands and personal property, and refuse to make any partition of them, or to account for them. Seaborn Keith was also to account for $300.00 for land which he had purchased of his father Cornelius Keith in his lifetime. There was also a small tract of land near the Table Rock which is subject to partition . . . The heirs were: Allen Keith, Mary B. Keith, Cornelius Keith Jr. Marquis D. Keith, Temperance Keith, Rebecca Keith, Elizabeth Keith, Stephen D. Keith residing in Pickens District, S. C. and G. W. Keith residing in Greenville District, S. C. William L. Keith resides in the State of Alabama.

Filed March 21, 1864. . . . George W. Keith was killed after the filling of this bill . . . Elizabeth Keith had intermarried with George K. Hendricks.

HUNDLEY EVATT PACK. 118 (EQUITY)
CLERK OF COURTS OFFICE, PICKENS, S. C.

Elizabeth Evatt of Pickens District states that her husband Hundley Evatt died in 1853 . . . He owned 500 acres lying on waters of Twelve Mile River adjoining lands of Russell, J. N. Arnold, A. Weems and others and a negro girl called Amy now about 15 years of age. His widow also states that she is now old and infirm and physically unable to attend properly to her affairs, and that the slaves and other property bequeathed to her for life are in a manner profitless, troublesome and annoying to her. That the said land and slave are subject to partition amongst the next of kin and heirs at law of Hundley Evatt viz. Elizabeth the widow, who is entitled to one third, and his 4 children viz. Thompson Evatt, William M. or W? Evatt, Mary C. Evatt, Sarah A. Evatt and his 2 grandchildren viz. Abbey Rilla Evatt and James F. S. Evatt and the personal representative and heirs at law of Hundley E. Campbell a grandson of said decd. who lately died intestate . . . F. N. Garvin, J. N. Arnold & wife Mary, J. T. S. Evatt, James Chapman & wife Sarah, and Wm. McCurry & wife Matilda, Wm. T. M. Campbell were ordered to appeae in court . . . Thompson Evatt resided out of the state. Filed Mar. 23, 1860. . . .

SLAVE PAPERS PACK. 119
CLERK OF COURTS OFFICE, PICKENS, S. C.

NO. 1

On May 13, 1863 Jacob Phillips appeared before H. J. Anthony a Magistrate for Pickens Dist. and swears that he does believe that Melissa a slave belonging to Elzie L. Keith did on the night of April 16th come to his house and break open his door which was locked which he said he and his family was absent and did steal some bacon & middlings, 1 trunk containing two razors, & $12.30 all of which has since been recovered from the premises of Elzie L. Keith by the hand of the said negro girl, except the trunk & razors which said Jacob Phillips found in the barn of Elzie L. Keiths . . . Jacob Phillips states that the negro girl Melissa came to his house and wanted him and his wife to come over. He did so and after he went there Mrs. Keith said he would write an order for her boy Tom to go for some whiskey and while he was there, Mrs. Keith said what if your house was to be broken open tonight and he said that there was no danger. Mrs. Keith said something about some of sal Phillips geting lonseome that night . . . After the articles were missing the next day he and John Phillips and found the things in Mrs. Keith's barn. He told her that this was aterrible scrape and she said what, and he said that he believed her negro had done it, and Mrs. Keith said that she would see about it. About sundown Mrs. Keiths negro girl came to his house with the money he had left and John Phillips helped count the money. Mrs. Keith came over afterward and ask him if he had got all his money back and he said yes. On cross examination Jacob Phillips said that he first told Polly Phillips his sister of the robbery of his house . . . John Phillips being sworn sayeth that he went to his Uncle Jacob Phillips house and he told him about what had happened . . . Martha Jane Keith said that she stayed in the field all day and did not miss the negro or that night wither.

NO. 2

Stephen Todd saith that Clint Arter came to his house with a hat which he said he got at an auction at Mr. Kirkseys and brought it here to sway it. It was a white Panama hat. He was not wearing it when he came. He wore it in the field but did not wear it away. He said that Mr. Williams refused to swap it.

W. S. Williams sworn saith, That on the 20th day of April Clint Arter a free man of color came to his store and did steal a fine hat from him. That he was walking about in the store and was looking at the hat and that the hat that was missing was worth about $3.00. Ann Arter sworn, Sayeth that he found the the hat in the road. I was with him. He left the hat beside the road and hung it up with a jug he had brought . . . The court found him guilty and that his sentence shall be, that he pay Mr. Williams $3.00 for the hat and a fine of $23.00 and receive 20 lashes well laid on his back. May 11, 1861. . . . In another paper found in same package the jury v. James and Berry slaves of the Widow Blassingame, on a charge of accusing Joseph Richards of stealing fruit from the orchard of their mistress. Found Berry not guilty, and find James guilty and order that he receive 10 lashes well laid on in a way not to cut the flesh, and to be whipped with a switch not to measure more than one inch round the but, and to be whipped on the bare back. Sept. 17, 1861. . . .

NO. 3

On Aug. 13, 1860 John Daniels states on the 4th day Inst. Fill Poole & Frank Poole the servants of C. P. Poole did come to his houseand there and then did violently beat and abuse him. States that he was at home in his yard and that Mr. Poole and his two boys Fill & Frank came over to give his boys peaches, and I told Pool that this would not do, the fence must be put up & then turned and went into the house. I then started to Mr. Whitfields? & met them. Fill struck me with a rock and knocked me down. Frank had a knife in his hand. I tried to catch the knife & he cut my throat, then I dont know which beat me worse. I was then led after the fracas by my sister. . . . Daniels also stated that he did not say he would make Pool afraid of him. There was nothing said about the orchard till after I moved. Pool showed a pistol which Daniel said was his and that he does not know where Pool got the pistol. Says that Pool told Fill to take hold of me & kill me. The latter part Mr. Pool admits to be true. The jury found that the negroes were acting according to their master.

"SLAVE PAPERS," PACK. 119
CLERK OF COURTS OFFICE, PICKENS, S. C.

NO. 4

On Nov. 21, 1862 W. O. Brock states that he believes that Aggy a negro slave of G. W. Brock did on the 18th Inst. in day time enter into the house of said G. W. Brock & did take there from some two bushels of wheat and that Steward a slave belonging to the heirs of Dr. F. W. Symmes was an accessory to the theft. Wm. C. Brock says that he was at Symmes Mill on wednesday last and saw Caleb a negro boy go to a stable and bring his wheat—and he went in with Caleb and saw him get the wheat & go towards the mill . . . Farmer Brock says went on tuesday last from the house some 2 hours and when she returned saw that a case of wheat had been opened and that she left no person there but Aggy & Mandy Aggy had been left in charge of the premises until she returned. Edward Symmes said that he was at the mill on tuesday last and saw and heard Steward tell Brock to bring him him his wheat. Said that Tilly Symmes gave permission to Stewrd to go to free Mary Ann to get the wheat & saw Steward clean & grind the wheat, that Steard was not off of the place on last tuesday last from 8 oclock till dark. I was present during the whole transaction. The jury found the slaves Aggy & Steward not guilty. . . .

NO. 5

On May 9, 1857 Warren D. Keith states that Jerry a slave the property of Nathaniel Reid, throw down his fence and went tp plowing on his land where it was broke up and leave a license of him and also left the fence down leaving all his corn that was planted, Wheat 7 rye to the mercy of all outside stock without leave of said Keith on the 8th instant . . . The jury found Jerry not guilty of any misdeamenor of his own accord. . . .

NO. 6

On May 18, 1859 Robert A. Lathem appeared before Larkin Hendricks a Magistrate and sworn says, that Abram a slave the property of Richard Burdine Sen. had in his possession about 2 bushels of wheat which said slave stole or got the wheat in the fall of 1858. Also states that Lewis the property of James McAdams did steal from Jas. McAdams in the fall 1858 2 bushels of wheat and took the same to Abram a slave the property of Richard Burdine Sen. . . . The jury found Abram and Lewis guilty and sentenced each to 20 lashes well laid on, on their bare back.

NO. 7

On May 31, 1858 Wm. S. Williams says that he has good reason to velieve that Dan Rouse a free man of color and Sam and Henry and Jessey slaves of Thos. Hallum are in the habit of retailing spiritious liquors from time to time. . . .

NO. 8

On Nov. 27, 1857 J. J. Hunt states that Tom Arter a free boy of color did on the 22nd of this month while he was doing his lawful duty as Capt. of patrol at one Simons House a slave came up to him and in an angry and threating manner pull off his coat and curse him at a tremendous rate and further said that he should not hurt his brother Clint Arter who said Hunt had in his custody to correct for his impudenece . . . Also Tom said that he would see his brother imposed upon, and said Hunt told him, that if he came any nearer that he would rock him down with a rock . . . S. A. Major states that while him and Hunt were patrolling at Simon Cannons they found Clint Arter there and while endeavoring to correct him for threats and impudence Tom Arter came running or walking fast with his coat drawn off and said he would be damned if he would see his brother Clint Arter imposed upon, where upon J. J. Hunt Capt. of Patrol told him that if he came any nearer he would stop him with a rock which he had in his hand. I think that the threat with the rock stopped him. The jury found Tom Arter guilty and sentenced him to 30 lashes laid on his bare back. . . .

NO. 9

On Aug. 22, 1854 Hanke Gissel made oath that Caesor is a runaway slave and was taken up in Pickens Dist. on the night of the 21st instant . . . Later John B. Earle made oath that Caesor was his property . . . Hanke Gissel recd. a $50.00 reward from A. Bryce the Sheriff for the arrest of the within slave. . . .

NO. 10

On Sept. 15, 1857 Levi Taylor said that he had been informed that Any a slave belonging to Jeremiah Prator had been threating his property, that his 2 colts should never do him any good and that his negro woman Kitty should leave there, his colts are since both dead and he has since sold the woman and has also been informed that he has threatend Wm. Claytons property and he has said that he has killed 2 persons by poisoning the spring and that he has threatened several of his neighbors. The slave was arrested and broke custody and has been out of the state. . . .

NO. 11

On Aug. 17, 1857 Melinda Russell says that Solomon a mulatto boy belonging to Ira G. Campbell of Anderson Dist. did on last friday night at her own house about 8 or 9 oclock viloently and by force commit a rape on her person by using severe blows on her body and with many threats of taking her life, and I uteerly pary that a warrant for the arrest of said boy may be granted and I further certify that I do not crave a warrant for any malice against the boy except that of the crime for which he committed . . . The jury found him guilty and sentenced him to be hung the second friday in Nov. next . . . Which is the 14th Nov. on which day between the hours of ten oclock in the forenoon and two oclock in the afternoon, you are to be taken to the place of public ececution and there hung by the neck, until you are dead, and may god have mercy on you . . . Malinda Russell says, That on friday night she went obed as she always did, went to sleep and was waked up some one hollowing at the door by saying get up, several times by a person that seemed to be very angry. I jumped up, screamed and said Lord, Lord, the person hollowing were on the western side of the house. She jumped at the door on the south side of the house, doors of the house are on opposite side. By the time she opened the door, the person was in the door, took hold of me by the shoulders and shook me almost to death and if she hollowed he would kill her. He picked up a chair then and struck her on the left arm. The person then picked up another chair which he raised on her head several times he would kill her if she hollowed and thenstruck her She was then pushed by the person from the piaza on the ground. She was then struck on the left side of her head by the fist of the person which knocked her down and choked her and said he would her if she hollowed. She was choked until she could not see. At that time she lying in the yard. She jumped up as quick as she could and screamed. The person then kicked and knocked her about until he got out in the cover some distance, caught her by the mouth to keep her from hollowing out, she was beaten and cuffed about. and was pushed or fell down. This person said he would kill her, said that he came there and would do as he pleased, he made an effor to do so. Made all the attempts that any body could make to commit a rape but did not commit the rape. Stayed at my house some time, not very long, he was actively engaged while there. She was left in the cover, as this person left her he said God damn you, and struck her in the head. He left in a hurry appeared to be frightened off by something. I got up as this person left and ran off to William Grants about ½ mile from my house. The moon was shinning full that night and she had seen this person several times before. Solomon the defendant. She lived one mile from Gambrell, she never knew who it was until she got out into the piaza. She then knew that it was Solomon. When she got to Wm. Grants she told what had happened at her house. She went to Grants and then back to her house about as quick as they could go. She had 2 children who she found under the bed when she came back to the house. She did not know at that time that Solomon had run away. She went before Esquire Stribling on saturday. A search was made for the person that disturbed her the next day after. . . . Mr. Grants people were up when she got there, they had been in bed, were just getting up, had heard her screaming and coming. First time she had seen Silomon she and her sister were going to a meeting she was going towards Gambrell. Her sister told her that he was a new negro of Mr. Gambreell, did not stop to talk to him. This was in the summer. Next time she saw him was between her fathers & her house.

NO. 12

On April 25, 1859 Samuel J. Verner sworn says, that he has grounds to suspect and does believe that Peg Oglesby, Sarah Oglesby and Tom Oglesby all free persons of color at some time between Dec. 1st and the 15th Inst. did steal and privately carry away a quanity of some bushels of wheat from him or did encoirage and procure slaves to steal the same, and deliver it to them . . . On April 25, 1859 Samuel H. Johns made oath that he does believe that Sam Oglesby a free person of color did in company with others on the night of the 21st inst. willfully break into the house store of said company and robbed the place of 75 or 80 dollars on bank notes and at the same time set fire to the house . . . Known as the S. H. Johns & Co.

The jury found Sam Oglesby guilty & confined him in the jail of Pickens Dist. until Friday the 24th June 1859 and that he be brought to the Cross Road, 3 miles north of Bachelors Retreat at 2 P. M. on that day and be hung until he is dead by the sheriff or any lawful Constable of the district.

JAMES PARSONS PACK. 120 (EQUITY)
CLERK OF COURTS OFFICE, PICKENS, S. C.

The State of South Carolina   (WILL)

In the name of God Amen. I James Parsons Calling to mind the certainty of death and the uncertainty of life do make and appoint this my last will and testament viz. First, I will and desire that all my just debts be paid by my Executors. Second, I will and bequeath to my beloved wife Maria L. Parsons during her natural life or widowhood the home tract of land on which I now live containing two hundred and fifty acres more or less, commencing at a Stake corner between me & Eneas Hunter thence a Strait line near East to a Maple corner thence a Strait line near East to a Rock corner between me and D. Grice then following the line between me and D. Grice to J. C. Parsons land, one two horse wagon and harness one Mule called Rube and one Horse called Ball, Four horned Cattle of her own Selections Two Stock Sows to be Selected by my Executors, and also all the corn, wheat, oats, fodder, and provender on the place at this time also all the Meat now killed, also my negro boy Joe and Caroline, also all the household and kitchen furniture, also that She has the Sole right of disposing of all the property she brought here, as She may wish. And the said property herein before given to my beloved wife, she is to have during her life or widowhood and after her death or marriage to be sold by my Executors and equally divided amongst my children each according to what he or She has received heretofore. Third, I will and bequeath that the remainder of my property not herein before Specificataly willed after my death Shall be Sold by my Executors and divided equally among my children according to what they have received heretofore. Fourth, I give to my beloved wife Maria L. Parsons all the ready money I may have at my death to be delivered to her by my Executors. Fifth, I appoint my two Sons Samuel Parsons and J. C. Parsons my Executors to carry this my last will and testament into affect. Signed Sealed published and declared on the 25 day of Oct. 1855 in presence of us as the last will and testament of James Parsons.

D. Grice   James Parsons (SEAL)
J. C. Grice
J. C. Boggs
Z. Smith
South Carolina

Pickens District) Personally appeared Z. Smith, who being duly sworn Saith on oath that he was present and did see James Parsons Sign and Seal the foregoing as, and for, his last will and testament, and that D. Grice, J. C. Grice and J. C. Boggs were present and witnessed the Same, in presence of each other and the testator. Sworn to before me August 18th 1862.
W. E. Holcombe O. P. D.   Z. Smith
South Carolina
Pickens District) In Ordinary

I W. E. Holcombe Ordinary of Pickens District Certify that the foregoing is a true copy of the last will and testament of James Parsons Deceased on record in my office. Given under my hand and Seal of office this 28th day of March 1864.

                                W. E. Holcombe O. P. D.

In Equity paper ment. as heirs were: Samuel Parsons, J. C. C. Parsons, F. C. Parsons, Watson Stewart & wife Mailinda who reside in Pickens Dist. J. B. Parsons, Wm. J. Parsons who resides in Texas, Thomas Parsons who resides in Arkansas, Benjamin Neighbors & wife Cynthia who reside in Alabama, James Adcock a minor son of Sallie Adcock decd. Elisha Dean & wife Caroline, Jessee Garner & wife Eliza, and Polly Mayfield who reside in Mississippi. James Adcock.

WILLIAM KIRKSEY SR. PACK. 21 EQUITY
CLERK OF COURTS OFFICE, PICKENS, S. C.

William Kirksey owned land on Golding Creek & 12 Mile River adjoining lands of William Hunter, Thomas Garvin Sr. & others whereon he had long resided. He conveyed the land to his son Elhanon W. Kirksey, therein & thereby reserving to himself the said Wm. Kirksey the use and enjoyment & possession of the said land during the term of his natural life. Afterwards Elhanon W. Kirksey departed this life intestate, unmarried & without issue, & subs equent thereto the said Wm. Kirksey also departed this life. The land is now subject to dovision amongst the heirs of the said E. W. Kirksey, consisting of his brothers & sisters viz. Nancy wife of David Garvin, Jared Kirksey who died in the lifetime of intestate, leaving 3 children, all of whom are of age viz. Jared Kirksey, Isaiah Kirksey, Mary Kirksey. 3. William Kirksey, Jr., Robert Kirksey, Christopher Kirksey, Catherine wife of Thomas J. Hallum, Penelope wife of Benjamin F. Holland. There were 2 other borthers Fair Kirksey and Silas Kirksey both of whom died unmarried & without issue, the former in the lifetime of the intestate and the latter since his death . . . The tract of land contained 300 acres. Filed Dec. 19, 1854.

LETTER OF ATTORNEY

Georgia

Lumpkin County) Know all men by these presents that I Nancy Garvin of the county and state aforesaid, for divers good causes and considerations me hereunto moving, have made, ordained and appointed, and by these presents do make ordain and appoint David Garvin, of the said state and county my true and lawful attorney for me and in my name, and for my own proper use and benefit, to ask, demand, sur for, recover and receive from Robert A. Thompson Clerk in Equity for Pickens District South Carolina, all my right, title and interest in my Fathers real estate, the late William Kirkey of the state and District last named, to receive, receipt for and do all things in the said premises, as if I were personally present my self In witness whereof I have here unto set my hand and affixed my seal this Febry 9th 1857.

Signed sealed and acknowledged before us.
Addela Garvin
R. F. Mays J. P.
State of Georgia

Nancy Garvin (LS)

Lumpkin County) I James Rusherford or Rutherford? Clerk of the Inferior court of said County and state aforesaid, do certify that Robert F. Mays, who genuine s ignature appears to the above and foregoing was at the time of signing the same and acting justice of the in and for said time of sining the same is Entitled to full faith and credit.

Given under my hand and seal of office this 10th day of Februy 1857.
James Rusherford? C. I. C.

Georgia

Lumpkin County) I Malcom J. Walker one of the justices of the Inferior Court of said county do hereby certify that James Rutherford? whose name appears to the foregoing certificate as Clerk of the inferior court of said county is the clerk of said said court and duly commissioned and qualified as such that his signature is geinuine and full faith and credit should be had to his attestations as such and that the same is in due form. Given under my hand this 10th day of February 1857.

Malcolm J. Walker J. I. C. L. C.

B. F. & PENELOPE HOLLAND PACK. 21
CLERK OF COURTS OFFICE, PICKENS, S. C.
DEED OF INT. IN REAL ESTATE

State of Georgia

Whitfield County) Know all men by these presents that we B. F. Holland and Penelope Holland his wife formerly Penelope Kirksey legal heirs and representatives of William Kirksey Dect. of the State of Georgia Whitfield County for and consideration of the sum of two hundred and fourteen dollars to me in hand paid by Thomas D. Garvin in Pickens District and State of South Carolina Have granted bargained sold and released and by these presents do grant bargain sell and release unto the said Thomas D. Garvin his heirs and assigns forever all our individual interest in all that certain piece or parcel of land situated in Pickens District and State afor said and lying on watters of Golden Creek and Twelve Mile River watters of Seneca River containing three hundred Acres more or less it being the same tract of land where the said William Kirksey formerly lived and up to the time of his Death The said William Kirksey having in his lifetime conveyed the said land to his son E. W. Kirksey Dect. which deed was to be valid at the Death of William Kirksey and the E. W. Kirksey died without heirs before he came in possession of said land and as such the said land become liable for partition amongst the other heirs adjoining lands of W? Hunter Thomas D Garvin and others Reference being had to the original papers will more fully appear Together with all and singular the rights members and appertainces there unto belonging or in any wise incident or appertaining to have and to hold all and singular our undivided interest in the said premises unto the said Thomas D Garvin his heirs and assigns forever and do hereby bind ourselves our heirs Executors or Administrators to warrant and forever defend our undivided interest in the said premises unto the said Thomas D Garvin his heirs and assigns against ourselves our heirs and against all manner of persons Lawfully claiming or to claim the same or any part thereof In Witness whereof we have set our hands and seals this the Sixth Day of Dec 1855 and in the year of our Lord one thousand Eight Hundred and fifty five and Eightyth year of Americian independence.

B. F. Holland (SEAL)
Penelope Holland (SEAL)

Sighned Sealed and delivered in the presence of
C. Kirksey
Fair Kirksey
The State of South Carolina

Pickens District) Personally appears before me C. Kirksey and makes oath that he was present and did see B. F. Holland and Penelope Holland sign seal and deliver to Thomas D. Garvin the foregoing deed for the uses and purposes therein set forth and that Fair Kirksey who was also present and saw the same, together with himself were subscribing witnesses to the same.

C. Kirksey

The above affidavit sworn to and subscribed before me this fourteenth day of December Eighteen Hundred and fifty five.

W. J. Gantt A Magistrate for Pickens District South Carolina.

RECORDED IN BOOK H PAGE 97. CERTIFIED the 25th SEPT. 1856.

C. KIRKSEY TO T. F. GARVIN PACK. 21
RELEASE FOR HIS INT. REAL ESTATE
CLERK OF COURTS OFFICE, PICKENS, S. C.

State of South Carolina

Know all men by these presents that I Christopher Kirksey of the State of Georgia and County of Whitfield for and in consideration of the sum of Two Hundred and Fourteen Dollars to me in hand paid by Thos. D. Garvin of Pickens District and State aforesaid Have granted bargained sold and released and by these presents do grant bargain sell and release unto the sd. Thos. D. Garvin his heirs and assigns forever all my undivided interest of all that certain tract of land situate in Pickens District and State aforesaid and Lying on Goldens Creek and Twelve Mile River waters of Seneca River containing Three Hundred Acres more or less it being the same tract of land whereon Wm. Kirksey Decd. formerly lived and up to the time of his death The said Wm. Kirksey having in his lifetime conveyed the sd land to his son E. W. Kirksey Decd. which Deed was to be valid at the death of Wm. Kirksey (and the said E. W. Kirksey died without heirs before he came in possession of the sd. land and as such the said land becomes liable for partition amongst the other Heirs) adjoining lands of Wm. Hunter Jun. Thos. D. Garvin and others reference being had the original papers will more fully appear Together with all and singular the rights members hereditaments and appertenance there unto belonging or in any wise incident or appertaining to have and to hold all and singular my undivided interest in the said premises unto the said Thos. D. Garvin his Heirs and assigns Forever and I do hereby bind my self my heirs Executors or Administrators to warrant and forever defend my undivided interes in the said premises unto the said Thos. D. Garvin his heirs and assigns against my self my heirs and against all manner of persons whomsoever Lawfully claiming or to claim any part thereof. In witness whereof I have set my hand and seal this 11th day of September in the year of our Lord one thousand Eight Hundred and Fifty-five and Eightyeth year of Americian Independence.

C. Kirksey (SEAL)

Signed Sealed and delivered in the presence of W. L. Keith, Robt. A. Thompson.

South Carolina
Pickens District) Before me personally appeared W. L. Keith and made oath that he was present and did see C. Kirksey sign seal and deliver the within deed for the use and purposes there in mentioned and Robt. A. Thompson with himself witnessed the same. Sworn to before me this 22d day of Decr. 1855.
Thos. J. Keith Dept. Clk.
RECORDED IN BOOK G PAGE 687. CERTIFIED 22 Decr. 1855.

THOMAS J. & CATHERINE HALLUM PACK. 21
LETTER OF ATTORNEY TO JOHN H. TREWELL?
CLERK OF COURTS OFFICE PICKENS, S. C.

The State of Texas
County of Upshur) Know all men by these presents that we T. J. Hallam and his wife Catharine Hallam of the county and state aforesaid for divers good causes and considerations have made constituted authorized and appointed and by these presents do make constitute authorize and appoint John H. Trowell? (check this name) of said county and state our true and Lawful attorney for us and in our names place and Stead to ask demand and receive and recover of and from the proper authorities in the State of South Carolina or from any person having the same in possession all money, goods chattels or property of any description or interest of whatsoever nature which we or either of us of right have in and to a certain Trust Estate created by Deed of T. J. Hallum executed to Fair Kirksey as Trustee for Catharine Hallam in Anderson District in the state of South Carolina on the 25th day of March A. D. 1843 and all of the same Estate which was reinvested in other property By the Deed or instrument of B. F. Sloan and George Seaborn made and executed to said Fair Kirksey on the 12th day of November A. D. 1844 giving to our said attorney full power to sue for settle compromise or to arrange in the Best manner our entire interest in said Trust Estate and to receipt for us and in our names the proper persons having any of said Estate in possession and to sign our names to any instrument of writing necessary for the settlement of said Estate as the protection of our interest therein we also authorize and empower our said attorney to ask demand sue for and receive and recover of and from Thomas D. Garvin the Trustee of said Estate appointed by the Court of Equity for Pickens District in said State of South Carolina all the interest of said Estate controlled by him or in his possession and also my other money or property of any description belonging to us which he may have in his possession or in any wise control and we also hereby fully authorize and empower our said attorney to ask demand and receive of and from the Commissioner in Equity for Pickens District in said State of South Carolina all the money property or interest of any description of said Estate which the said commissioner may have in charge, or control and authorize our said attorney to receipt for the same and we also authorize and empower our said attorney to ask demand sue for receive and recover of and from the proper authority or person our distributive share or the interest of

right belonging to us or either of us in the Estate of William Kirksey deceased also authorize him to ask demand sue for receive and recover of and from the proper authority or person our distributive share or the interest belonging to us or either of us in the Estate of E. W. Kirksey deceased also give our said attorney the same authority in the Estate of Fair Kirksey deceased and also in the Estate of Richard Hallam deceased and also hereby give to our said attorney full and general power in the premises and also full and general power to do and transact any Business in the state of South Carolina in which our interest may in any manner be concieved authorizing him in all cases to use discretionary power if necessary in effecting any settlement or compromise and to employ attorneys if necessary and sign our names in cases where the same may be required Hereby ratifying and holding firm all the acts our said attorney in and about the premises In Testimony whereof we hereunto set our hands and seals using scrawls for seals the 11th day of May A. D. 1857.

T. J. Hallum (SEAL)
CATHARIne Hallum (SEAL)

In presence of A. H. Abney, J. G. Cromer?

The State of Texas
The State of Texas

County of Upshur) Personally appeared before me A. H. Abney one of the Subscribing Witnesses to the above and foregoing Power of Attorney and after being duly Sworn Says that he did see T. J. and Catharine Hallum Sign Seal and deliver the same and that they acknowledged the same to be their act and deed for the purposes and considerations therein stated Given under my hand this the 11th day of May AD 1857.

S. C. Hart Justice of the Peace

The State of Texas

County of Upshur) I G. E. Warren Clerk of the County Court in and for the County of Upshur and State aforesaid do hereby certify that S. C. Hart whose name appears to the above Certificate of authentication is an acting Justice of the Peace for Upshur County duly commissioned and sworn and that his Signature to the same is genuine and that his said act is entitled to full faith and credit. Given under my hand with the seal of the County Court hereon impressed at my office in the Town of Gilmer on this the 11th day of May AD 1857.

G. E. Warren Clerk of U. Co. T.

BENJAMIN F. LAWRENCE PACK. 22 EQUITY
CLERK OF COURTS OFFICE, PICKENS, S. C.

Adaline Lawrence wife of Benjamin F. Lawrence of Pickens District by her son Joseph R. Lawrence states that, Rachel Lawrence the grandmother of her husband by deed, dated the 28th Decr. 1844 gave to James Lawrence her fatherinlaw who resides in said district the sum of $800.00 with the accruing interest in trust for her Adalines use, "only separtae use and behoof" during her natural life and fater her death for the heirs of her body share and share alike etc. that the said James Lawrence accepted in writing the said trust about five days after the date of the said deed, recd. the trust fund and then had the said deed and acceptance duly proved and recored. That the said fund has not been paid to her by the James Lawrence. That altho the burden of the support of the family has devolved on her on account of the unprovidence of her otherwise kind and industrious husband caused by his unfortunate love of spiritious liquors, yet rather than enter suit against her fatherinlaw now in his 78th year and consquently feeble & infirm, she would have struggled on with poverty and want feeling that the said fund was accumulating for her children but her said trustee altho he faithfully promised her since the close of the late war to secure the said trust fund by confession of judgement, being as he informed her then, and as she is informed believes and charges that he now is in very doubtful circumstances, has never the less subsequently to his said promise and very recently set up and pretended that a certain negro girl slave by the name of Rachel, bought by the said James Lawrence and loaned to his son Benjamin F. Lawrence her husband was bought with the said trust fund . . . Filed May 9, 1867.

B. F. Lawrence states that Wm. L. Keith was appointed trustee for his wife the said Adaline Lawrence in her interest in the estate of her late father Stephen C. Reid.

RACHEL LAWRENCE TO JAMES LAWRENCE PACK. 22
DEED OF GIFT
CLERK OF COURTS OFFICE, PICKENS, S. C.

Deed of Gift
State of South Carolina

Pickens District) Know all men by these presents that I Rachel Lawrence of the District of Pickens and State aforesaid for and in consideration of the love and affection which I have for and towards my Grand Daughter Adaline Lawrence wife of Benjamin F. Lawrence and in consideration of other good causes and the sum of Five dollars to me in hand paid my son James Lawrence of the same district and state the receipt and payment whereof I do hereby acknowledge have this day given and by these presents do give and in plain and openly give and deliver unto the said James Lawrence Trustee the following amount of money to wit Eight hundred Dollars in cash to have and to hold the said Eight hundred dollars together with the interest of the same that may arise therefrom unto the said James Lawrence and to his heirs assigns and executors as Trustee to the only separated use benefit and behoof of the said Adaline Lawrence during her natural life and after her death to the only separate use benefit and behoof of the heirs of her body and it is herein provided that James Lawrence the above named Trustee shall have full power to purchase any lands slaves or other valuable property if he should deem it necessary and expedient for the interest of the said parties and invest the same to the only seperate use and behoof of the said Adaline Lawrence during her life and at her death to the use of her Heirs of her body or to keep the same amount of money at using as he may think best for the interest of the said parties during the life of the said Adaline Lawrence and after her death to the heirs of her body share and share alike and should my said Trustee die or remove the said Adaline Lawrence has full power to chose other trustee or Trustees to act in his place and at all times to appoint

Trustee or Trustees whenever necessary to act for her in the same matter. In witness whereof I have hereunto set my hand and seal this Twenty eighth day of December in the year of our Lord one thousand eight hundred and forty four and in the sixth ninth year of Americian Independence. Signed sealed and delivered in presence of

           her
       Rachel X Lawrence (SEAL)
          mark

Rachal Craig
David T. Lewis
State of South Carolina

 Pickens District) Know all men by these presents that I James Lawrence the Trustee named in the within deed of Trust do hereby signify my acceptance to the trust therein specified witness my hand and seal this econd day of January in the year of our Lord one thousand eight hundred and forty five. Signed sealed and acknowledged in the presence of us

         James Lawrence (SEAL)

J. L. Kennedy
E. E. Alexander
South Carolina

 Pickens District) Before me personally appeared Revd. J. L. Kennedy and made oath that he was present and did see James Lawrence sign seal and acknowledge the acceptance to the trust within mentioned and E. E. Alexander was present and a subscribing witness with himself to the due execution of the same. Sworn to & Subscribed before me Jany 1845.
W. L. Keith C. C.
            J. L. Kennedy
State of South Carolina

 Pickens District) Before me personally appeared Mrs. Rachal Craig and made oath that she was present and did see Rachal Lawrence sign seal and acknowledge the within deed of trust by making her mark to James Lawrence for the uses and purposes therein mentioned and David T. or F? Lewis with this deponent witness the same in presence of each other. Sworn to and subscribd before me this 3d January 1845.
W. L. Keith CC
            Rachal Craig
 RECORDED JANUARY 3, 1845.

JAMES McKINNEY PACK. 23 EQUITY
CLERK OF COURTS OFFICE, PICKENS, S. C.

 James McKinney departed this life several years since, intestate leaving a widow Mary McKinney & the following heirs, John McKinney, Elizabeth Lay & her husband James Lay, James McKinney, William McKinney, Sarah McKinney and James McKinney her husband, Preston McKinney, Mary Earnest, Ester Robinson & her husband James Robinson, sons, daughters and soninlaws of James McKinney decd. Eliza Knox & her husband Robert Knox, Rosa Morton, Sarah McKinney & her husband Chesley McKinney, John McKinney, Evaline McKinney and Sarah McKinney children of Charles McKinney who was a son of the said James McKinney and is now dead, Nancy McKinney widow of David McKinney and his children. Jesse & Wilson McKinney were also sons of said James McKinney decd . . . Filed June 2, 1857.

SILAS KIRKSEY PACK. 50 EQUITY
CLERK OF COURTS OFFICE, PICKENS, S. C.

Silas Kirksey's will was probated in court Oct. 14, 1853. In his will he had willed to his nephew William Silas Kirksey son of Robert Kirksey the following negroes viz. Vina a negro woman & her children viz. Wesley, Mahala, Brareale, Harriet, Julia Ann, Eli & Sarah Elizabeth and to his nephew Silas R. Holland son of B. F. Holland & his sister Penelope the following negroes Drilla & her children viz. Harrison, Mary & George. And to his father William Kirksey Sr. his negro man Sam during his natural life and at his decease to his brother Robert Kirksey forever. And to his nephew Silas Garvin son of David Garvin & his sister Nancy the following negroes Jincy a negro woman and Tom a negro man. He owned a tract of land near the village of Pickens & also 3 town lots in the village of Pickens. Estate divided between Robert Kirksey, Wm. Kirksey, Alexander Bryce & Wm. Silas Kirksey a minor over 14 years, all residing in Pickens District & his other brothers & sisters.

Filed March 31, 1858.

W. Kirksey Jr.
    to
W. L. Keith   Trust Deed

The State of South Carolina

Know all men by these presents that I William Kirksey Jr. of the District of Pickens and State aforesaid, for and in consideration of good will natural love and affection I have and do bear towards my beloved wife Eady Katharine Kirksey and my Daughter Rebecca Kirksey and Joseph B. Kirksey and in consideration of the sum of Five dollars to me in hand paid by W. L. Keith of the State and District aforesaid the receipt whereof is hereby acknowledged Have granted bargained and released and confirmed and by these presents do grant bargain release and confirm in plain and open market unto the said W. L. Keith Trustee the following property to wit, all those Houses and lots in the Village of Pickens and State aforesaid, formerly occupied by my brother Silas Kirksey and sold by his Executor to me, also I convey unto my said trustee W. L. Keith for the use of my said wife and children as aforesaid all the goods money Stock and chattels real and personal Estate that may be in the hands of W. L. Keith Administrators of the Estate of S. Kirksey decd. that may be due me or coming from said Estate as one of his legal Heirs or in the hands forever or possession of any other person said W. L. Keith is authorized to draw the same and to hold as trust Estate for my said wife and children to invest the same in any other kind of property that will be more advantageious in his judgment to my said wife and children. I hereby further authorise the said Trustee to sell and dispose of all those Houses and lots above mentioned and to reinvest the same in any other kind of property he may think fit and proper for my said wife and children or to retain the money for there use as he may think best her further hereby authorised and impowered to appoint other trustee or Trustees to act for them in his place and stead then the said Trustee shall be fully discharged from any further liability in the said deed of trust. Witness my hand and seal this Sixth day of March in the year of our Lord one thousand eight hundred and fifty four and in the Seventy eighth year of American Independence.

                                          Wm. Kirksey Jr. (SEAL)

Signed sealed and delivered in the presence of
A. Bryce
P. Alexander
South Carolina

Pickens District) I W. L. Keith the Trustee named in the annexed or within deed of Trust do hereby signafy my acceptance of the trust therein specified and stated.

Given under my hand & seal this 6 day of March Anno Domini 1854.
A. Bryce   W. L. Keith (SEAL)
P. Alexander
Proven April 12, 1854.

JOHN GILSTRAP PACK. 54 EQUITY
CLERK OF COURTS OFFICE, PICKENS, S. C.

John Gilstrap owned 170 acres on Rices Creek, waters of Twelve Mile River in Pickens District, adjoining lands of John Arial, Joseph Young & others. He sold the said lands Dec. 15, 1854 to Harvey Tripp of said district for $600.00. Harvey Tripp paid half of the money and refused to pay the rest. . . .

Filed May 26, 1858.

Harvey Tripp was a porr man engaged in dailey labor as a freight conductor upon the Greenville & Columbia Railroad and the tract aforesaid is the home of his family, from whom he is for the most part seperated by the nature of his business. . . .

Georgia

Forsythe County) To Robert A. Thompson

Sir you will please make a title to the land that I bought at sale from you to E. P. Smith as I have sold him the land by his paying you your cost as I have settled James Hagood & Jacob P. Reed cost as yours is all that is behind an oblige &c this 2nd January 1860.

                                                        John Gilstrap

Harvey Tripp states that the first subpoena in this case was handed to him at Cokesbury in Abbeville District on the 8th June last which was the first notice he had had of this suit. Since then he had made 2 tripe to Greenville to see his attorneys but due to their absence failed to do.

JOHN SHARP JR. TO ELIZABETH McALLASTER DEED PACK. 58
CLERK OF COURTS OFFICE, PICKENS, S. C.

South Carolina

Pickens Judtial District) Know all men By these presents that I John Sharp Junr of the State and District Aforesaid in Consideration of the Sum of Three hundred and Fifty Dollars to me in Hand paid by Elizabeth McAllaster of the State and District Aforesaid, Have granted Bargained Sold and Released and by these presents do grant Bargain sell and Release unto the said Elizabeth McAllaster all that Plantation or tract of land situate in the District Aforesaid on the Oconey Creek waters of Little River Containg one Hundred and Twenty acres Be the same more or less Beginning on a spannish oak 3x near said creek thence south 10 W. 6 to A black oak thence N. 85. W 50 to a black oak 3x thence S 55 W 12.50 to A black oak 3x thence S 28 W 34.50 to aread oak 3x N 5 E 47 to a post oak 3x thence A north East Coars along A conditional line to a large Black oak 3x thence to a large pine 3x thence toA small Red oak 3x standing close to the Maple Stump the old corner thence down the creek to A crab apple Tree corner thence down the manders of the creek to the Begining Corner. Together with all and Singular the rights members Hereditaments & Appertances to the said premises Belonging or in anny wise Incident or appertaining to Have and to hold all and Singular the premises Before mentioned unto the said Elizabeth McAllaster Her Heirs and Assigns for Ever And I do hereby Bind my Self my Heirs Executors Administrators to warrant And for Ever Defend all and Singular the said premises unto the said Elizabeth McAllaster Her Heirs and Assigns against my self and against Every person whom soever Lawfully claiming or to claim the same or anny part thereof as Witness my Hand and Seal this Eleventh Day of Sember in the year of our Lord one Thousand Eight Hundred and Twenty Eight and in Fifty Second year of the Independence of the Unighted States of America.

John Sharp (LS)

Signed Seal and Delivered in the presence of
William Hammond
John Capehart
South Carolina

Pickens Judical District) Personally appeared Before me and Made Oath William Hammond that he saw John Sharp Sign Seal & as his act & Deed Deliver the within Deed for the use and perpose therein mentioned and that John Capehart with him self was A subscribing witness to the Same. Sworn to this 11th Day of Septr 1823. (NOTE. At this place the year was written 1823 instead of 1828, must be the ordinarys mistake).

William Hammond

Before me
Jacob Capehart J. P. Q.
South Carolina

Pickens Judical District) I Jacob Capehart one of the Justices of Quorom for Sd. District and State Aforesaid do hereby Certify unto all whome it may Concern that Catharine Sharp the wife of the within named John Sharp Did this Day appear Before me and upon Being privately & Seperately Examined by me did declare that she does freely voluntarily & without anny Compulsion Dread or fear of anny person or persons whomsoever Renounce Release & for Ever Relinquish unto the within named Elizabeth McAllaster her heirs & Assigns all her interest & Estate and also all her Right & Claim of Dower of in or to all & Singular the premises within mentioned & Released. Given under my Hand & Seal this 11th Day of September 1828.

Jacob Capehart J. Q. Catharine Sharp

RECORDED IN BOOK A PAGE 206. CERTIFIED DEC. 7, 1829.

FRANCES JENKINS TO JOHN SHARP JR. PACK. 58 DEED
CLERK OF COURTS OFFICE, PICKENS, S. C.

South Carolina
Pendleton Destrict) Know all men By these presents that I Frances Jenkins of the State and Destrict Aforesaid in Consideration of the sum of Four

Hundred Dollars to me in Hand paid by John Sharp Junier of the State & Destrict Aforesaid Have granted Bargained Sold and Released and By these presents do grant Bargain Sell and Release unto the said John Sharp Junier all that Plantation or tract of Land Situate in the Destrict Aforesaid on the Oconey Creek waters of Little River Containing one hundred and Twenty Acres Be the Same more or less Begining on A spanish oake 3x neare Said Creek thene S. 10 W. 6 Black oak thene N. 85 W. 8.50 to a black oak 3x thene S. 55 W. 12.50 to a black oak thence S. 28 W. 34.50 to a read oak 3x N. 5 E 47 to a post oake 3 x thene A north East corse along A Conditional line to A large Black Oak 3 x thene to A large pine 3 x thene to a small Red Oak 3x Standing Close to the Maple Stump the old corner thence Down the Creek to a Crab apple Tree Corner thene Down the Manders of the creek to the Beginning Corner Together with all and singular the rights members, Hereditaments and Appertainances to the Said premises, velonging, or in any wise incident or Appertaining to have and to hold all and Singular the premises before mentioned unto the said John Sharp Jun'r his Heirs and Assigns for Ever. And I do hereby Bind my self my heirs, Executors, And Administrators to warrant And for ever Defend, all and Singular the said premises unto the said John Sharp Jun'r His heirs And Assigns, against my Self and Against Every person whomsoever Lawfully claiming or to Claim, the Same or any part thereof Witness my Hand And Seal this third Day of June in the year of our Lord one Thousand Eight Hundred and Twenty Three And in the Forty Seventh year of the Independence of the Unighted States of America. Sighnd, Seald and Delivered in the presence of

James Jenkins Frances Jenkins (SEAL)
Nancy Jenkins
South Carolina

Pendleton District) Personally appeared James Jenkins Before me and made oath he did see Frances Jenkins Signe Seal and as his act & Deed Deliver the within Deed for the use and purpose therein mentioned and that Nancy Jenkins with himself was a Subscribing witness to the same Sworn to and Subscribed Before me this 3d Day of Jun anno Domini 1823.

Jacob Capehart J. Q. James Jenkins
South Carolina

Pendleton Destrict) I Jacob Capehart one of the justice of the Quorum of the State and District Aforesaid do hereby Certify unto all whom it may concern, that Polly Jenkins the wife of the within Frances Jenkins did this day appear Before me and upon being privately & Separately examined By me did declare that she does freely voluntarily and without any compulsion dread or fear of any person or persons whomsoever Renounce Release, forever Relinquish unto the within named John Sharp Jur. His Heirs and Assigns, all her interest and Estate and also all her Right and Claim of Dower, of in or to all and Singular the premises within mentioned and Released. Given under my Hand and Seal this 3d Day of June Anno Domini 1823.
Jacob Capehart J. Q.

                                              her
                                    Polly X Jenkins
                                          mark

CERTIFIED SEPT. 1, 1825.

CAPT. DAVID SLOAN PACK. 58 EQUITY
CLERK OF COURTS OFFICE, PICKENS, S. C.

William C. Sloan & John T. Sloan states that their father David Sloan died in October 1834. That he owned the following plantations or tracts of land viz. 400 acres on Cane Creek where David Sloan lately lived known as the Moultrie tract, 260 acres on Cane Creek being part of two tracts, one originally granted to Benjam in Lawrence, the other to John Crosby & known as the Scott tract, 150 acres whereon Thomas McDonald lives lying on Conneross Creek bounded by Thos. McDonald, James H. Dendy & Nathaniel Hull, 130 acres lying on Crooked Creek being part of a tract originally granted to James Barton & known as the Garret tract, 310 acres known as the Crosby tract being part of 2 tracts, one originally granted to Joab Lawrence & the other to John Crosby. 120 acres lying on Oconey Creek known as the McAllister tract, 400 acres lying on waters of crooked creek, formerly owned by Andrew Mullinax & adjoining the Crosby tract, 150 acres lying on the north side of (?) Creek & known as the Voyles tract etc. . . . Left a widow Nancy Sloan, John W. A.? Blassingham in right of wife Sarah M.? George W. Bowen in right of his wife Emily C. late Sloan, Susan A. Sloan, Lucy C. Sloan, Thomas J. Sloan, Benjamin F. Sloan, Wm. D. Sloan, John T. Sloan . . . Filed June 27, 1835. . . .

Nancy Sloan

Benjamin F. Sloan was an infant under 14 years & wanted his Uncle Benjamin F. Sloan to be his guardian . . . Lucy C. Sloan, Thomas J. Sloan were infants under 14 years & Nancy Sloan wanted their Uncle Thomas Sloan to be their guardian . . . Susan Sloan was a minor over 14 years and wanted her Uncle Benjamin Sloan to be her guardian . . . Capt. David Sloan died on or about the 29th Oct. . . .

McALLISTERS DEED TO CAPT. DAVID SLOAN PACK. 58
CLERK OF COURTS OFFICE, PICKENS, S. C.

South Carolina

Pickens District) Know all men by these presents that we Andrew McAlister & Elizabeth McAlister of District aforesaid for and in consideration of the sum of forty one dollars twenty four cents to us in hand paid the receipt whereof is hereby acknowledged hav Granted Bargained and sold and by these presents doth Grant Bargain Sell and release unto David Sloan of said State & District allthat Parcell or Tract of Land whereon we now live containing one hundred and twenty acres more or less runing as follows beginning ona spanish oak 3x near the creek runing thence South 10 W 6 to a Black oak thence N. 85 W. 50 to a black oak 3x thence S 55 W. 50 to a Black oak 3x thence S 28 W. 34.50 to a Red oak 3x thence N. 5 E 47 to a post oak 3x thence a north coarse along a conditional line to a Large Black oak 3x thence to a large Pine 3x thence to a small Red oak 3x standing close to the maple stump the old corner thence down the creek to a crab apple tree corner thence Down the Meanders of the creek to the begining corner Reference to Sharps Deed to Elizabeth McCalister will fully shew the same To have and to hold the said Tract of Land together with every privilege thereto be longing or in any wise incident we do hereby bind ourselves our Heirs Executors and Administrators to warrant and defend the same and every part thereof unto the said David Sloan his heirs and assigns against us our Heirs Executors and

Administrators and all other Lawful claims whatsoever in witness whereof we have hereunto set our hand and seal this ninth day of February in the year of our Lord one thousand Eight hundred and thirty.

                                his
                      Andrew   X   McAlister (SEAL)
                                mark
                                her
                    Elizabeth   X   McAlister (SEAL)
                                mark

Signed Sealed and Delivered in presence of R. Cox.
Robert Jackson
The State of South Carolina

Pickens District) Personally appeared Jacob R. Cox before me and made oath that he saw Andrew McAlister & Elizabeth McAllister Sign Seal and deliver the within deed of conveyance to Capt. David Sloan for the use and purposes within mentioned and that Robert Jackson with himself witnessed the due execution of the sa,e Sworn to the 3rd May 1830 before William L. Keith.

                                                        JR Cox

RECORDED IN BOOK A PAGE 282. CERTIED JUNE 7, 1830.

JEREMIAH WILLIAMS PACK. 64 EQUITY
CLERK OF COURTS OFFICE, PICKENS, S. C.

Paschal K. Williams of Pickens District states that his father Jeremiah Williams died on or about the 14th March 1855 intestate. Owned 573 acres on the waters of 23 Mile Creek adjoining lands of David K. Hamilton & others. Also one half of a h ouse & lot situated at Salubrity held in joint tenants by the said Jeremiah Williams & William S. Williams his son. Owned 27 slaves, also a stock of horses, cattle, hogs & Plantation implements are subject to division amongst his heirs viz. his widow Charity Williams & 14 children viz. William S. Williams, Frances Williams, Nancy Williams, Benjah Williams, Thomas P. Williams, Graham F. Williams, Christian B. Williams, Reginald O. or C? Williams, Mary E. Williams, Cynthia M? Williams, Elvira G. Williams, Paul E. A. Williams all of whom reside in Pickens District and are all of full age, except the last 4 mentioned who are minors over the age of 12 years. David Williams a Son of the said Jeremiah Williams died in November 1854 which was before the death of his father. He was of full age and unmarried and owned considerable real estate. One tract of 195 acres on both sides of 18 Mile Creek . . . Catherine Williams a daughter married James C. Welborn. . .
Filed May 20, 1855.

JAMES HOLDEN PACK. 68 EQUITY
CLERK OF COURTS OFFICE, PICKENS, S. C.

Jacob Alexander & his wife Polly Alexander who was formerly Polly Holden states that James Holden her father died in May 1854 intestate. That he owned 585 acres of land on both sides of Big & Little Crow Creek, waters of Keowee River. adjoining lands of E. Alexander & others. Owned 250 acres on Big Crow Creek adjoining lands of Henry Grogan & the home tract & others & known as the Humphries Tract. Owned 152 acres on Little & Big Crwo Creek adjoining lands of William Alexander & others. Subject to distribution among his children as follows, Joshua Holden who resides in Pickens

District, Lucy Maloy who married Andrew Maloy & resides in Louisiana, the husband however has not been heard from for many years. The children & representatives of Malinda Roe formerly Malinda Holden viz her husband Watson Roe & her children, David Roe, James Roe, Ruthy Roe names & numbers of the others not known now in Alabama . . . Salina Alexander formerly Salina Holden who married James Alexander & resides in Alabama. Jannetta Ray formerly Janetta Holden who married Emory Ray & resides in Georgia, Arvy or Anadoe Holden a minor who resides in Alabama, John Holden who resides in Alabama, Nancy Moody formerly Nancy Holden who married Abraham Moody and resides in Alabama. Letty Nix formerly Letty Holden who married Tyre Nix & resides in Alabama. Elizabeth Ann Nix formerly Elizabeth Ann Holden who married Daniel Nix & resides in Alabama, Fanny Bynum formerly Fanny Holden who married Elijah Bynum & reside in Alabama . . . Filed April 12, 1856. . . .

CHARLES C. MORGAN PACK. 71 EQUITY
CLERK OF COURTS OFFICE, PICKENS, S. C.

John H. Reed & his wife Susan M. Reed before marriage Susan M. Morgan states that her father Charles C. Morgan died in 1847 leaving as his heirs his widow Sarah Morgan & 6 children viz. John J. Morgan, Mary A. Morgan, Charles M. Morgan, Licena C. Morgan, Sarah F. Slater then Sarah F. Morgan who has since married Edward Slater . . . That John J. Morgan, Mary A. Morgan, Charles M. Morgan & Licena C. Morgan are minors . . . Letters of Administration were granted on the personal estate of Charles Morgan by Wm. D. Steele Esq. Ord. of Pickens District on Oct. 18, 1847, to Sarah Morgan & John Rankin. That on Sept. 5, 1842 the court sold for partition in several tracts the real estate of Thomas Richards, one tract containing 600 acres was purchased at said sale by Edward Rankin for the sum of $400.00. That Susan Reeds father soon after the sale, previous to his death, and before any part of the purchase money except the cost was paid contracted to purchase a portion supposed to be one half or about 300 acres of said land bought by Edward Rankin, at the valuation of $250.00 and agreed to pay the purchase money on the bond to said Rankin to the Commissioners of the Court of Equity. But alas before he was able to make the first payment he was removed by the hand of death, but not before he had accumulated a sufficiency of money and other personal estate to pay all his debts, among which we reckon the amount due for the tract of land, and to leave a small amount of money to be divided among his heirs at law . . . Filed May 12, 1858. Mary A. Morgan married Charles Mayhew.

EDWARD RANKIN TO SARAH MORGAN PACK. 71 DEED
CLERK OF COURTS OFFICE, PICKENS, S. C.

Edward Rankin   Release for 500 Acres Land
   to
Sarah Morgan
State of South Carolina

Pickens District) Know all men by these presents that I Edward Rankin of the State and District aforesaid for and in consideration of the sum of two hundred and fifty dollars to me paid by Sarah Morgan of said state and District the receipt whereof is hereby acknowledged, have granted, bargained and sold and by these presents do grant bargain sell and release unto the said Sarah Morgan her heirs and assigns a part of the plantation or tract of land, land which I purchased at the sale of the Richards lands and a deed being made to me by the Commissioner in Equity for Pickens District South Carolina on the 5th day of September 1842 Containing as supposed not having been run out about Three Hundred acres more or less a conditional line commencing on the South side of Oconey Creek said line commences and runs a straight line by a double Chestnut to a pine, thence a straight line to a post oak stump on the ridge near Grogans shop, thence a straight line to the mouth of the creek, thence up the creek to a Small Chestnut, on the point of the Bluff, thence a straight line to a post oak, thence a straight line to Gum, thence a straight line to where the back line across the Brasstown trail and thence the old line round to the beginning of the conditional line. To have and to hold all and singular the premises above mentioned unto the said Sarah Morgan her heirs and assigns against myself my heirs and against every other person lawfully, claiming or to Claim, the same or any part thereof. In witness whereof I have hereunto set my hand and seal this twenty seventh day of November AD one thousand Eight hundred and forty eight and in the seventy second of the Sovereignty and Independence of the United States.

            his
          Edward X Rankin (SEAL)
            mark

In Presence
Silas Kirksey
John Rankin
South Carolina

Pickens District) I Edward Rankin agree to give the said Sarah Morgan her Heirs & C Priviledge of a Road to run straight through the field where it crosses the creek run to her plantation and bind myself my heirs and assigns to warrant that privelege to thes aid Sarah Morgan. Given under my hand & seal the 27th day of November 1848. In presence of

            his
         Edward X Rankin (LS)
            mark

Silas Kirksey
John Rankin
State of South Carolina

Pickens District) Before me Personally appeared Silas Kirksey and made oath in due form that he was present and did see Edward Rankin sign seal & as his act and deed deliver the foregoing deed to Mrs. Sarah Morgan & her heirs for the use & purpose therein mentioned and that John Rankin was also present and subscribed his name, as a witness to the same in presence of each other. Sworn to and subscribed before me this third day of February 1857.

                Silas Kirksey

L. N. Robins Not Pub
State of South Carolina

Pickens District) I Levi N. Robins Notary Public & Ex off a magistrate in and for the District aforesaid do hereby certify to all whom it may concern that Mrs. Mary Rankin, the wife of the within named Edward Rankin, did this day appear before me and upon being by me privately and separately examined did declare that she does freely voluntarily and without any compulsion dread or fear of any person or persons, whomsover renounce release and forever relinquish unto the fore mentioned Mrs. Sarah Morgan & her heirs all her right title, & interest, of in, or to, all and singular the forementioned premises and also all the Claim of Dower to the forementioned and described premises & Released.

         Mary X Rankins her mark

Given under my hand and seal this 31 January AD 1857.

HUDSON GREENWOOD TO GEORGE CALHOUN PACK. 71 BOND
CLERK OF COURTS OFFICE, PICKENS, S. C.

South Carolina

 Pickens Dist) Know all men by these presents that I Hudson Greenwood of the State of Tennessee and in the County of McMinn am held and firmly bound unto George Calhoun his heirs administrators and assigns in the sum of one thousand dollars well and truly to be paid. The condition of the above obligation is such that should the above named Hudson Greenwood make or cause to be made a full relinquishment of a part or claim to a certain tract or parce 1 of land which claim is one fourth of said tract and is agreeably to James Yowells will the property to Elizabeth Yowell daughter of Joshua Yowell deceased which part with the balance of said tract was this day conveyed by said Greenwood to said Calhoun, and the said part is to be released by the time said Elizabeth Yowell is of age or sooner if it can be done agreeably to Law. Also the said Greenwood bind himself to relinquish or to cause his wife Sarah to relinquish her Dowry to the above mentioned tract of land this day conveyed. The conditions being punctually complied with, the above bond to be null and void, also in case of failure I Hudson Greenwood have herein bound myself to relinquish the right of a certain tract of land on the head waters of Mill Creek waters of Tugalo River in the aforesaid State & District containing one hundred & sixty acres more or less & formerly was the property of James Yowell deceased in case the fourth part of the above tract is not relinquished the one hundred & sixty acre tract only as a part of the compensation for said tract on Tugalo River, which Land I agree to give George Calhoun a right & title to, in case of failure. If the annexed is complied with as stated this Bond shall be of no effect, but if to the contrary to remain in full force and virtue agreeably to Law. In testimony whereof the said Greenwood hath hereto set his hand & seal this ninth day of April A. D. one thousand eight hundred & twenty nine.

Test   Hutson Greenwood (LS)
Claud Barton
James Eddins

SARAH E. MITCHELL PACK. 72 EQUITY
CLERK OF COURTS OFFICE, PICKENS, S. C.

 James M. Reid of Pickens District states that his mother Mrs. Sarah E. Mitchell who died on or about the 4th June 1852 was seized and possessed at the time of her death of an individual interest in joint tenancy with her hus-

band F. M. Mitchell in a certain tract of land situate in Pickens Dist. containing 265 acres adjoining lands of Stephen Watson, Wilson? Gilliand & others & known as the Pickensvills tract, which said land was part of the estate of the late Stephen C. Reid. That at the death of Sarah Mitchell her undivided interest was subject to partition among her distributees viz. one third thereof to said husband F. M. Mitchell, and the remaining to be divided between her eight children viz. George M. Reid, Adeline D. Lawrence & her husband B. F. Lawrence, Joseph B. Reid, Mary Reid, Esther Reid, Stephen C. Reid, James M. Reid and Benjamin Mitchell. The last five mentioned are minors.
Filed June 2, 1857.

In same package, probably by mistake. James Blythe states that sometime in the year 1840 he purchased from James McKinney a tract of land on Cheowee Creek at the price of 42 hundred dollars of which he paid all but about one thousand & 11 hundred dollars. A claim has been set up and suit brought therefrom by Sally Lawrence formerly Sally (looked like Sally M. Cholsom am not positive writing was to bad.)
Filed Oct. 13, 1841.

MAGER OR MAJER COLE PACK. 72 EQUITY
CLERK OF COURTS OFFICE, PICKENS, S. C.

George W. Phillips states that on or about the 28th January 1860 he purchased from Mager Cole a citizen of Franklin County, Georgia three negro slaves, Margaret, John and Berry aged 30, 14 and 7 years old & with the said slaves recd. from Mager Cole a bill of sale in writing by which the said Mager Cole warranted the title to the slaves for ever, he paid the said Cole 14 hundred dollars and also gave him a joint and several sealed note signed by both of them payable by the 25th Decr. 1860. That soon after the note became due, suit was commenced thereon by the Mager Cole and at the Oct. term of court, judgment was obtained, no defence having been made, and execution entered in the Sheriffs office in favor of the said Cole against him. That soon after the entry of the said execution, he paid 500 dollars thereon but there still remains a considerable sum to be paid. He further shows that the said slaves have been emancipated & taken from his possession & are of no longer any value to him. He further states that the said Mager Cole died in Georgia & left the following heirs viz. Willey P. Cole who is within this state, Aaron Cole, Lewis Cole, Morgan Cole who are residents in Georgia, also children and a widow whose names are unknown. Filed Nov. 14, 1866.

NATHANIEL LYNCH PACK. 72 EQUITY
CLERK OF COURTS OFFICE, PICKENS, S. C.

Gideon M? Lynch, Banister S. Lynch, Nathaniel Lynch, Henry Lynch states that their father Nathaniel Lynch died Feb. 20, 1861 intestate leaving as his heirs at law a widow Jane Lynch & 13 children viz. Harriet who married Cornelius Keith & resides in Pickens District, Eliza who married John Robinson & resides in Georgia, Nancy who married Richard Robinson & resides in Georgia, Sarah who married William Baker & resides in Texas, Mary who married John Lewis & resides in Georgia, Elizabeth who married Jason Gillespie & resides in North Carolina, Wm. J. Lynch, (F. or T?) C. Lynch, Calvin Lynch. All of whom are of age. Owned 161 acreslying on Oulenoy Creek & adjoining lands of Sutherland, Alexander Edens & others. . . .

JOSIAH PERKINS PACK. 73 EQUITY
CLERK OF COURTS OFFICE, PICKENS, S. C.

Josiah Perkins states that his father Joshua Perkins died owning a tract of land in the fork of Tugalo River & Chauga Creek adjoining lands of Jabez Jones, Robert Gilmer & others containing 319 acres. He had never had titles executed to him because he had not paid all the purchase money & there still remains due to Wm. W. Mitchell the sum of about $310.89. Letters of Admnrs. were granted to his son the said Josiah Perkins and his widow Hannah Perkins. His other heirs are the following children, Josiah Perkins, William Perkins, Augustus Perkins, over the age of 21 years and Mary Perkins, Moses Perkins, Samuel Perkins, Harriet E. Perkins & Martha Adaline Perkins who are minors. Filed Aug. 29, 1859 . . . Letters of admnr. were granted Dec. 15, 1856.

In same package was the following.

Know all men by these presents that I Larkin Cason of the County of King? & (word) State of Virginia hath this day Sold unto John Couch three negroes namely Clary & Mehaley & Mary for inconsiderations of the sum of five Hundred & seventy five dollars to me in hand paid which the right and title of the above named negroes & doe warrant and defend from the claim of myself my heirs & from the Lawfull Claim of each & every person whatsoever as witness my Hand this eighteenth day of April 1821.

test   Larkin Cason (SEAL)

Benj Rucker?
      his
Saml   X   Jones
      mark

WILL OF JESSE STRIBLING PACK. 73
CLERK OF COURTS OFFICE, PICKENS, S. C.

South Carolina

Pickens District) Know all men by these presents that I Jesse Stribling of State and District aforesaid being in feeble health and well stricken in years but of sound mind and desirous of disposing of my worldly effects do hereby in Consequence of the affection I entertain towards my beloved wife and the great confidence I entertain in her making an equitable distribution of the effects I do invest her with amongst my children at her decease do give and bequeath to my wife Elizabeth Stribling all the property I am now or may here after be possessed of without any reservation whatsoever together with all Bonds Notes accounts &c except so much as shall be necessary to pay my funeral expenses and all just debts and against me. And in order the better to carry out this my last Will and Testament I do hereby appoint my Wife Elizabeth Stribling my sole executrix. Signed and sealed this twentieth day of April one thousand Eight hundred and forty one.

In the presence of   J. Stribling (LS)
R. D. Maxwell
Wm. W? Stribling
Wm. Sloan

Jonathan Gilleson
CERTIFIED JUNE 13, 1857.

ALMON POWELL PACK. 77 EQUITY
CLERK OF COURTS OFFICE, PICKENS, S. C.

Sarah Ann Cantrell wife of D. W. Cantrell sheweth that her father Almon Powell died in the year 1857 intestate leaving a widow, Elizabeth Powell & 6 children viz. Mary Ann who married Burrell Broom, Asel Powell, Robert Powell, Thomas Powell, Caroline who married Joseph McIntyre all of whom are of full age. Letters of Administration were granted to Robert Powell. Owned 200 acres on Tugaloo River adjoining lands of Harvy Davis, William Leathers & others. Filed March 20, 1858. Sept. 10, 1858 To Edgefield Advertiser.

To Adr. Sale of land for partition in case of D. W. C. Cantrell vs. Mrs. E. Powell & others $5.25.

ANDREW BODDAN TO JAMES BLAIR PACK. 77 DEED
CLERK OF COURTS OFFICE, PICKENS, S. C.

State of South Carolina

Pendleton County) Know all men by these presents that I Andrew Boddan of Camden District and State aforesaid for and in Consideration of the Sume of Twenty eight pounds to me in hand paid by James Blair of pendleton County and State of South Carolina have Granted. barganed sold and Released and by these presents do Grant bargain Sell and Release unto the said James Blair all that plantation or Tract of land Containing Two Hundred acres more or less situat in the District of Ninety Six in pendleton County on a north branch of Toxaway Creek Bounded on all Sides by vacant land Surveyed originally for James Madison the Second day of aprile one thousand Seven Hundred and ninety three and granted to John Calvert by his Excellency Arnoldus? Vanderhorst Governor &c on monday the sixth of July one Thousand Seven Hundred and Ninety five Together with all and singular the rights, members Hereditaments and apertenances to the said premises belonging or in any ways incident or apertaining to Have and to hold all and Singular the premises before mentioned unto the said James Blair His Heirs and assigns for ever and I do hereby bind myself my heirs Executors & administrators to warrant and forever Defend all and singular the said premises unto the said James Blair His Heirs and assigns against me and my heirs Executors administrators and assigns and all other persons whatsoever lawfully Claiming a right or title there unto Witness my hand and seal this ninth day of August one Thousand Seven Hundred and Ninety Seven and the Twenty Second year of the Independence of the United States of America. Signed Sealed and Delivered in presence of

Jas. Wyly   Andrew Boddan (SEAL)
Thos. Crews

State of South Carolina

Pendleton County) pershonely Came Thomas Crews and made oath that he saw Andrew Bodden sign seal and deliver the within Deed to James Blair andthat James Wiley was a Consigning witness with himself to sd deed sworn to before me this 29th Day of August 1797.

CERTIFIED AUGUST 30, 1797.

RICHARD HOLDEN TO ALMOND POWELL PACK. 77
DEED OF CONVEYANCE
CLERK OF COURTS OFFICE, PICKENS, S. C.

The State of So Carolina

Pendleton District) Know all men by these presents that I Richard Holden of the County of Habersham and State of Georgia for and in consideration of the Sum of one Hundred dollars to me in hand paid by Almond Powell of the State and District first mentioned have granted bargained sold and released and by these presents do grant bargain Sell and Release unto the said Almond Powell a certain Tract or Parcel of land Situate in said district being part of a tract of land originally owned by John Smith Beginning on a red oak on the conditional line made between Saml. Isaacs and Thomas Gibson Thence running on a marked line northwardly which is a conditional line made between William Fowler and John Smith to where it intersects the land now owned by the said Powell thence following the Said Powell line back to the beginning corner containing by estimation Twenty acres be the same more or less Together with all and Singular the rights members hereditaments and appertainances to the said premises belonging or in any wise incident or appertaing to have and to hold all and Singular the premises befor mentioned unto the Said Almond Powell his heirs and assigns forever and I do hereby bind myself my heirs executors administrators and assigns to warrant and for ever defend all and Singular the premises above mentioned unto the said Almond Powell his heirs and assigns against my self my Heirs executors and administrators and against the Lawful Claims of all persons whomsoever claiming or to claim the same or any part thereof In witness whereof I have hereunto set my hand and seal this (no date given) day of April in the year of our lord one thousand eight hundred and Twenty Three and the forty Seventh of American Independence.

Signed sealed and acknowledged in presents of

            Richard Holden (SEAL)

Test
John T. Humphreys
   his
Jesse X Biram
   mark

JOHN T. HUMPHRIES TO ALMOND POWELL PACK. 77
DEED
CLERK OF COURTS OFFICE, PICKENS, S. C.

The State of So. Carolina

Pickens District) Know all men by these presents that I John T. Humphreys of the State & District aforesaid for and in consideration of the sum of four hundred and fifty dollars to me in hand paid by Almond Powell of the State & District aforesaid, have granted bargained sold and released and by these presents do grant bargain sell & release unto the said Almond Powell a part of several tracts of land, viz. Frederick Ward, John Smith and Richard Holden beginning on a stake where the said Powell & Hervey Davis lands corner thence following the middle of a ditch to the first bend in said ditch thence following a well marked line which is a conditional line betwixt myself &

Hervey Davis to the West corner of Edmund Thoms ? land thence following the said Thoms? line on the south side to his lower corner of his old tract thence a strait line to the Brasstown Road near the Black Jack stand thence following the said road down to where it intersects the line that I sold to Balew thence following said line back to the east corner of said Powells bounty tract thence following the said Powells line back to the beginning I do hereby bind myself my heirs and assigns to warrant and forever defend all and singular the premises before mentioned unto the said Almond Powell his heirs and assigns against myself and my heirs & against the lawfull claim of every other person whomsoever Given under my hand & seal this 21st day of September in the year of our lord eighteen hundred & thirty five.

Test   John T. Humphreys (LS)
Thos. J. Humphreys
Robert Ballew

THOMAS F. GORDON TO ALMOND POWELL PACK. 77
DEED
CLERK OF COURTS OFFICE, PICKENS, S. C.

The State of So. Carolina

Pendleton District) Know all men by these presents that I Thos. F. Gordon of the State and District aforesaid for and in consideration of the sum of Sixty dollars to me in hand paid by Almond Powell of the state and district aforesaid have granted bargained sold and released and by these presents do grant Bargain sell and release unto the said Almond Powell a certain Tract or parcel of land Situate in said District being part of a tract of land originally granted to Norman Martin beginning on a Sassafras on the River bank thence a strait line to a pine thence to a post oak thence to a Beach which is a line tree? of the originally Survey made for Normon Martin thence following the said original line from the Beach back to the river thence up the river to the beginning sassafras containing by estimation Four acres be the same more or less together with all and singular the rights members hereditaments and appertainances to the said premises belonging or in any wise incident or appertaining to have and to hold all and singular the premises before mentioned unto the said Almond Powell his heirs and assigns forever and I do hereby bind myself my heirs executors administrators and assigns to warrant and forever defend all and singular the premises above mentioned the said Almond Powell his heirs and assigns against myself my heirs executors and administrators and assigns and against the Lawful Claim of all persons whom soever claiming or to claim the same or any part thereof In witness whereof I have hereunto set my hand and affixed my seal this 26th February in the year of our lord one thousand eight hundred and Twenty four and in the Forty eighth of american independence Signed Sealed and delivered in presents of   Thomas F. Gordon
Stephen Bates
Grief Williams

ROBERT A. HAWTHORNE PACK. 78 EQUITY
CLERK OF COURTS OFFICE, PICKENS, S. C.

Moses Cain, William Hardin & John Baylis Myers & H. A. Cole, assignee of William Hardon as follows. That Robert A. Hawthorne of Pickens District on the 14th February 1859 sold to the above a tract of land in Pickens District, which formerly belonged to the estate of Josiah F. Perry decd. & which was purchased by him at the sale of Perrys estate, sold by the Commissioner of Equity for partition amongst the heirs of said Perry. The tract of land lies on the branches of Snow Creek, waters of Conneross Creek, waters of Seneca River. Robert A. Hawthorne & Thoms D. Long made and executed their bond at the date above mentioned in the sum of 2 thousand dollars to the above. To Moses Cain 91 acres, to John B. Myers 96 acres to William Hardin 92 acres. Wm. Hardin sold & transfered his land to H. A. Cole of Pickens District. Robert A. Hawthorne soon after the execution of the bond entered the Army of the Confederate States of America & was killed in the battles around Richmond whilst gallantly charging at the head of the Company of Infantry which he commanded. After his death E. P. Verner Esq. took out letters of administration upon his estate. The said Captain R. A. Hawthorne died leaving a widow Mrs. Emma Hawthorne & one infant daughter, his only heirs at law. Filed May 5, 1864. Ida Hawthorne was his infant daughter.

AARON ROPER SENIOR PACK. 79 EQUITY
CLERK OF COURTS OFFICE, PICKENS, S. C.

Tyre L. Roper, Marcus Roper, Aaron Roper & Marena Roper who married Simeon E. Burgess states that Aaron Roper Sr. died in 1855. Owned 300 acres lying on Saluda River adjoining lands of Samuel Earle & others. His wife died about the same time he did and was buried about the same time. Left 10 children viz. Lemuel Roper, John Roper, Matilda Roper wife of Joab Lankford, the heirs of Jane Hagood who died some years before her parents viz. Benjamin Hagood the names and numbers of the others unknown if any, the heirs of Tilmon Roper who died before his parents leaving the following children viz. Catherine Roper a minor over the age of 12 years, John, James, David & Tilmon Roper each minors under 14 years . . . The heirs of Charles Roper decd. who died in 1855, and the above Tyre L. Roper, Marcus Roper, Marena Burgess. Hamilton Roper decd. Clarinda Roper was the widow of Hamilton Roper. Lemuel Roper died leaving a widow Jane Roper & 4 children, William Noble Roper, Bailey Roper under 14 years, Martha Roper & Elmina Roper under 12 years all of whom reside in Georgia. Filed March 27, 1856 . . . Hamilton Roper died leaving no children. Clarinda Roper admits it to be true that she did live separate and aprt from her husband Hamilton Roper 18 months prior to his death, but she postively denies that this separation and apart from him was in ac cordance with her wishes and avers that it had its origin in no fault of hers and that its continance was against her will and beyond her power to remedy. andshe claims that there was nothing whatever in the said separation which at all conflicts with her right to a share in her decd. husbands real estate. She was married to him in Greenville District in January 1853 and lived with him until June 1854, during which time she had a male child by him which died when but a few weeks old. Her said husband was unfortunately addicted to intemperate habits, and from the results of this he became cruel and unkind towards her, and frequently inflicted blows upon her person. He at length drove her from his house threatening her with severe personal violence if she did not leave and ordering her never to return under these circumstances. She went to the house of her father Benjamin Turner in Greenville District where she has ever since resided. After thus driving her from his house he never s olicited or expressed his willingness for her to return & never contributed towards her support & maintenance. She avers that this unkind treatment was entirely undeserved by her, that she had ever been kind affectionate & faithful towards her said husband and would gladly have resided with him as his wife, had she been permitted to do so. That she is deeply pained and mortified in thus being compelled to disclose these unhappy transactions which she had hoped were buried forever in the grave of her unfortunate husband, but the covert and injurious attack which has been made upon her rights and her reputation, have imposed upon her the necessity of making her defence by a true statement of the facts. She carried to her husband at their marriage, articles of furniture of considerable value only a portion of which has been returned to her.

ANNA HAWTHORNE PACK. 79 POWER OF ATTORNEY
CLERK OF COURTS OFFICE, PICKENS, S. C.

The State of South Carolina

Pickens District) Know all men by these presents that I, Anna Hawthorne of the State and District aforesaid have nominated constituted and appointed and by these presents do nominate constitute and appoint Joseph J. Norton Esq. my true and lawful attorney for me and in my name to institute proceedings in the Court of Equity for the recovery of certain monies in the hands of Lemuel Reid Executor of the Estate John R. Wilson decd. late of Abbeville Dist. in said state for me or for the appointment of a trustee for me in that behalf as may be deemed most advisable, and also to receive and receipt the said Lemuel Reid Executor for the said monies. Witness my hand & seal this day of May AD 1866.

Anna Hawthorne

Anna Hawthorne states that she and her husband moved to Pickens District before the death of the latter, which ocurred about 7 years ago. Filed June 1, 1866.

JAMES W. GRAY VS. J. B. FISCHESER PACK. 80
BILL TO FORECLOSE MORTGAGE

James W. Gray master in Equity of Charleston District sheweth that J. B. Fischeser of South Carolina but now resding in (no county given) on March 30, 1858 was indebted to him in the sum of $371.25 to be paid in 2 equal instalments with interest, the last payment which was due on March 30, 1860. being the purchase money for two lots of land situated in the town of Walhalla containing one and one half acre, before that time sold and conveyed to the said defendant. Filed March 23, 1860. On March 28, 1860 he the said J. B. Fischeser was mentioned as residing out of the state . . . The lots were known as No. 9 and 40 situated in the Town of Walhalla and fronting on Main Street between D. Biemann's and the Post Office.

NEGRO TRIAL CASES PACK. 82
CLERK OF COURTS OFFICE, PICKENS, S. C.

No. 1. On July 31, 1845 the state tried Tom a negro slave of Mary Keith of Pickens District for assault and Battery said to have been committed on a free white man Balis Hester. Balis Hester sworn said that Tom was riding past him & said to him, dam you, you need not look at me. I told him to go to hell & he said I had threatened him some time & now come to whip him if he wanted to & laid a rod over him & told him how he could whip him, but did not strike & Tom jerked it out of his hand & caught him by the collar & jerked him down & that he (word) got a stick & the person took it from him & he Hester said he would have him whipped & the person said he did not care for that nor for hell & damnd notion further saith he drawed his knife on prisoner to defend him self & that prisoner knocked the knife out of his hand in some way, which was before he got the stick. When asked on cross examination if he thought that the prisoner wanted to hurt him he said he does not but says he did not but thinks he did as the prisoner appeared to be mad. and that it was committed in Pickens District on the evening of 16th Inst. Jeptha Rigdon sworn saith that he saw the prisoner and Balis Hester pulling & shoving each other across the road by the arms. Says that he did not know at the time whether they were mad or not. Did not see them begin, says he some some hundred yards from them. Saw Hester go to the house & brought out a gun and the prisoner went off. The jury found the prisoner guilty and sentenced him to 10 stripes on his bare back. In this case the court fee was $6.04. The whipping $.75.

NO. 2

On Sept. 22, 1847 William Young stated that on the 20th of this instant a negro boy by the name of Jake belonging to Samuel Johnston at a unreasonable time of the night, his dog attacked him, he believes he was in his yard or near his house, he incouraged his dog, the dog pursued the negro, he found him concealed in the bushees. He would not give any account of him self but very fancy language. He was found prowling about the said Youngs yard at an untimely hour in the night after 10 o'clock and when hailed would not speak. The jury found him not guilty.

NO. 3

On June 17, 1841 information was given to Bryan Boroughs J. P. by James Garner that a negro man named Reuben the property of Aaron Boggs did in the time of 2 or 3 months past in Pickens District committ the crime of posioning a negro man named Luke the property of Henry Garner whereas the said Negro man Reuben has been committed by meto the safe keeing of John Gunter constable in order to be brought to his trial for the said offence. His trial was to be at Williamses store.

NO. 4

On Sept. 18, 1836 Pleasant Alexander Sheriff of Pickens District made oath that he has good reasons to believe that a negro man by the name of Ben the property of Col. Joseph Grisham of Falls did on the night of the 17th came to the jail of Pickens Dist. and climbed by a ladder in at a window in the lower room of said jail and then went to the door of the petition and broke the lock and then went to the door of two of the prisoners viz. John Cone & Solomon Gibson. Cone charged with robbing the U. S. Mail & Gibson charged with Larceney and then and there broke two locks and open the door & released the 2 prisoners. The prisoner pled guilty to the charge and sentenced to receive 25 lashes around the legs and be removed from the state within 2 months.

NO. 5

On April 18, 1848 Zachariah Masters of Pickens District states that a negro man named Joseph the property of David Cherry did on the 1st March aforesaid felloniously & without his leave or consent take his beast in the night time and rode the same to his his injury. John Masters states that Zachariah Masters & himself saw 2 boys come to David Cherrys each leading Zachariah Masters mare and saw them turn the animal thru the gate & when questioned about it said they had found the mare a short distance from the gate, but says he did not know either of the boys and cannot say which one had the mare or which one turned him thru the gate. A. C. Pickens sworn says that his boy told him that he overtook Joe on the road coming from Mr. Calhouns and soon afterwards they over took a gray mare which they turned into David Cherrys pasture.

No. 6

On April 27, 1839 Esli Hunt states that from information from one of his tenants that a negro man named Kin a slave of Jeremiah Looper Sr. did on the 26th instant with his own free and against the interest of said Hunt went into the said Hunts plantation then and there violently went into the creek, cut and threw out an obstruction which said Hunt put therein to keep the ditches from filling up with sand so that the bottom lands of said plantation may not over flow with water.

NO. 7

On Oct. 1, 1846 Nathan Boon Cornoner of Pickens Dist. states that a murder has been committed onthe body of Jack, a slave of the property of Mrs. Martha Lawrence by a slave named Willis also the property of the said Martha Lawrence on the 30th Sept. 1846 at the residence of the said slave Willis striking the said slave Jack with a large stick on the head . . . A slave Mary sworn says, "She was not at the commencement of the affray. Saw Willis strike Tom with an ear of corn. Told him if he hit with an ear of corn she would not not run. He then threw an ear at her and then she threw one at him and then he made at Tom. She asked him if he wantedto kill another negro. Then Jack and Willis with their fists, afterwards Jack took yp a piece of plank. Jack struck Willis first on the arm, then threw the stick at him and runed, and he Willis pursued with a waggon standard in his hand and knocked him down as they ran. Says that Willis did nothing afterwards only stand at the place. Says that he did not lie at the place long. Got up himself and both went back to shucking corn. Says blood was running from his nose, but waled as well as usual. Saw Jack and Willis both laugh after throwing the corn, but thought they were angry at first. Says she was not told to go to the corn pile that morning. Says the first thing she did after getting there was to ask what he was fighting Tom Ben for. Jack struck Willis first with his fist, only two blows passed . . . Willis told Tom Ben to up on the corn pile. Tom told him if he went up he would hit him with an ear of corn & Willis said he would hit him anyway. Says he went up & Willis hit him and he hit Willis. Jack and Willis did not say anything till Mary came down. When she did she told Willis if he hit her, she would hit him. Willis hit Mary and she hit him. Then Jack threw an ear of corn at Willis & he hit Jack. Jack struck Willis first with his fist. & blows passed between them. Thomas R. Brackenridge says that he gave Willis authority to make the negroes work and to whip the small ones if they did not work. Never had seen him abusing them, Conducted himself peaceably. Willis never showed any disposition to quarrelsome on any occasion. When he got to the corn pile Jack was standing leaning against the stable. John Lawrence said he would give Jack 100 lashes after breakfast. Willis said he was sorry he struck him. Says that he knows they (the negroes) have no good feelings toward Willis. The boy later died . . . Willis was given 50 lashes on the bare back and then set at liberty. . . .

NO. 8

On Nov. 7, 1845 Daniel Durham states that on sunday night last of an unlawful assembly, rioting, drinking, quarrelling & fighting of free negroes and slaves at the house at Jackson Arter a free negro, all against the peace & diginity of the state. The magistartae had the trial at A. Hunters store at Wolf Creek.

NO. 9

On March 20, 1841 Cate a slave of Mrs. Cannon gave a runaway slave her victuaks one time while she lying out, and that her slave Mary said that she could sleep in the masters barn that night. She was a slave of Andrew Hunter. The court sentenced Cate to have 2 lashes and Mary five lashes. Polly Burdine, Eleanor Waters free negroes were tried Aug. 19, 1841 for retailing spiritous liquor to slaves & white persons on the sabbath as well as other times without any authority whatever, and keeping about their house riotious assemblies of negroes to the teror of the neighborhood. Hardy Gilstrap says that he was at Polly Burdines house and saw her sell half pints of whiskey to slaves on the sabbath. William Eads says he saw Polly Burdine sell whiskey to the slaves that there was some 15 or 20 slaves and free negroes assembled all drunk or nearly so and that they were rioting and keeping a terrible noise. The jury could not find anything to convict Eleanor Waters but found Polly Burdine guilty of them all and sentenced her to 12 lashes.

LEONARD CAPEHART PACK. 85 EQUITY
CLERK OF COURTS OFFICE, PICKENS, S. C.

Sarah Capehart widow states that Leonard Capehart did on or about the 3 July 1848 make his last will of which is a copy.

State of South Carolina
District of Pickens
In the name of God, Amen.

I Leonard Capehart of the District and State aforesaid being in usual health, and of sound Mind and disposing memory, and knowing the certainty of death, do make this my last Will and Testament. (Viz)

First, I will and bequeath unto my beloved wife Sarah all her wearing apparel, the Bed and Furniture which she had when I married her, and all other property of every description which She may have had when I married her.

Second. I will and bequeath, that after my death, all of my property of every description, (except that heretofore and above disposed of) be Sold by my Executors hereinafter named, at public or private sale, at their discretion, and the proceeds applied, first to the payment of all my just debts and the remainder, if any, divided as follows Viz.

Third. I will and bequeath unto my beloved wife Sarah one third part of the remainder of my Estate after the payment of my debts as above directed to have and use during her natural life, for her Support, and after her death to be given under the direction of my said Executors to my daughter Elizabeth Eveline Capehart.

Fourth. I will and bequeath that the remaining two thirds of my Estate be equally divided, between my Son Harvey, one fifth part, the lawful heirs of my Son John one fifth part, to be between them equally divided, my Son Samuel one fifth part, and the children of my daughter Nancy who was married to James Rogers, and is dead, Viz. Leonard, James, Diver, John and Nathan Rogers one fifth part, to be divided equally between them and to my daughter-in-law Mary Ann Capehart (the Widow of my Son B. W. F. Capehart) and her Son Hamilton Brevard the remaining fifth part to be between the two equally divided.

Fifth. I do hereby Constitute and appoint my friends Col. Jephtha Norton, Capt. Levi N. Roberts and Miles M. Norton my Executors to carry into effect this my last Will and Testament, according to the true intent and meaning thereof, hereby revoking all other wills made by me.

Witness my hand and Seal this third day of July one thousand eight hundred and forty eight.

                                  his
                    Leonard   LC   Capehart (SEAL)
                                  mark

Signed Sealed and acknowledged in the presence of us
E. Alexander
W. S. Grisham
W. J. Nevill
South Carolina
Pickens District) In the Court of Ordinary

I Certify that the foregoing is a true copy of the last Will and Testament of Leonard Capehart decsd. which has been duly probated in the Court of Ordinary, the original will now remaining in my office.

Given under my hand and Seal of office this 22nd day of March AD 1866.
                                       W. E. Holcombe O. P. D.

Equity . . . Elizabeth E. is still an infant about the age of 19 years who married Waddy T. Hester who is now dead, his son Henry who is now dead and whose heirs names & numbers unknown, & the place of their residence is unknown to Sarah Capehart, the heirs of his son John Capehart who died before his father, names & numbers and residence unknown, except Hamilton A. H. Gibson a son of the said John Capehart who had his name changed from Capehart to Gibson by order of the court, Samuel Capehart of this state, the children of his daughter Nancy who married James Rogers and is dead to wit, Leonard Rogers & John Rogers who reside in Pickens District, Nathan Rogers who died before his grandfather & left no family, James Rogers who died after the testator and left the following heirs in this state to wit,

Emily C. Rogers widow, Sarah A. Rogers, Nathan Rogers who are infants under 21 years and upon whos estate the said Leonard Rogers took out Letters of Administration, W. Diver Rogers who died after the testator Leonard Capehart & left the following heirs in this district to wit, Sarah Rogers widow, Nancy L., Frances M., Mary K., & Margaret J. Rogers minors under 21 years, and upon whose estate A. Diver Rogers took out letters of administration and whose residence is now unknown, the heirs of his son B. W. F. Capehart to wit, Mary Ann Capehart widow, & son Hamilton B. Capehart. Filed March 27, 1866. . . .

LAWRENCE C. CRAIG PACK. 87 EQUITY
CLERK OF COURTS OFFICE, PICKENS, S. C.

Lawrence Coatsworth Craig of Pickens District states that Elliot M. Keith about the 21 March 1857 was indebted to him in the sum of $300.00. That he made and executed unto him by the said E. M. Keith two tracts of land situate and lying in said district on the west side of Keowee River and known as the Merritt tract, containing together 360 acres. Filed May 26, 1860.
    Mortgage For 2 Tracts Of Land On Keowee River
E. M. Keith
    to
L. C. Craig
    In this morgage mentioned one tract was known as the Pleasant Alexander tract. In 1857 L. C. Craig was Sheriff of Pickens District and E. M. Keith was an Attorney at Law.

GIDEON MARTIN PACK. 88 EQUITY
CLERK OF COURTS OFFICE, PICKENS, S. C.

Gideon Martin died in 1840 owning considerable real estate, consisting of land, negroes and other personal property. Leaving neither wife or children but left a mother Elizabeth Martin and a brother David Martin and five sisters viz. Sarah the wife of Garner Evans, Rachel the wife of James Mauldin, Polly the wife of Joseph Edwards, Ruth the wife of John Hendrix, Peggy the wife of Claibourn Wilkinson and the children of a decd. brother Absalom Martin to wit. Rachel, Betsy, Peggy, Lydia and Mary . . . They state during his during his illness one Sarah Parsons induced the said Gideon Martin to execute a deed conveying to the said Sarah Parsons during her natural life a tract of land containing 213 acres to her two children Loyd Belton Parsons & Baylis Miffin Parsons. By the said deed he also gave to the 2 children all the residue of his estate after the payment of his debts and constiuted Thomas D. Garvin trustee with directions. Filed May 10, 1841. On one paper Sarah was written Sally Parsons . . . Sarah Parsons states that she hoped the court would let her keep the land and not deprive those who are helpless and were dependant for support upon the said Gideon Martin of that pittance whicha fathers kindness and humanity is commanded. . . .

SIMPSON L. FOUNTAIN PACK. 91 EQUITY
CLERK OF COURTS OFFICE, PICKENS, S. C.

Simpson L. Fountain states that in 1858 that he was much in debt and pressed by his creditors he applied to Alexander Bryce Senior and his nephew J. Gambrell Bryce both then residing in Pickens District, whom he concieved to be his friends, for a loan of money to extricate him from his embarrassment. After some negotation the sum of $550.00 or near that sum, was advanced to him by J. Gambrell Bryce aforesaid, who to secure the payment of the money, suffered two of his negro slaves who were of peculiar value to wit, Leah a woman of about 40 years of age and her child named Eade about 1 years old to go into the possession of the said J. Gambrell Bryce. Was to keep them until he got the money to pay it back. The said J. Gambrell Bryce and Alexander Bryce Sr. was combining and confederating with one Edwin M. Cobb of Anderson District a dealer on slaves & with other persons unknown to him, hastened to remove & actually did remove in a clandestine manner the said slaves without the limits of this state. He charges that the said Edwin Cobb was instrumental in the removal of the slaves and that he had a full knowledge of all the circumstances under which they went into possession of the said J. Gambrell Bryce. Filed Oct. 4, 1859.

ROBERT JOHNSON PACK. 100 EQUITY
CLERK OF COURTS OFFICE, PICKENS, S. C.

Robert Johnson states that in the year 1818 he was residing in Ireland when he received a letter from his brother Thomas Johnson informing him that he had bought a tract of land in the upper part of South Carolina and requesting him to remove to the United States and to take possession of and cultivate the same. Robert Johnson decided to accept the same and landed with his family in Charleston on the 3rd Decr. in the same year. In a few days he left Charleston for Pendleton District. Where the land was situated. Previous to his coming to Charleston where his brother Thomas resided, he made a contract with his brother that he should go and take possession of the land which his brother Thomas had bought of Co. Dickison at the price of $4V3, which sum was to be paid by the hire of the sons of Robert Johnson as the said Thomas Johnson might from time to time employ at the rate of $8.00 per month. When Robert Johnson arrived upon the land and had resided upon it some time, he found it entirely exhausted and worn out and altogether inadequate to the incumberance of his family. Thereupon he informed his brother that he could by no means think of settling himself and wasting his time and labor upon such land, but informed him that a man by the name of Cunningham owned a tract adjoining which if he could purchase, he would then be willing to take both tracts on the terms as to payment agreed on as to the tract bought of Col. Dickson. After some time he was informed by his brother Thomas that he had purchased Cunninghams land where upon he determined to settle himself upon the lands. He built a tolerable log house upon the land, he cleared the land and ditched and reclaimed a piece of bottom land, in all he thinks was near 20 acres, and then from time to time in various ways, paid to his brother upwards of 11 hundred dollars. In the year 1821 he recieved a letter from the said Thomas Johnson acknowledging certain payments which had been made to hom on account of these tracts of land and requesting him to preserve the letter as a memorandum of their contract which was therein recited as above stated, that on payment of the purchase money and interest that titles to the said lands were to be made to him. Robert Johnson has been and is now ready to pay the ballance of the purchase money for the above mentioned lands according to his contract. He further states that some time in the year 1831 the above lands were sold by the Sheriff of Pickens District as the property of Thomas Johnson when it was true that the legal title existed, but subject to the equitable claim of him. He forbid the sale and stated his claims to the land. The land was however sold and was purchased by Col. Robert Anderson who having had notice of the equitable claims of Robert Johnson purchased the same subject to these equitable claims . . . Filed March 15, 1833.

THOMAS J. KEITH, L. C. CRAIG VS. J. R. HUNNICUT
PACK. 101 CLERK OF COURTS OFFICE, PICKENS, S. C.

Thomas J. Keith, and L. C. Craig sheweth that on the 12th Jan. 1860 they sold to J. R. Hunnicutt a certain tract of land lying and being on Long Nose Creek in the State and District aforesaid, adjoining lands of Wm. B. Dixson, J. J. Cotes, J. G. Hightower & others. Containing 360 acres. To secure the payment of the purchase money J. R. Hunnicutt gave the following notes viz. one note on John Hawkins for $105.00 dated the 22nd Sept. 1859 and due the first day June 1860. Filed April 22, 1861. James M. Hunnicutt Jr. admnr. of J. R. Hunnicut states that he died intestate on the 5th May 1863 leaving his wife Elizabeth & four children surviving him . . . On Sept. 15, 1863 James M. Hunnicut, Elizabeth Hunnicut, John J. Hunnicut, Jobery Hunnicut, Newton Jasper Hunnicut & Lewis Reese Hunnicut were ordered to appear in the court of equity.

IRA R. NICHOLSON PACK. 103 EQUITY
CLERK OF COURTS OFFICE, PICKENS, S. C.

Isaac Holden & Jane Holden his wife formerly Jane Nicholson sheweth that Ira R. Nicholson of Pickens District died, owning considerable real estate viz. Tract No. 1 The Chattooga old Town tract containing 600 acres lying on Chattooga River in Pickens District on the Georgia line. No. 2 containing 300 acres adjoining the said tract No. 1. The lands are now subject to division amongst the heirs of the said Ira R. Nicholson viz. his widow Jane Nicholson and 12 children to wit, Evan Nicholson, Mary Barker wife of Josiah Barker, Sarah Loveless who married James Loveless, Martha Nicholson who married William Holden, Harriet Nicholson who married James Jackson Pell, William Nicholson, Malinda Nicholson who married Mordecai Cox, Mira Nicholson who married Jesse Lay, Silas Nicholson, Bailey Nicholson, Bailus Nicholson and the said Jane Holden wife of Isaac Holden. Filed March 15, 1851 . . . Evan Nicholson was appointed guardian of Bailey Nicholson a minor over the age of 14 years . . . Evan Nicholson, James Loveless and wife, William Holden and wife, William Nicholson, Mordicai Cox and wife, Bailus Nicholson were all living in Georgia. . . .

JOHN B. PITTS PACK. 104 EQUITY
CLERK OF COURTS OFFICE, PICKENS, S. C.

Pleasant S. Mahaffey and his wife Catherine Mahaffey sheweth that her father John B. Pitts died the 27th Sept. 1862 leaving considerable real estate. Upon which admnr. was granted by the Ordinary of Pickens District to Andrew Bolt who is proceeding to settle up the estate. At the time of his death was in possession and occupancy of a certain tract of land situated on the waters of Conneross Creek, bounded by lands of John Maxwell, & others containing 160 acres. John B. Pitts bought this land from one John Maxwell. Left a widow Elizabeth Pitts & the following heirs viz. Catherine Mahaffey wife of Pleasant S. Mahaffey, Andrew Bolt & his wife Martha Jane Bolt, Nathan A. Gray & wife Lucinda S. Gray, Drury Y. Pitts, William M. Pitts, Mary T. Pitts, Sarah A. Pitts, the three last named of whom are minors, and all of whom resides in Pickens District except Andrew Bolt and his wife who reside in Laurens District.

Filed 18 May 1863.

THOMAS M. CLYDE PACK. 113 EQUITY
CLERK OF COURTS OFFICE, PICKENS, S. C.

Thomas M. Clyde died in Pickens District where he had resided for many years and was living at the time of his death. He left a widow and children. Charles E. Clyde a son who died at Gettysburg after the death of his father, leaving a widow Sally Clyde but no living children. Thomas M. Clyde also left 2 minor sons William A. Clyde and Leonard Clyde also his heirs at law. The said Thomas M. Clyde died intestate leaving no will and making any position of his property. He left no debts due at his death. Thomas T? Clyde administrated on his estate. His widow was Harriet L. Clyde. Left 8 children. viz. Joseph B. Clyde, Edgar W. Clyde, Samuel C. Clyde, Thomas T. Clyde, Sally Clyde widow of Charles E. Clyde, Luvina or Lecina? M. Clyde wife of W. A. Alexander. Owned 35 acres more or less lying on 18 Mile Creek near the residence of the late Col. Thomas M. Clyde Filed Oct. 10, 1863 . . .

ALLEN ROBERTSON PACK. 126 EQUITY
CLERK OF COURTS OFFICE, PICKENS, S. C.

Jeremiah Robertson of Pickens District states that his father Allen Robertson of said district died on or about the 28th March 1854 intestate owning considerable real estate. One tract of land situated in Pickens District on both sides of Carpenters Creek and on the south side of the south fork of Saluda River containing 784 acres, adjoining lands of Joseph Williams etc. Left a widow Catharine Robertson and 13 children. or their representatives viz. James Robertson who resides in Greenville District, Randall Robertson who resides in Texas, Joseph Robertson who resides in Mississippi, Anna Robertson who married Jeremiah Whitmire and resides in Pickens District, Martha Robertson who married Thomas Hitt and resides in Cherokee County, Georgia, Lidia Robertson now widow of Osborne Hagood and resides in Gilmer County, Georgia, Lucy Robertson who married Bailey Barton and resides in Pickens District, Malinda Robertson who married Wilson Jones and resides in Pickens District, John A. Robertson who resides in Pickens District, the heirs at law of Elizabeth Reese formerly Elizabeth Robertson, names unknown and residing in Mississippi when last heard from, the heirs at law of Hardy Robertson names and residences unknown, the heirs at law of George Robertson voz. George Robertson who resides in Alabama, and the heirs at law of William Robertson a son of George Robertson names unknown, but residing in Georgia . . . And the said Jeremiah Robertson. Filed April 23, 1855 . . . Elizabeth Reese was the wife of Absolom Reese. . . .

WILLIAM DAVIS TO ALLEN ROBINSON DEED PACK. 126
CLERK OF COURTS OFFICE, PICKENS, S. C.

Georgia

This indenture made this 11th Day of November 1809 between William Davis of the State aforesaid & County of Jefferson of the one part & Allen Robinson of the State aforesaid & County of Putnam of the other part Witnesseth that the sd. William Davis for & in consideration of the sum of one Thousand Dollars to him in hand paid, at, & before the sealing & delivery of these presents, the receipt whereof he doth here by acknowledge to be well content, hath granted, Bargaind, Sold. Ateemd? Conveyd, & confirmed, And by these presents doth Grant, Bargain, Sell, Convey & confirm unto him the Sd. Allen Robinson, his Heirs & assigns All that Tract or parcell of Land containing Two Hundred & Two & one half Acres Situate lying & being in Putnam County (formerly Baldwin County) in the State aforesaid, Bounded N. E. by Lot No. 171 N. West by Lot No. 167 S. West by Lot No. 137 & S East by Lot No. 169 & known in the plan by Lot No. 168 in the Fourth District Baldwin County & was drawn in the name of Benjamin Bridge of Warren County, Surveyed on the 4th Day August 1804 reference being had to sd. Grant will more fully appear, To have & to hold the sd. parcell or Tract of Land as before described, with all & singular the Rights Members & Appertenances what so ever, to the sd. parcell or Tract of Land being, belonging or in any wise appertaining, with the remainder & remainders Reversion & Reversions, Rents, Issues & profits thereof, to the only proper use, benefit, & behoof of him the Sd. Allen Robinson, his Heirs & assigns forever in fee simple. And, the sd. William Davis, his Heirs, Executors & Administrators, the sd. Bargain & Tract, or parcell of Land, aforesaid, to the sd. Allen Robinson, his Heirs, Executors, Administrators & Assigns against him the sd. William Davis his Heirs Exrs. Admnrs & Assigns & all & every other person & persons whatsoever shall & will Warrant & forever defend by these presents. In Witness whereof the sd. William Davis hath hereunto set his Hand, & Sign'd Seald & delivered in presence of

              his
         William X Davis (LS)
test   mark

James Robinson
Moses Newton J. P.

Georgia

Jefferson County) To all whom these presents shall come Greeting. Know ye, that on the 11th Day of Novr. 1809 Before me personally appeared Sarah Davis the Wife of the within nam'd William Davis, & on her private, & Seperate examination acknowledged & declared her fee & voluntary relinquishment of Dower or thereto in the within mentioned Tract or parcell of Land, & that she was not Influenc'd so to do, by the Dread, Fear, or Coercion of her Husband or any other person whatsoever. In Testimony whereof she, the S'd Sarah Davis hath here unto set her Hand & seal, the Day & year aforesaid

In presence of   Sarah Davis (LS)
Moses Newton J. P.
Georgia

Putnam County) Personally appeared before me Jas. Robertson and being duly Sworn saith that he is a Subscribing witness to the within Indenture of bargain and Sale and that he saw William Davis sign and acknowledge the same to be his act and Deed and as such to be Recorded Sworn to before me this 15th of Novr. 1810.

Danl. W? Zachry J. P.   Jas. Robinson

RECORDED IN THE CLERKS OFFICE OF PUTNAM SUPERIOR COURT IN BOOK B. folio 163& 164 the 17th Day of April 1811.

                                                                 Wm. Williams CLK

ALLEN ROBINSON TO RANDOL ROBINSON PACK. 126
DEED. CLERK OF COURTS OFFICE, PICKENS, S. C.

State of South carolina

Pickens District) Know all men by these presents and to whome it may conccarn that I Allin Robinson of the State and district aforesaid do give unto my Son Randol Robinson of the same State and District afore said a certain tract or parcel of land whereon my Son Randol now lives on vallued at five hundred Dollars Suppose to be one hundred acres more or less the corners and lines as follows Begining corner on a red oak on South Saluda river above the indian ford wher Martin Whitmires lands corners thence Down the said river to the mouth of Carpernters creek thence along Joseph Williams line to a stake corner thence a conditional line a west course to the said creek thence along across fence to a drean thence up the drean to the head of said Drean thence a conditional line a north course to a Stake corner on Martin Whitmires line thence along said line to the begining corner on the river to have and to hold for ever on certain Conditions that is at my death when the distribution of my property among my lawful heirs if it does not amount to five hundred each the said Randol Robinson my son is bound to pay back to the estate so much as will make the rest of my heirs Equal with him and the conditions is further that the said tract of land is to stand good to my other lawful heirs for their Equal proportion of my estate if required and on my Son Randol Robinson Complying with these conditions this instrument of writing shall be his lawful titles to the said tract or parcel of land forever after my death in witness whereof I have set my hand and seal this the 30th day of August 1838.

test   Allin Robinson (LS)

James Robinson

THOMAS ROBERTSON TO ALLEN ROBERTSON PACK. 126
DEED OF CONVEYANCE
CLERK OF COURTS OFFICE, PICKENS, S. C.

South Carolina

Pendleton District

This indenture made this the twentyeth day of December and in the year of our Lord one thousand Eight Hundred and five between thomas Robertson of the State & District aforesaid and allin Robertson of the same the said thomas Robertson Doth Bargain and sell to the said Allen Robertson of the State and District aforesaid one tract of Land Containing one Hundred and fifty Acres more or less Begining on the South Corner of the land that Charles Gates sold to the said Allen Robertson and runs S. to a red oak corner on the washbarn road thence along the said road E to a pine Corner a corner of a tract of land formerly granted to Joseph Whitner thence N. E. to a red oak Corner thence West to the begining corner The S'd thomas robertson doth Warrant and defend the said land from all Persons or manner of persons to the said Allen Robertson and his Heirs for Ever Given under my hand the Day and date above written.

             his
         Thomas X Robertson
            mark

Test
Jas. Hagood
William fendley
South Carolina

 Pendleton District) Personally Came Wm Findley before me James H. Foster one of the justices assign to keep the peace for said District & made oath that he saw thomas Robertson sighn & deliver the within deed of Conveyance for the use & purposes therein mentioned & he saw James Hagood sighn his name at the same time with this deponant as witnesses to the same Sworn to & Subscribed this 17 of December 1810.
James H. Foster JP   J or I? William fendly
 Registered 21st March 1818 in the Mesne Conveyance office for Pendleton District Book O Page 87.
          John Lewis C. C. & R. M. C.

WILLIAM ELLETT TO MOSES FENDLEY PACK. 126 DEED CLERK OF COURTS OFFICE, PICKENS, S. C.

THE STATE OF SOUTH CAROLINA

 Know all men by these Presents that I William Ellett of the District of Edgefield in the state aforesaid, in consideration of five hundred dollar to me paid by Moses Fendley of the District and State aforesaid, have granted bargained sold and released and by these Presents, do grant bargain sell and release unto the said Moses Fendley all that tract or parcel of Land containing five hundred acres more or less as the same may be originally granted to William Ellett the thirty first day of August in the year of our Lord one thousand seven hundred and Seventy four, thence conveyed to his son William Ellett Situate lying and being in the District and State aforesaid on Middle Creek a Branch of Savannah River and a Branch of Stephens Creek bounded N. E. and E by Lands of Alexander Smiths and by lands of Isaiah Blackwells, and S.W. by lands of John Richseys Together with all and Singular the rights members Hereditaments and appurtenances to the said Premises belongin or in any wise incident or appertaining to have and to hold all and singular the Premises before mentioned unto the said Moses Fendley his Heirs and assigns forever. And I do hereby bind myself my Heirs Executors and Administrators to warrant and forever defend all and singular the said Premises unto the said Moses Fendley his Heirs and assigns against my self and my Heirs and against every other Person whomsoever lawfully claiming or to claim the same or any part thereof. Witness my hand and seal this Twenty seventh day of August in the year of our Lord one thousand Eight hundred and in the 25th year of the Independence of the United States of America. Signed

Sealed and acknowledged in Presence of
Hezekiah A. Boyd   William Ellett
Allin Robinson

PHILIP COOPER TO JAMES ROBERTSON PACK. 126 DEED
CLERK OF COURTS OFFICE, PICKENS, S. C.

South Carolina

Pendleton District) Know all men by these presents that I Philip Cooper of the State and District afore Said am held and firmly bound unto James Robertson of the State of Georgia Putman County the sum of Two thousand four hundred Dollars Which payment I do bind myself my heirs Executors administrators to be well and truly made herto the said James Robertson his heirs or assigns in witness I have here unto set my hand and seal this sixth September 1818.

The Conditions of the above obligation is such that if the above bound Philip Cooper doth on the receipt of Six? hundred Dollars make or cause to be made unto James Robertson good and Lawful titles to the Tract of Land that said Cooper now lives on by the first day of January then this obligation to be nul and void, otherwise to remain in full force & power in same? in the presents.

Name not plain.   Philip Cooper

ALLEN ROBINSON TO JAMES H. FOSTER PACK. 126
DEED. CLERK OF COURTS OFFICE, PICKENS, S. C.

The State of South Carolina

Know all men by these presants that I Allen Robinson of Pendleton District and State aforesaid in consideration of the Sum of Twelve hundred dollars to me in hand paid James Hoggatt? Foster of Greenville District and State afore said Have granted Bargained Sold and Released and by these presents do grant bargain sell and Release unto the Said James Hoggatt? Foster all that plantations tracts of parcel of Lands Containing three hundred and fifty acres Situated in pendleton District on the South Side of Salluday River. The Beging corner a black oak on said River above the old Indian Ford, thence Running S. 65 W. 44.73 to a post oak corner Thence S 25 E 44 to a Stake thence Running to a pine it being a station tree thence Running a conditional line fresh marked to a Read oak it being a conditional corner on Washbuns Road—Thence down washbuns Road It being a conditional line to pine corner—thence a strait line from the pine corner to Read oak corner, Moses Fendleys corner, thence the said line to Read oak bush it being a conditional corner thence a conditional line to a pine stake intersecting the line of the original two hundred acres granted to Charles Gates, thence Gates old line to a stake corner thence a strate line to the mouth of Carpenters on the River, thence up the meanders of the river to the begining corner, Be there the Same moore or less. Together with all and singular the Rights members heriditary an appertainences to the said premises belonging or in any wise incident or appertaining there unto. To have and to hold all & singular the premises before mentioned unto the Sd. Jas. H. Foster his heirs and assigns for Ever. And I do hereby bind myself my heirs Executors and administrators to warrant and forever defend same all and Singular the premises unto unto the said James H. Foster his heirs and assigns against myself my heirs and every other person Claiming or to Clame the same or any part thereof witness my hand and seal this seventeenth of September AD one thousand Eight hundrd & Seven and in the Thirty seven of Americian Independancy.

Assigned in the presents of us

                                                Allin Robinson (SEAL)

      his
Gideon   X   Hagwood
      mark
James Robinson
Robert C. Foster
South Carolina

Pendleton Dist) personaly apeared Gideon Hagwood or Haywood? before me the Subscribing Justice and being duly sworn saith that he saw Allen Robertson sign seal and acknowledge the with in Deed to James Foster Like wise he saw James Robertson and Robt. C. Foster with himself sign their names as witnesses Sworn and Subscribed this 2d of January 1808.

                                                his
                                       Giden   X   Hegood
                                                mark

John McClure JP
The State of South Carolina

I John McClure one of the Justceas of the Quorum do hereby certify unto all whom it may concern that Sarah Robinson the wife of Allin Robinson did this day appear before me and upon being privately and seperately Examined by me did declare that that she does freely and voluntarily and without any Compulsion dread or fear or aney person or persons whomsoever Renounce Release and forever Relinquish unto James Foster his heirs and assigns all her interest and Estate also all her Right and claim of Dower of in or to all and singular the premacies sold by said Robinson to Foster by Deed. Given under my hand and Seal this twelth of November 1807.
John McClure J. P.   Sarah Robinson (SEAL)
RECORDED IN THE CLERKS OFFICE OF PENDLETON DISTRICT R. M. C. BOOK J PAGE 192. CERTIFIED APRIL 4, 1808.

CHARLES GATES TO ALLEN ROBINSON PACK. 126
DEED. CLERK OF COURTS OFFICE, PICKENS, S. C.

State of South Carolina

Pendleton District) Know all men by these presents that I Charles Gates Planter of the state and Deastrict Before mentioned in Consideration of one thousand Dollars to me in hand paid by Allin Robinson of the same Deastrict have Bargained Granted sold and by these preasants do grant Bargain and sell unto the said Allin Robinson his heirs Executors Administrators and assigns all the following plantations Parsels or Tracts of Land as will appear by a plat and grants being in two Different surveys the one of Two hundred Acres Granted to Charles Gates the Twenty first day of January one thousand seven hundred and Eighty five, the other a Tract of Forty Acres Being part of a one hundred and Eighty Acres Tract granted to the above Gates the

Fifth Day of June one thousand seven hundred and Eighty six Lying and being in the State and Deastrict and on Saludy waters and on the south side of Saluda River as will appear by a Plat of Each survey the one Tract of Forty acres taken out of the one hundred and Eighty Acre Tract by a conditional line adjoining the Two hundred Acree Tract on the North in all Two hundred and forty acres Together with all and singular the Rites members herediti- ments and appertinances belonging or in any wise appertaining thereunto for Ever unto the only proper use beneyfit and behoof of him the said Allin Rob- inson his heirs Executors administrators or assigns to warrant snf forever de- fend all and singular the Primacies afore mentioned unto the said Allin Rob- inson his heirs Executors and assigns and From Every other person or per- sons whom so ever Lawfully claiming or to claim the same or aney part there of in witness hereof I have hear unto set my hand and seal this Twenty third day of November and in the thirtyeth of the Independencey of America and in the preasants of us as suscribing witnesses (no year given).

Travers? N? Hill   Charles Gates (SEAL)
William Ellett
South Carolina

Pendleton Destrict) Personally apeared Travers Hill and William Ellett before me John McClure Justice of the Quorum and being Duly Sworn Sayeth that he saw Charles Yates sign and deliver the within deed to Allen Robertson and the Subscribed their names as witnesses Sworn and Subscribed this 23th day of November 1805 before me.
John McClure J. O.

                                                                                  William Ellett
South Carolina

Pendleton District) I John McClure Justice of Quorum do hereby Certify unto all whome it may Concern that Ann Gates the wife of the within named Charles Gates did this day apear before me and upon being privaitly and seperately Examined by me did declare that she does freely voluntery and without any Compultion Dred or fear of any person or persons whomsoever renounce release and forever relinquish all her interest and Estate and also all her right and Clame of Dowry of in or to all and singular the premises within mentioned and released Given under my hand and seal this twenty third day of november 1805.

                                                                    hir
                                              Ann   X   Gates
                                                           mark

John McClure JQ
    CERTIFIED JANUARY 14, 1806.

HENRY GARNER PACK. 128 EQUITY
CLERK OF COURTS OFFICE, PICKENS, S. C.

James Garner states that Henry Garner died in Pickens District in 1848. Owned 100 acres lying on the waters of 18 Mile Creek purchased from Robert Anderson Jr. Another tract of 96 acres he purchased from Robe rt Baker lying on the north branches of 18 Mile Creek. Another tract of 130 acres he purchased from Thomas Garvin lying on the west side of litle fifteen mile creek. Left a widow Nancy Garner & 6 children viz. Polly Boggs formerly

Polly Garner widow of Thomas Boggs decd. Mahala Fennel who married Hardy Fennel, Ruhama widow of Barnett Neighbors decd. Matilda Garner who intermarried with John Garner, James Garner, and the legal heirs & representatives of Sylvania Boggs decd. the wife of Aaron Boggs to wit, Josiah N. Boggs, James A. Boggs, William Garner & wife Matilda, formerly Garner, Henry G. Boggs, Munroe Boggs, John Mullenax & wife Elizabeth, Madison Boggs and Martha Boggs. Filed June 21, 1849 . . . On Feb. 7, 1849 Aaron Boggs states that Martha Boggs is over the age of 12 years. That Madison Boggs is over 14 years of age. . . .

POWER OF ATTORNEY

Know all men by these presents that we William A. Mullinax & Sylvania Mullinex his wife all of Monroe County & State of Mississippi do hereby nominate constitute and appoint Aaron Boggs of the District of Pickens State of South Carolina our true and lawful attorney for us and in our names to draw from the Commissioner in Equity of Pickens District South Carolina or from any other person or persons any Sum or Sums of money due us as the Heirs at law of Henry Garner deceased late of said District and more particularly to draw from Miles M. Norton Commissioner in equity of Pickens Dist. S. C. or from any other person any sum of money due us from the sale of the Real Estate belonging to the said Henry Garner in his lifetime, late of said county. We hereby authorize our said attorney to sign our names to any Deed, Bill, Bond, recept, acquitance or any other instrument necesary to be signd in order to enable him to draw said money and in general to do all other acts & deed in the premises in as full ample & perfect a manner as we could do were we personally present hereby ratifying each & every act of my said attorney in the premises. In testimony whereof we have here unto set our hands & affixed our seals on this the 17 day of December AD 1850.

        Wm. A. Mullinnex (SEAL)
        Sylvania Mullinnex

Acknowledged before me at Aberdeen, Miss. this 17 day of Decr AD 1850.

        D. W. Sadler (SEAL)
        Justice of the peace
        Monroe County Miss

The State of Miss
Monroe County) I hereby certify that D. W. Sadler esquire before whom the foregoing acknowledgements were made was at the time of so doing an acting justice of the peace in & for said county duly sworn & commissioned & that his said signature is genuine. In testimony whereof I have here unto set my hand & affixed my seal as Clerk of Probate Court Monroe County, Miss this 17 day of December AD 1850.

        T. W. Williams Clerk

EZEKIEL PILGRIM PACK. 131 EQUITY
CLERK OF COURTS OFFICE, PICKENS, S. C.

Ezekiel Pilgrim died in Pickens District. Owned 300 acres on the waters of 23 Mile Creek & adjoining lands of R. Russell, Mrs. Whitten, Henderson Ekes & J. Wilson decd. He died intestate leaving a widow Mary Pilgrim & 8 children all alive viz. William Pilgrim, Amos Pilgrim, Ezekiel Pilgrim, Elijah Pilgrim, Jefferson Pilgrim, Elizabeth who intermarried with Alfred Smith,

Sidney Pilgrim & Nancy who intermarried with Alfred Ekes. All the children are still alove and over 21 years of age . . . Ezekiel Pilgrim his son resides without the state. (Not given).

Filed Feb. 4, 1831.

COL. JOHN C. KILPATRICK PACK. 134 EQUITY
CLERK OF COURTS OFFICE, PICKENS, S. C.

In the name of God Amen—

I John C. Kilpatrick of Pickens district in the State of South Carolina, being of sound mind and memory, but advanced in years and feeble in health, am desirous of settling all my worldly affairs, and do ordain and establish the following as my last will and testament. In the first place, I desire that sufficient property may be sold to pay all my just debts and I wish if practicable, that my Executors may dispose of the mills and the lands adjoining, reserving the tract on which I live, for the children of my deceased son John C. Kilpatrick Junr. to be divided equally or equilably between them when they become of age, or at such time as may be deemed advisable. I vest in my Executors full power to dispose of such negroes, at public or private sale, as they may think proper, for the settlement of debts.

The remaining negroes I wish equally divided between the two children at a proper time, with the exception of those hereafter mentioned, Viz. Fanny I desire by request of my wife to give to Clara, and Delilah to Whitner the two children, and the families of these two women to be divided equally between them when either becomes of age, or the other division takes place.

The management of the property after the payment of the debts, I leave to the discretion of my Executors, believing that they will so manage it as to render it most beneficial to my Grand children. And reposing full trust and confidence in my friends John S. Lorton, John Maxwell and F. W. Symmes I hereby appoint them Executors of this my last will and testament which revoking all others I hereby acknowledge to be such.

Given under my hand & seal the 21st day of November in the year of our Lord one thousand Eight hundred & forty three, & in the Sixty eighth year of the Sovereignty & independence of the United States.

(Signed) J. C. Kilpatrick (SEAL)

In presence of
Tilmon C. Megee
John Coates
Elizabeth H. Maxwell
John Arnold?

South Carolina
Pickens District) By James H. Dendy
Ordinary of Pickens District

Be it Remembered that on the Eighteenth day of December Anno Domini 1843 the enclosed Last will and Testament of John C. Kilpatrick Deceased was proven by the oath of Tilmon C. Megee one of the subscribing witnesses to the said will and at the same time Qualified John S. Lorton as Executor of the same.

J. H. Dendy O. P. D.

I James H. Dendy Ordinary of Pickens Dist. do hereby certify the above and foregoing signed J. C. Kilpatrick to be a true copy of His original Last Will & Testament.

Jas. H. Dendy O. P. D. (LS)

Certified Jan. 10, 1844.

———————

On Jan. 15, 1857 F. Whitner Kilpatrick states that he is a minor over the age of 14 years and prays that his friend Judge J. N. Whitner be appointed his guardian.

Will of John C. Kilpatrick Jr.

In the Name of God Amen.

I John C. Kilpatrick Jr. being of sound and disposing mind and memory, but weak in body and calling to mind the uncertainty of life, and being desirous to dispose of all such worldly estate as it has pleased God to bless me with do make and ordain this my last Will & Testament in manner following Vizt. Item 1st I desire that my Executors herein after named shall make provision for the payment of all my debts by the sale of such property as they may think best for the interest of the Estate. If, However, after my decease, the debts should not be pressing, and the times will not justify the sale of valuable property without a sacrifice, it is my will and desire, provided my principal creditors will consent to a further indulgance, to postpone the sale of such property which may be necessary for the payment of my debts, until a more propitious season, but this I leave discretionary with my executors having full confidence in them that they will consult the true interest of my Estate—or of my debts should not be pressing, and my creditors will consent to such indulgence as will enable my hands to work out of debt, I submit it to my Executors exercesing as I know they will do, a sound descretion, or resort to the sale of property to make provision for the payment of my debts.

Item 2d I desire that the residue of my property which will remain after the payment of my debts, consisting of the Tract of Land on which I now reside including such metes and boundaries as my beloved father has marked out for me, and all my personal property of whatsoever kind and description shall remain in common stock and undivided, untill my oldest daughter Clarissa or Clara arrives at age or marries, and then I desire that my Executors shall* cause to be appraised by three or more disinterested and good men all my Real and personal property (except so much of it, as I acquired by my wife) which may belong to my Estate at that time and divided into four equal shares, each of my children, Clara, Franklin Whitner and Amanda, and my beloved wife Amanda to receive a share, which portion of my Estate so divided I do give, devise & bequeath unto my three children above named and to the heirs of their body forever, and the portion to my wife during widowhood.

3d. I do also in addition to the above legacies, give and bequeath unto my beloved wife all the property given unto her by her father and such property as she may hereafter receiveffrom his Estate, to have and to hold forever and to dispose of at her pleasure without any control from this my Will and Testament.

Item 4th. If either of my children should die before they arrive at age or without issue, it is my will and desire that the share or portion they would have been entitled to shall be divided between their brother or sister as the case may be.

Item 5th. If my wife should marry again it is my will and desire that the portion allowed her in Item 2d shall be equally divided between our three children or in case of the death of any of these without issue between the survivor or survivors.

Item 6th. It is my will and desire that the income arising from the property untill distribution shall be appropriated to the maintenance of my family & education of my children, and I must enjoin particularly upon my beloved wife and my Executors to have my children well educated.

Item 7th. It is my will & desire that my family should remain in this country and I do enjoin upon my Executors not to permit my property to be removed out of the state and if my land should not be sufficient to work the hands to advantage I do hereby request and empower them to purchase or make such investment as they may think advantageous.

Item 8th I appoint my father John C. Kilpatrick, Joseph N. Whitner, John Maxwell and Aaron Shannon of Alabama Executors of this my last will & Testament In witness whereof I have hereunto set my hand and affixed my seal this 30th day of May 1840.

J. C. Kilpatrick Jr. (SEAL)

Signed Sealed published & declared in presence of
Robert A. Maxwell
F. W. Symmes
Tilmon C. Megee

ROBERT BOWEN PACK. 135 EQUITY
CLERK OF COURTS OFFICE, PICKENS, S. C.

Robert Bowen died in Pickens District. Owned 244 acres on the east side of 12 Mile River and south side of Town Creek. His wife died shortly after he did, Hminor children were, Eliza Ann P. Bowen over the age of 12 years, Dorcas J. Bowen, O. E. Bowen, Louisa A. Bowen, Martha Ann J. Bowen each under the age of 12 years, Bailey A. Bowen, John Caldwell C. Bowen each under the age of 14 years . . . Filed June 25, 1847 . . . The home tract was sold to John Bowen for $1485.00. . . .

BENJAMIN STARRETT TO JAMES STARRETT PACK. 136
CLERK OF COURTS OFFICE, PICKENS, S. C.

South Carolina

Pendleton District) To all whom these presents shall come greeting Whereas I Benj Starrett have Borrowed of James Starrett the sums of money hereafter mentioned viz. Fifty dollars cash also four hundred & thirty dollars Recd. of Capt. James Wood, also four Hundred and fifty five dollars more making in the whole nine hundred & thirty five dollars which are to Bear lawfull interest agreeable to notes given for the aforesaid sums I the said Benjamin Starrett do mortgage & sell unto the sd James Starrett one tract of land containing 300 acres where on I now live one sorrel stud horse one B horse one old sorrel mare one young sorrel mare aged three years old, thirteen head of cattle together with all my household Furniture Including the Profits arising by cultivating the aforesaid plantation to the proper use and behoof of him the said James Starrett his heirs & assigns forever on the Express condition and provided nevertheless that if the said Benjamin Starrett or his heirs shall well & truly pay unto the said James Starrett the sum of nine Hundred and thirty five dollars with the interest and cost which may grow and become due thereon on or before the twenty fifth day December next, then and in that case the aforesaid property to Revert Back and Becomes the Right of the said Benj Starrett his heirs and assigns forever, But and if the said Benjamin Starrett my heirs or assigns s hou'd happen to make Default in the payment of the said sums at the time above Stipulated unto the said James Starrett then and in that case I do hereby authorize the said James Starrett to go into my houses and land and use and Possess the property above mentioned without any molestation or Interruption on the part of me the said B. Starrett and to take the said Bargained property & land, into his own Possession and his own Right and property in witness whereof I have hereunto set my hand & seal this Twenty fourth day of March 1806 and of the American Independence the 31st year.

B. Starrett

James Wood
Joseph B. Earle
State of South Carolina

Pendleton District) Came personally before me the Subscribing Justice Capt. James Wood and made oath as the Law directs and on his oath states that he saw the within Namd Benjn Starrett Jur sign & seal the with Instrument of writing and that he was a subscribing witness and in his presence saw the other witness sign his name also Sworn to before me this 7th Day of April 1806.

James C. Griffin JP James Wood
   Certified June 4, 1806.

State of South Carolina

Know all men by these presents that I Peter Gray of Spartan District for and in consideration of one hundred and fifty dollars to me paid by Benj'n L. or S? Starrett of Pendleton County and State aforesaid, have granted bargained sold released and by these presents do grant bargain sell and release unto the said Benj'n or L? Starrett all that plantation or tract of land containing three hundred acres which was the Bounty right for the said state to the said P. Gray for Services during the late war—Situated on the waters of Connerossee (ninety Six District) and hath such form marks butting & boundings, as the annexed plat will represent—Together with all and singular members heriditaments and appurtenances to the said premises belonging or in any wise incident or appertaining to have and to hold all and singular the premises before mentioned unto the said Benjn S? Starrett his heirs and assigns forever, and I do hereby bind my self my Heirs my Executors and administrators to warrant and forever defend all and singular the said premises unto Benjn, Starrett his Heirs and assigns against my self and my Heirs and against every person whomsoever lawfully claiming or to claim the same or any part thereof. Witness my Hand and Seal this 18 day of October 1803.

Peter Gray

   Executed in presents of us

Banjn Hawkins
William Montgomery

(Hannah Gray was the widow of Peter Gray. The rest of this paper too dim to copy).

Benjamin Starrett purchased from Capt. Peter Gray his bounty of 300 acres Land on Richland Cr took a Title dated 18th October 1803. about 1805 William Steele obtained judgment vs. B. Starrett for about $75 besides Int and cost which still remains unsatisfied in the Clerks office of Anderson Dist. The Exor was renewed several times not levied nor does there appear to be any cr on it. But Deft paid Pltff $25 about 24 March 1806 B. Starrett Mortgaged this land to his Father for $50 cash $430 Recd. of Capt. James Wood also $450 more in all $930 dated 24 March 1806 The Mortgage Recorded 4 June 1806 and is unpaid, but the notes are misplacd—about 1807 or 1808 B. Starrett moved to Ga. he left his lands to pay Steele & his Father or abandoned it, as it is not now worth $1000. perhaps on a cr may bring 6 to 900 $. He has often said he intended the land to pay Steele. about 1821 in July W. Steele died leaving I? C. Griffin, J? L. or S? Steele & B. Dickson Executors and after specific Legacies gave the residue or Remainder of his Estate to Mary L. or S? Steele, Elizabeth Steele, Joseph L. Steele & Jas. Steele Griffin & Steele qualified collected what they could without difficukty paid legacies & divided the bal. about 1824 J. L. Steele died the case vs. B. Starrett unattended to. Jos. Grisham married Mary L. Steele, Elijah Alexander married Elizabeth Steeleand as Jos. or Jas? L. Steele died intestate his part of his Fathers Estate as well as his own was to be divided between his mother Estaher Steele 2 sons of his bro. Aaron Steele, Wm. Steele, James Steele, Jos. Grisham & Elijah Alexander. The amt being small no one was willing to undertake to attend to this old debt & it still remains uncollected. James Starrett is dead & his papers & debts transferred to his son John Starrett the Mortgage unpaid. About 1838 or 1839 Benj. Starrett died in Franklin County G leaving a widow Cynthis Starrett and Eleven children.

1. Polly Ann who married a Bell.
2. James S. Starrett
3. Bethenia who married Alfred Dawkins
4. Volinder Starrett
5. Patsy who married James Ellard
6. William Starrett
7. Susannah who married a Summerville
8. Benjn. J. Starrett
9. Preston C. Starrett
10. Clark S. Starrett
11. John R. Starrett

THOMAS M. JOHNSON PACK. 137 EQUITY
CLERK OF COURTS OFFICE, PICKENS, S. C.

Thomas M. Johnson of Pickens District states that he purchased from George W. Rankin assignee of Frederick N. Garvin a certain tract of land lying on the waters of Crow Creek, adjoining lands of Wm. Crenshaw, Daniel Alexander, Micajah Alexander & others containing about 225 acres, paying therefor $115.00 but that owing to the xciting state of public affairs, which directed the attention of the people to a great extent from their private affairs the title thereto was not executd to the said J. W. Grant until the 20th Dec. 1863, but on that day was duly executed by George W. Rankin and placed upon record according to law. On Feb. 28, 1863 J. W. Grant fairly and openly granted and sold to him 115 acres acres being part of the above dscribed tract. He also states that both he and the said J. W. Grant being away from home in the army, and being absorbed with public affairs, the matter in question was neglected until the death of the said J. W. Grant who left a widow Rebecca M. Grant and 4 minor children, Sarah M. Grant, James N. Grant, Lydia F. Grant, Rebecca W. Grant in Pickens Dist.

Filed April 6, 1867.

INQUESTS PACK 138
CLERK OF COURTS OFFICE, PICKENS, S. C.

NO. 1 JAMES LOWRY

An inquest was held at the house of James Lowry Aug. 12, 1833 or 1855 (this writing was bad, could not make out numbers plain) in Pickens Dist. before Mathias Tally a Justice of the Quorum for said district upon the view of the body of the said James Lowry. Miles Darnel or Daniel says that he and and James Lowry were crossing Whetsone Creek and the said Lowrys nag made a blunder & he fell off and washed down the creek and was found drowned by Conrad Weaver and said Darnel. The jury brought it out that the cause of his death was by his own venturing into the creek.

NO. 2

An inquest was held Dec. 12, 1845 on the dead body of William Waldrop. The jury brought it out that he came to his death by the visitation of God, at the house of Ira G. Gambrell on the 11th Decr. 1845 . . . R. A. Frasure states that on Decr. 11, 1845 he over took the decd. and came into the house of Ira G. Gambrells, sat down and ate dinner. The decd. ate harty and appeared to be well & after dinner he walked out with the decd. into the yard, stood and talked some time, looked round and saw the decd. fall on his back in the yard, They picked him up and brought him into the house, by that time he was dead. I thought it was a fit, but not like the common fits. James Frasure says that he was at Mr. Gambrells house. The decd. appeared to be in good health, took dinner, rose from the table, sat down by the fire and smoked his pipe, then went out into the yard and talked some to him. I saw the decd. fall on his back. Mr. Gambrell raised him up and he was dead. Then they brought him into the house. Mr. Gambrell states that the decd. came to his house and he asked him how he was. The decd. said he was well and sat by the fire, smoked his pipe, went out into the yard and talked and appeared quite jovel standing by the grindstone. I heard him fall, turned around and he was lying on his back. I raised him up felt gor his pulse but found none and brought him into the house. Laid him by the fire and he gaped 2 or 3 times after he was laid down on the pallet. I do not think the fall was hard enough to kill any person.

SARGENT GRIFFIN PACK. 132-A EQUITY
CLERK OF COURTS OFFICE, PICKENS, S. C.

Avarilla Griffin of Pickens District states that her husband Sargent Griffin died in 1858. Owned 1100 acres of land on To wn Creek waters of Twelve Mile River adjoining lands of Samuel Brown, J. E. Hagood, George Hendricks & others. Heirs at law viz. Thomas Griffin, E. H. Griffin, H. J. Anthony & wife Avarilla Anthony formerly Avarilla Griffin. J. B. Mansell & wife Vashti Mansell formerly Vashti Griffin who reside in Georgia. Barton Griffin, Benjamin Griffin, Sargent Griffin, R. H. Griffin who reside in Alabama, the heirs at law of Dorcas Alexander decd. formerly Dorcas Griffin who married Prior Alexander, namely Minerva Billingsley formerly Minerva Alesander & her husband H. A. Billingsley who reside in Georgia, Prior Alexander, E. B. Alexander, Sargent Alexander & Thomas P. Alexander who reside in Pickens District. The heirs at law of Bailey Griffin to wit, his 3 children Sargent J. Griffin, Joseph Griffin, Avarilla Griffin minors residing in Alabama. The children of William Griffin a decd. son namely, Avarilla A. Griffin, Nancy V. Griffin, Elihu H. Griffin, Rosanna M. Griffin, G. B. Griffin, Mary L. M? Griffin, Bailey B. Griffin, Thomas V. Griffin, Margaret T. Griffin, Martha F. D. Griffin, Jane M. S. Griffin, the last 9 named children all being minors reside in Alabama, Anderson Griffin residing in Edgefield District. Fi led Aug. 16, 1858. William Griffin died in 1857 leaving a widow Mahaney Griffin & 11 children all in Alabama.

NATHANIEL DAVIS TO SARGANT GRIFFIN PACK. 132-A
CLERK OF COURTS OFFICE, PICKENS, S. C.
RELEASE FOR 500 ACRES LAND

South carolina

Pickens Destrict) Know all men by these presents that Nathl. Davis of the state and Destrict afore sd. for and in consideration of the sum of five hundred dollars to me paid by Sargent Griffin of sd. state and destrict have bargained granted and sold and and by these presents do bargain grant sell and release unto the sd Sargent Griffin a certain tract or parcel of land situate in the district afore sd on town creek waters of twelve mile River containing five hundred acres be the same more or less according to the following boundary beginning on a hickory on Rebinses (probably meant for Robinson) old line on the fox squirrel Roadthence a Conditional line line between Nathl. Davis and Sargent Griffin straight to a sweet gum near the Creek, thence to a white oake a few Rods up the creek thence straight to a stone by the grave yard thence straight by a stone at the root of a peach tree untill it strikes a Conditional line made beetweeen Nathl Davis and J. Roper thence on Sd. line to a stone x thence S 63 W 11.90 to a poplar thence N 60 W to the creek thence up the creek to the mouth a Branch which is Conditional line with Wm. Crane thence up the sd branch to where Earlses old line Crosses it thence along sd. line to a stone x thence N. 30 E 7.60 to a pine oak thence N 45½ W 16.30 red oak thence S 81½ W 14 to a pine N 25 w 20 to a stake thence N 30 E 71 to astake thence S 60 to the beginning it being part a tract granted to Balis Earl and two tracts granted Wm Robins together with all and singular the Rights and privileges of the sd previleges unto the sd Sargeant Griffin and his heirs for ever to have and to hold and I do hereby bind my self my heirs and assigns to warrant and forever defend the sd premises unto the Sd. Sargeant Griffin and his heirs for ever against my self my heirs and against all and every other person Claiming or to Claim the same not with standing Signed and Delivered this 29 Day of october 1832 in the presence of us.

                                            Nathl Davis (LS)

Elihu H. Griffin
William Griffin

The State of So. Carolina

Pickens district) before me the subscribing Justice for the said district personally came and appeared Elihu H. Griffin and being sworn in due form of law deposeth & sayeth that he saw Nanth Davis assign seal and deliver the within as his act and deed and sayeth on oath that William Griffin was present and a subscribing witness to the due Execution of the same with himself swon to and subscribed this 20 day of January 1833 before me.

Bailey Barton J. Q.   Elihu H. Griffin

The State of So. Carolina

Pickens District) I Bailey Barton Esqr. one of the Justices of the Quorum or the said district do hereby certify to all whoom it may concern that Emily Davis the wife of the within named Nathl Davis did this day appear before me and upon being privately and seperately Examined by me did declare that she does freely voluntarily and without any compulsion dread or fear of any person or persons whoomsoever renounce release and forever relinquish all her right interest and Estate and also all her her right and claim of dower of in or to all and singular the premises within mentioned and perticularly discribed given under my hand and seal this 10th day of Nov. 1834.

Bailey Barton J. Q. (SEAL)

                                                    her
                                      Emily   X   Davis
                                              mark

RECORDED IN BOOK C PAGE 150. CERTIFIED MARCH 14, 1836.

NATHANIEL DAVIS TO SARGEANT GRIFFIN PACK. 132-A
DEED. CLERK OF COURTS OFFICE, PICKENS, S. C.

The State of South Carolina

Pickens District) Know all men by these presents that I, Nathanie Davis of the district of Pickens & State affour Said in Consideration of the Sum of Eight Hundred dollors to me in hand Paid by Sargent Griffin of the State and district affour said, the Recipts where of is here by acknowledged, have granted Bargained Sold & Released & by these presents do grant, bargin, sell & Release, unto the said Sargent Griffin all that tract plantation or tract of land, Situate Lying & being on Town Creek waters of twelve mile river, in the State and District affoursaid Containing two hundred & fifty acres, be the same more or less & buting & bounding on North by Lands belonging to Lewis Browns & N. & N. E. by Henry Griffin & Williams land & on E. & South West by the said Sargent Griffins land, beginning on a Conditional Hickry Corner on the old line near the fox Squerl Road made by the said Sargent Griffin & Nathaniel Davis, thence S. 60 E. along the said old Line to pine Corner thence N. 7 W. to Black Jack & then S. 47 W. along said old line to a conditional Corner, thence Strate line to a Conditional White oak on the bank of Sd. Creek thence down Said Creek to a Conditional Sweat gum, made by the said Davis & Griffin thence Strait Line to the beginning corner together with all & Singular the Rights Members, Heraditaments & apertainances to the said primisses Belonging or in any wayes incident or appertaining to the Said, To have & to hold, all & Singular the primises before mentioned unto the said Sargent Griffin his heirs & assigns for Ever & I do, Here by bind my Self my heirs ExEcutors & Administrators to warrant & for Ever defend, all & Singular the primises before Mentioned unto the said Sargent Griffin his heirs & assigns against my Self & my heirs and against Every other person, whom so ever may Lawfully Claim or to Claim the same or any part thereof. Witness my hand and Seal this Seventeenth day of November in the year of our Lord one thousand Eight Hundred & thirty six A. D.

                Nathl. Davis (SEAL)

In presence of
Benjamin H. Davis
Sergent Griffin Jr.
State of South carolina

Pickens District) Before me the Subscribing Justice of the quorum for the said district personally appeared Benjamin H. Davis and made oath in due form of Law and Say on his oath that he saw the within named Nathaniel Davis Sign Seal & deliver the within deed of Conveyance to the within named Sargent Griffin for the use & purposes therein mentioned & that him self & Sargent Griffin, Jr. were present & subscribed their names thereto, to the dew Execution of the same. Swon to & Subscribed this 17th day of November 1836 before me.

Joseph B. Reid (J. Q.)   Benjamin H. Davis
State of South carolina

Pickens District) I, Joseph B. Reid of the Justice of the Quorum for the district affour said do Certify that Milley Davis the wife of the within named Nathaniel davis did this day appear before me & upon being privately & seperately Examined by me, did Declare that she does freely, & voluntarily, and without any fear or Compulsion or dread, of any person or persons, whome soeve, Renounce Release & for Ever Relinquish unto the within named Sargent Griffin his heirs & assigns, all hur intrest and all so all hur Right & Claim of dower and also all hur intrest & Estate of in and to all and Singular the primises within named and Released. Given under my hand & Sea¹ this 17th day of November one thousand Eight hundred & thirty Six.

 before me Joseph B. Reid (J. Q.)

              her
            Milley X Davis (SEAL)
              mark

RECORDED IN BOOK C PAGE 319. CERTIFIED MARCH 6, 1937. (NOTE. On the other deed her name was written EMILY DAVIS).

     LAWRENCE C. CRAIG PACK. 94 EQUITY
    CLERK OF COURTS OFFICE, PICKENS, S. C.

The State af South Carolina

In the Name of God Amen. I Lawrence C. Craig of Pickens District and State aforesaid, being of sound mind and disposing memory, do make ordain publish and declare this to be my last Will and Testament, That is to Say. 1st. I desire that my body be decently buried. 2nd. I desire that all my just debts be paid by my Executors hereinafter named as soon after my death as practicable. 3rd. I will and bequeath to Sarah E. Craig the wife of W. N. Craig my negro girl Susan and her future increase, during her natural life if she survives her said husband, if she should die after the death of W. N. Craig without living issue, then the said girl Susan and her increase to go to my Father and Mother, but in case of her leaving living issue at the time of her death, it is my will that said issue shall hold and enjoy said girl Susan and her increase to them and their heirs forever, in case said Sarah E. Craig should die before her husband W. N. Craig without living issue, I desire that he shall have the said girl Susan and her increase. 4th. All the rest, residue and remainder of my Estate Real and personal, I will desire and bequeath to my Father and Mother, the one that survives the other to hold and enjoy said property for and during his or her natural life and at the death of the Survivor to be equally divided among my brothers and sisters, and if any of them be dead then the child or children of such deceased brother or sister to take the share amongst them respectively, that the parent would have been entitled to if living. 5th. It is my will and desire that my Father and Mother if both or either of them should survive me, shall take my friend Thomas R. Brackenridge, and give him a comfortable Support, during his natural life, as I feel it my duty to make some provision for him, for his care and attention to my affairs during my lifetime, and in case he Should survive my Father and Mother, it is my my Will that he Select his home among the family and that they be paid out of my Estate reasonable compensation for the necessary care and attention they may give him. 6th. I hereby nominate constitute and appoint my Father Robert Craig and my friend James E. Hagood Executors to this my last will and Testament. In witness whereof I have hereunto Set my hand and and Seal this 13th day of December AD 1862.

L. C. Craig (SEAL)

In presence of
E. E. Alexander
W. E. Holcombe
      his
Wm. A.   X   Evatt
      mark

South Carolina
Pickens District) In Ordinary

I Certify that the foregoing is a true copy of the last will and testament of Lawrence C. Craig decsd. & which was duly Probated in the Court of Ordinary on the 19th day of October 1864, the original will remaining in my office. Given under my hand and Seal of office March 3rd 1868.

W. E. Holcombe O. P. D.

Lawrence C. Craig died in Oct. 1864, unmarried. Left as his heirs his father and mother, Robert & Rachel Craig. The following brothers and sisters viz. Martha C. Griffin wife of Thomas Griffin, William T? Craig, John C. Craig, Arthur R. Craig, Esther M. Craig, Laura Baker widow, Sarah E. Craig, Josephine E. Craig. All of age except Josephine E. Craig who is 18 years of age. His estate was large. Owned 1 tract lying and being in Pickens District, known as the "Howard Lands" adjoining lands of John Howard, Jeremiah Looper & others containing 800 acres. Another tract on the Cedar Rock, adjoining lands of Robert Craig, & others, containing 35 acres. Owned 10 negro slaves, stock of horses, mules, cattle, hogs &c. household and kitchen furniture. Also an interest in the firm known as the L. C. Craig & Co. and L. C. & W. N. Craig. The largest portion was left in their hands from sales they made while the war was raging between the northern and southern states, but which was of no value now. Much of their poses sions were swept away durin g the war, and of no value now, slaves, money etc. Filed April 28, 1868.

JAMES MOODY & WIFE TO JOEL MOODY PACK. 76
POWER OF ATTORNEY
CLERK OF COURTS OFFICE, PICKENS, S. C.

The State of Alabama

DeKalb County) Know all men by these presents, that for divers good and sufficient reasons hereunto, us moving, and for the the sum of Five Dollars to us in hand paid the receipt wherof, is hereby acknowledged we, James Moody and Nancy Moody his wife (late Nancy Holden) child and heir at law of John & Mary Holden, late of Pickens District, South Carolina) of DeKalb County and State of Alabama have this day nominated, constituted and appointed, and by these present do nominate, constitute and appoint, our true and trusty friend Joel Moody of Jackson County North Carolina, our true and lawful Attorney for us, and in our name to demand and receive from Elisha Holden, and the Clerk in Equity, of Pickens District South Carolina, or from any other person, or persons whatsoever, any money, goods wares, or property of any and every description that may be due or coming to us as heirs, legatees or Distributees of the estate of the said John and Mary Holden Decd. here by ratifying and confirming all the acts of our said Attorney, the Same as if we were personally present doing the same. In testimony whereof we have hereunto set our hands & seals this the 5th day of May AD 1856.

         James Moody (SEAL)
           her
       NANcy X Moody (SEAL)
          mark

Test.
N. S. Penn?
Wm. J. or K? Glazner

The State of Alabama

DeKalb County) Before me L. P. Ward a justice of the peace in and for the county and state aforesaid, this day personaly appeared James Moody and Nancy Moody his wife, who acknowledged that they signed, sealed and delivered the foregoing power of Attorney to Joel Moody, and for the purposes therein contained. Given under my hand & seal this 5th day of May AD 1856.

            L. P. Ward (SEAL)

State of Alabama

DeKalk County) I Reuben Estes Judge of the Probate Court of the County and State aforesaid hereby certify that L. P. Ward whose Genuine signature is affixed to the above acknowledgement was at the time of signing the same a Justice of the peace duly authorized by law to take such acknowledgement and that full faith and credit are due to all his official acts as such. Given under my hand and seal of office at office this 7th day of May A. D. 1856.

R. Estes, Judge of Probate

SAMUEL MEANS TO MICHAEL SMITH PACK. 76
DEED FOR 129 ACRES LAND
CLERK OF COURTS OFFICE, PICKENS, S. C.

The State of South Carolina

Know all men by these presents that I Samuel Means of Pendleton County in the state aforesaid for and in consideration of the sum of Thirty Dollars to me paid by Michael Smith of the State and County aforesaid have granted Bargained Sold and Released and by these presents do grant bargain Sell and Release unto the said Michael Smith all that parcel or Tract of Land Lying in Pendleton County on the waters of Brushy Creek containing one hundred and Twenty nine acres more or less Beginning on a Black oak Corner and running on John Boyds line N. 72 W. 66 chains then cornering on a Stake and running S. 9 W. 37 Chains then corner on a Red Oak and running N. 80 E. 62 Chain And from thence a Conditional line to the Beginning Corner It being a part of a Tract of Land granted to the aforesaid Samuel Means on the ninth Day of May one thousand seven hundred and ninety two, Together with all and singular the rights, members, hereditaments and appurtenances to the said premises belonging or in any wise incident or appertaining to have and to hold all and Singular the premises before mentioned unto the said Michael Smith his Heirs and assigns for ever And I do hereby bind my my self my heirs Executors and administrators to Warrant and for ever defend all and singular the said premises unto the said Michael Smith his Heirs and asigns against myself and my heirs, and against every person whomsoever lawfully claiming or to claim the same, or any part thereof. Witness my hand and seal this Twelfth day of February in the year of our Lord one thousand seven Hundred and ninety six, and in the Twentieth year of the Sovereignty and Independence of the United States of America.

Signed Sealed & Delivered in presence of
J. McGehee   Saml Means (SEAL)
Wm. Gunn

State of South Carolina

Pendleton County, to wit) Memorandum, that on the Tenth day of November in the year of our Lord one thousand seven hundred and Ninety Six. Personnally came Jno. McGehee before me Geo. Washington each a Justice for sd. County and being duly Sworn, made oath that he saw Saml. Means sign, seal, and as his act and deed deliver the within, deed of Conveyance to Michael Smith for the use therein Mentioned and that Wm. Gunn with this Deponent was a Subscribing witness to the same. Sworn to the day above.
Before Geo. W. Earle   J. McGehee
   Filed Nov. 10th, 1796.

JOHN HOLDEN PACK. 76 (EQUITY)
CLERK OF COURTS OFFICE, PICKENS, S. C.

Elias Norton & his wife Mary Norton formerly Mary Holden states that her father John Holden died in 1852, seized and possessed of several tracts of land. Tract No. 1 situated in Pickens District and lying on Nicholsons fork of Little River containing 420 acres. Tract No. 2 lying on the north fork of Little River containing 240 acres. Tract No. 3 containing 250 acres. Tract No. 4 adjoining tract 3 lying on Keowee River containing 50 acres. His widow recently died. Left 11 children viz. Nancy Moody who married James Moody & resides in Alabama. William Holden who resides in Georgia. Jackson Holden who resides in North Carolina. Elisha Holden who lives in South Carolina. Catherine Moody who married Joel Moody & resides in North Carolina. Sarah Abbett who married Anson Abbett. James Holden, Elijah Holden, John Holden, Franklin Holden all of whom reside in this state and the last of whom is a minor about the age of 18 years, & Mary Norton who married Elias Norton.

Filed March 19, 1853.

Release for 50 Acres

Richard Holden
   to
John Holden

The State of South Carolina

Pickens District) Know all men by these presents that I Richard Holden of the State and District aforesaid for and in consideration of the Sum of two hundred dollars to me in hand paid by John Holden have bargained Sold and released a certin tract or parcel of land cituate on Kewee River in the State and District aforesaid and by the presants do bargan Sell and release the Said tract of land containing fifty acres be the Same more or less beginning on the River bank thence S. 12. E. ten chanes to a stake thence S 25 E. thirty canes to a Stake thence E to the River thence up the river to begining it being part of a tract granted to Sd. Fenly and hath Such Shapes formes marks as the above mentioned plat represents together with all and Singular the rights members heraditryaments and appertainnances to said premises belonging or in any wise insident or appeartaining to have or to hold all and Singular the premises before mentioned unto the Said John Holden his heirs Executors and assigns forever and I do hereby bind my Self my heirs Executors administrators and asigns jointly and Severly to warant and defend all and Singular the Sd. premises unto said John Holden his heirs & asigns against my Self my heirs & against every person or persons who so ever lawfully claiming or to claim the Same or any part thare of whare unto I have Set my hand and Seal this April the fifteenth one thousand Eight hundred and thirty three Singned Sealed and delivered in the presants of us.

                                      his
                        Richard   X   Holdn (LS)
                                   mark

Charles D. Adair (LS)
    her
Hannah   X   Nicholson
    mark
State of South Carolina

    Pickens District) Personally apeared Charles D. Adair before me and made oath he did see Richard Holden sign seal and as his act and deed deliver the within deed for the use and purposes tharin mentioned and that Hannah Nicholson with him self was a Subscribing witness to the same sworn to and subscribed before me this 16th day of September 1833.
N. Boon J G (SEAL)   Charles D. Adair
    RECORDED IN BOOK C PAGE 47. CERTIFIED FEB. 23, 1835.
    Isaac Holden recd, a share of said estate. Mary Holden was the widow of John Holden.

WILLIAM HOOD TO NATHANIEL REID PACK. 76
RELEASE FOR 88 ACRES
CLERK OF COURTS OFFICE, PICKENS, S. C.

The State of South Carolina
    Pendleton District) Know all men by these presents that I William Hood of the above state & District for & in consideration of the sum of Sixty Dollars to me in hand paid by Nathaniel Reid of the same District and state have granted bargained and sold to the said Nathl. Reid two tracts of Land intersecting each other one containing Eighty Eigth acres garnted to the Sd. Nathl. Reid by his Excellency John Drayton and dated in the year 1802 December 6th Day Surveyed November 25 in the year 1802 Begining at a post oak thence N 83 W 30 chs to a stake thence S. 15 chs. to B. O. thence S. 63 E. 52 50 to a stake thence N. 25 W 40 chs to the begining corner a P. oak. Begin the other tract being part of a tract granted to James Jett Esqr. by his Excellency Paul Hamilton Dated first Day of September in the year 1806 Surveyed 21st of august 1806 and conveyed from said James Jett to said William Hood the within mentioned part begining at a stake on the twelve mile road and runing thence S. 72 W till it comes parrellel with what is comonly Call.d Sally fords branch thence to the nearest water in said branch and Down the source of said branch by conditional line till it intersects with a conditional line near a large shoal made between said W. Hood & Stephen Adams thence along that Conditional line till it intersects with a conditional line made between said W. Hood and said Nathl. Reid which line is to run from the begining corner parrellel with two certain trees Marked by Each party Namely a chesnut and B. oak till it intersects with the conditional line made between S. Adams and said Hood this tract surrounding and includes the old acre tract on all sides and containing two Hundred acres Be the same more or less holding to the above mentioned bounds as agreed on by Each party Together with all and singular the right members Hereditaments and Apurtenances to the said premises belonging or in anywise appurtaining to have and to hold all & singular the premises before mentioned unto the said Nathl. Reid his heirs & assigns for Ever and I do hereby bind myself my heirs Executors & Admnrs. & assigns to warrant and for ever Defend all and Singular the premises before Mentioned Unto the said Nathl. Reid his

heirs and assigns for the tract of Eighty Eight acres against myself my heirs and against every other person whom so ever Lawfully Claiming or to Claim any part thereof and also I do hereby bind myself to Warrent and defend said tract of two Hundred acres more or less to the said Nathl. Reid his heirs and assigns against myself my heirs & assigns from the date of his deed but no farther given under my hand and seal the 25th Day of May Anno domini one thousand Eight hundred and Eight.

Sign.d Seald & Delivered in presents of us.

                William Hood (SEAL)

John Carson
Lucinda Brown
State of South Carolina

Pendleton District) This day Appeared before me a Subscribing Justice of the peace for said District John Carson And Made oath as the Law directs that he did see William Hood sign seal and Deliver the within Deed of Conveyance to Nathaniel Reid as his act and Deed and that he saw Lucinda Brown assign her name as a witness to the same Sworn to this 7th Day of April in the year of our Lord one thousand Eight hundred and Ten.
Colin? Campbell J. P.   John Carson

WILLIAM HOOD TO NATHANEEL REID PACK. 76
RELEASE FOR 350 ACRES
CLERK OF COURTS OFFICE, PICKENS, S. C.

State of South Carolina

Pendleton District) Know all men by these presents that I William Hood of the above state and District for and in consideration of the sum of one hundred & seventy Six Dollars to me in hand paid by Nathaniel Reid of the above state and District have granted bargained sold & released unto the said Nathl. Reid A certain parcel of land lying and being in the above state & District on Carpenters Creek waters of main Saluda and waters of oolinoie a south branch of Saluda river containing three Hundred and fifty acres more or less agreeable to bounds it being part of two tracts one granted to John Yager by his Excellency William Moultrie and Conveyed to william Reid & from Sd. Reid to william Hood bearing date July 1st 1793 the other granted to James Jett Esqr. by his Excellency paul Hamilton bearing Date 1st Day of December 1806 and Conveyed to william Hood by said James Jett the part of the tract Conveyed from John Yager & William Reid (Note. this was probably meant to be Hood) beginning at a post oak and runing thence Each way (Viz) a Direct Course with west End of said plat of 380 acres till it strikes each original line which is S. 10 W. and North 10 E thence on the original line N. 79 west to stake thence S 10 W. 40.50 to a stake thence S. 80 E to where it intersects with the first crossline stake on the original line this part containing two Hundred acres more or less the other part Containing one Hundred & fifty acres more or less being part of a tract granted to James Jett and Conveyed to William Hood the now (word) Conveyance having such bounds as agreed on (Viz) beginning on a stake on the west End of said Yagers line making a straight line agreeable to a black Jack & pine the pine being a corner thence by Condition Near North along a certain old path to conditional B. O. corner thence by Condition by a pine & Cowcumber tree as Conditional between S. Adams & sd. Hood Near or about a Shoal on Adams Creek thence by Condition between sd Hood & James Statifield marking a tall pine from the shoal and Sd Creek thence direct to a black oak on a path thence to a chesnut thence to a stake on Sd line granted to sd Jett thence S. 75 west to stake thence N. 18 E to Yagars line Together with all & Singular the rights members hereditaments and Apurtenances to the said premises to have & to hold belonging or in any wise Apertaining all & Singular the rights Memembers and Appurtenances before Mentioned housing ways & waters in fee simple of the above two hundred acres more or less as granted to John Yager for Ever and I do hereby bind myself my heirs Executors & admnrs to warrant & for Ever Defend all and Singular the premises of the above 200 acres granted to John Yager unto the said Nathl. Reid his heirs & assigns against myself my heirs & assigns from and against all maner of persons Claiming or to claim any part thereof as to the other part granted to James Jett as above Mentioned I do warrant & Dend from my self my heirs and assigns from the Date of the original grant but no farther Witness my hand and Seal this 5th Day January in the year of our Lord one thousand Eight hundred and nine and in the 33rd year of the independence of America.

William hood (SEAL)

Signd Seald & Delivered in the presence of us.
Stephen Adams
George Keith

VIOLET BOWMAN PACK. 67 (EQUITY)
CLERK OF COURTS OFFICE, PICKENS, S. C.

Leonard Towers states on or about the 15th June 1854, that he was the agent and attorney of Violet Bowman now decd. delivered and paid by the direction of the said Violet Bowman of her monies to one Joseph R. Sheeler of Pickens District. the sum of $450.00 & then instructed and directed him, to place the same to the credit of said Violet Bowman and John M. Bowman.

Filed May 17, 1858.

JOHN M. BOWMAN & VIOLET SMITHSON
Marriage Settlement Agreement
Marriage Settlement

South Carolina

Pickens District) Articles of Agreement between John M. Bowman of the first part and Violet Smithson of the second part as followeth, Whereas the said Violet Smithson seized and possessed of certain lands negroes and other property in the District of Pickens and state aforesaid and whereas a marriage is shortly intended to be had and solemnized between the said John M. Bowman and the said Violet Smithson, it is therefore covenanted and agreed between the said parties to these presents, in manner and form following that in case the said marriage shall be had and solemnized, the said Violet Smithson shall have entire control of the Property of which she is now possessed, with full power to dispose of the same, in manner and form, as she may think proper, and the said John M. Bowman confines on his part all the wright, she now has to the same. Given under our hands and seals this 11th day of July 1851 in the presents of

Dewitt Cantrell   John M. Bowman (SEAL)
Leonard Towers   Violet Smithson (SEAL)

State of South Carolina

Pickens District) Before me personally appeared Capt. Leonard Towers and made oath that he was present and did see John Bowman and Violet Smithson sign seal and acknowledge the within as their act and deed for the uses and purposes therein mentioned and Dewitt Cantrell with himself witnessed the execution of the same. Sworn to and Subscribed before me this 5th Jany 1852.

W. L. Keith C. C.   LEONARD Towers

State of South Carolina

Pickens District) Office Court of Common & General Sessions. I J. E. Hagood Clerk of the Court of Common Pleas and General Sessions and Ex officio Register of Mesne Conveyance for the State and District aforesaid hereby certify that the above doth contain a true copy of a certain marriage Settlement between John M. Bowman and Violet Smithson as recorded in the registers office aforesaid as appears by the BOOK G PAGE ____ in which was registered remaining in my office. Given under my hand and seal of said court at Clerks office Pickens Court House this the 28th day of June AD 1859.

J. E. Hagood C. C. P. & R. M. C.

A. O. NORRIS TO JOHN McWHORTER NO. 37 (DEED)
CLERK OF COURT'S OFFICE, PICKENS, S. C.

The State of South Carolina

This indenture made the fifth day of November in the year of our Lord one thousand eight hundred and fifty five between Andrew O. Norris, Esquire Commissioner of the Honorable Court of Equity, for Anderson District at Anderson in the said State, of the one part, and John McWhorter of Pickens district and State aforesaid of the other part. Whereas, William Vanwyck and wife Lydia A. Vanwyck did on or about the twenty seventh day of February one thousand eight hundred and fifty four, did exhibit their Bill of Complaint in the Court of Equity at Anderson Court House, in the said State, against Samuel A. Maverick, Gray Jones Houston and wife Elizabeth A. M. Houston and others, on a Bill of Partition of Real Estate, &c., amongst other things praying that a Writ in Partition should issue which said Writ did issue, and upon the return thereof. And the cause being at issue before the Honourable Court, came on to be heard at June Term, one thousand eight hundred and fifty five when the said Court, after full hearing thereof, and mature deliberation in the premises, did Order, Adjudge and Decree, that the said Tract No. 1 of land as described in the proceedings of this case in Pickens district and State aforesaid should be sold at Public Auction, by the Commissioner of the said Court, on the terms and for the purposes mentioned in their Decretal Order, as by reference thereto, in the Registry of the said Court, will appear. And the said Andrew O. Norris as Commissioner of the said Court, after having duly advertised the said Tract No. 1 for sale, by public outcry, on the said fifth day of November first above mentioned, did then openly and publicly and according to the custom of Auctions, sell and dispose of the said Tract No. 1 of Land below described, unto the said John McWhorter for one hundred and Ninety five dollars, he being at it that price, the highest bidder for the same. Now THERETHIS INDENTURE WITNESSETH, that the said A. O. Norris, as Commissioner of the said Court, under and by virtue of the said Decree, and in consideration of the sum of one hundred and Ninety five dollars paid him by the said John McWhorter, the receipt whereof is hereby acknowledged, hath granted, bargained, sold and released and by these presents, doth grant, bargain, sell and release unto the said John McWhorter his Heirs and Assigns, ALL THAT Tract No. 1 of land containing one hundred and thirty acres, situate in Pickens District, on waters of Eighteen Mile Creek, and bounded by lands of Jeremiah Prater, F. N. Garvin, John McWhorter and others, as will more fully appear by reference to a Copy plat herewith attached made by Thomas D. Garvin, D. S. dated the 29th June 1853, the original of which is on file in the office of the Commissioner in Equity, in the above stated case. Together with all and singular, the hereditaments, rights, members and appurtenances whatsoever to the said Tract No. 1 of land, belonging, or in any wise appertaining, and the revervions and remainders, rents, issues and profits thereof, and also all the estate, right, title, interest, dower, possession, property, benefit, claim and demand whatsoever, both at Law and in Equity, of the heirs and representatives of the said Samuel Maverick deceased, and of all the parties to this suit, and of all other persons rightfully claiming or to claim the same or any part thereof by from or under them, or either of them. To have and to hold the said Tract No. 1 of land with its hereditaments, privileges and appurtenances, unto the said John McWhorter his heirs and assigns, to him and their only proper use behoof, forever. In witness whereof the said Andrew O. Norris, as Commissioner of the said Court, under and by Virtue of the said Decree, hath hereunto set his hand and Seal of the Court, on the day and year first above written.

A. O. Norris C. E. A. D.
SIGNED, SEALED, AND DELIVERED IN THE PRESENCE OF
Elijah Trible
John Martin
State of South Carolina

Anderson District) Personally appeared John Martin before me, and made oath that he saw A. O. Norris Commissioner in Equity for Anderson District sign seal the within deed for the use and purposes within mentioned and that Elijah Trible, was a subscribing witness with himself to the Same Sworn to before me this 27th November 1855.
Elijah Trible Clk. Eoff. M. A. D.   John Martin
Recorded in Book H Page 172. Certified Jan. 15, 1857.

J. J. HOLLINGSWORTH TO JOHN McWHORTER NO. 37 (DEED)
South Carolina
Pickens District) Know all men by these presents that I J. J. Hollingsworth of the State and district aforesaid for and inconsideration of the sum of thirty ? eight Dollars and Twenty five cents to me in hand Paid by John Mc-

Whorter of the district and State aforesaid Have Granted bargained sold and Released unto the said John McWhorter his heirs and assigns Forever all that piece parcel or tract of Land situate in said District on a branch of the 18 mile creek waters of Savannah River containing Four & half Acres be the same more or Less it being part of a tract of Land originally Granted to Thomas Roberts the 1st Jany. 1785 Begining on a Rock 3x Runs S 50 W 3.50 to a rock 3 x Thence N 28 W 15.60 to aRock 3x thence N 71 E3.60 to a Rock 3 x on the bank of the branch Thence down Said branch to the begining corner Together with all and Singular the rights members hereditaments and appertainances to the said premises belonging or in any wise appertaining To Have and To hold all and Singular the said premises before mentioned unto the said John McWhorter his heirs and assigns forever and I do hereby bind my self my heirs Executors and administrators to warrant and forever defend all and Singular against myself my heirs Executors and administrators and against all other person or persons Lawfully claiming or to claiming the same or any part thereof in Witness my hand and Seal the 11th day of Augst 1851.

Signed Sealed and declared in presence of us

John McWhorter Jur   J. J. Hollingsworth (SEAL)
Thomas D. Garvin
South Carolina

Pickens District) Personnaly appeared John McWhorter Jun before me and made oath in due form of law deposeth and Saith that he did see the within named J. J. Hollingsworth sign seal and as his act and deed deliver the within Deed for the use and purpose therein set forth and that Thos. D. Garvin was a subscribing witness to the same. Swore to and subscribed before me this 25th day of December 1856.

Thos. H. Boggs M. P. D.

Recorded in Book H Page 174.
Certified Jan. 15, 1857.

JESSE STRIBLING NO. 41 (EQUITY)
CLERK OF COURT'S OFFICE, PICKENS, S. C.

South Carolina

Pickens District) to their Honows the Chancellors of said State. Humbly complaining shews unto your Honors your orators and oratrixes, Benjamin F. Kilpatrick and Rebecca C. his wife, Robert Stribling, William H. Stribling, W. W. Stribling, Thomas R. Sheeler and Susan A. his wife, Thomas Stribling, Thomas R. Sheeler and Susan A. his wife, Thomas Stribling, Elizabeth C. Stribling, David S. Stribling, Willis Roberts and Elizabeth S. his wife, William W. Winn and Mary A. his wife, William Jones, Adam Jones and Hartwell Jones. That Jesse Stribling late of the District and State aforesaid departed this life 18 . . (no dates) being seized and possessed at the time of his death of a considerable real estate, consisting of about 14 hundred acres of land situate in Pickens District on Cane Creek bounded by lands of Robert Maxwell Jr., William H. Stribling and others, and exceeding in value one thousand dollars. That the said Jesse Stribling executed his last will and testament, leaving the same in full force and virtue, by which he bequeathed his whole real estate to his widow during life and at her death the same became subject to distribution amongst his children and grandchildren, as his heirs at law. Your orators further shew that the said Jesse Stribling & Elizabeth Stribling left the following children surviving them, Rebecca C. wife of Benjamin F. Kilpatrick, Robert Stribling, William H. Stribling, W. W. Stribling, Susan H now the wife of Thomas H. Shealor, Thomas M. Stribling, Elizabeth C. Stribling, Nancy now the wife of Henry N. White, M. S. Stribling, David S. Stribling being 10 in number, and also the children of a decd. child named Mary formerly the wife of Hartwell Jones(who is now living) to wit, your oratrix Elizabeth S. now the wife of Willis Roberts, your oratrix Mary A. wife of William W. Winn, your orators William jones, Adam Jones, Hartwell Jones who are of full age, also Thomas H. David, Susan C., Lucinda J. Rebecca C., Nancy, Martha M., and Matilda C. Jones who are minors and reside out of the state who are entitled to distribution of the real estate of the said Jesse Stribling.

H. C. Young (Comp. Sol.)

Filed Nov. 7, 1850.
State of Georgia
  Cobb County) We Hartwell Jones of said County, Elizabeth Roberts formerly Elizabeth Jones, and Willis Roberts her husband, William Jones son of said Hartwell Jones, Adam Jones son of said Hartwell Jones, Mary Winn formerly Mary Jones daughter of Sd. Hartwell Jones and Hilliard W. Winn her husband and Hartwell Jones Guardian for the balance of his children who are minors under the age of twenty one years to wit, Thomas H., David–Susan C.–Lucinda J.–Rebecca C.–Nancy–Martha M. & Matilda C. Jones all being heirs and distributees of the real and personal estate of Elizabeth Stribling decd. late of Pickens District, State of South Carolina consent that an order be granted by the proper court, for the sale of the said estate real and personal for distribution. June 17th 1850.
  Signed and attested in open Court now in session.

W. C. Greene J. J. C.
S. Lawrence J. J. C.
J. M. Carruth J. J. C.
Willis Roberts
Elizabeth S. Roberts
Hillard W. Winn
Mary A. Winn
William Jones
Adam Jones
Hartwell Jones

(NOTE: On the other paper William W. Winn was written, but on this paper Hilliard W. Winn was written.)
State of Georgia
County of Cobb
  I, Thomas H. Moore Clerk of the Superior Court of said County, do hereby certify that the within and foregoing instrument was duly signed, sealed and delivered before me, as such clerk, by the parties therein named. Given under my hand & the seal of said court this 17th June 1850 at Marietta in the County aforesaid.

Thomas H. Moore C. S. C.
  The home tract on which Jesse Stribling lived and died on Cane Creek

was said to be one of the best Cotton Farms in the district. On another paper was the following. No date to paper tho.

Rebecca C. wife of Benjamin F. Kilpatrick living in Mississippi. Robert Stribling in Georgia. (The W. W. Stribling must be for Warren W. Stribling.)

JOHN COUCH NO. 40 (EQUITY)
CLERK OF COURT'S OFFICE, PICKENS, S. C.

The State of South Carolina
Pickens District   In Equity

To their honors the Chancellors of the said state. Humbly complaining sheweth unto your honors your oratrix Mary Ann Couch of the State and District aforesaid. That her late husband John Couch of the same state and district departed this life in the year 1857. intestate. That he was seized and possessed of considerable real estate as follows, One tract of land situate in the State and District foresaid, known as the Home Place, lying on Brushy Creek containing 450 acres more or less and adjoining lands of Thomas Montgomery, Samuel Cruikshank and others. One other tract situate in same State and District on Brushy Creek containing 483 acres more or less and adjoining lands of Thomas Montgomery, Joel Ellison and others. That the said lands are subject to distribution amongst his heirs at law viz a widow and nine children as follows. Robert Couch who resides in the state aforesaid and district of Pickens, Henry Hendrix and wife Margaret Hendrix formerly Margaret Couch who also resides in Pickens District. Spencer Stegall and wife Mary Ann Stegall formerly Mary Ann Couch who also resides in Pickens District. William M. Jameson and wife Dorcas P. Jameson formerly Dorcas P. Couch who also resides in Pickens District, Alexander Orr and wife Melinda Orr formerly Melinda Couch who reside in Anderson District. William Couch who resides in Pickens District. John Couch and Sidney Couch each of whom reside in Pickens District, and the representatives of Ellender Baker formerly Ellender Couch who died before her father viz eight children and a grandchild as follows. John Baker who resides in Texas the representatives of Mary Ann Williams formerly Mary Ann Couch, names unknown, last heard of in Texas, Elizabeth Forrester and (no name) Forrester her husband who reside in Florida, William Baker, Lucinda Baker, Robert Baker, Richard Baker, Crawford Baker and Lewellen Baker the last four of whom are said to be minors and reside in Texas, and your oratrix the widow of the said John Couch. Your oratrix further charges and believes that a fair and just partition of the said Real Estate would be advantageous to all the distributees, whereupon your oratrix respectfully prays that a Writ in Partition may be issued in the usual form.

Harrison
Filed April 30, 1857.   Comp Sols

ALLEN KEITH PACK. 55 (EQUITY)
CLERK OF COURT'S OFFICE, PICKENS, S. C.

The State of South Carolina
Pickens District) To their Honors the Chancellors of said State. Humbly complaining sheweth unto your Honors your orator and oratrice, Alexander Edens and wife Margaret Edens as follows. That Allen Keith the father of your oratrice departed this life on the 5th Aug. 1861, leaving considerable

real & personal estate, situate in the District & State aforesaid. That administration of the personal estate, was duly granted by the Ordinary of Pickens District to Larkin Hendricks and your orator Alexander Edens, the former who died about 1862 leaving your orator the sole administrator, who in the discharge of his duties as such, has possessed himself of personal assets for more than sufficient to satisfy all debts and, liabilities, existing against the estateof his intestate. That the land of the said Allen Keith deed, consists of two tracts, situate in Pickens District to wit, Tract No. 1 lying on Adams Creek waters of Oolenoy River, adjoining lands of the estate of Cornelius Keith decd., estate of Matthew Keith, estate of John B. Deith decd. & others, containing 250 acres more or less. Tract No. 2 lying on the South Fork of Saluda River adjoining lands of Nathaniel Reid, John B. Southerland & others, containing 450 acres more or less, which lands are distributed amongst the following named persons who are the children & grand children of intestate, and his only heirs at law, to wit, Rosey Hendricks widow, Rebecca Keith decd. an infant & Monterey Adaline Keith, all of whom are minors. The heirs of Jane Hendricks decd. late wife of G. W. Hendricks formerly Jane Keith who reside beyond the limits of this state, & the number & names unknown. Sworn to May 18, 1863.

DAVIS HUNT TO JOHN W. LEWIS PACK. 55
CLERK OF COURT, PICKENS, S. C.
(FOUND IN EQUITY RECORD OF ALLEN KEITH DECD.)

State of South Carolina

Greenville District) Know all men by these presents that we, Davis Hunt and John W. Lewis both of the District and state aforesaid, thinking it to be to our mutual advantage to cut off some lands on South Saluda, on that part of Sd. River which is now the dividing line between S. Hunt & Lewis, for the purpose of making the River more straight, have mutually agreed and by these presents do agree upon the following conditional line, Viz. Beginning about one hundred yards below the Ash corner (the lower corner of the Elias Earle & Earle & the upper corner of the Hagood place) at the mouth of a ditch, thence up sd. ditch to where it intersects the River, thence with the River to the lower end of the ditch lately cut Eli & Elihu Howard, with sd. ditch to the River thence with the river about two hundred yards to a blazed sycamore on the north bank of the river thence across two bends where a ditch is to be cut about two hundred and fifty yards (nearly straight) to a cherry tree on the south side of Saluda River by which line J. W. Lewis gets of sd. Hunt three bends containing in all three or four acres be the same more or less, and the sd. Hunt gets two bends containing two or three acres more or less, and forty five Dollars to boot the Receipt whereof is hereby acknowledged all the sd. bends the sd. Lewis gets being on the south side of said conditional line, and the bends the sd. Hunt gets being on the north side of Sd. conditional line, the title of which bends both on the north & south side of sd. line be here by relinquish to each other as described, and for the due and faithful performance of this agreement together with the support of titles to the land as above described we bind ourselves, our heirs Executors &. In

witness whereof we have hereunto set our hands & affixed our seals this 27th day of March 1834. Signed & sealed in presence of
>Thomas Payne
>Nathl. Reid
>>John W. Lewis (L. S.)
>>Davis Hunt (L. S.)

DAVIS HUNT TO JOHN W. LEWIS PACK. 55
South Carolina
Pickens District) Before me personally appeared Nathl. Reid and made oath that he did see John W. Lewis & Davis Hunt sign seal and acknowledge the within as their act and deed as agreed on line by ditches to each other and Thomas Payne was with him and in his presence a subscribing witness to the due Execution of the same Sworn to the 1st day of Jany. 1838 before
Bailey Barton J. P. Nathl. Reid
Copied from original. Recorded in Book C Page 482.

EDWARD NORTON Esq. No: 46
CLERK OF COURT'S OFFICE, PICKENS, S. C.
The State of South Carolina
To the Honorable the Chancellors of Pickens District. Humbly complaining sheweth unto your Honors your orator James Mulliken and wife Malinda formerly Malinda Norton that Edward Norton of the State of South, Carolina Pickens District, departed this life intestate to wit on the day of 18 (no dates given) seized and possessed of a valuable real estate consisting of one tract in Pickens District containing 356 acres more or less. your orator and oratrix further shew unto your honors that the said real estate is subject to division among Martha Norton the widow of the the said Edward Norton decd. and 8 children to wit, The heirs of Zepporah Forbes deed. who inter married with one William Forbes leaving children viz. Elmina Forbes, Adolphus Forbes & Nelson Forbes, the names of the others if any being unknown to your orator and oratrix, residing as your orators are informed in the State of Mississippi. 2. The heirs at law of Malissa Forbes formerly Malissa Norton now decd. who intermarried with one Samuel Forbes, being 4 in number to wit, Jepthah, Eliza and George, the name of the fourth being unknown to your orators who are residing in the State of Georgia. 3. Sarah Wilson formerly Sarah Norton who intermarried with Robert Wilson. 4. Your oratrix Malinda Mulliken. 5. Jeptha Norton. 6. Elizabeth Wilkinson formerly Elizabeth Norton who intermarried with William Wilkinson. 7. Lucinda Taylor formerly Lucinda Norton who married Joseph Taylor. 8. Mathurza Emmerson formerly Norton who married Robert Emmerson all residing in South Carolina.
>Perry & Keith Comp. Sols.

Filed Feb. 20, 1851.
Edward Nortons land was about three miles from Pickensville.

JAMES M. MURPHEY & MARY ALEXANDER to JOSEPH CASS PACK 96
CLERK OF COURT, PICKENS, S. C. (BASEMENT)
The State of South Carolina
Pickens District) Know all men by these Presents that we James M. Mur-

phree & Mary Alexander Executor & Executrix of the last will and testament of William Murphree late of Pickens District deceased for and Inconsideration of one hundred & thirty seven dollars and fifty cts to me in hand paid by Joseph Cass all of the same State and District the Receipt whereof we do hereby acknowledge do grant bargain sell and release unto the said Joseph Cass his heirs and Assigns for ever all that pece parcel or tract of land lying and being in the District and State aforesaid containing one hundred and ten acres Be the same more or less it being part of a tract of land originally granted to Hamilton Reid survey for him 3rd day o fAugust 1791 as reference to the plat annexed will fully shew together with all and singular the Rights members hereditaments and appertainences thereunto belonging or in any wise incident or appertaining to have and to hold all and Singular the said premises unto the said Joseph Cass his heirs and assigns for ever and we do hereby bind ourselves our heirs Executors and Administrators to warrant and forever defend all and singular the said premises unto the said Joseph Cass his heirs Executors & Administrators and against all other Person or persons whomsoever may Lawfully Claim the same or any part thereof In witness whereof we have hereunto set our hands and seals the twenty third day of July AD 1856 and the 81st year of the Independence of the United States of America.

         David M. Murphree (SEAL)
         Mary Alexander (SEAL)

 Signed Sealed and Delivered in the presence of us
James M. Stewart
William Stewart
South Carolina
 Pickens District) Personally appeared William Stewart and made oath in due form of law that he was present and saw James M. Murphree and Mary Alexander sign seal and deliver the within deed for the use and purposes therein mentioned and that James M. Stewart was present and saw it and that they both did sign their names as witnesses to the same.
                William Stewart
 Sworn to before me the 23rd day of July A. D. 1856.
W. J. Parsons O. P. D.

  WILLIAM H. ANDERSON TO WILLIAM WILSON PACK. 96
   CLERK OF COURT, PICKENS COUNTY, S. C. (EQUITY)
South Carolina
Pickens District) In Equity.
 Humbly Complaining sheweth unto your Honors your orator William H. Anderson that William Wilson the defendant on or about 1857 applied to and requested your orator to advance for him the sum of $200.00 on security of the premises hereinafter described, which your Orator consented to do and accordingly advanced the said sum of $200.00 to and for the use benefit and behoof of the said William Wilson. Whereupon and in order to secure the repayment thereof to your Orator with legal interest the said William Wilson executed a certain mortgage bearing date the 15th May 1857 and and made or expressed to be made between the said William Anderson the complainant on the one part and part William Wilson the defendant on the other part. And that thereby after reciting as therein mentioned it was witnessed that for and in consideration of the said sum $200.00 by the said complainant paid laid

out and expended to and for the use benefit and behoof of the said defendant, he the said defendant did grant bargain sell and release unto the said William Anderson all that plantation or tract of land containing 110 acres more or less situated in the District of Pickens and State aforesaid which was conveyed to the said Wm. Wilson by A. Hunter together with all and singular the appurtenances to have and to hold the said premises unto the said William Anderson subject to a proviso for redemption upon payment by the said Wm. Wilson to the said Wm. H. Anderson of the sum of $200.00 on or by the 25th Dec. 1857 and 1858 by two equal instalments sd in and by the said mortgage. Your orator further shows that the said sum was not paid at the times for that purpose limited by the said mortgage for the payment of the same, and that thereby the estate of your orator in the said mortgaged premises became absolute at law.

Filed March 10th 1860.
South Carolina
Pickens District) Know all men by these presents that I Andrew Hunter of the State and Dist aforesaid for and in consideration of the sum of two Hundred dollars to me in hand paid by William Wilson of the State and Dist aforesaid the Rect. whereof I hereby acknowledge do grant Bargain Sell and Release unto the said Wm. Wilson his heirs and Assigns forever all that piece parcel or tract of land lying and being in the District and State aforesaid containing one Hundred and ten Acres more or less It being part of a tract of land originally granted to Hamilton Reid on the 3d day of Aug. A. D. 1791 and has Refference to the plat annexed commencing on a Black oak x thence S. 19 to a P. O. x dead thence S. 28.W. 24.50 Sp. ox thence x 30 x thence N. 66 E. 32.50 to a Rock x thence N. 73 E. 8.50 to a pine thence N. 53 E. 16.50 to a stake near Road thence along said Road to B. O. thence S. 72 W. 58.25 x thence S 82 W 1540 to the Begining corner together with all and singular the Rights members hereditaments and appearainces thereunto belonging or in any wise incident or appertaining to have and to hold all and singular the said premises unto the Wm. Wilson his heirs and assigns forever and I do hereby bind my self my heirs Executors and Administrators to warrant and forever defend against any person or persons whomsoever may lawfully claim the same or any part there of in witness whereof I have hereunto set my hand & seal this the 29th day of April A. D. 1857 and in the Eighty first year of the Independence of the United States of America.

Signed Sealed and delivered in the presence of
G. F. Steading   Andrew Hunter (SEAL)
C. Durham
On March 10, 1860 the said Wm. Wilson was residing out of the state.

ANDERSON, S. C.

In The name of God amen.

I, Handy Harris of So. Carolina in the District of Pendleton Being sick & weak in body, but of sound and disposing mind, memory; & understanding, thanks be to God for the same, do make & declare this my last Will & testament in manner & form following; that is to say I give unto Sister Anna McCurdy The Tract of Land on which she now lives, the prinsapal part of which land was granted unto McCurdy in his life time & the rest was granted unto me The whole of sd lands I give & bequeath to her forever Except that part which I sold unto Mr. John Montgomery: upon his paying me or my Executors the sum of four hundred & five Dollars Ninety three Cents with lawful Interest from the first of January one Thousand Eight hundred & five until the sd Sum of four hundred & five Dollars & ninety three Cents is paid allowing her ten years to pay sd money in. I give & bequeath unto my beloved Wife Ann all my personal Estate my goods Chattles Bonds Notes & Book accounts to be at her disposal after she has paid all my just debts, also I give unto my son Nathaniel Harris all my lands in Pendleton District lying on the Little Beaver Dam Creek allowing my Wife the use of the same her life time & the use of all the rest of my lands which Is not willed to sister McCurdy or disposed of by me I give & bequeath unto my two daughters a Tract of Land in Abbeville District which I purchased of William Callaham to be theirs at the Death of my wife. It is my will that my Executors have the tuition & Direction of My Son Nathaniel untill he arives to the Age of Twenty one years. I also Will that my Executors purches for my two Daughters when they come of Age out of that part of my Estate which I have Left my wife Each of them one well bound Bible A Hymn Book that shall be best approved of by the General Afsembly of the presbyterian Church Pike & Howards Case of contions the villige Sermons & Dickenfons Letters alfo one Half Dozen of Silver Tabel Spoon & one half Dozen Tee-fspoons. & do hereby nominate, conftitute & appoint my wife Ann Brother John & Brother Thomas Harris with Brother Jofeph Irwen my Executors of this my Last Will and Testamint in witnefs whereof I have hereunto Set my hand & seal this twenty Seventh Day of May 1805.

Signed Sealed, Delivered & Published by the above Handy Harris as his last will & testament, in the presents of us who at his request & in his presents have subscribed our names as witnefses thereto.

William Davis   Handy Harris
Mary Harris
Martha Harris

State of So Carolina)
Pendleton District)

By John Harris, Esqr. Ordinary of
Pendleton District

Perfonally appeared before me Martha Harris who being duly sworn on the Holy Evangelistic of Almighty God, doth make oath & say that she saw Doctr. Handy Harris Sign Seal & Pronounce the within Will to be & contain his Last Will & Testament & that sd Handy Harris was then of sound & disposing mind, memory, & understanding, to the best of the Deponent's knowledge & belief: & that she Martha Harris with the other two witnefses did sign their names as witnefses there to at the Request of the Testator & in his presence & in the Presence of Each other. And at the same qualified Ann Harris Thomas Harris and as Executors given under my hand this 17th Day of July 1805.

John Harris O. P. D.

WILLIAM JAMESON NO. 39 (EQUITY)
CLERK OF COURT'S OFFICE, PICKENS, S. C.

The State of South Carolina In Equity.
Pickens District.

To the Honourable the Chancellors of the said State. Humbly complaining sheweth unto your honors your orators William A. or M.? Jameson and Joshua Jamuson that William Jameson of the State of South Carolina and District of Pickens departed this life intestate on the 4th day of April 1850, seized and possessed of a considerable real estate consisting of five tracts of land. 1. The Home Tract situate on the said state & district on Georges Creek waters of Saluda River and containing 768 acres. 2. The Singleton Tract situate in said district and lying on Georges Creek, containing 146 acres. 3. The Bowen Tract situate in said district and lying on Georges Creek, containing 15 acres. 4. The Cedar Rock Tract situate in said district and lying on head waters of Georges Creek, containing 662 acres. 5. The Medlock Tract situate in said district and lying on the waters of Twelve Mile River, containing 221½ acres. 6. Barnett Tract containing 50 acres lying on waters of Georges Creek. Your orators further shew unto your honors that the said lands are subject to division amongst Rebecca Jameson the widow of the decd. the said William Jameson and 10 children to wit. Frances Perry the wife of William H. Perry, formerly Frances Jameson, Madison Jameson, Wilkinson Jameson, John Jameson, your orator William Jameson Westly Jameson, your orator Joshua Jameson, McElroy Jameson, Louisa J. Jameson and Carrol Jameson a monor over the age of fourteen to wit twenty years old. Your orator further shews unto your honors that P. B. Jameson one of the heirs of the said William Jameson decd. departed this life in 1846 near four years previous to the death of his father William Jameson decd. leaving no heirs or legal representatives save his mother and brothers and sisters, never having intermarried, and your orators submit that the real estate of the said of the said William Jameson decd. is to be divided among the 10 living children above named. Your orators further charge and believe that the said lands are not susceptible of division without manifest injury to some of the parties in interest allotting a share to each and that the same may not be equally distributed otherwise than by sale.

Perry & Keith Comp. Sols.

Filed Nov. 13, 1850.

JOHN CRANE TO JAMES MANSELL. PACK. 53
CLERK OF COURT'S OFFICE, PICKENS, S. C.

The State of South Carolina

Know all men by these presents, That I John Crane, of Pickens district & State aforesaid for & in consideration of one hundred & Seventy dollars to me paid by James Mansell of the Same place, have granted Bargained sold & released & by these presents do grant bargain sell & release unto the said James Mansell a certain tract or parcel of land Situate in Pickens District on the Waters of Dobbys Creek, beginning on a Post oak, running thence with Arthur Braswells line to Henry Hesters or Londons line thence with their line to Stephen Reeds line, thence with his line, to said Mansells line, thence on the lines of his land, to the lands belonging to the Estate of Robt. H. Briggs decd. thence with the lines of Sd. Briggs land to the Beginning, containing three hundred acres more or less, originally Surveyed for a Mr. Cunningham, as will appear by the record of the Surveyor generals office of this State. The above lands having encured to me by possesion as will appear from a decree of this Court of Common Pleas at Spring term AD 1840. Together with all & Singular the rights members hereditaments & appurtenances to the said premises belonging or in any wise incident or appertaining, to have & to hold all and Singular the premises aforesaid unto the said James Mansell his heirs & assigns forever. And I do hereby bind myself my heirs Executors & administrators to warrant and forever defend all & Singular the premises aforesaid unto the said James Mansell his heirs and assigns, and against all Singular the claim of every other person or persons whomsoever lawfully claiming or to claim the same or any part thereof. In testimony whereof I have hereunto set my hand and Seal this the 2 of Sept. day of 1840 in the year of our Lord one thousand eight hundred &forty.

his
John   X   Crane (L. S.)
mark

Signed Sealed & delivered in presence of
Henry Davis
Nathan Davis

South Carolina

Pickens District) Before me James Robinson one of the Justices assigned to keep peace in and for Pickens District personally came Nathan Davis and made oath in due form of law saith that he saw John Crane Sen. sign seal and deliver the within and above deed of conveyance unto James Mansel for his own use and purposes therein mentioned and that Henry Davis was a Subscribing witness with him to the same this sworn and subscribed to before me February 15th 1841.
James Robinson J. Q.   Nathan Davis

JAMES MANSELL TO JOHN CRANE PACK. 53
CLERK OF COURT'S OFFICE, PICKENS, S. C.
(BOND FOR TITLES)

The State of South Carolina

Know all men by these presents that I James Mansell of Pickens district & State afsd. am held & firmly bound unto John Crane in the full Sum of three hundred & forty dollars, for the payment of which Sum administrators firmly by these presents Sealed with my Seal and dated this 2 of Sept day on one 1840 in the year of our Lord one thousand eight hundred & forty. The condition of the above obligation is such that whereas the said Crane hath this day given to said Mansell his promissory note for the Sum of one hundred & Seventy Dollars payable Christmas day next, now if the said Crane shall puntually pay or cause to be paid the full amt. of said note by the time it falls due, then the said Mansell is to make to him a lawful title to a tract of land where on Said Crane now lives, which will make the above bond void or in the event the Said Crane Should fail, to pay the amt. of the note above

specified at the time it falls due that is to Sitiate? & make void the obligation.
James Mansell (L. S.)

Signed Sealed & acknowledged in presence of
Henry Davis Nathan Davis

WILLIAM KIRKSEY JR. PACK. 127 1844
BILL FOR RELIEF
CLERK OF COURTS OFFICE, PICKENS, S. C.

William Kirksey Jr. states that he intermarried with Catharine Reed daughter of Joseph B. Reed in June 1840. That he continued to live in the family of Joseph B. Reed until the latter part of December 1840 or the first of January 1841, when he moved to a house in the neighborhood and commenced keeping house. Joseph B. Reed than gave to them the following slaves viz. Jacob a boy 21 or 22 years old, Patty a girl some 14 or 16 years old, Jinny a girl 12 or 13 years old. Wm. Kirksey states that at the time Joseph B. Reed gave to them the slaves he was a man in good circumstances & propserpous condition, owning and carrying on business as a merchant with one Chillion Packardand doing as any one supposed a profitable business. J. B. Reed had no futher children. Wm. Kirksey further states that previous to his marriage he had made considerable money, he had been for a number of years engaged in merchanddizing he had collected in after his marriage a large portion of which he lent to the said Joseph B. Reed at various times. Chillion Packard now resides out of the state . . . Filed April 1, 1844 . . . Wm. Kirksey lived some half a mile distant on a piece of land which belonged to his fatherinlaw. Chillion Packard in answering for him self says that the defendant resided in Barnwell District. While at Reids house in Feb. 1841 he did regard Reids property as sufficient to pay his debts, altho his confidence in the man was greatly impaired by reason of his intemperate habits.

COPY OF MEMORANDUM OF PARTNERSHIP

Memorandum of an agreement made this twenty seventh day of August one thousand Eight Hundred and thirty six by & between Chilion Packard on the one part and Joseph B. Reid of the other part, both of Pickens District South Carolina as follows. The said Parties agree to associate themselves together to carry on a joint Mercantile business at the stand now occupied by the said Packard & to trade in in the same wares and commod ities, that the said Packard now deals in,to commence on the twenty Eighth day of September next and to continue two years. The said Packard on his part agrees and contracts & convenants to furnish two thirds of the Capitol & to attend to the purchasing and forwarding of the goods & to sell such produce as may be sent to him to sell for the joint concern & to keep a book in which he may make for the joint concern & all other transactions in relation thereto & to exhibit the said Book to the said Reid whenever called upon to do so either for the purpose of copying or Examination. The said Reid on his part agrees, contracts & covants to furnish one third of the capitol & the Store House & to attend to the sale of the goods and to sell such articles as may be taken in barter or to forward them to to the said Packard or to market as the case may require & to keep a sales book in which shall be regularly entered every article sold with the cost of it & the amount for which it sold & also to keep a book on which shall be kept a correct account of all articles taken in on a payment &

also to keep an account of all expenses which he may pay for the benefit of the joint concern & to exhibit the said Books & accounts to the said Packard and all other accounts & papers relating to the joint concern, whenever called upon to do so, either for the purpose of copying or Examination & it is mutually agreed that the above specified acts to be done & services to be rendered free of any charge fo so doing. It is further agreed, mutually by & between the said Packard & Reid, that the profits of the business shall be equally divided between the parties & that the parties shall bear equal parts of all expenses of transportation and all other expenses not fore mentioned. And it is further mutually agreed that in case either of the parties shall neglect or fail to perform faithfully the duties assigned to him in this instrument the other party shall be entitled to have the joint concernimmediately closed if he desire it & that if the parties do not agree on the terms of closeing the concern, it shall be settled by an arbitration of the Merchants, one to be chosen by each of the parties who shall have power to choose an umpire. The party aggrieved shall give the other reasonable notice of his appointment of an arbitration & the place of meeting & the other shall comply with it & it is further agreed that all differences that may arise between the parties in relation to the joint concern, shall be settled by the same arbitration & it is also agreed that when the concern is to be closed, the parties shall each take out the same amount of capitol that they put in it & it is agreed that if either of the parties should die during the continuance of the partnership, that the concern shall be closed forthwith in the manner pointed out above and that the Executors or administrators of the deceased shall have the same rights and privileges in settling up the concern as the party himself would have had if he had been living at the Expiration of the partnership & it is also agreed that the business of the concern shall be carried on, under the name and title of J. B. Reid & Co. & that the stock of goods that may be in the store of the said Packard on the 28th Septr next shall be taken by the concern at private cost & carriage except those that may not be in good order and condition, which shall be taken at the valuation of Arbitrators chosen one by each party. It is mutually agreed that the profits shall not be divided oftener than once in six months, without the consent of both parties, nor shall either party be at liberty to draw out the profits, so as to leave the amount invested in trade less than two thousand dollars. And it is further agreed that each of the parties shall make out & forward to the other by mail at least once in three months a statement of the amount of sales & purchases & an amo/unt of all monies received and expended for the benefit of the concern. In testimony whereof we have hereunto set our hands & seals on the day & date first above written.

                              (Signed) Joseph B. Reid (LS)

Witnesses   (Signed) C. Packard (LS)
S. Patten
Char C. Packard

JOSEPH B. REID TO CHILLION PACKARD PACK. 127
MEMORANDUM OF DISSOLUTION
CLERK OF COURTS OFFICE, PICKENS, S. C.

Pickens District So. Ca.)

1st Febry 1841) Know all men by these presents that we Joseph B. Reid and Chilion Packard have this day dissolved the partnership heretofore existing between us under the firm of J. B. Reid & Co. and have settled with each as follows viz. The said Packard agrees to give up to the said Reid all his share of the profits of the joint business for the sum of seven hundred Dollars & to relinquish to the said Reid all his right interest and control in & over all manner of business connected with the said firm & the said Reid on his part Covenants & agrees to pay the said Packard the sum of seven hundred dollars for his share of the joint profits and also to pay to the said Packard the sum of seven hundred dollars for the joint profits and also to pay to the said Packard the sum of two thousand eight hundred & thirteen dollars & 33 cents which is the amount of capitol which the said Packard had put into the concern as his part of the capitol stock which two sums make up the amount of three thousand five hundred & thirteen dollars & 83 cents with interest on the same till paid, the payments to be made at the bank of Hamburg by depositing the money there to the credit of the said Packard as follows two thousand dollars on or before the first of September next Eight hundred dollars, on or before the first of January next seven hundred & thirteen ($713.33) Dollars & 33 cents on or before the first of April one thousand forty-two & the said Reid further agrees to pay all outstanding claims against the firm of J. B. Reid & Co. & to take on himself all the trouble & expense of collecting & settling up the business of the firm. The seven hundred dollars for the profits is not to draw interest till after the first of January next & whenever the sum of one hundred dollars is deposited or more than that sum, the interest on that amount so deposited shall stop.

(Signed) J. B. Reid
(Signed) C. Packard

Test
Wm. Kirksey Jr.

WILLIAM M. JAMESON PACK. 126 (EQUITY)
CLERK OF COURTS OFFICE, PICKENS, S. C.

Dorcas P. Jameson widow of William M. Jameson states that her husband died on or about the 12th May 1864, that he was killed while bravely fighting the battles of his country. That he owned several tracts of land at the time of his death. No. 1 the "home tract" situated in Pickens District on waters of Georges Creek containing 130 acres, adjoining lands of Elias Hollingsworth, William Couch, Malinda Archer & others ... Tract No. 2 of 112 acres on waters of Georges Creek adjoining lands of H. T. Harper, Moses Hendrix, Elias Hollingsworth & others ... Tract No. 3 of 110 acres on waters of Georges Creek, adjoining lands of Margaret Archer, William Couch, A. A. H. Moon & others ... Left 5 children viz. John Jameson, A. P. Jameson, William C. Jameson, Mary J. Jameson, Martha Jameson all who reside in this state, the last 3 of whom are minors above 14 years ... On Sept. 30, 1864 Dorcas Jameson obtained Letters of Admnr. ... Tract No. 3 was on the Greenville Road ... Filed May 29, 1866 ... On May 17, 1871 Mary Jane Stegall & Sydney Stegall recd. $43.60 of their share of estate ... On June 1, 1871 D. P. Robison recd. $109.00 as her third of said estate ... On another paper Spencer Stegall was written ... Louisa J. and Leaner Jones her husband were mentioned as creditors of estate.

CROSS INDEX TO NAMES

—A—

Name	Page
Abbeville	188-202-243
Abbott, Ann	4
Abbott, Sarah	230
Abbott, Bird W.	133-137
Abbott, Anson	230
Abbott, Thomas H.	4
Abrams, William	111
Abraham, Pleasant	111
Adair, John	63
Adair, Charles D.	231
Adair, Robert	111
Adams, John	64
Adams, Jane	64
Adams, Lidiah	64
Adams, Mark	71
Adams, William	64
Adams, Stephen	231
Adcock, James	180
Aiken, Dr.	111
Air line Rail Road	16
Albertson, Samuel	130-151
Alabama	85-174-180-193-210-224-230
Jefferson County	113
DeKalb County	228
Talladega County	113-167
Alexander, Ann	66
Alexander, Dorcas	224
Alexander, Daniel	222
Alexander, David	153
Alexander, Elijah	88-90-222
Alexander, E. E.	24-186-192-227
Alexander, E. B.	224
Alexander, Mary	240
Alexander, Eliza	222
Alexander, John	65
Alexander, Jacob	192
Alexander, James	193
Alexander, Lucena	210
Alexander, Micajah	222
Alexander, Mr.	90
Alexander, Minerva	224
Alexander, Polly	192
Alexander, Prior	224
Alexander, Pleasant	83
Alexander, P.	188
Alexander, Robert	66
Alexander, Salina	193
Alexander, Sargent	224
Alexander, W. A.	210
Alexander, William	94-192
Allen, Eliza Luella	9
Allen, Elizabeth Wigfall	64
Allen, James	65
Allen, LaFayette	9
Allen, Thomas	65
Allgood, William	169
Allred, Levi	100-102
Allison, James	109
Allison, Richard	109
Allison, Sarah	109
Amory, Ann	1-2
Amory, Jonathan	1
Amory, Martha	1-2-3
Amory, Robert	1-2-3
Amory, Sarah	1-2
Amory, Thomas	1-2
Anderson District	22-27-28-33-34-183-208-235-238
Anderson Court House	234-242
Anderson, Dr.	84
Anderson, Colonel Robert	209
Anderson, Thomas	110
Anderson, William H.	241
Anderson, William	110
Anthony, Avarilla	224
Anthony, H. J.	103-151-174-224
Andright, William	86
Araial, John	23-108
Archer, Margaret	248
Arden, Edward	66
Arden, Joseph	67
Arden, Mary	67
Aredn, Margaret	67
Arkansas	180
Arnold, J. N.	174
Arnold, John	218
Arnold, M. M.	12
Arnold, Mary	174
Arter, Clint	175
Ash, John	67
Ash, Mary	67
Ash, William	68
Atkin, Ann	3
Atkins, James	146

—B—

Name	Page
Bagley? Joab	114
Bagwell, Allen	107
Bagwell, James Madison	107
Bagwell, Josiah	107
Bagwell, John	107
Bagwell, Nancy	107
Bagwell, Sarah	107
Bagwell, Simsford	107
Bagwell, Rachel	107
Bagwell, William	107
Bagwell, Winkfield	107
Baker, Sarah	196
Baker, William	196-238
Baker, Laura	227
Baker, John	238
Baker, Ellender	238
Baker, Lucinda	238
Baker, Robert	238
Baker, Richard	238
Baker, Crawford	238
Baker, Lewellen	238
Baldwin, Isaac	125
Baldwin, Daniel	150
Baldwin, Stephen	134-142

Name	Page
Ball, R. J.	117
Ballew, Robert	200
Ballentine, John H.	63
Barker, Josiah	158-209
Barker, Mary	209
Barnette, Richard	43
Barnette, Frances Parham	43
Barnette, John Allen	44
Barnette, Joseh Josiah	44
Barnette, Joel S.	44
Barnette, Francis	72
Barnes, Morning	82
Barratt, Francis	72-85
Barratt, L. T.	102
Barnwell District	76-246
Barton, James H.	50
Barton, William	12
Barton, Bailey	83-210-225
Barton, Jane	83
Barton, J. M.	98
Barton, David	123
Barton, Thomas	149
Barton, Peter L.	163
Barton, James	191
Barton, Claud	195
Barton, Lucy	210
Bates, Joseph A.	14
Bates, Stephen	200
Batt, Mary	67
Batt, Samuel	67
Beasley, Clark	111
Beasley, O.	111
Beatty, W. C.	39
Beck, J. H.	63
Beard, Mr.	169
Beard, William	170
Berkley County	28
Bellinger, Edmund	68
Belloo, Franklin	88
Bellomy, Timothy	64
Benson, John P.	122
Bennett, James	170
Bennett, Rhoda	171
Berry, William	51
Berry, Hudson	75-76
Berry, Micajah	75-76
Berry, Nathan M.	125
Beach, Laban G.	77
Bell, Adam	111
Bell, Polly Ann	222
Biemann's, D.	202
Billingsley, Minerva	224
Billingsley, H. A.	224
Biram, Jesse	199
Bird, A. S.	95
Bishop, Abel	162
Bivens, Mary Ann	113
Bivens, Valentine	113
Black, Thomas	78
Blair, James	198
Blake, Joseph	3-66
Blake, Elizabeth	68
Blakely, James	62
Blassingame, W. G.	12
Blassingame, John W.	191
Blassingame, Sarah	191
Blassingame, Widow	175
Blythe, James	196
Boatwright, William	138
Boddan, Andrew	198
Boggs, Aaron	217-203
Boggs, Henry G.	217
Boggs, J. C.	179
Boggs, James A.	217
Boggs, Josiah N.	217
Boggs, Polly	216
Boggs, Sarah L.	163
Boggs, Sylvania	217
Boggs, Thomas	217
Boggs, Thomas H.	236
Bolt, Andrew	209-210
Bolt, Martha Jane	210
Bolton, Martha	32
Boon, Nathan	204
Bond, Elizabeth	65
Bond, George Paddon	65
Bond, Jacob	65
Bond, Susannah	65
Bonnette, John Allen	44
Bonnette, Joel S.	44
Bonnette, Joseph Josiah	44
Bonnette, Frances P.	44
Boren, Caroline	23
Borlan, John	67
Boroughs, Bryan	203
Bowman, Violet	23-233
Bowman, John	23-233
Bowen, R. A.	12
Bowen, R.	85
Bowen, Robert	220
Bowen, Eliza Ann P.	220
Bowen, Martha Ann J.	220
Bowen, Dorcas J.	220
Bowen, O. E.	220
Bowen, Louisa A.	220
Bowen, John Caldwell	220
Bowen, John	220
Bowen, George W.	191
Bowen, Emily C.	191
Bowen, R. E.	162
Boyd, Joseph	35
Boyd, Sara	35
Boyd, Mary An	35
Boyd, James Lee	35-36
Boyd, Sally	35
Boyd, Jinny Clark	35
Boyd, Eliza Livena	35
Boyd, Peggy	35
Boyd, T. M.	49
Boyd, Rufus J.	48
Boyd, Jane	40-48-49
Boyd, Mary	40-48
Boyd, Margaret	48
Boyd, Jincy	48
Boyd, Permilia	48
Boyd, Thomas Sr.	39

Name	Page
Boyd, Nancy	39-40
Boyd, Elizabeth	39-40
Boyd, John	29-40
Boyd, Thomas Jefferson	40
Boyd, James	40
Boyd, William	40
Boyd, Robert	40
Boyd, Bennet Franklin	40
Boyd, Rachel	40
Boyd, Louisa	40
Boyd, Hezekiah A.	214
Bradberry, Jesse	28
Bradeen, A. R.	15
Bradley, D. F.	21
Bradley, Thomas R.	86
Brackenridge, Thomas R.	9-16
Brem, W. D.	74
Brewer, Sintha	76
Brewer, Benjamin	76
Brasstown Road	200
Briggs, M. C.	11
Briggs, Robert H.	244
Bridges, Thomas	47
Bridges, Edmond	47
Bridges, Robert	47
Bridges, Dicy	47
Bridges, William	47
Bridges, Benjamin	211
Brock, W. O.	176
Brock, G. W.	176
Brock, William C.	176
Brock, Farmer	176
Brook, John	108
Broom, James	170
Broom, Burrell	198
Broom, Mary Ann	198
Brown, Jasper	34
Brown, Prudence	45
Brown, Samuel G.	46
Brown, William	58
Brown, Isaac	71
Brown, Robberd	97
Brown, Lewis	97-101-225
Brown, Jeremiah C.	169
Brown, Lucinda	232
Bryan, Lewis	76
Bryan, Joseph	76
Bryce, Alexander Jr.	70
Bryce, Alexander	105-120-187-207
Bryce, Thomas	106
Bryce, J. Gambrell	207
Buckhuster, Joel	170
Buchanan, Owen	147
Burdine, Perry	23
Burdine, John	26
Burdine, A.	85
Burdine, Revd. John	142
Burdine, Richard Sr.	176
Burdine, Polly	205
Burgess, George R.	13
Burgess, Simeon E.	19-201
Burgess, Joshua	111
Burgess, Benjamin	111-114
Burgess, Mary Ann	111-114
Burgess, Marena	201
Burns, Jim	167
Burton, Mary	57
Bull, William	33
Bush, R. O.	31
Bush, Edward	76
Bynum, Fanny	193
Bynum, Elijah	193
Byres, Ja.	68
Byrd, John F.	16

—C—

Name	Page
Cady, Joshua	103
Cairey? Edmund	118
Cain, Aaron	155
Cain, Moses	200
Callebuff, Stephen	31
Calladon, James	33
Callaham, William	243
Calhoun, John C.	127
Calhoun, Sarah	172
Calhoun, George	195
Calvert, John	198
Camden District	198
Campbell, William	36-41
Campbell, Mrs. E.	167
Campbell, G. T.	167
Campbell, Hundley E.	174
Campbell, William T. M.	174
Campbell, Colin	232
Cane Creek	191
Cannon, Henry	82
Cannon, Ellis	83
Cannon, I. D.	107
Cannon, Rachel	107
Cannon, John R. M.	141
Cannon, Mrs.	205
Cannon, Simon	177
Cantrell, William	82-121-134
Cantrell, D. W. C.	198
Cantrell, Sarah Ann	198
Cantrell, Dewitt	234
Cape, William	141
Capehart, Leonard	24-205-120
Capehart, Sarah	205
Capehart, Eliza. Eveline	206
Capehart, Harvey	206
Capehart, John	156-189-206
Capehart, Jacob	190
Capehart, Samuel	206
Capehart, Nancy	206
Capehart, Mary Ann	206
Capehart, B. W. F.	206
Capehart, Hamilton A. H.	206
Capehart, Mr.	172
Carpenters Creek	232
Carr, S. R.	31
Carson, T. C.	128
Carson, John	232
Carruth, J. M.	237
Carver, Susannah	24
Carver, Andrew	63
Casey, R. M.	14

Name	Page
Cason, Larkin	197
Cass, Joseph	240
Catawba River	55
Cathcart, H. I.	44
Cauthen, John	43
Cedar Rock	14-16-17-90
Charlotte Bank	55
Chambers, Lucius	88
Chambers, Philip	159
Chambers, Spencer	130
Chandler, Polly	76
Chandler, Batey	76
Chandler, James	148
Chandler, Jesse	91-92
Chandler, Mary	91-92
Chandler, Delilah	92
Chapman, Samuel	24-25-26
Chapman, Jsohua	24-25
Chapman, Joel	24-25
Chapman, Jacob	24-25
Chapman, Elizabeth	24-25
Chapman, Joseph	118
Chapman, Rachel	24
Chapman, Isaac A.	24-25-90
Chapman, Margaret	24
Chapman, Giles	24-25
Chapman, John F.	24-25-26
Chapman, Amelia	25
Chapman, Sarah	25-174
Chapman, Thomas H.	25
Chapman, J. W.	25
Chapman, Mary E.	24-25-26
Chapman, Della	25
Chapman, John	25
Chapman, Rhodey	25
Chapman, Benjamin	25
Chapman, Green E.	25
Chapman, Lucy Eleanor	25
Chapman, Caroline	26
Chapman, Joseph Sr.	26
Chapman, George	26
Chapman, William	26
Chapman, Jeremiah	26
Chapman, Enoch	26-77-87
Chapman, James	174
Chapman, Archibald	26
Chapman, M. R.	74
Cheowee Creek	196
Chester District	60
Cherry, David	142-153-204
Charleston	1-2-3-4-28-29-202-208
Cholsom, Sally	196
Child, John	64
Chumner, William	74
Chitty, Ann B.	32
Clark, Thomas	36
Claiborn, P. D.	115
Clauson, Ann D.	57
Clayton, John B.	6
Clayton, Stephen	146
Clayton, Martha A.	11
Clayton, William	177
Clayton, F. V.	14-16
Clayton, S. W.	16
Clayton, Carter	25
Clayton, Balis	90
Clements, Jerry M.	162
Cleveland, William	27-69
Cleveland, George	69
Cleveland, Nancy	69
Cleveland, Thomas	69
Cleveland, Elizabeth	69
Cleveland, Fanny	69
Cleveland, Monroe	70
Cleveland, Clark	71
Cleveland, Green	71
Clinkscales, T.	34
Clyde, William A.	210
Clyde, Leonard	210
Clyde, Harriet L.	210
Clyde, Joseph B.	210
Clyde, Edgar W.	210
Clyde, Samuel C.	210
Clyde, Thomas T.	210
Clyde, Thomas M.	210
Clyde, Sally	210
Clyde, Charles E.	210
Clyde, Luvina M.	210
Cobb, Mary Jane	63
Cobb, Edwin M.	208
Cobb, Ephraim	139
Cock, John Sr.	66
Cock, John Jr.	66
Cokesbury	188
Colber, Edward	88
Coates, John	218
Cole, Mrs.	28
Cole, H. A.	200
Cole, Majer	196
Cole, Willey P.	196
Cole, Aaron	196
Cole, Lewis	196
Cole, Morgan	196
Coltharp, H. H.	57
Coffe, J. E.	172
Collenton County	6-67
Collins, James—1857	86
Collins, Watson	83
Cooper, Philip	214
Cooper, James	86-93
Cook, John R.	168
Corbin, John	104
Cotes, J. J.	209
Cornog? Wallace W.	27
Costello, Young	169
Couch, F. M.	18
Couch, Mary Ann	238
Couch, John	103-169-238
Couch, Robert	238
Couch, Margaret	238
Couch, Dorcas P.	238
Couch, Melinda	238
Couch, William	238-248
Couch, Sidney	238
Couch, Ellender	238
Couch, Elizabeth	238

Coyle, John	166
Cox, Elizabeth	28
Cox, Jacob R.	150-192
Cox, James	161
Cox, Malinda	209
Cox, Mordecai	209
Craig, Robert	12-21
Craig, John	16
Craig, John C.	227
Craig, W. N.	94-227
Craig, Davy	94
Craig, Rachel	196-227
Craig, Thomas	111
Craig, Lawrence C.	207-209-226
Craig, Sarah E.	227
Craig, Martha C.	227
Craig, William	227
Craig, Arthur R.	227
Craig, Esther M.	227
Craig, Laura	227
Craig, Josephine E.	227
Cothran, M.	162
Crawford, James M.	22
Crawford, John	143
Croskeys, Joseph	1-3
Crosby, John	191
Crooked Creek	191
Crow Creek	192
Crow, Willis	89
Crenshaw, Jesse	15-84
Crenshaw, William	222
Crenshaw, Jane	84
Crenshaw, Henry	164
Creek, Shoal	25
Crews, Thomas	198
Cruikshank, Samuel	238
Crane, John	244
Cunningham	208
Cunningham, James	93
Cunningham, Mr.	245
Curriers, James	79
Currence, Hugh	50
Curlay, Edward	166

—D—

Dachres, Robert	3
Dalton, Jefferson	153
Daniels, John	175
Darby, Zadock	36
Darby, Mary	36
Darby, Jane	36
Darby, Delilah	36
Darnal, James	43
Darnal, Susan	43
Darnal, William	43
Darnal, Hanah	43
Darnal, Cinthy	43
Darnal, Ekizabeth	43
Darnal, Franklin	43
Darnal, John	43
Darwin, John Sr.	78-79
Darwin, Payton B.	78
Darwin, George	79
Davis, Treat	85

Davis, William Sr.	49
Davis, Martha	49
Davis, Francis C.	49
Davis, Anne	49
Davis, John	49
Davis, Thomas	49
Davis, William	49-211
Davis, William Sr.	49
Davis, Martha E.	49
Davis, Sarah	211
Davis, Harvy	198-199-245
Davis, Nathaniel	198-199-245
Davis, Nathan	245
Davis, Benjamin H.	226
Davis, Milley	226
Davis, Emily	225
Davidson, Mary L.	55
Davidson, John S.	55
Dawkins, Bethenia	222
Dawson, Rev. Thomas	123
Dickson, Mary	11
Dickson, Ann	11
Dickson, Col.	208
Dickson, William B.	209
Day, William	4
Day, Austin	14-72
Day, Nathaniel	62
Day, Allen	62
Dean, Elisha	180
Dean, Caroline	180
Dendy, James H.	25-191
Denton, Joshua	79
Devils Fork	6
Dill, Mary	29-30
Dill, Elizabeth	29-30
Dillard, James	81-111
Dillard, Seborn	111
Dodd, Dennis	22
Doddy Creek	85
Douglass, George	49
Douglass, Elizabeth	50
Douglass, Thomas H.	50
Douglass, Dowdle	169
Douthit, Solomon	111
Douthit, Rebecca	111
Douthit, Davis	111-116
Douthit, Eleanor	111
Douthit, Robert	111
Douthit, Silas	111
Douthit, John	111
Douthit, Andrew	111
Douthit, Mary Ann	111
Douthit, Margaret	111
Douthit, Lucy	111
Douthit, Lilly Ann	111
Douthit, Samuel T.	111
Douthit, Levica A.	111
Douthit, Polly	112
Douthit, James R.	114
Doyle, J. A.	25
Douxsaint, Paul Esq.	33
Drake, James	34
Drayton, John	231

Name	Page
Drennon, Harvey H.	42
Duckett, Regnold	102
Dulin, Frances	51
Duncan, J. V. B.	14
Duncan, Marshall	80-110
Duncan, David	103
Dunkley, William	88
Dunn, Nehemiah	161
Durham, Jane	51
Durham, John	50
Durham, Isaac	16
Durham, J. V.	17
Durham, Benjamin	23
Durham, Mary	51
Durham, William	51
Durham, Margaret	52
Durham, Elizabeth	15-51
Durham, George G.	50-51
Durham, Lorenzo Young	26
Durham, Sarah Ann	27
Durham, Julius Newton	26-27
Durham, Charles Newton	27
Durham, Charles	27
Durham, Hortence	27
Durham, Rebecca	27
Durham, Courtnay McIlroy	27
Durham, Mrs. M. M.	164
Durham, Daniel	205
Durham, Janie	27
Durham, C.	242
Durham, William Homer	27
Durham, Charles Harold	27
Durham, Frances	51
Dutart, Isaac	33

—E—

Name	Page
Eads, William	205
Eakin, Alexander	50
Earle, Eliza Ann	5-7
Earle, William Robison	8
Earle, Dr. James W.	9
Earle, Dr. James B.	5
Earle, J. R.	27
Earle, Elias	105-239
Earle, John B.	177
Earle, George W.	229
Earle, Samuel	201
Earle, Joseph B.	221
Earnest, Mary	186
Easleys Bridge	20
Eastatoe Creek	77
Eaton, Lewis	83
Eaton, James	159
Edens, Margaret	111-238
Edens, James	195
Edens, Alexander	111-197
Edgefield District	109-213-224
Edwards, Polly	207
Edwards, Joseph	207
Edgar, Edward F.	150
Ehney, Catharine	32
Evans & Evins, Lucy E.	25
Evans, Sarah	31
Evans, Lucy	166

Name	Page
Evans, Garner	207
Evatt & Evett, Hundley	99-174
Evatt, Adam	165
Evatt, Elizabeth	174
Evatt, William	166-174
Evatt, William A.	227
Evatt, Mary C.	174
Evatt, Sarah A.	174
Evatt, Abbey Rilla	174
Evatt, James F. S.	174
Eve, Abraham	66
Evliegh, Mr.	65
Ekes, Henderson	217
Ekes, Nancy	218
Ellard, Patsey	222
Ellett, William	213-216
Elfe, Benajmin	32
Elford, Charles J.	85
Ellis, John	36
Ellis, Robert	58
Ellis, Mary	58
Ellis, Sally	58
Ellis, Benjamin	59
Ellis, Rebecca	59
Ellis, Thomas	59
Ellis, Reuben	73
Ellis, Gideon	73
Ellis, G.	103
Ellison, Joel	238
Elliott, John	32
Elliott, William	64
Emerson, Moses S.	17
Emerson, Robert	240
Emerson, Mathurza	240
Emory, Mrs.	165
England	1-67
Erwin, Lucy	111
Erwin, Samuel	111
Estes, Reuben	228
Ewing, David	77

—F—

Name	Page
Fall, William	167
Farley, Philip	92
Fair Play	167
Farr & Fair, G. W.	24
Farr, George Washington	63-162
Fendley, Moses	214-213
Fendley, William	213
Feemster, James	45
Feemster, James D.	45
Feemster, William	45
Feemster, Joseph	45
Feemster, Mary	45
Feemster, Nancy	45
Feemster, Prudence	45
Feemster, Letitia	45
Fennell, Martha E.	25
Fennell, Mahala	217
Fennell, Hardy	217
Ferguson, Riley	12-18
Ferguson, Judge G.	72-73-85
Ferguson, John	73
Ferguson, Jane	85

Ferguson, James	95-99-103
Ferguson, J.	101
Ferguson, James T.	105
Field, Jeremiah	6
Fields, John Sr.—1842	98
Field, A. G.	144
Field, John Sr.	98
Fidling, Fra.	1
Filput, Ann	4
Filput, Thomas	4
Fischeser, J. B.	202
Fitts, David	77
Fitzpatrick, Michael—1861	168
Flat Rock Tract	85
Floridie	238
Flowers, Adaline	56
Foley, Edward	167
Ford, Dolly	74
Ford, Capt. Manly	74
Ford, Daniel	75-76
Ford, Mary	75
Ford, Elizabeth	75
Ford, Stephen	75
Ford, John	75
Ford, William	76
Folger, Della	11
Folger, Corrie	11
Folger, M. P.	11
Fountain, Simpson L.	23-207
Forrester, Elizabeth	238
Fort George	94
Foster, J. J.	46
Foster, John	87
Foster, James H.	214
Foster, Robert C.	215
Forbes, Zepporah	240
Forbes, William	240
Forbes, Elmina	240
Forbes, Adolphus	240
Forbes, Nelson	240
Forbes, Melissa	240
Forbes, Samuel	240
Forbes, Jeptha	240
Forbes, Eliza	240
Forbes, George	240
Fowler, William	199
Franklin, William	112
Fraser, William	105
Frazier, Natt	71
Frederick, Jacob	149
Fretwell, Bryan	132
Freeman, David	26
Freeman, Julia Ann	72
Freeman, Meredith	72-85
Freeman, Juliet	85
Frick, W. H.	88
Frick, Mathias	148
Frick, Joseph	149
Friend, Ann	32

—G—

Gadsden, December	71
Galloway, Levissa S.	113
Galloway, Miles	170
Gambrell, Ira G.	223-177
Gant, Sarah	22
Gant, Nancy Clarintine	22
Garison, Pamela	41
Garner, John	26
Garner, James	203
Garner, Henry	203-216
Garner, Jesse	180
Garvin, Thomas D.	6-77-236-235-207-181-182
Garvin, Frederick N.	6-25-26-104-222-235-174
Garvin, David	20-187
Garvin, Silas	187
Garvin, Nancy	20-187-180
Garvin, Thomas Sr.	180
Garvin, Addela	180
Garrett, David	24
Garrett, Elizabeth	24-25
Garrett, Fed.	71
Garrett, Widow	111
Garrett, Mary	111
Garrett Tract	191
Garrison, W. D.	20
Garrison, O. W.	20
Gaston, Lettitia	45
Gassaway, N.	85
Gassaway, William	93
Gassaway, John W.	150
Gates, Charles	215
George, James	9
Georgia	69-85-111-196-201-224-238-230-210-240-209-193
Georgia, Cobb County	25-237
Georgia, Hall County	26
Georgia, Franklin County	27-196
Georgia, Habersham County	28-199
Georgia, Cherokee County	85-210
Georgia, Fannin County	111
Georgia, Lumpkin County	111-180
Georgia, Forsythe County	188
Georgia, Jefferson County	11
Georgia, Putnam County	214
Georgia, Whitfield County	181
Georges Creek	72-98-101-103
Glazner, William J.	228
Glenn, John	37-41-48
Glenn, Franklin	37
Gibson, Thomas	199
Gibson, Hamilton A. H.	206
Godfrey, Ansel	89
Godfrey, Mahaly	89
Godfrey, Alfred	90
Godfrey, Robert W.	90
Goldens Creek	90
Gough, Will	30
Gordon, Harriett	74
Gordon, John C.	118
Gordon, Thomas J.	200
Gormon, Widow	85
Goodlett, Spartan	35
Goodlett, Martha N.	35
Gossett, John T.	20-21-162

Name	Page
Gossett, John	63
Gossett, John R.	162
Gossett, Pinckney	162
Grant, Noah	62
Grant, George Darwin	79
Grant, G. W.	223
Grant, Rebecca M.	223
Grant, Sarah M.	223
Grant, James N.	223
Grant, Lydia F.	223
Grant, William	178
Granville County	4
Graveley, John Jr.	136
Gray, William	3-4
Gray, John	3-4
Gray, Alexander	3
Gray, Martha	3
Gray, Ann	3
Gray, Capt. Peter	221
Gray, James W.	202
Gray, Nathan A.	210
Great Britian	4
Greene, W. C.	237
Greene, dr.	172
Greenville	173
Greenville Court House	89
Greenville District	34-75-112-201-210-239
Greenville Road, Pickens Co.	17-21-248
Greenwood, Hudson	195
Grice, D.	179
Griffin, E. H.	18-224-146
Griffin, E. R.	21
Griffin, Elihu	23-224-225
Griffin, James C.	221
Griffin, Seargent	223-225
Griffin, Avarilla	224
Griffin, Thomas	224-227
Griffin, Vashti	224
Griffin, Barton	224
Griffin, R. H.	224
Griffin, Dorcas	224
Griffin, Joseph	224
Griffin, William	224-225
Griffin, Nancy V.	224
Griffin, Rosanna M.	224
Griffin, G. B.	224
Griffin, Mary L.	224
Griffin, Bailey B.	224
Griffin, Thomas V.	224
Griffin, Margaret T.	224
Griffin, Martha F. D.	224
Griffin, Jane M. S.	224
Griffin, Anderson	224
Griffin, Mahaney	224
Griffin, Henry	225
Griffin, Seargeant Jr.	226
Griffin, Martha C.	227
Grimball, Thomas	64
Grogan, Henry	192
Grisham, John O.	119
Grisham, William S.	123-206
Grisham, Joseph	124-222
Grisham, Mary L.	222
Grisham, Col. Joseph	203
Grisham, Major Wm. S.	149
Grisham, Revd. Joseph	160
Grissop, John	129-156
Gilham, John	90
Gillespie, Esquire	84
Gillespie, Eliza	196
Gillespie, Jason	196
Gillespie, James	170
Gilliam, Mary S.	11
Gilliam, Jessie L.	11
Gilliam, Carrie C.	11
Gilliland, R. J.	19
Gilliland, David	154
Gilliland, Wilson	196
Gilmer, Robert	197
Gillison, Mr.	165
Gilstrap, Benson	17
Gilstrap, Hardy	21-205
Gilstrap, William	85
Gilstrap, John	188
Gingles, Delilah	36
Gissel, Hanke	177
Guerard, Peter Esq.	64
Gunn, William	229
Gunter, John	203

—H—

Name	Page
Hadden, W. M.	6
Hagan, James S.	80
Hagood, J. E.	6-15-17-24-84
Hagood, Col. Benjamin	26
Hagood, Gideon	76-215
Hagood, James	188-213
Hagood, Lidia	210
Hagood, Osborne	210
Hagood, Jane	201
Hagood, Benjamin	201
Haley, Archibald	62
Hall, Z. Jr.	165
Hallum, Thomas J.	180-183
Hallum, Catharine	180-183
Hallum, Cato	16
Hallum, Thomas	133
Hallum, Richard	184
Hamilton, Thomas	33
Hamilton, Andrew	33
Hamilton, David K.	192
Hamilton, Archibald	34
Hamilton, Major Andrew	127
Hamilton, Paul	231
Hammett, John	131
Hammond, William	189
Hampstead Village	32
Hancock, Hardy	113
Hancel, John	89
Harkness, James	34
Harkness, Letitia	34
Harrell, Zachariah	76
Harbin, Major Morgan—1851	157
Hardin, William	200
Hart, S. C.	184

Harris, Harriet	22
Harris, John	33-243
Harris, C. B.	102
Harris, James	105
Harris, Handy	242
Harris, Anna	242
Harris, Ann	243
Harris, Thomas	243
Harris, Joseph	243
Harris, Mary	243
Harris, Martha	243
Harrison, Genl. J. W.	6
Harrison, Nancy	70
Harrison, E. W.	70
Harrison, Thomas	70
Harrison, Larkin	70
Harrison, James	70
Harrison, Elizabeth	70
Harrison, Harriett B.	70
Harrison, James W.	126
Harrison, Major James W.	146
Hawkins, John	209
Hawkins, Benjamin	222
Hawthorne, Anna—1866	202
Hawthorne, Robert A.—1864	200
Hawthorne, Sarah A.	27
Hawthorne, Jasper N.	27
Haynes, Sheriff	105
Haynes, Nathaniel	105
Haynes, Mary	105
Haynes, Harrison	105
Haynes, Jesse	105
Haynes, Nancy	105
Haynes, Harper	105
Haynes, Rebecca	105
Haynes, Andrew	105
Haynes, Parthenia	105
Haynes, Dorcas	105
Haynes, William	162
Hazard, B. J.	31
Hearne, Joane	1
Hemphill, James S.	42
Henderson Place	79
Henderson, Nathaniel	50
Henderson, Jackson	71
Henly, Sally	108
Hendricks, G. K.	13
Hendricks, Elizabeth	11
Hendricks, E. B.	18
Hendricks, John W.	18
Hendricks, Moses	25
Hendricks, Balis	164
Hendricks, Ruth	207
Hendricks, John	207
Hendricks, Rosey	239
Hendricks, G. W.	239
Hendricks, Henry	238
Hendricks, Margaret	238
Hendricks, Capt. William	31
Hendricks, Larkin	84-111
Hendricks, Jane	84-239
Hendricks, Joseph C.	84
Hendricks, L.	96
Hendricks, George	101-103
Hendricks, William	111
Hendricks, Rosa	111
Hendricks, Eliza	174
Hendricks, George K.	174
Henson, John	26
Herndon, E. L.	27
Hering & Herrin & Herren,	
Edward	82
Marian	82
Morgan	82
Frederick O.	168
Joshua	126
Hester, J.	13
Hester, J. B.	19
Hester, Alfred	68
Hester, Eady	68
Hester, Henry	244
Hester, Eliza E.	206
Hester, Waddy T.	206
Hester, Balis	203
Hewitt, James H.	113
Hicks, John	163
Hiett, Mary	167
Higgin, John	85
Higgin, G. W.	103
Hightower, J. G.	209
Hill, W. R.	52
Hill, Mahala	217
Hill, Ruhama	217
Hill, Travers?	216
Hill, Matilda	217
Hill, Sylvania	217
Hill, Lewis	22-72-85
Hill, Henry	216
Hill, James	216
Hill, Samuel B.	58
Hill, William	110-217
Hill, Nancy	216
Hill, Polly	216
Hinkel, Elijah	89
Hinkel, Silas	89
Hinrickson, B.	32
Hinton, Synthia	25
Hinton, Jeremiah	87
Hix, Jean	69
Hix, Baylus	69
Hix, Francis	70
Hix, Milton	70
Hix, Elizabeth	164
Hix, John	164
Hoggatt, James	214
Holcombe, W. E.	5-14-17-227
Holcombe, Jonathan S.	168
Holden, James—1856	192
Holden, William	209-230
Holden, Mary	228-230
Holden, Elisha	228-230
Holden, Jackson	230
Holden, Catharine	230
Holden, Sarah	230
Holden, Elijah	230
Holden, Franklin	230

Name	Page
Holden, Richard	230-199
Holden, Isaac	231-209
Holden, Joshua	192
Holden, Lucy	193
Holden, Malinda	193
Holden, Jannette	193
Holden, Arvy	193
Holden, John	193-228-230
Holden, Nancy	193-228-230
Holland, B. F.	20-187
Holland, Penelope	20-180-181-187
Holland, Nancy	70
Holland, Robert	70
Holland, Julia	70
Holland, William	70
Holland, Catharine	70
Holland, Benjamin	70
Holland, Lucinda	70
Holland, Benjamin F.	180-181
Holland, Silas R.	187
Holland, E. D.	142
Holland, W. T.	164
Holland, Jannette	165
Holland, J. E.	165
Hollingsworth, A.	14
Hollingsworth, Clinton	25
Hollingsworth, Elizabeth	25
Hollingsworth, Elias	248
Hollingsworth, J. J.	235
Holman, Thomas	4
Holman, Mary	4
Holmes, Sarah	29
Holmes, John	29
Holmes, William	86
Honea, William	105
Hood, John P.	42
Hood, William	231-232
Hopkins, Martin	87
Horan, James	167
Horlbeck, Dan	4
Horlbeck, Henry	4
Horlbeck, Ann G.	4
Horton, John	111
Huston, Gray Jones	234
Houston, Eliza A. M.	234
Howard, John	16-161-228
Howard, Mr.	90
Howard, John Jackson	137
Howard, Eli	239
Howard, Elihu	239
Hudson, Green	171
Hughs & Hughes,	
John	4
Sarah	11
Mary	11
L.	21
Edward	154
Henry R.	158
Hull, Nathaniel	191
Hunnicut, Miles M. N.	71
Hunnicut, J. M.	16
Hunnicut, Milton R.	118-136
Hunnicut, J. R.	209
Hunnicut, James M. Jr.	209
Hunnicut, Eliza	209
Hunnicut, Newton Jasper	209
Hunnicut, Lewis Reece	209
Hunt, J. J.	13-176
Hunt, Charles W.	70-72
Hunt, William H. H.	71
Hunt, Hulet	72
Hunt, Henson	72
Hunt, H. C.	162
Hunt, Davis	239
Hunt, S.	239
Hunt, Esli	204
Hunter, William	24-180
Hunter, Bill	90
Hunter, William Jr.	182
Hunter, James J.	168
Hunter, Andrew	205-242
Hunter, Aenas	91
Hunter, Eneas	179
Hutchison, James	43
Hutchison, Leroy	43
Hutchison, John	59
Hyde, Ezra	123
Hyde, Bennett	132
Hawthorne, Ida	201
Hawthorne, Emma	201
Hawthorne, Anna	202
Hawthorne, Robert A. Capt.	200
Hitt, Martha	210
Hitt, Thos.	210
Humphries, Thomas J.	200
Humphries, John T.	199

—I—

Name	Page
Indiana	83
Irby, Col.	81
Irwin, Joseph	243
Ireland	4
Inlow, Nancy	74
Isbell, Robert—1842	148
Isebell, Robert	27-70-147
Isebell, Lucinda	70
Isaacs, Samuel	199

—J—

Name	Page
Jacks, Isaac	81-111
Jacks, Anne	108
Jacks, John	111
Jackson, Susanna	3
Jackson, Robert	192
James Island	28
Jameson, William	46-95-244-248
Jameson, Joshua	73-244
Jameson, Carrol	96-244
Jameson, William M.	238
Jameson, Dorcas P.	238
Jameson, A. P.	248
Jameson, Rebecca	244
Jameson, Frances	244
Jameson, Madison	244
Jameson, Wilkinson	244
Jameson, John	244-248
Jameson, Westly	244
Jameson, McElroy	244

Jameson, Louisa J.___244
Jameson, P. B.___244
Jameson, William C.___248
Jameson, Mary J.___248
Jameson, Martha___248
Jameson, Dorcas___248
Jett, James Esq.___231
Jenkins, J. A.___10
Jenkins, Henry___71
Jenkins, Frances___189
Jenkins, Jesse___152
Jenkins, James___190
Jenkins, James T.___172
Jenkins, Nancy___190
Jenkins, Polly___190
Jocassee Road___87
Jordan, James___86
Johnston & Johnson,
   William H.___49-105
   George Esq.___4
   Benjamin J.___16
   David___35-37
   Captain___63
   Eliza J.___105
   John___47
   Nathaniel___68
   Amanda___74
   Samuel___105-203
   Mary H.___105
   James T.___135
   Elijah M.___105
   Robert___105-208
   Edward___105
   Joseph W.___105
   Margaret___105
   John M.___112-116
   Thomas___208
   Thomas M.___222
Johns, James___105
Johns, Henry___105
Jolley, Mr.___169
Jones, H.___11
Jones, Louisa___11
Jones, Elizabeth___11
Jones, William M.___15-19
Jones, Jabez___197
Jones, William___236
Jones, Adam___236
Jones, Hartwell___236
Jones, Thomas H.___237
Jones, David___237
Jones, Susan C.___237
Jones, Lucinda J.___237
Jones, Nancy___237
Jones, Lewis___16-33
Jones, J. S.___19
Jones, John___20
Jones, Joel___143
Jones, Dudley___143
Jones, Malinda___210
Jones, Wilson___210
Jones, Dr. W. R.___162
Jones, Samuel___197
Jones, Mary___237
Jones, Martha M.___237
Jones, Matilda C.___237

Jones, Louisa J.___248
Jones, Leaner___248
Julian, John___15
Jumping Off Rock___89

—K—

Kahoe, John___169
Kees, Elijah___28
Keith, John R.___5-6-7
Keith, Eliza Ann___5
Keith, Mary Isabella___5
Keith, Mary R.___6
Keith, Flora C.___6
Keith, Elliott M. Jr.___6
Keith, William___63-69
Keith, Cornelius___68-173-196-239
Keith, Eady___68
Keith, Mary___69
Keith, James___69-71-117
Keith, Allen___69-117
Keith, Sarah___69
Keith, Rebecca___69-111-239
Keith, Anderson___69
Keith, Col. William C.___5
Keith, William C.___5-6-7
Keith, William L.___4-5-7-20-24-25
   26-69-101-145-183-185
Keith, Elliott M.___5-6-7-8-9-207
Keith, Thomas J.___5-6-7-209
Keith, John___69
Keith, George___69
Keith, Lucinda___69
Keith, Mathew___69-111-116
Keith, Elizabeth___69-174
Keith, Virginia Elvira___6
Keith, Elizabeth M.___6
Keith, Marvel L.___5-6-7-8
Keith, Broadwell___8
Keith, Elizabeth Brown___4-5-8
Keith, Mary J.___7
Keith, John D.___173
Keith, Margaret___111-238
Keith, Rosa___111
Keith, Jane___111
Keith, Nancy___173
Keith, Stephen D.___173
Keith, Allen___173-238
Keith, Willis J.___173
Keith, Lemuel S.___173
Keith, Calhoun William___6-7
Keith, Mary___8
Keith, S. D.___19
Keith, Marquis D.___173
Keith, James M.___173
Keith, Seaborn___173
Keith, Mary B.___174
Keith, Temperance___174
Keith, George W.___174
Keith, Elzie L.___174
Keith, Martha Jane___175
Keith, Warren D.___176
Keith, Harriet___196
Keith, Matthew___239
Keith, John B.___239
Keith, Rosey___239
Keith, George___233
Keith, Monterey Adaline___239

Name	Page
Keith, Jane	239
Kelly, Lucinda	24
Kelly, Henry	86-93
Kennedy, N. P.	46
Kennedy, Elias	71
Kennedy, William	111
Keith, Rev. J. L.	186
Keith, Susannah	108
Kennemore, Elias	18
Kennemore, Lot	18-124
Kennemore, John	61
Kennemore, James	61
Kentucky	83
Keowee River	6-77-94-192
Kern, John Frederick Sr.	109
Kern, John F. Jr.	109-111
Kern, Alfred A.	109
Kern, Col.	111
Kirksey, W. S.	12
Kirksey, J. Brown	13-19
Kirksey, Silas	20-180-187-194
Kirksey, William Sr.	20-180-187
Kirksey, William Silas	187
Kirksey, Nancy	20-180-187
Kirksey, Jared	20-180
Kirksey, Isaac	20
Kirksey, Mary	20-180
Kirksey, Isaiah	180
Kirksey, Elhanon W.	180-181-182
Kirksey, William	181-182
Kirksey, William Jr.	246
Kirksey, Rebecca	187
Kirksey, Joseph B.	187
Kirksey, Robert	20-180-187
Kirksey, William Jr.	20-180-187
Kirksey, Catharine	20-180-246
Kirksey, Christopher	20-180-182
Kirksey, Eady Katharine	187
Kirksey, Penelope	20-180-187
Kirksey, Fair	20-180-182-183
Kilpatrick, John C. Jr.—1840	219
Kilpatrick, John C.	106-118-218
Kilpatrick, F. Whitner	218-219
Kirksey, Amanda	219
Kirksey, Col. John C.	218
Kirksey, Clara	218
Kirksey, Benjamin F.	236
Kirksey, Rebecca C.	236
Kincade, James	112
Kinloch, James	68
Kings Mills	12
King, W. W.	22
Kink, William	28-158
King, James	145
Knight, W. W.	22
Knight, John	93
Knox, Eliza	186
Knox, Robert	186
Kuykendal, James	39

—L—

Name	Page
Ladd, William	26
Ladd, Polly	26
Laney, John A.	49
Langston, Isaac	18
Lancaster District	56
Lark, Henry	162
Lathem, Robert A.	176
Laughridge, Benjamin	69
Laughridge, Mary	69
Laurens District	108-210
Law, William	33
Lawrence & Laurence,	
E. H.	13
J. N.	25-89
A. G.	44
James	101-184-185
Martha	139-204
Benjamin F.	184
Adaline	184-186
Joseph R.	184
Rachel	184-185
S.	237
John	205
B. F.	196
Sally	196
Joab	191
Benjamin	191
Lawson, Andrew	1
Lay, C.	22
Lay, C. M.	169
Lay, William A.	70
Lay, Mira	209
Lay, Jesse	209
Lay, Elizabeth	186
Lay, James	186
Leathers, William W.	140
Leathers, William	198
Leathers, Nimrod	139
Lee, E.	85
Leech, Jane	45
Leech, G. M.	74
LeGrand, Thomas H.	125
Lemon, Robert	34
Lesley, Sarah	11
Lesley, Justina	11
Letson, G. H.	48
Lewis, Jacob	21
Lewis, Tarlton	104
Lewis, Capt. R. L.	71
Lewis, Delilah M.	129
Lewis, David T.	186
Lewis, Mary	196
Lewis, John	196
Lewis, John W.	239
Lindsay, H.	111
Linderman, R. W.	163
Lindershine, Catharine	32
Lincoln County	56
Linn, Mary Ann	113
Lightwood Knot Springs	63
Loden, Jesse P.	125
Logan, George	1
Logan, George Esq.	66
Logan, Joseph	78
Long, J. C.	70
Long, Thomas D.	201

Jameson, Louisa J. 244
Jameson, P. B. 244
Jameson, William C. 248
Jameson, Mary J. 248
Jameson, Martha 248
Jameson, Dorcas 248
Jett, James Esq. 231
Jenkins, J. A. 10
Jenkins, Henry 71
Jenkins, Frances 189
Jenkins, Jesse 152
Jenkins, James 190
Jenkins, James T. 172
Jenkins, Nancy 190
Jenkins, Polly 190
Jocassee Road 87
Jordan, James 86
Johnston & Johnson,
  William H. 49-105
  George Esq. 4
  Benjamin J. 16
  David 35-37
  Captain 63
  Eliza J. 105
  John 47
  Nathaniel 68
  Amanda 74
  Samuel 105-203
  Mary H. 105
  James T. 135
  Elijah M. 105
  Robert 105-208
  Edward 105
  Joseph W. 105
  Margaret 105
  John M. 112-116
  Thomas 208
  Thomas M. 222
Johns, James 105
Johns, Henry 105
Jolley, Mr. 169
Jones, H. 11
Jones, Louisa 11
Jones, Elizabeth 11
Jones, William M. 15-19
Jones, Jabez 197
Jones, William 236
Jones, Adam 236
Jones, Hartwell 236
Jones, Thomas H. 237
Jones, David 237
Jones, Susan C. 237
Jones, Lucinda J. 237
Jones, Nancy 237
Jones, Lewis 16-33
Jones, J. S. 19
Jones, John 20
Jones, Joel 143
Jones, Dudley 143
Jones, Malinda 210
Jones, Wilson 210
Jones, Dr. W. R. 162
Jones, Samuel 197
Jones, Mary 237
Jones, Martha M. 237
Jones, Matilda C. 237

Jones, Louisa J. 248
Jones, Leaner 248
Julian, John 15
Jumping Off Rock 89

—K—

Kahoe, John 169
Kees, Elijah 28
Keith, John R. 5-6-7
Keith, Eliza Ann 5
Keith, Mary Isabella 5
Keith, Mary R. 6
Keith, Flora C. 6
Keith, Elliott M. Jr. 6
Keith, William 63-69
Keith, Cornelius 68-173-196-239
Keith, Eady 68
Keith, Mary 69
Keith, James 69-71-117
Keith, Allen 69-117
Keith, Sarah 69
Keith, Rebecca 69-111-239
Keith, Anderson 69
Keith, Col. William C. 5
Keith, William C. 5-6-7
Keith, William L. 4-5-7-20-24-25
  26-69-101-145-183-185
Keith, Elliott M. 5-6-7-8-9-207
Keith, Thomas J. 5-6-7-209
Keith, John 69
Keith, George 69
Keith, Lucinda 69
Keith, Mathew 69-111-116
Keith, Elizabeth 69-174
Keith, Virginia Elvira 6
Keith, Elizabeth M. 6
Keith, Marvel L. 5-6-7-8
Keith, Broadwell 8
Keith, Elizabeth Brown 4-5-8
Keith, Mary J. 7
Keith, John D. 173
Keith, Margaret 111-238
Keith, Rosa 111
Keith, Jane 111
Keith, Nancy 173
Keith, Stephen D. 173
Keith, Allen 173-238
Keith, Willis J. 173
Keith, Lemuel S. 173
Keith, Calhoun William 6-7
Keith, Mary 8
Keith, S. D. 19
Keith, Marquis D. 173
Keith, James M. 173
Keith, Seaborn 173
Keith, Mary B. 174
Keith, Temperance 174
Keith, George W. 174
Keith, Elzie L. 174
Keith, Martha Jane 175
Keith, Warren D. 176
Keith, Harriet 196
Keith, Matthew 239
Keith, John B. 239
Keith, Rosey 239
Keith, George 233
Keith, Monterey Adaline 239

Name	Page
Keith, Jane	239
Kelly, Lucinda	24
Kelly, Henry	86-93
Kennedy, N. P.	46
Kennedy, Elias	71
Kennedy, William	111
Keith, Rev. J. L.	186
Keith, Susannah	108
Kennemore, Elias	18
Kennemore, Lot	18-124
Kennemore, John	61
Kennemore, James	61
Kentucky	83
Keowee River	6-77-94-192
Kern, John Frederick Sr.	109
Kern, John F. Jr.	109-111
Kern, Alfred A.	109
Kern, Col.	111
Kirksey, W. S.	12
Kirksey, J. Brown	13-19
Kirksey, Silas	20-180-187-194
Kirksey, William Sr.	20-180-187
Kirksey, William Silas	187
Kirksey, Nancy	20-180-187
Kirksey, Jared	20-180
Kirksey, Isaac	20
Kirksey, Mary	20-180
Kirksey, Isaiah	180
Kirksey, Elhanon W.	180-181-182
Kirksey, William	181-182
Kirksey, William Jr.	246
Kirksey, Rebecca	187
Kirksey, Joseph B.	187
Kirksey, Robert	20-180-187
Kirksey, William Jr.	20-180-187
Kirksey, Catharine	20-180-246
Kirksey, Christopher	20-180-182
Kirksey, Eady Katharine	187
Kirksey, Penelope	20-180-187
Kirksey, Fair	20-180-182-183
Kilpatrick, John C. Jr.—1840	219
Kilpatrick, John C.	106-118-218
Kilpatrick, F. Whitner	218-219
Kirksey, Amanda	219
Kirksey, Col. John C.	218
Kirksey, Clara	218
Kirksey, Benjamin F.	236
Kirksey, Rebecca C.	236
Kincade, James	112
Kinloch, James	68
Kings Mills	12
King, W. W.	22
Kink, William	28-158
King, James	145
Knight, W. W.	22
Knight, John	93
Knox, Eliza	186
Knox, Robert	186
Kuykendal, James	39

—L—

Name	Page
Ladd, William	26
Ladd, Polly	26
Laney, John A.	49
Langston, Isaac	18
Lancaster District	56
Lark, Henry	162
Lathem, Robert A.	176
Laughridge, Benjamin	69
Laughridge, Mary	69
Laurens District	108-210
Law, William	33
Lawrence & Laurence,	
E. H.	13
J. N.	25-89
A. G.	44
James	101-184-185
Martha	139-204
Benjamin F.	184
Adaline	184-186
Joseph R.	184
Rachel	184-185
S.	237
John	205
B. F.	196
Sally	196
Joab	191
Benjamin	191
Lawson, Andrew	1
Lay, C.	22
Lay, C. M.	169
Lay, William A.	70
Lay, Mira	209
Lay, Jesse	209
Lay, Elizabeth	186
Lay, James	186
Leathers, William W.	140
Leathers, William	198
Leathers, Nimrod	139
Lee, E.	85
Leech, Jane	45
Leech, G. M.	74
LeGrand, Thomas H.	125
Lemon, Robert	34
Lesley, Sarah	11
Lesley, Justina	11
Letson, G. H.	48
Lewis, Jacob	21
Lewis, Tarlton	104
Lewis, Capt. R. L.	71
Lewis, Delilah M.	129
Lewis, David T.	186
Lewis, Mary	196
Lewis, John	196
Lewis, John W.	239
Lindsay, H.	111
Linderman, R. W.	163
Lindershine, Catharine	32
Lincoln County	56
Linn, Mary Ann	113
Lightwood Knot Springs	63
Loden, Jesse P.	125
Logan, George	1
Logan, George Esq.	66
Logan, Joseph	78
Long, J. C.	70
Long, Thomas D.	201

Long, Pamelia	70
Louisiana	193
Looper, Jeremiah	13-18-204-228
Looper, James Perry	17-21
Looper, Joseph	69
Looper, Margaret	69
Lorton, John S.	218
Loveless, Sarah	209
Loveless, James	209
Lowery, James	223
Lumpkin, Dickinson	147
Lumpkin, Mr.	165
Lumpkin, D. L.	165
Lusk, Elizabeth	44
Lusk, Robert	44
Lusk, Samuel	44
Lusk, Elizabeth	44
Lusk, Margaret	44
Lusk, James	45
Lyles, Samuel	27
Lyles, Mary	27
Lyles, D. L.	27
Lyles, Martha Ann	27
Lynch, William	26
Lynch, Nathaniel	196
Lynch, Gideon M.	196
Lynch, Banister S.	196
Lynch, Jane	196
Lynch, Harriet	196
Lynch, Eliza	196
Lynch, Nancy	196
Lynch, Sarah	196
Lynch, Mary	196
Lynch, Calvin	197

—M—

MaHaffey, Pleasant S.	209
MaHaffey, Catharine	209
McAdams, James	176
McAllaster, Elizabeth—1828	188
McAllister, D. B.	10
McAllister, Andrew	191
McAllister, Eliza	191-188
McAllister Tract	191
McCrackin, Samuel A.	16
McCrackin, John	150
McCurry, William	174
McCurry, Matilda	174
McElroy, Elizabeth	75
McElroy, James	75
McElroy, John	75-76
McCall, John D.	49
McClanahan, Capt.	83
McCord, John	111
McCollum, Duncan	51
McCollum, David	98
McConnel, J. B. W.	22
McConnel, Sarah Ann	22
McCorkle, Frank	63
McCleland, Hugh	44
McCleland, Elizabeth	44
McClure, John	215
McCrackin, Samuel A.	16
McCrackin, John	150

McCurdy, Anna	242
McDade, William	13-18
McDaniel, Archey	165
McDonald, Thomas	191
McFarlen, William	86
McFarland, William	93
McFadden, Isaac	61
McGehee, John	229
McGill, John	41
McGinnis, John	170-169
McGraw, John	93
McGuffin, Joseph B.	163
McIntire, Mrs.	173
McClure, Robert B.	111
McClure, Lilly Ann	113
McClure, Reece J.	113
McLure, Robert	69
McLure, Mary	69
McIntyre, Joseph	198
McIntyre, Caroline	198
Mathis, Jesse	82
Maxwell, Samuel E.	128-155
Maxwell, John	138-210-218-220
Maxwell, Robert Jr.	236
Maxwell, R. D.	197
Maxwell, Elizabeth H.	218
Massingale, Green	91-92
Mauldin, Joab	18
Mauldin, Amelia J.	25
Mauldin, William A.	25
Mauldin, James	207
Mauldin, Rachel	207
Mauldin, Tyre B.	128-130-149-160, 161
Maverick, Samuel	121-124-234
Maverick, Samuel A.	140
Mays, Abucy	110
Mays, Robert F.	180
Maybank, Joseph	65
Mayfield, Israel	24
Mayfield, Polly	180
Mayhew, Mary A.	193
Mayhew, Charles	193
Means, Samuel	229
Megee, Tilmon C.	218
Meek, James B.	80
Meek, William B.	80
Meredith, Abraham	28-141-133
Merck, Joseph	24
Merck, Susannah	25
Merritt Tract	207
Merrimon, Thomas M.	31
Methodist Camp Ground	72
Mims, M. A.	11
Mims, E. R.	11
Miller, John	37-111
Miller, James G.	37
Miller, Dickson	37
Miller, Thomas	37
Miller, Calvin	37
Miller, Mildred	39
Miller, Dr. H. C.	14
Miller, Th.	47

Name	Page
Miller, Caroline	74
Miller, Micah	102
Miller, Martha Ann R.	102
Miller, Tillman	162
Mitchell, M. F.	6-9-63-196
Mitchell, Sarah E.	195
Mitchell, Benjamin	196
Mitchell, William W.	197
Miscellaneous Records	62-70
Mississippi	210-180-238-240
Mississippi, Monroe County	217
Moore, Reuben—1805	76
Moore, William	41-76
Moore, Jefferson L.	62
Moore, Elizabeth	76
Moore, Margaret	76
Moore, Maria	76
Moore, Matilda	76
Moore, Thomas	76
Moore, Catharine	76
Moore, Gordon	78
Moore, John	78-79-145
Moore, Wm. Thompson	79
Moore, Jacob Alexr.	79
Moore, Minerva	79
Moore, Colnee	80
Moore, Temander	80
Moore, Diana	80
Moore, Thomas H.	237
Moody, James	228-230
Moody, Joel	228-230
Moody, Nancy	228-193-230
Moody, Nancy	228-230-193
Moody, Catharine	230
Moody, Abraham	193
Moreland, James	47
Montgomery, John	243
Montgomery, Thomas	169-238
Montgomery, William	222
Morgan, B. F.	15
Morgan, William	87
Morgan, Charles C.	193
Morgan, Susan M.	193
Morgan, Sarah	193
Morgan, John J.	193
Morgan, Mary A.	193
Morgan, Charles M.	193
Morgan, Licena C.	193
Morgan, Sarah F.	193
Morton, Rosa	186
Morton, John	168
Morris, James H.	112
Moultrie Tract	191
Moultrie, William	232
Moseley, Samuel	133
Moseley, Leonard	156
Mount Pleasant Church	74
Mullinix, Abner	18
Mullinix, William A.	217
Mullinix, Sylvania	217
Mulliken, James	240
Mulliken, Malinda	240
Munro, William	71
Murphey & Murphree, Thomas	23
Charles T.	80
Elijah	96-101
Levi	96
James M.	241-242
David	241
Murray, William	62
Muster Ground	87
Myers, Sophia C.	55
Myers, William R.	56
Myers, John S.	55
Myers, John Baylis	200
Mansell, Joshua—1854	72
Mansell, Robert	72-85
Mansell, Samuel	72-85
Mansell, Lemuel	72-85
Mansell, Frances	72-85
Mansell, Richard H.	72-85
Mansell, John	72-85
Mansell, Mahala	72
Mansell, Camilla Jane	73
Mansell, Tinsa Emmer	73
Mansell, Thomas Fletcher	73
Mansell, Abi	73
Mansell, Bailey	73
Mansell, Malinda Alice	73
Mansell, Anny	73
Mansell, Green	73
Mansell, Harriet	73
Mansell, Amanda	74
Mansell, Perry	74
Mansell, Merida	74
Mansell, James	74-85-244
Mansell, Caroline	74
Mansell, Jane	85
Mansell, Julia	85
Mansell, J. B.	224
Mansell, Vashti	224
Maret, B. J.	27
Maret, E. C.	27
Maret, John	152
Marshall, Revd. Samuel	1
Mason, John W.	27
Mason, W. C.	27
Mason, Julia	27
Mason, Carry C.	27
Mason, Joel	27-134
Mason, Frances	27
Mason, Charles W.	27
Mason, Ambrose	28
Mason, Nancy	28
Mason, Lucinda	28
Mason, Ester	28
Mason, Mary	28
Mason, Kitty	28
Mason, James	28
Mason, Elizabeth	28
Masters, Zachariah	204
Martin, William N.	22
Martin, John	164-235
Martin, Norman	200
Martin, Gideon	207

Martin, Elizabeth	164-207
Martin, David	207
Martin, Sarah	207
Martin, Rachel	207
Martin, Polly	207
Martin, Ruth	207
Martin, Absolom	207
Martin, James	170
Martin, Mary Jane	171
Martin, Mary	207
Martin, Lydia	**207**
Martin, Betsy	207
Matthews, John	29
McJunkin, Samuel	70
McJunkin, Martha	70
McJunkin, Eleanor	111
McJunkin, Daniel	111
McJunkin, Margaret	111
McJunkin, James	111
McKnight, Thomas K.	46
McNeely, Robert	46
McNeely, James	46
McNeely, Jemima	46
McNeely, Eliza Ann	46
McNeely, Margaret	46
McNeely, Mary	46
McNeely, Jane	46
McKenzie, Joseph Jr.	49
McKenzie, Edwin	49
McKinney, Thomas	25-87
McKinney, Mary	25-87-186
McKinney, Henderson	71
McKinney, Wilson	87-186
McKinney, John	88-186
McKinney, James	104-186-196
McKinney, Elizabeth	186
McKinney, William	186
McKinney, Sarah	186
McKinney, Preston	186
McKinney, Ester	186
McKinney, Ford	88
McKinney, Rosa	186
McKinney, Chesley	**186**
McKinney, Evaline	186
McKinney, Charles	186
McKinney, Nancy	186
McKinney, David	186
McKinney, Jesse	186
McTier, William	4
McWhorter, Janie	27
McWhorter, W. A.	164
McWhorter, John	235
McWhorter, John Jr.	236
Maddens, Mrs.	16
Maddox, John C.	86
Madison, James	198
Magee, Solomon	26
Magee, Elizabeth	26
Major, Joab	34
Major, Ida Tecoa	34
Major, Laura Cannon	34
Major, S. A.	177
Makin, Francis	86
Maloy, Lucy	193
Maloy, Andrew	193
Mannon or Mannor,	
Mary An	35
Robert	36
Mansell & Mancill,	
Sarah	22-72-73-85
Joseph	72-85
Julia Ann	72
William	72-85
Mathew	72-85
Joshua	72-85

—N—

Negro Trials	202
Neeley, Samuel	45
Neelys Creek	60
Neighbors, Barnett	217
Neighbors, Ruhama	217
Neighbors, Benjamin	180
Neighbors, Cynthia	180
New York, Bank of	56
Newman, Martha	4
Newman, John	4-92
Newman, George	4
Newman, Alexander	4
Newman, Alexr. Shaw	76
Newman, Ann	4
Newman, Susannah	4
Newton, Moses	211
Nevell, James A.	136
Nevell, W. J.	206
Nichols, John	63
Nichols, James	63
Nichols, Alexander	63
Nicholsons Fork	230
Nicholson, Hannah	|231
Nicholson, Evan	127-209
Nicholson, Ira R.	209
Nicholson, Mary	209
Nicholson, Sarah	209
Nicholson, Martha	209
Nicholson, Harriett	209
Nicholson, Bailus	209
Nicholson, William	209
Nicholson, Bailey	209
Nicholson, Melinda	209
Nicholson, Mira	209
Nicholson, Silas	209
Nix, William B.	77
Nix, Letty	193
Nix, Tyre	193
Nix, Eliza Ann	193
Nix, Daniel	193
Nimmons, J. B.	13-14
Nimmons, James	14
Noble, Thomas	1
Norrell, Isaac	109
Norris, Robert	95
Norris, Edward	162
Norris, Andrew O.	234
North Carolina	68-84-85-91-197-230
County	5
Northampton County	59

Jackson County	228
Mecklinburg County	36
Norton, Joseph J.	5-6-202
Norton, J.	85
Norton, Miles M.	101-132-206
Norton, Jeptha	151-240
Norton, Col. Jeptha	206
Norton, Edward	240
Norton, Malinda	240
Norton, Martha	240
Norton, Zepporah	240
Norton, Malissa	240
Norton, Sarah	240
Norton, Elizabeth	240
Norton, Lucinda	240
Norton, Mathurza	240
Norton, Elias	230
Norton, Mary	230

—O—

Oconee Creek	191
Oconee County	27
O'Dell, Laura	11
O'Dell, Martha	11
O'Dell, Calvin	18
O'Briant, John	25
O'Briant, Carr	165
O'Briant, Thomas	165
Oolenoy	8
O'Neal, George W.	11-12
O'Neal, John	69
O'Neal, Mary	69
Orr, Col.	63
Orr, Alexander	238
Orr, Malinda	236
Owens, Thomas	75
Owens, Milley	75
Owens, Patsey	75
O'Hara, Charles	169
O'Hara, Patrick	166

—P—

Packard, Chillion	246
Parish, Augustus	61
Parker, John	78
Parker, Susan	79
Pardue, James M.	48
Parris, R. J.	19
Parsons, W. J.	24-25-26
Parsons, Sarah	207
Parsons, John Belton	207
Parsons, Loyd Miffin	207
Parsons, James	179
Parsons, Thomas	180
Parsons, Samuel	180-179
Parsons, J. C. C.	179-180
Parsons, F. C.	180
Parsons, William J.	180
Parsons, Maria L.	179
Patterson, Nancy	26
Patterson, Joel	156
Patterson, Eleanor	126
Payne, Jenny	28
Payne, Thomas	240
Peak, James	63

Pelfrey, James	164
Pendleton Road	13
Pell, Harriet	209
Pell, James Jackson	209
Perkins, Thomas	21
Perkins, Josiah	197
Perkins, Joshua	197
Perkins, William	197
Perkins, Augustus	197
Perkins, Mary	197
Perkins, Moses	197
Perkins, Samuel	197
Perkins, Harriet E.	197
Perkins, Martha Adaline	197
Perry, Frances	244
Perry, William H.	244
Perry, Josiah F.	201
Perry, Nathaniel	95-96
Pettus, George	57
Pettus, Jeane	57
Pettus, Rebakah W.	57
Pettus, Sarah	57
Pettus, Sinthay	57
Pettus, Susanna	57
Pettus, Elizabeth	57
Pettus, John D. O. K.	57
Pettus, Ann D.	57
Pettus, Stephen	57
Pettus, Mary	57
Pettus, Jane	57
Pettus, Sarah	57
Petition of the Females of Pickens County—1871	10
Pickle, Jacob	19
Pickens, A. C.	204
Pickensville Tract	196
Pilgrim, John	65
Pilgrim, Ezekiel	217
Pilgrim, Mary	217
Pilgrim, William	217
Pilgrim, Amos	217
Pilgrim, Elijah	217
Pilgrim, Jefferson	217
Pilgrim, Elizabeth	217
Pilgrim, Sidney	218
Pilgrim, Nancy	218
Pitts, William R.	23
Pitts, Robert	111
Pitts, Martha Jane	210
Pitts, Lucinda S.	210
Pitts, Drury Y.	210
Pitts, William M.	210
Pitts, Mary T.	210
Pitts, Sarah A.	210
Pitts, John B.	209
Pitts, Catharine	209
Phillips, Wesley	9
Phillips, Polly	175
Phillips, G. W.	155
Phillips, George W.	196
Phillips, Mary	62
Phillips, Jacob	174
Philson, Mrs.	111

Philson, Elizabeth	111
Philpot, H.	12-14
Plaxco, James	41-42
Plaxco, John T.	41-42
Plaxco, James G.	41
Plaxco, Jane	41
Plaxco, Henry G.	41
Plaxco, John S.	42
Plaxco, George	47
Plexca, James	78
Poole, John	74-111
Poole, Washington	108
Poole, Frank	175
Powell, Almond	172-197-199-200
Powell, Sarah Ann	198
Powell, Mary Ann	198
Powell, Elizabeth	198
Powell, Asel	198
Powell, Robert	198
Powell, Caroline	198
Powell, Thomas	198
Powers, William K.	63
Prater, Jeremiah	235-177
Pressely, William	52
Price, Isaac	36
Prichard, Jefferson	62
Prichard, Ruth	105
Prince, John	95-96
Pumpkintown	19
Puckettt, G. B.	20
—Q—	
Queen, Timothy	62
Queen, Frankling	62
Quelch, Elizabeth	32
Quelch, Capt. Andrew	32
Quelch, George	65
—R—	
Raine, Thomas	32
Rankin, George W.	104-222
Rankin, Edward	135-152-193-194
Rankin, John	193
Rankin, Mary	195
Rankley, J. M.	19
Ramsey, Alexander E.	136
Ratchford, John	47
Ratchford, H. Catherine	48
Ray, William	91-92
Ray, Fanny	108
Ray, Blaseton	108
Ray, Emory	193
Ray, Janetta	193
Reeder, A. P.	152
Reid & Reid, Joseph B.	5-69-246-196-226
Nathaniel	5-62-176-239-240-231-232
J. P.	5
A. E.	34
Rebecca	69
Reid, John	71
Reid, Adaline	185
Reid, Stephen C.	185-196
Reid, Rachel	186
Reid, Hamilton	241-242
Reid, Catherine	246
Reid, John H.	193
Reid, Susan M.	193
Reid, James M.	195
Reid, George M.	196
Reid, Mary	196
Reid, Ester	196
Reid, Jacob P.	188
Reid, Lemuel	202
Rembly, Elizabeth	69
Remington, Jacob	32
Reese, Lewis	83
Reese, Elizabeth	210
Reese Absalom	210
Reeves, William	59
Rhett, Capt. William	1-2
Rhett, Sarah	1-2-3
Rhett, William Jr.	2
Richey, John	213
Richards, Thomas	193
Rigdon, Mr.	160
Rigdon, Jeotha	203
Rivers, John E.	26
Rivers, Capt. Robert	29
Rivers, Joseph	30
Roberts, Jane	63
Roberts, Thomas	236
Roberts, Willis	236
Roberts, Elizabeth S.	236
Robbins, Levi N.	148-194
Roddy, John	61
Rodgers & Rogers, Leonard	89-206
William L.	12
Nancy	206
James	206
Diver	206
Emily C.	207
Sarah A.	207
Nancy L.	207
W. Diver	207
Frances M.	207
Mary K.	207
Margaret	207
Robertson, Robinson, Robison,	
Thomas	59-212
D. P.	248
James	186-210-211-214
Ester	186
John	196
Nancy	196
Richard	196
Sarah	215
Allen	210-211-212-214
Catherine	210
Jeremiah	210
Randall	210-212
Joseph	210
Anna	210
Martha	210
Lidia	210
Lucy	210
Malinda	210

John A.	210
Elizabeth	210
George	210
William	210
Roe, Malinda	193
Roe, Watson	193
Roe, David	193
Roe, James	193
Roe, Ruthy	193
Rohledder, John	147
Roper, Toliver	25
Roper, Mary E.	25
Roper, Lucinda	69
Roper, Meredith	69
Roper, Sarah	69
Roper, Abe	69
Roper, Ira T.	74
Roper, Aaron	201
Roper, Tyre	201
Roper, Marcus	201
Roper, Marena	201
Roper, Lemuel	201
Roper, John	201
Roper, Matilda	201
Roper, Jane	201
Roper, Catharine	201
Roper, James	201
Roper, David	201
Roper, Tilmon	201
Roper, Charles	162-201
Roper, Hamilton	201
Roper, Clarinda	201
Roper, Wm. Noble	201
Roper, Bailey	201
Roper, Martha	201
Roper, Elmina	201
Royer, Rebecca	31
Rucker, Benjamin	197
Russell, Stephen	29
Russell, E. H.	62
Russell, R.	217
Russell, Melinda	177
Rutherford, James	180
Rya, Peter	31
Rya, William	31
Rya, Richard	31

—S—

Sadler, D. W.	217
Saint Peter Parish	32-33
Saluda River	85
Salubrity	192
Samvays, Mary	29
Sandiford, Ann	29
Sandiford, John	29
Sargent, Abraham	24
Sargent, A. B.	138
Satterfield, William	33
Satterfield, Thomas W.	33
Satterfield, Rachel	33
Satterfield, Elijah	33
Satterfield, Thedford H.	86
Scott, Tract	191
Scott, Anne	49
Scipworth, Tho.	64
Seaborn, George	104
Seven Mile Fort?	89
Sharp, Peter	87
Sharp, Elam	128
Sharp, John Jr.	188-189
Sharshal, Frederick	87-93
Shaw, Alexander	3
Shaw, Martha	3-4
Shaw, Ann	3
Shanklin, Joseph V.	131
Sheers, William	31
Sheeler, Joseph R.	233
Sheeler, Thomas R.	236
Sheeler, Susan A.	236
Sheilds, Lambert	33
Singleton, David	71
Sims & Symmes	
George	135
Dr. F. W.	135-218-22
Tilly	176
Simpson, James T.	100
Simpson, John	108
Slabtown	18
Slater, Sarah F.	193
Slater, Edward	193
Slave Papers	22-174
Sloan, B. F.	183
Sloan, William	197
Sloan, Capt. David	191
Sloan, William C.	191
Sloan, John T.	191
Sloan, Nancy	191
Sloan, Sarah	191
Sloan, Emily C.	191
Sloan, Susan A.	191
Sloan Lucy C.	191
Sloan, Thomas J.	191
Sloan, Benjamin F.	191
Sloan, William D.	191
Sloan, Thomas	191
Smithson, Violet	233
Spartanburg District	74-82-90
Smith, Z.	21-174
Smith, William	25-40-95
Smith, Elvira	25-40-95
Smith, Daniel	79
Smith, Harvey	87
Smith, Lewis C.	87
Smith, Nancy	91
Smith, Wm. John	92
Smith, E. P.	188
Smith, Mahaley	112-116
Smith, Capt. John W.	139
Smith, John	199
Smith, Michael	229
Smith, Andrew N.	48
Smith, Martha	4
Smith, Mary	11
Smith, E.	11
Smith, A. S.	14-17
Smith, Zadock D.	36
Smith, Jane	36

Name	Page
Smith, Nancy	39
Smith, Rhoda	78
Smith, Mabel	78
Smith, John—1858	169
Snead, Philip—1850	160
Spencer, Oliver	30
Spencer, Rebecca	30
Spencer, T. C.	20
Spencer, Elizabeth	30-31
Spencer, Martha	30
Spencer, Hannah	30-31
Spencer, Susannah	30
Spencer, Robert	31
Spencer, Isaiah	31
Spencer, Emeline	31
Spencer, William	28-29-30
Spencer, Sarah	28-31-29
Spencer, John	28-30-31
Spencer, Ann	29-30-33
Spencer, Joseph	29-30-33
Spencer, Sebastian	32
Spencer, Jane Mary	33
Springs, John	52
Springs, Margaret	55
Springs, Julia Amanda	55
Springs, Richard A.	55
Springs, Leroy	55
Springs, Mary L.	56
Springs, Sophia	56
Springs, Adaline	56
Springs, Adam A.	56
Springs, Richard C.	56
Springs, Andrew B.	56
Springs, Eli B.	55
Southerland, John B.	239
Stribling, John	67
Stribling, Elizabeth	197
Stribling, William	197
Stribling, David S.	157
Stribling, Jesse	197-236
Stribling, Robert	236
Stribling, William H.	236
Stribling, W. W.	236
Stribling, Warren W.	238
Stribling, Rebecca C.	236
Stribling, Susan A.	236
Stribling, Thomas	236
Stribling, Eliza C.	236
Stribling, David S.	236
Stribling Elizabeth S.	236
Stribling, Mary A.	236
Stribling, M. S.	237
Stribling, Nancy	237
Stanley, John	96-98
Stanyarne's, John	28
Steading, G. F.	242
Stegall, William	17
Stegall, Mary Jane	248
Stegall, Sydney	248
Stegall, Spencer	238
Stegall, Mary Ann	238
Steel, William D.	25-137-139-154
Steel, Archibald	42
Steel, Thomas	94
Steel, Robert E.	172
Stewart & Stuart, A. J.	13-14
Watson	180
Malinda	180
Robert	89
Isaac	89
Jackson	89
James M.	241
Shourdan, Phillip	92
Stoll, Catharine	32
Stent, Samuel	30
Stevenson, Hugh	52
Stevenson, Mary	51
Stevenson, Jane	51
Stone, Mary	32
Sturgis, Susan	43
Sturgis, William	43
Stumphouse Tunnell	93
Starrett, Cynthia	222
Starrett, Polly Ann	222
Starrett, Bethenia	222
Starrett, Voliner	222
Starrett, Patsy	222
Starrett, William	222
Starrett, Susannah	222
Starrett, Benjamin J.	222-220
Starrett, Preston C.	222
Starrett, Clark S.	222
Starrett, John R.	222
Starrett, James	220
Slattery, Dennis	166
Sugar Creek	56
Suddeth, P. F.	20
Sugg, Jesse	97
Sullivan, Samuel	26
Sullivan, Polly	75
Sullivan, Vicy	76
Sullivan, Mike	167
Sullivan, Charles	76
Sumner, Sally	58
Summerville, Susannah	222
Suit, John	88
Sutherland, J. B.	19
Sutherland, Sarah	69
Sutherland, Wiliam	69
Sutherland, Mary	69
Sutherland, Amos	69
Swords, Rebecca	25
Stephens, Mary	168
Stuart, Robert—1857	89
Symmes, Dr. F. W.—1845	135

—T—

Name	Page
Table Mountain	13-174
Table Rock Hotel	15
Tally, Mathais	223
Target, Joseph	58
Tatum, Hugh	97
Tatum, Frank	169
Taylor, J. C.	86
Taylor, Lucinda	240
Taylor, Joseph	240
Taylor, Levi	177

Taylor, Capt. C. H.	163
Tennessee	25-111
Tennessee, McMinn County	195
Terrell, Aaron	144
Texas	210-238-180-196
Texas, Upshur County	183
Thoms?, Edmund	200
Thomas, George B.	11-12
Thomas, Rebecca	102
Thomas, Samuel	110
Thomas, D. Ann	163
Thomas, Aaron	163
Thompson, Keziah	76
Thompson, William	76
Thurston, William	34-35
Thurston, Rebbecca	34
Thurston, John	34-35
Thurston, Street	34-35
Thurston, Lewis	35
Thurston, Beverly	35
Thurston, Richard	35
Todd, Dr. Thomas	1
Todd, A.	138
Todd, Archibald	159
Todd, Stephen	175
Tompkins, David	25
Tompkins, Mary	25
Towers, Leonard	233-234
Trannum, George	162
Tranham, John	162
Trible, Elijah	235
Tripp, Harvey	188
Trott, Jane	3
Trott, Nicholas	3
Trotter, Sarah	73
Trotter, John R.	73-100-103
Trotter, Isaiah	94-101
Trotter, Josiah	94-98-100-101
Trotter, Clemtine	100-103
Trotter, Arminda	100-103
Trotter, A. C.	100
Trotter, Joseph	100-102
Trotter, Benjamin	101
Trotter, Jane	103
Trotter, Andrew	103
Trowell, John H.	183
Tunnell Hill	86-92-93
Turner, Clary	24
Turner, Clarinda	201
Turner, W. N.	162
Turner, Benjamin	202

—U—

Union District	78
Unity Church	55

—V—

Van, William	62
Van Wyck, Lydia A.	234
Van Wyck, William	117-119-120-121
	122-129-154-234
Vanderwicke, Mary	29
Varnor, Henry	31
Vannay, John Mul	166
Vandergrift, Andrew J.	12-13

Verner, Ebenezer P.	126-131-201
Verner, Samuel J.	178
Vickery, J. W.	16
Vills?, John	28
Vills?, Milandy	28
Visage, Thomas	158
Visage, James W.	158
Virginia	197-84
Virginia, Norfolk	83
Virginia, Jamestown	83
Virginia, Culpepper County	83
Virginia, Stafford County	83

—W—

Walhalla	23-27-202
Walker, J. H.	48
Walker, Jack	71
Walker, Malcom J.	180
Walker, Matilda	169
Waldrop, William	223
Wallace & Wallis, William	33
Letitia	34
Robert H.	34
John T.	34
Mary Jane	34
Ebenezer	34
Lilly Ola	34
Wm. Augustus	34
S. A.	34-48
Margaret	52
Rebecca	75
Anenias	75
Walsh, William	104
Warren, Lot	33
Warren, G. E.	184
Ward, Frederick	199
Ward, L. P.	228
Waring, Thomas	67
Washington, George	229
Waters, Eleanor	205
Watkins, William	162
Watson, David	51
Watson, Stephen B.	19-196
Watson, William	65
Welch, William	168
Welborn, Thomas M.	18-19
Welborn, James C.	192
Welborne, Thomas W.—1872	18
Welborn, Catharine	192
West, Wm. Gimerson	103
West, John	104
West, A.	168
Wetherick, Elizabeth	64
Wharey, Dorcas	45
Wherry, William	42
Wherry, Andrew	42
Wherry, Elizabeth	42
White, James	24
White, Hugh M.	57
White, Henry F.	60
White, Elizabeth	61
White, Dicy	47
White, Nancy	237
White, Henry N.	237

Whiteside, Margaret	44
Whiteside, Hugh	44
Whitmore, Capt.	111
Whitten, Lindsay	80-108-110
Whitten, Nancy	81-110
Whitten, John	81-111
Whitten, Alfred	81
Whitten, John Sr.	108
Whitten, John Jr.	108
Whitten, Sally	108
Whitten, Anne	108
Whitten, Mrs.	217
Whitten, Fanny	108
Whitten, Susannah	108
Whitfield, Rebecca	168
Whitmire, Martin	212
Whitmire, Anna	210
Whitmire, Jeremiah	210
Whitner, Joseph	213-220
Whisenant, B. C.	27
Whisenant, Milly	27
Wier, Thomas	111
Wigfall, Elizabeth	64
Wigington, Obadiah J.	25
Wigington, Ruth	25
Wilkinson, Elizabeth	240
Wilkinson, William	240
Wilkinson, Peggy	207
Wilson Meeting House	33
Wilson, J. F.	13
Wilson, Levi	116
Wilson, J.	217
Wilson, John R.	202
Wilson, Sarah	240
Wilson, Robert	240
Wilson, William	241
Wilson, T. W.	217
Williamson, Dr. Atkin	1
Williams, Isaac	13
Wiliams, Mathew H.	42
Williams, John T.	93-103
Williams B. J.	93-103
Williams, Benjamin J.	98-100
Williams, William S.	144-175-176-192
Williams, Grief	200
Wiliams, Mary Ann	238
Williams, Joseph	210-212
Williams, Jeremiah	192
Williams, Paschal K.	192
Williams, Charity	192
Williams, Frances	192
Williams, Nancy	192
Williams, Benjah	192
Wiliams, Thomas P.	192
Wiliams, Graham F.	192
Williams, Christian B.	192
Williams, Reginald	192
Williams, Mary E.	192
Williams, Cynthia	192
Williams, Elvira G.	192
Williams Paul E. A.	192
Williams, David	192
Williams, Catharine	192
Wingo, Y. J.	74
Winn, William W.	236
Winn, Mary A.	236
Winn, Hillard W.	237
Withers, G. B.	57
Wood, F. H.	39
Wood, Milly	92
Wolf Creek	205
Wool Factory	13
Woody, William	91
Workman, Martha	45
Workman, Robert	59
Workman, John	59
Wright, James W.	70
Wright, Mary	70
Wright, Nancy	70
Wright, Olive	70
Wright, Catharine	70
Wright, Lilburn	70
Wright, Frances	70
Wright, George	71
Wright, Dr.	78
Wyly, James	198
Wylie, William	60
Wylie, Caroline	60
Wylie, Elizabeth	60
Wylie, Thomas G.	60

—Y—

Yager, John	232
Young, C. W.	14
Young, Rebecca	27
Young, James Sr.	28
Young, L. C.	62
Young, Henry	71
Young, Dolly	74
Young, Sally	74
Young, Phillip	77
Young, Joseph	85
Young, George	89
Young, E.	136
Young, John S.	157
Young, Joseph	188
Young, William	203
Youngblood, William A.	62
Yow, Thomas A.	120
Yowell, Elizabeth	195
Yowell, Joshua	195
Yowell, James	195

—Z—

Zackary, James	23

www.ingramcontent.com/pod-product-compliance
Lightning Source LLC
Chambersburg PA
CBHW020057020526
44112CB00031B/232